"You're Next!"
Loss of Identity in the Horror Film

Frankenstein Must Be Destroyed

"You're Next!"

Loss of Identity in the Horror Film

edited by
Anthony Ambrogio

Midnight Marquee Press, Inc.
Baltimore, Maryland, USA

Copyright © 2008 by Anthony Ambrogio
Interior layout and cover design by Susan Svehla

Without limiting the rights under copyright reserved above, no part of this publication may be reproduced, stored in or introduced into a retrieval system, or transmitted, in any form, or by any means (electronic, mechanical, photocopying, recording or otherwise), without the prior written permission of the copyright owner or the publishers of the book.

ISBN 13: 978-1-887664-80-6
ISBN 10: 1-887664-80-7
Library of Congress Catalog Card Number 2007932979
Manufactured in the United States of America
Printed by Odyssey Press
First Printing by Midnight Marquee Press, Inc., May 2008

Dedication

"In my practice I've seen how people have allowed their humanity to drain away. Only it happens slowly instead of all at once. They didn't seem to mind....All of us, a little bit. We harden our hearts, grow callous. Only when we have to fight to stay human do we realize how precious it is to us." From *Invasion of the Body Snatchers* (1956), screenplay by Daniel Mainwaring.

To individuals everywhere who have found themselves fighting that fight, in offices, classrooms, pews, and prison cells, we dedicate this book.

"You're Next!"

Introduction

Fear of the dark, fear of death, fear of the unknown and the unseen. Commentators have analyzed at length these terrors of the psyche and how they figure prominently in the horror film. But one particular fear, one particular fate worse than death, which manifests itself time and again, has rarely been discussed in detail or depth.

Loss of identity, submergence of self, death of the soul—under various names and in various guises—befalls individuals trapped in a horror/sf/fantasy universe. An examination of the ways in which this fundamental terror is visited upon people in the movies—and what it does to them—could provide a new perspective on and greater understanding of the films that employ it and perhaps lead to a deeper appreciation of what it means to be human and why losing that defining aspect of our lives is so profoundly frightening.

Loss of identity in fantastic films is most closely associated with science fiction, particularly of the 1950s. *Invasion of the Body Snatchers* (1956) probably stands as the quintessential treatment of the subject. But loss of identity (sometimes identified as LOI in these pages) assumes many forms—mind control, hypnosis, metamorphosis, brain-washing, possession, zombification, etc.—and has been a staple of the fantastic-film genre since at least 1919, when *The Cabinet of Dr. Caligari*'s evil mesmerist controlled the hapless Cesar. Rhona Berenstein, in her 1996 book *Attack of the Leading Ladies*, heightened our awareness of LOI by identifying the "hypnotism" subgenre, wherein an individual (usually female) is held in thrall to the antagonist's will: She cites *Dracula* (1931), *Svengali* (1931), *White Zombie* (1932), and *The Mummy* (1932) as prime examples. It's easy to see how a major component of the terror that is *The Exorcist* (1973) is the possession of a child by a demonic force, transforming her into something entirely Other. From there, it's not so hard to realize that human-into-animal scenarios, like *The Wolf Man* (1941) and *Cat People* (1942, 1982), and the many versions of and variations on *Dr. Jekyll and Mr. Hyde* deal, at their core, with a loss of humanity in a very real, tangible way. Including in this study such movies as *It's a Wonderful Life* (1946) and *Eternal Sunshine of the Spotless Mind* (2004) may at first seem a bit of a stretch, until you think about it and read what our contributors have to say.

The arrangement of materials in this book betrays the editor's fondness—nay, *weakness*—for movie guides. But there's a reason why Leonard Maltin's annual *Movie Guide*, John Stanley's *Creature Features*, and other such works are so popular. And LOI lends itself to similar treatment.

The 201 films herein are listed alphabetically, for easy reference, and discussed, in shorter and longer entries, in the context of LOI, in the hope that the writers' analyses of LOI in the films will cast these often much-discussed pictures in a new light and illuminate the nature of both LOI and the movies themselves. We could have opted to cover LOI with a series of learned treatises on the subject—in-depth articles on individual films or themes, a chronological history of LOI, etc.—but we chose instead to take an encyclopedic approach, along the lines of Phil Hardy's *Horror Film Encyclopedia* or, perhaps more pertinently, Alain Silver and Elizabeth Ward's *Film Noir: An Encyclopedic Reference to the American Style*, which employs an ABC approach to examine

Blade Runner**, starring Rutger Hauer and Darryl Hannah, is a perfect example of loss of identity in the science fiction film.**

that hard-to-pin-down genre. Such a method gives readers the option to read the book from cover to cover or to skip around, pick and choose, and discern for themselves the connections that surely exist and which our contributors point out; it permits patterns to unfold and methods to manifest themselves, providing for a cumulative effect. (We prefer to stint on "pure" theory and expand upon practice—to apply the theory and let you, the reader, see LOI in action—so we can all form conclusions through an examination of the concrete.)

We cannot pretend that this book covers every single film that deals with LOI, but it offers a more than representative sampling. (The editor and contributors themselves didn't realize the extent of this theme and its many permutations until they came to work on this book.) The publishers hope, of course, for a positive reception to this volume, and welcome readers' comments about other movies that employ this theme so that, assuming reader interest, future editions of this book can be even more comprehensive.

[The editor would like to take this space to thank Midnight Marquee Press—Susan and Gary Svehla—for indulging him in this project. I hope it proves worthy of your faith and support. He would also like to thank the contributors, who brought such a broad perspective and depth of knowledge to the subject and to crave their indulgence over his editing. No matter how much I tweaked your wording, folks, I strove to keep your identities intact. Finally, the editor would like to thank his spouse and daughters for being there and being who they are. Anca, Olivia, and Beatriz, I love you. (Yes, even you, Ms. B!)]

Key

The apparatus for these films is not all inclusive, partly because we wished to cut down on space that could then be allotted to essays, and partly because so much information about films these days is readily available elsewhere—over the Internet, for example (if you have access to a computer). Each entry takes the following form:

> ***Title of Film (Alternate Title[s], if Any)*** (Year of release) [**type of LOI**] Country of origin, if not USA: Production Company, if different from distributor (Producer-Distributor). *D:* Director(s). *S:* Screenwriter(s), Source Writer(s). *Cast:* Performer (Character); Performer (Character); etc.
> Contributor's comments (ca. 200-1,000 words).—*Initials of Contributor*

We've included what we consider to be the important information for identifying the film (identity is important) but have left out commonly included items such as a film's running time, whether it's in color or black and white, and the producer's name. If any of these other elements are crucial, the contributor mentions them in his/her remarks. You will also note that—because the players and their roles are listed up front, in the essays themselves—we have, for the most part, avoided the common (and often useful) practice of identifying the actor who plays the character about whom we are speaking. Thus, instead of writing "Baron Frankenstein (Peter Cushing) needs the help of fellow mad scientist Dr. Brandt (George Pravda)," we write simply "Baron Frankenstein needs the help of fellow mad scientist Dr. Brandt." When writers wish to call attention to a performer, they do so.

These omissions are all done in the service of the subject. Loss of identity is what we want to explore here. We incorporate other material only insofar as it pertains to LOI.

We have tried to be accurate in the information that we do include. Any errors are the fault of your editor falling down on the job.

The opinions expressed in the entries are those of their contributors. (Occasionally, because your editor cannot keep his nose out of things, he will insert some additional material [in brackets] into an entry. These additions are not always clearly marked as his, but please don't blame the contributors for them.)

The inclusion of the bolded LOI category is so that, if a reader is of a mind, s/he can turn to Appendix I, "LOI by Subject," and look up all the other films that make up any of our (admittedly arbitrary) categories.

With the demise of the studio system, the major Hollywood studios have more and more become distributors, and production companies are formed sometimes for the purpose of producing a single film, and sometimes three or four companies will be credited on a single film. This can certainly cause a confusion of identity, but (again, arbitrarily) we have decided that unless such production companies have some significance we will omit them from our apparatus and, wherever possible, identify a film (American films in particular) via its U.S. theatrical distributor.

Throughout the book, when we want to point you to another entry, we use *q.v.* (*qq. v.* for more than one entry), the abbreviation for the Latin *quod vide*, or "which see." Sometimes we use *cf.*, the abbreviation for the Latin *confer*, or "compare." The meanings of these abbreviations are probably self-evident, but it never hurts to elaborate.

Entries are listed in alphabetical order. Alphabetization follows standard dictionary form, wherein spaces are ignored. Thus *Identity* comes before *I Married a Monster from Outer Space*, and *It's a Wonderful Life* comes before *I Was a Teenage Werewolf*. (If we were following the flawed computer-generated method of alphabetization, the order would be *I Married a Monster…*, *I Was a Teenage…*, *Identity…*, and then *It's a Wonderful Life.*). Movies beginning with numbers (e.g., *28 Days Later*) are treated as if the number were spelled out ("Twenty-eight") and follow alphabetically that way. Movies beginning with an abbreviation (e.g., "Dr.," for the various versions of *Dr. Jekyll and Mr. Hyde*) are treated as if the word were spelled out and follow alphabetically that way. (Thus *Dr. Jekyll and Sister Hyde* comes *before* the entry for *Doctor X*, whose "doctor" is spelled out in the title, which comes before *Donovan's Brain*. Sorry if this is counter-intuitive.)

Identities

ABJ: Andrew (Barton) Jones
AFA: Anthony (Frank) Ambrogio
AJB: A(lex) J. Ballard
AJL: Arthur (Joseph) Lundquist
BMS: Bryan (McCluer) Senn
CCS: Cindy Collins Smith
GJS: Gary J(oseph) Svehla
JDT: Jeffrey (Dillard) Thompson
JML: Jonathan Malcolm Lampley
JSM: Jeffrey (Scott) Miller
LJ-C: Laurel Jenkins-Crowe
MDC: Mark Daniel (aka "Danger") Clark
OVA: Olivia V(lasopolos) Ambrogio
RJT: Robert (John) Tinnell
SAS: Susan (Aurelia) Svehla
SGT: Steven (Gary) Thornton
SMD: Shane M. Dallmann

ANTHONY AMBROGIO (AFA), when he's not unsuccessfully looking for a job or receiving rejections from publishers, gets to write film-book reviews for *Video Watchdog* and articles and reviews for *Monsters from the Vault* and *Midnight Marquee*. He edited Midnight Marquee Press' Rondo-nominated *Peter Cushing* (2004) and received a Rondo honorable mention for "Tell Me When It's Over: The Rise and Fall of the Downbeat Ending," an article about horror films' excesses and abuses of the post-*Rosemary's Baby* shock finish, *Midnight Marquee*, 67/68 (Spring 2003). He received no awards but enormous satisfaction from his greatest work, co-created with poet and novelist Anca Vlasopolos—namely, their daughter, Olivia Vlasopolos Ambrogio. And he didn't do it just so she could contribute to this book. Honest! (No offense to his younger, adopted daughter, who has an identity—and mind—of her own, and to whom he says, "Start writing, Beatriz!")

OLIVIA V. AMBROGIO (OVA) has been published in the journals *Café Irréal*, *Fugue*, *Controlled Burn*, *Yemassee*, *Yuan Yang*, and *The Bathyspheric Review*, among others, and the book *Abandon Automobile: An Anthology of Detroit Poets* (Wayne State University Press). For a while she edited (and was the main contributor to) a political newsletter, *The Weekly Grudge*, but lately she can't stop yelling about the news long enough to write about it. She is currently pursuing a Ph.D. at Tufts University, where she studies the sex lives of marine snails. For her research, that is. Not just for fun.

A.J. BALLARD (AJB) was born in Liverpool, U.K., in 1978. Since then, he has indulged in a wide range of pursuits both worthwhile and questionable. Such activities include being a professional musician on the road with the likes of Motorhead, Ice T, and Napalm Death, in addition to working as a freelance journalist and self-taught scholar in the undead, all of which contrasts somewhat to the smoking of copious amounts of marijuana and generally wasting time during his formative years of adulthood. After finally "pulling his finger out" and leaving such exploits behind, he is presently engaged as a news reporter in Bangor, North Wales (UK). On weekends, he covers Liverpool F C football matches ("soccer games" to us Yanks) for a national daily. In his "spare time" he is learning how to cook and to speak Mandarin and Welsh. Ballard is also hard at work on several book projects and the odd short screenplay, as well as contemplating various devious schemes to gain funding for said activities. He'd tell you more, but then he'd have to kill you.

MARK CLARK (MDC)—as he is now known—is the author of *Smirk, Sneer and Scream: Great Acting in Horror Cinema* (McFarland), and a contributor to several Midnight Marquee Press books and other genre publications. He has no memory of what occurred prior to the Accident, and is puzzled by the scarring and runic tattoos left on his ears and toes. He currently lives in an undisclosed location in the American Midwest and usually wears a tin hat to foil spy beams from intelligence satellites. Other than that, he's a pretty normal guy.

SHANE M. DALLMANN (originally from Valparaiso, Indiana, but a California resident for many years now) never lost his identity as a fantastic-film fanatic, but he's gained a couple of extra identities in the meantime. He became a first-time published writer while inspired by the cinematic career of Paul Naschy—and has written for *Fangoria, Deep Red, Blood Times, Psychotronic Video, Video Junkie,* and *Screem Magazine.* He is currently a regular contributor to *Video Watchdog.* His alter ego has hosted the weekly creature-feature program *Remo D.'s Manor of Mayhem* since January 2002 (it's viewable on-line at www.ampmedia.org). His best and greatest role has been as the husband of Lisa and the father of Rebecca and Cameron. And he still thinks that the "he was dead the whole time" finale [see his entries] needs a bit of rest.

LAUREL JENKINS-CROWE (LJ-C) is a creative writer, folklorist-in-training, and Memphis expeatriate completing her Ph.D. coursework at the University of Louisiana Lafayette, where she also studies film. Her fiction has appeared in *The Vincent Brothers Review, Scrivener Creative Review, edificeWRECKED,* and *The Pinch*; her poetry in *Gulf Coast* and *Tattoo Highway.* A steady childhood diet of Creature Features and drive-in movies ruined her for academia until age 33, when the existence of courses and study areas like popular culture and film in English departments allowed her to return to college and give up her day jobs (veterinary assistant, pizza-joint salad goddess, actress, art model, hand model, cartoonist, Elvira look-alike, etc.). Her hobbies and obsessions include the Marx Brothers; adoption; foreign, cult, animated, and horror films; mythology; juggling; circus freaks; being Louisiana's only friend to the nutria; Elvis; Guy Maddin; and a growing compulsion to sum up her life for complete strangers in the third person.

ANDREW JONES (ABJ), whore to intoxicants, subsequent seer of things and visions (and consequently, gutters), prone to bitch rants and ravings. Sometime artist and writer, always morbid obsessor and collector of original *Night of the Living Dead* theater and press material. Hopeful we as a "civilization" will face a slow-moving zombie apocalypse; resolved to witnessing the joys of corporate tyranny and enslavement (but where the hell is the *Rollerball*?). Currently displaced in Pennsylvania, which in itself is an exercise in LOI.

JONATHAN MALCOLM LAMPLEY (JML) is the co-author (with Ken Beck and Jim Clark) of *The Amazing, Colossal Book of Horror Trivia: Everything You Ever Wanted to Know About Scary Movies But Were Afraid to Ask* (1999). He is a contributor to such

Midnight Marquee books as *Vincent Price, We Belong Dead, Peter Lorre,* and *Peter Cushing*. His articles have appeared in such publications as *Scarlet Street, Movie Club,* and *American Spirit*. Jonathan currently teaches developmental writing at Tennessee State University, gives tours of Belmont Mansion, and contributes movie reviews to *All the Rage,* all in Nashville. He completed his dissertation, *"Much of Madness, and More of Sin": Vincent Price, Gender, and the Poe Cycle, 1960-1972,* and received his doctorate in English from Middle Tennessee State University in May 2007. Check out his latest news and movie reviews at jonathanlampley.com.

ARTHUR JOSEPH LUNDQUIST (AJL), a second-generation monster kid (he was Gary Svehla's student in high school) juggles many identities: secretary, actor (*The Regenerated Man* [1994]), and writer. "Diary of a Slasher—or—How I Found Myself Killing People in a Movie Called *A Hazing in Hell,*" *Midnight Marquee,* no. 37 (Fall 1988), details his experiences on the film eventually released as *Pledge Night*; "Battle-Scarred Horrors," *Midnight Marquee* 65/66 (2002), examines the effect of WWI on horror films of the 1920s and 1930s. He has edited a one-man play, *To The War Was Called,* from the poetry of the Trench Poets of WWI and is working on a stage adaptation of Cyrano de Bergerac's 17th-century novel *Voyage to the Moon.*

JEFF MILLER (JSM) has written for *Midnight Marquee, Mad about Movies, Television Chronicles,* and *Filmfax* magazines and is the author of *The Horror Spoofs of Abbott and Costello*. He currently manages Rocket Video, Hollywood's greatest video store. He has contributed to Midnight Marquee's *Peter Cushing* volume and hopes to contribute to many future books as well. As you can see by his entries in *this* book, he is obsessed with Abbott and Costello and the Incredible Hulk.

By day BRYAN SENN (BMS) is a seemingly normal individual who works as a psychometrist at a Seattle-area children's hospital; by night he becomes a cinematic masked crusader viewing countless hours of drive-in dreck so *we* don't have to. He has reported his findings in such magazines as *Filmfax, Shivers, Midnight Marquee,* and *Monsters from the Vault*. Of course, he enjoys the good as well as the bad, and has authored the books *Golden Horrors: An Illustrated Critical Filmography of Terror Cinema, 1931-1939* (McFarland), *Drums of Terror: Voodoo in the Cinema* (Midnight Marquee Press), *Fantastic Cinema Subject Guide* (McFarland; with John Johnson), and the late-2007 one-man encyclopedia, *A Year of Fear: A Day-by-Day Guide to 366 Horror Films* (McFarland). He lives in the beautiful Pacific Northwest with his forgiving wife and movie-loving son (already a fan of Godzilla, Santo, and hopping Asian vampires), several cats, and a boa constrictor named Fang.

CINDY COLLINS SMITH (CCS) is a writer/editor with contributions in several Midnight Marquee/Luminary Press books. She is known in Ripper circles as owner and writer of the *Hollywood Ripper* website, which covers nine decades of Ripper and Faux-Ripper movies. She is also publisher of the e-book edition of *The Curse Upon Mitre Square* (the first published piece of fiction inspired by the Ripper killings) and is a serial contributor to *Ripperologist* magazine. In her day job, Ms. Smith edits a magazine, a newsletter, and conference publications for a professional association. She lives with her husband, fellow writer Brian Smith, in Falls Church, Virginia.

GARY J. SVEHLA (GJS), the 2006 inductee to the Rondo Awards' Monster Kid Hall of Fame, certainly deserves the honor. One of the original monster-kid progeny of *Famous Monsters of Filmland,* he forged a horror-film/horror-fan identity for himself by creating *Gore Creatures* in 1963, which developed into *Midnight Marquee* magazine, the longest continuously published horror-film journal in the world. Not content to rule the horror-film magazine world, he established Midnight Marquee Press in 1995 to publish books of quality film criticism (like this one). Somehow, he also finds time to teach high-school English in Anne Arundel County, Maryland: 2007-2008 marks his 36th year.

SUSAN SVEHLA (SAS) has been aiding and abetting her husband Gary for over 20 years. She creates the distinctive cover montages and photo layouts that grace *Midnight Marquee, Mad About Movies*, and Midnight Marquee books (like this one). She spent over one year layering and transforming photos into her first graphic novel, based upon *Spawn of Skull Island*. But graphic design, layout, and editing were not enough of a creative outlet for her talents, and she has recently devoted her energies to feature-film writing, editing, and directing as the auteur of *Terror in the Tropics* (2005) and *Terror in the Pharaoh's Tomb* (2006), DTV films that seamlessly combine contemporary actors with famous monsters of filmland.

JEFF THOMPSON (JDT) teaches English at Tennessee State University in Nashville. He has written chapters for *Peter Lorre, Peter Cushing, Dark Shadows*: *The Comic-Strip Book,* and *Tools for Academic Excellence.* He has written articles for *Midnight Marquee, Scarlet Street, Paperback Parade,* and *Mad About Movies.* His writings about popular culture and education appear on several Internet websites. An acknowledged Dan Curtis expert, Jeff completed his dissertation on the man's film and television career (*Dark Dreamer: Dan Curtis and Television Horror, 1966-2006*) and received his doctorate in English and popular culture from Middle Tennessee State University in May 2007. At home, Jeff has a "Dark Shadows" guest bedroom, a Joan Bennett wall, and a *Psycho* bathroom.

STEVEN THORNTON (SGT) is a man of many identities. As a genre writer, he has had his work appear in the pages of *Midnight Marquee, Mad About Movies, Monsters from the Vault,* and *Little Shoppe of Horrors.* As a musician, he is an accomplished guitar, bass, and keyboard player and can be seen onstage with local rock and blues bands. As a stage performer, he has appeared in community-theater productions of *Ten Little Indians, Joseph and the Amazing Technicolor Dreamcoat, Guys and Dolls,* and Disney's *Beauty and the Beast.* When not pursuing such creative endeavors, Steven works for a major IT consulting firm located in Michigan, where he lives with Rosanne, his wife of 15 years. Sometimes he also believes that he is Napoleon. But that usually passes quickly.

ROBERT TINNELL (RJT) works in both the film and comic-book industries. His film credits include *Frankenstein and Me* (1996) and *Kids of the Round Table* (1995). Tinnell's graphic novel *The Black Forest* won the 2006 Rondo Award for best horror comic (which is why his *The Wicked West* didn't), while his semi-autobiographical comic-strip collection *Feast of the Seven Fishes* was a 2006 Eisner Award nominee for Best Graphic Album – Reprint. His graphic novel *Sight Unseen* and his sequels, *The Black Forest 2* and *The Wicked West 2*, were all published in 2007. He resides in WV with his wife Shannon and their two children. Among his current projects is another based-on-autobiography webstrip, *The Chelation Kid*, recently nominated (June 2007) for a Harvey award.

The Films

Abbott and Costello Meet Dr. Jekyll and Mr. Hyde (1953) [**metamorphosis**] (Universal). *D:* Charles Lamont. *S:* Lee Loeb and John Grant, based on stories by Sidney Fields and Grant Garrett. *Cast:* Bud Abbott (Slim); Lou Costello (Tubby); Boris Karloff (Dr. Jekyll and Mr. Hyde); Helen Westcott (Vicky Edwards); Craig Stevens (Bruce Adams); Reginald Denny (Inspector); Eddie Parker (Mr. Hyde in most scenes, uncredited).

In the original story *The Strange Case of Dr. Jekyll and Mr. Hyde*, author Robert Louis Stevenson posits that all men have dual natures—one good and one evil. Kind Dr. Jekyll ingests a potion to bring out his darker side, Mr. Hyde. Hyde quickly gains control of Jekyll and ruins his life, for, once unleashed, man's evil side is too difficult to contain or control. Jekyll suffers a true loss of identity when he becomes Hyde; Hyde is Jekyll's polar opposite despite the fact that he resides within Jekyll's subconscious.

In *Abbott and Costello Meet Dr. Jekyll and Mr. Hyde*, the comedians play Slim and Tubby, bumbling American police officers who have joined the London force to study British crime-solving methods. The city is being terrorized by Mr. Hyde (called "the Monster" by the public at large), who is, in reality, the kind and respected Dr. Jekyll. Jekyll transforms into Hyde to kill his fellow scientists who mock his work. Now he has targeted reporter Bruce Adams, who has fallen in love with Jekyll's ward, Vicky. Though Vicky sees Jekyll as a father figure, the good doctor has long been in love with the beautiful girl. After being thrown off the force, Slim and Tubby team up with Bruce to track the monster. Tubby figures out that Jekyll is Hyde, but no one believes him. During a wild climactic chase, Tubby himself is transformed into a monster and leads Slim on a wild-goose chase while the real Hyde is killed trying to escape from Bruce and the police.

Boris Karloff and Mr. Hyde pose for this studio publicity shot for *Abbott and Costello Meet Dr. Jekyll and Mr. Hyde*.

Though not one of the duo's best horror-comedies, *Abbott and Costello Meet Dr. Jekyll and Mr. Hyde* is still a fun romp. Bud and Lou actually seem absent for much of the picture, and, when they are onscreen, they rely too much on slapstick and knockabout comedy. But most fans recall the pic fondly. One of the reasons the movie remains memorable is its frightening ending. Costello as the Tubby-Hyde bites a roomful of bobbies and his boss, the Inspector, before transforming back to his normal self. The officers themselves transform into monsters and chase the comedians out of the room for a final gag. For young children, this can be a frightening moment because the movie ends with new monsters on the loose and ready to terrorize their beloved comedians. In a way, the ending of the film foreshadows modern horror films which end with a cheap shock or final scare reminding the viewer that the monster has not been vanquished and will inevitably turn up for a sequel.

Straight adaptations of Stevenson's story have done very well in fleshing out the author's theme of the duality of man as well as the theme of loss of identity. But this spoof fails to do so. Boris Karloff's Dr. Jekyll briefly explains his theories about man's dual natures to Bruce and Vicky and claims his work is based on these ideas. He says every man is born with two sides to his personality—one good, the other evil. The good side keeps the evil side in check. But some are born with the inability to keep their darker side under control, and they commit violent crimes.

But the character of Jekyll and Hyde does not reflect the good doctor's theory. Karloff's Jekyll, though a respected citizen, is actually evil to begin with. He mistreats his servant. He raises his ward from a child, shaping her to be the perfect woman, solely to marry her and take her as his own. When she falls in love with Bruce, he plots to kill the reporter. Like a spoiled brat, he kills any of his peers who disagree with his theories. And he cold-bloodedly plots the murders of Slim and Tubby—his line reading of "Perhaps they should never leave this house" drips with delicious menace.

Hyde, then, is just a disguise for Jekyll so that he can commit his crimes without being recognized. Jekyll seems to have total control over Hyde, who is just Jekyll with an ugly face and a heck of a lot of hair. The whole theme of man's dual nature is lost, and, as a result, the film rings rather false.

Further proof that the film neglects its source and does not play by the rules of dual nature and loss of identity can be seen in Tubby's transformation. If Jekyll's potion truly brought out one's opposite nature (and caused loss of identity), Tubby would have become a murderous fiend. Instead, he becomes more of a prankster. He scares London's citizens, barks at some dogs, and bites some policemen on their fingers. Though he wreaks some minor havoc, he is simply trying to get away from his pursuers, who have mistaken him for the real Hyde. The Tubby-Hyde is rather a childlike innocent, like his regular self. The Tubby-Hyde is not a killer because Tubby is not evil. The Jekyll-Hyde is a killer because Jekyll is evil. Instead of trying to tie in the idea of man's duality, the film should have instead focused on the interpretation of appearance vs. reality. One cannot judge people by how they look, for an ugly face does not mean an ugly heart. The true measure of a man is what's on the inside. One may "smile and smile and be a villain": Jekyll's potion makes manifest what Jekyll is really like.

This lack of focus does not fully detract from the enjoyment of *Abbott and Costello Meet Dr. Jekyll and Mr. Hyde*. Despite its outer flaws, it has a good heart. It wants to make us laugh while at the same time scaring us—and, quite often, it does just that.—*JSM*

Abbott and Costello Meet Frankenstein (1948) [**metamorphosis; hypnotism**] (Universal). *D:* Charles T. Barton. *S:* Robert Lees, Frederic I. Rinaldo and John Grant. *Cast:* Bud Abbott (Chick Young); Lou Costello (Wilbur Gray); Lon Chaney, Jr. (Lawrence Talbot); Bela Lugosi (Dracula); Glenn Strange (the Monster); Lenore Aubert (Sandra Mornay); Jane Randolph (Joan Raymond); Frank Ferguson (MacDougal); Charles Bradstreet (Prof. Stevens); Vincent Price (the Invisible Man, uncredited).

For many (myself included), *Abbott and Costello Meet Frankenstein* remains the greatest horror-comedy of all time. Combining the zany antics of Universal's top comedy team with the play-it-straight scares of the studio's classic monsters, the film retains its power to this day, continuing to entertain new generations of movie buffs.

The plot by now is familiar: Baggage clerks Chick and Wilbur deliver the bodies of Dracula and the Frankenstein Monster to MacDougal's "house of horrors" museum. The Count, hoping to use the Monster to take over the world, needs to find a suitable brain so the Monster won't rebel against his master. Dracula enlists the aid of beautiful Dr. Sandra Mornay, who chooses Wilbur as the perfect brain donor. She pretends to romance him (which drives Chick crazy—he can't understand why a "classy dish" like Sandra would show any interest in tubby Wilbur). Lawrence Talbot—the Wolf Man—has discovered Dracula's plan and arrives in town to stop the vampire. A pretty insurance investigator named Joan Raymond also gets involved, and she, too, pretends to be in love with Wilbur in order to get information on the whereabouts of the museum's missing exhibits.

Two loss-of-identity themes play a part in this picture. First, there is the doomed lycanthrope Larry Talbot, who—despite being cured of his affliction in *House of*

Lawrence Talbot (Lon Chaney, Jr.) frantically searches for a cure that will stop his transformations in *Abbott and Costello Meet Frankenstein*.

The second loss of identity comes with Dracula's (Lugosi) hypnosis and control over Wilbur (Costello) in *Abbott and Costello Meet Frankenstein*.

Dracula (1945)—is now once again a werewolf. When he's not suffering from a lapse of humanity, Talbot is one of the good guys, trying to convince Chick and Wilbur that Dracula must be stopped. Unfortunately, Talbot's loss-of-identity problem continually gets in the way of thwarting the vampire. Initially, Talbot tries by phone to warn Wilbur against delivering the exhibits. But his transformation into the Wolf Man keeps him from finishing his message. Next, he wolfs-out in his hotel room after Wilbur locks him in. He almost kills the comic, but Wilbur's luck holds, and he just barely misses being slaughtered. Talbot's next metamorphosis occurs during a search for Joan, whom Dracula has spirited away. This time, the Wolf Man almost succeeds in killing Wilbur, as well as MacDougal. His appearance causes the gathered crowd to chase Chick and Wilbur instead of looking for Sandra and Joan. During his final appearance, as if to make up for all the added trouble he's caused, the Wolf Man instinctively goes after Dracula. The brief but exciting battle ends with the werewolf grabbing Dracula (in the form of a bat) and taking the Count with him to their mutual demise as they tumble from a castle window to the water below. Talbot finally conquers his loss of identity just enough to vanquish his foe and save the world.

In the Universal films, the audience always feels for Larry Talbot. Again and again, he reminds us that he has no control over his other self and that he would rather die than continue living as a lycanthrope. He's still complaining here, but this time Wilbur mocks his sad story. Talbot says he will transform into a wolf when the moon is full, and Wilbur replies, "I'm kind of a wolf myself." Later, Talbot again reminds Costello,

"When the moon is full, I turn into a wolf." Wilbur answers with the film's most quoted line: "You and 20 million other guys." Talbot's loss of identity has come a long way from *The Wolf Man* (1941 [*q.v.*])—it is now a source of humor. Maybe that's why Lon Chaney, Jr. was never a big fan of the film.

The second loss of identity comes with Dracula's hypnosis—and eventual control—over three of the picture's characters: Sandra, Joan, and Wilbur, all of whom fall under Dracula's spell: Sandra becomes a vampire when she does not follow the Count's wishes; Joan is put under Drac's spell to get her out of the way; Wilbur is hypnotized twice—once in the wax museum and again when he is trying to escape from the island. Interestingly, these three victims all have feminine traits: Joan and Sandra are obviously beautiful women while Wilbur exhibits less manly characteristics such as dancing with Chick, skipping, etc. In addition, these three characters are all romantically (perhaps even sexually) active. Wilbur is pursued by two different women, and he urges each of them on, much to the frustration of Chick, who's also attracted to them and can't understand their interest in Wilbur. (Chick tells Sandra he doesn't "get it"; she replies "And frankly you never will.") Sandra oozes pure sex when she seduces Wilbur (he is so lovestruck that he doesn't feel Chick smash him in the head with a heavy bag: "Nothing matters no more."). Joan uses her feminine wiles to attract Wilbur, but she also makes her attraction to Prof. Stevens very plain and clear. He seems interested but later coolly admits to Chick that he doesn't even try to understand women.

With these three characters being so openly "on the move" sexually, is it any wonder that they are easy targets for the monsters? For the film's first three-quarters, only Wilbur, Sandra, and Joan encounter or see the monsters—Chick and MacDougal scoff at the supernatural while Stevens is just plain oblivious. The film seems to be warning against promiscuity by showing romantically active characters losing their identities to Dracula. Because they are distracted by their baser instincts, they are ripe targets.

One last note: The magic of *Abbott and Costello Meet Frankenstein* lies in the fact that the monsters play it straight and remain frightening figures. Bud and Lou add the comedy through their scared reactions to the terror trio. But there is one instance where the Frankenstein Monster loses his fearsome identity and briefly becomes a buffoon. Seeing the hypnotized Wilbur, he recoils in fear. Dracula soothes him: "Don't be afraid. He won't hurt you." Though it breaks the continuity of the Monster's image and identity, it's a hilarious moment that reinforces my belief that *Meet Frankenstein* is one of the greatest movies ever made. My belief—and 20 million other guys'.—*JSM*

Abbott and Costello Meet the Invisible Man (1952) [**madness**] (Universal). *D:* Charles Lamont. *S:* Robert Lees, Frederic I. Rinaldo and John Grant; Original Story by Hugh Wedlock, Jr. and Howard Snyder, Suggested by the Novel *The Invisible Man* by H.G. Wells. *Cast:* Bud Abbott (Bud Alexander); Lou Costello (Lou Francis); Nancy Guild (Helen Gray); Arthur Franz (Tommy Nelson); Adele Jergens (Boots Marsden); Sheldon Leonard (Morgan); William Frawley (Det. Roberts); Gavin Muir (Dr. Philip Gray).

The hook in most Invisible Man movies that creates their connection to loss-of-identity fantasy films is the fact that the serum used to create invisibility also causes eventual madness. In *Abbott and Costello Meet the Invisible Man*, this holds true though the theme of loss of identity is barely a subplot. Instead, the film centers on the Invisible Man employing newly graduated private eyes Bud and Lou to prove he's innocent of

Bud Abbott and Lou Costello try to help Tommy Nelson (Arthur Franz), who is slowly descending into madness in *Abbott and Costello Meet the Invisible Man.*

a trumped-up murder charge. After all, the film was written around a scene where Lou is a boxer aided in the ring by an invisible cohort.

Tommy Nelson is a prizefighter who is framed for the murder of his manager after he refuses a gangster's "request" to throw a match. Luckily, his girlfriend's uncle is a scientist experimenting with the same invisibility serum created by Dr. John Griffin in the original *The Invisible Man* (1933 [*q.v.*]). In fact, a photo of Claude Rains is shown hanging on the wall. Tommy injects himself with the serum to better hide from the police. Together with Bud and Lou, he forms a plan to catch gangster Morgan, who ordered the hit on Tommy's manager. If all this sounds familiar, it's because the same plot (sans the boxing angle) was used in *The Invisible Man Returns* (1940)—in fact, entire sequences and lines of dialogue were lifted from that film and used in this one.

The catch in the plan is that the serum has not been fully perfected, and, if Tommy does not receive the antidote in time, he'll become a raging maniac just like Dr. Griffin. While this idea could have been used to create more suspense in the picture, it is instead pushed to the background. (This is, after all, an Abbott and Costello film.) There are hints of impending madness—mostly during the scenes where an inebriated Tommy shares dinner with Bud and Lou. Nelson speaks of being the ruler of an invisible empire, one where he will reward his friends and destroy his enemies. When Bud and Lou nervously remind him that they are his friends, Tommy says he doesn't need friends but worshippers. The boys' apprehension is understandable; they have been told what could happen to Tommy if he does not receive the antidote in time. And they know that Nelson's true identity is not that of a murderer but rather a decent athlete who has been mixed up in a situation beyond his control. Nelson's rants and raves are the same lines Vincent Price spouted in *The Invisible Man Returns*, but they sound rather random here—any loss-of-identity effect seems to come more from Tommy's drunkenness than from the serum. After recovering from his night out, he is back to normal.

In the end, everything turns out all right for everyone—except Lou, who literally has body parts turned around in a gruesome sight gag. After receiving some of the invisibility serum during a blood transfusion, Lou certainly does not lose any of his identity—he pinches girls and dreams of being the best private eye in the world.

So while the "eventual madness" plot device does not really explore loss of identity, there is some hint of the idea in the film's theme of appearance vs. truth. Throughout the film, characters refuse to see the underlying truth about their fellow players. The police (led by *I Love Lucy*'s William Frawley) do not see boxer Tommy as a good man framed for a crime he did not commit but as a vicious murderer. Morgan and his moll Boots do not see that Bud and Lou are detectives but accept their undercover identities of manager and boxer. The police who know that Bud and Lou are detectives do not see them as capable but rather as buffoons. The police also do not see that Morgan is the real murderer and a dangerous criminal. And Gray does not see Tommy as someone capable of handling the invisibility serum in his system. These are just a few examples of characters not seeing or realizing the true identities of those around them. Eventually, though, the truth is always revealed. Tommy is proved to be innocent and shows Gray up by avoiding the eventual madness from the serum. Bud and Lou prove to police and criminals alike that they are actually capable detectives. And Morgan is revealed to be the mastermind behind the evil doings in the boxing community. It all goes to show that loss of identity can in fact be a temporary condition and, with patience and fortitude, can be overcome. Sometimes, the truth can just not be plainly seen—just like Tommy Nelson.—*JSM*

Abbott and Costello Meet the Killer, Boris Karloff (1949) [**hypnotism**] (Universal). *D:* Charles T. Barton. *S:* Hugh Wedlock, Jr., Howard Snyder, and John Grant; Original Story by Hugh Wedlock, Jr., and Howard Snyder. *Cast:* Bud Abbott (Casey Edwards); Lou Costello (Freddy Phillips); Boris Karloff (Swami Talpur); Lenore Aubert (Angela Gordon); Gar Moore (Jeff Wilson); Donna Martell (Betty Crandall); Alan Mowbray (Melton); James Flavin (Inspector Wellman); Roland Winters (T. Hanley Brooks); Nicholas Joy (Amos Strickland); Mikel Conrad (Sergeant Stone).

Abbott and Costello Meet the Killer, Boris Karloff is a comic murder mystery that takes place at Crandall's Lost Cavern Hotel. Former clients of a prominent defense attorney have gathered there because they are being blackmailed by someone whom they think is the attorney himself—Amos Strickland. Strickland is murdered, and suspicion falls upon naïve bellboy Freddy Phillips, who lost his job after a run-in with the lawyer. Hotel dick Casey Edwards tries to convince the police that his pal Freddy isn't bright enough to commit murder. But the blackmail victims are happy to have a fall guy. After beautiful Angela Gordon tricks Freddy into signing a confession, Swami Talpur takes it upon himself to make sure Freddy disappears—by hypnotizing the hapless bellboy into committing suicide.

Swami (Karloff) tries to order Freddy (Costello) to plunge the knife into his chest in *Abbott and Costello Meet the Killer*.

In a way, a theme of loss of identity becomes prominent even before the hypnotism scene. Casey—and Freddy himself—keep trying to convince Inspector Wellman that Freddy is too dumb to commit a murder. Yet everyone, from the hotel manager to the other guests, believes that the childlike Freddy *is* capable of such a violent act. As the evidence piles up against Freddy, even he comes to believe that he may actually have it in him to kill. He questions who he is and his own identity. This leads to all kinds of comic mishaps including a sequence where Freddy is forced to disguise himself as a maid to avoid Wellman and dispose of a body that has appeared in his room. Under this loss of gender self, he even suffers sexual harassment from night clerk Abernathy. (But Freddy strikes a blow for women's lib by striking a blow against Abernathy!)

The scene that allows *Abbott and Costello Meet the Killer* to be included in this study (and which qualifies its inclusion in lists and studies of horror and fantastic films) is the hypnotism sequence. The Swami sneaks into Freddy's room and hypnotizes him. Ignoring the fact that people under hypnosis will not do what it is not in their nature to do normally, the Swami tries to force Freddy to commit suicide. Lou's mind and identity are now under the Swami's control. Or so he thinks!

Thankfully, luck—and Freddy's surprisingly strong self-awareness—wins out. The Swami has Freddy place his head in a noose and jump off the bed. But the fat comic grabs hold of the noose, and his weight pulls the rope—and pieces of the ceiling—to the floor. Next, the Swami orders Freddy to shoot himself with the gun he keeps in his room—only to be frustrated again when the gun in question turns out to be a harmless squirt gun. When the Swami asks Freddy how he would like to die, Freddy responds, "Old age."

The Swami orders Freddy to jump out the window, but Freddy refuses. Finding a knife, he gives it to Freddy and tells him to plunge the knife into his chest. Again, Freddy refuses. His sense of self-preservation is actually powerful enough to overcome his loss of control and identity! Even the Swami is taken aback. "Amazing," he says, "even under hypnosis, the will of an idiot to cling to life."

Finally, the Swami tells Freddy to plunge the knife into the heart of the man whose reflection Freddy sees in the mirror—not realizing that Freddy is looking at him! For a brief moment, Freddy truly does lose his identity as he becomes the murderer everyone believes him to be. With an evil grin, he chases Karloff with the knife, and the Swami finds he is unable to stop him. Talpur beats a hasty retreat just as Casey enters the room. Now becoming the man in the mirror, Casey is momentarily threatened by Freddy and his knife until he snaps Freddy out of the trance and the bellboy returns to normal. The old adage was right—people won't do under hypnosis what they would not do in waking life. But the fact that Freddy is even for a few seconds willing to stab Casey shows that he may harbor some deep resentment for his bullying partner. I think Freddy's identity actually does remains intact—while he is definitely too dumb to commit murder, he is not above scaring those authority figures who think they can control him, bully him, or steal his identity—hence his momentary killing instinct against the Swami and Casey. Freddy does not have a lot of opportunities to get revenge and has to get his jabs in wherever and whenever he can.

All in all, a good scene in a fun movie.—*JSM*

Alien³ (1992) [alien possession; eradication of self] (20th Century Fox). *D:* David Fincher. *S:* David Giler, Walter Hill, and Larry Ferguson, from a story by Vincent Ward, based on characters created by Dan O'Bannon and Ronald Shusette. *Cast:* Sigourney Weaver (Ellen Ripley); Charles S. Dutton (Dillon); Charles Dance (Clemens); Paul McGann (Golic); Brian Glover (Andrews); Ralph Brown (Aaron); Lance Henrickson (Bishop II).

In the 1979 hit *Alien*, Signorney Weaver plays Ripley, a blue-collar worker in a future world where the lives of its workers are considered without value. What self-value these laborers possess is earned working with the people around them. *Alien* ended with all Ripley's friends and co-workers (including a man with whom she shared the possibility of something more) killed by a malevolent creature from another world. The 1986 sequel *Aliens* begins by taking more from Ripley: a half-century and all former human contact. Awakened from cryogenic sleep when the shuttle she escaped in (in *Alien*) is found drifting in deep space, Ripley discovers that 57 years have elapsed. In the intervening time, virtually everyone Ripley had ever known has died, including her own daughter—a point dropped from the theatrical release of the film and made clear only in the subsequent LD/DVD extended versions.

The plot of *Aliens* takes Ripley from being a forgotten cog in the industrial future, haunted by nightmares about the creature who killed her friends, and returns her to the world where those nightmares first began. There she confronts her greatest terror and finds reservoirs of strength and resourcefulness she'd never known she possessed. The

Ripley (Sigourney Weaver) loses everything at the beginning of *Alien³*.

film concludes with her setting out once more for home, this time surrounded by a surrogate family who owe their lives to her, including an android friend (Bishop) who has earned Ripley's respect and affection (in contrast to Ash, the android who tried to kill her in *Alien*), a man with whom we notice the beginnings of a more intimate relationship, and a little girl who in the film's final note of triumph, has given Ripley the title "Mommy." Each member of this family represents a part of Ripley's self that had been lost at the film's beginning.

A lot of people in the world's audiences fell in love with what Ripley created for herself by the end of *Aliens*. In my opinion, that journey from Ripley's heart of darkness makes *Aliens* the finest of the series.

In 1991 another *Alien* sequel was in production, involving Ripley confronting her alien nemeses on a prison planet. There was only one problem. The script had no room for her new family.

And so, over the opening credits of *Alien³*, every one of them is killed off, and, in the process, Ripley is herself violated and impregnated by her worst enemy. When we finally join her, her hair has been sheared away, and she is given featureless garments to wear that evoke the clothing intended to dehumanize the inmates of concentration camps.

That blotting out of inconvenient accomplishments by the producers of *Alien³* is more terrifying than anything in the movie itself. That anyone could so cavalierly take everything Ripley had built for herself and throw it all away (before the opening credits have even ended, for chrissakes!) was so heartless, so disturbing for its audience, so bone-chillingly frightening that—well, let me put it this way: I, like everyone else in New York City, tried to see the film on its opening weekend in May of 1992. I couldn't even get into the theater. *Alien³* opened on 3,000 screens around the country, and in its first three days grossed more than $23 million. By the end of the week its gross had gone up to just under $27 million. It was a major hit. Then word of mouth got around. In its second week, playing just about the same number of screens, the film's box office dropped almost 60%. In its third week, it dropped about 50% again. When I finally saw it, in the heart of a Friday night three weeks after its smash opening, the Times Square first-run house was mostly empty.

It served the bastards right.—*AJL*

Alien Resurrection (1997) [**alien possession; scientific manipulation**] (20th Century Fox). *D*: Jean-Pierre Jeunet. *S*: Joss Whedon, Based on Characters Created by Dan O'Bannon and Ronald Shusett. *Cast:* Sigourney Weaver (Ellen Ripley); Winona Ryder (Annalee Call); Dominique Pinon (Vriess); Ron Perlman (Johner); Gary Dourdan (Christie); Michael Wincott (Frank Elgyn); Kim Flowers (Sabra Hillard); Dan Hedaya (Gen. Martin Perez); Brad Dourif (Dr. Jonathan Gediman).

Alien Resurrection is an extremely satisfying and engaging resolution to the *Alien* series, not just because it takes the bad taste of *Alien³* (1992 [*q.v.*]) from our cinematic mouths, but because it, unlike the third film, retains and works with the themes of the first two films. It builds on the concepts of corporate/scientific greed, technology, parent-child relationships, and creator-creation relationships in order to examine what it means to be human. It is the most disturbing of all the *Alien* movies, probably because of the ways in which it plays with and plays on our sense of belonging, of Self, of Other.

The terror of and preoccupation with loss of identity is present on a number of levels throughout the film. First, and perhaps most fundamentally, Ripley herself *isn't* Ripley herself, but a clone, the eighth one made from blood of the original Ripley. Second, she was only created as an incubator for the *real* prize—"Her Majesty," the queen alien—which the army wants to clandestinely develop as a biological weapon. (Never mind that the concept of using blood to clone Ripley *with the alien inside her*

Ripley (Sigourney Weaver) must destroy the deformed and suffering clone of herself as Call (Winona Ryder) watches in horror in *Alien Resurrection.*

is a misuse of science on the scale of inheriting acquired characteristics.) Ripley is no longer an independent individual or even a pawn of the Machine—instead, she's a medical discard, a subject the top brass insist on referring to as "it." Nor is she "herself" physiologically: She soon discovers that she's been changed by the cloning process, and that, when they took the alien out of her, they didn't take it "all the way out." She is now a hybrid of sorts, with somewhat acidic blood, some regenerative powers, preternatural speed, and an ability to sense the presence of the aliens. This hybridism ties into one of the second blows to established identity—because, unlike the invasive, penetrating figure of the first film or the opposing colonial force of the second film, the "alien" creatures in this film are much less foreign than they should be—and this shift in perspective is in itself terrifying. The question of Who's Worse was brought up once in *Aliens* (1986)—"at least they don't screw each other over for a lousy percentage"—but in *Resurrection* this question is always right below the surface. After all, the army and its scientists are amoral tamperers-with-nature who have no qualms about creating and discarding organisms in their search for the proper Ripley/queen combination, and the crew of the *Betty*, who become the "heroes" of the film, are scruffy space pirates who sold live people in their cryo-tubes to the army to be used as hosts for the queen's offspring. In fact, the only truly heroic people in the film are Ripley (in spite of some dark moments) and Call—one of whom is an alien hybrid and the other of whom is an android. "I should have known," the ironically amused Ripley states when she discovers Call's secret: "No human is that humane."

Perhaps the film's best illustration of human inhumanity is the nightmarish scene in which Ripley finds the room containing Ripley clones # 1-7, six of which have been so malformed that they've been preserved as specimens in solution: half-human, half-alien merges, with Ripley's features distorted by alien jaws, arms turning to claws, legs twisted, alien face on human torso ending in embryonic tail. Finally Ripley encounters

In order to save the crew, Ripley (Weaver) must destroy the human/alien creature that accepts Ripley as its mother in *Alien Resurrection*.

#7, the almost-Ripley, a woman only somewhat mutated, that the scientists not only operated on but kept alive in agony in their specimen room—this hall of horrors which is also a hall of mirrors that Ripley has to pass through before, weeping, she must kill her other self, her mirror image, at the woman's request. This scene, in which Ripley has to acknowledge these clones as herself, realize what's been *done* to her and what she's become, is one of the most effectively horrifying in the movie.

The other, final, horror is the Frankenstein monster-child, the live-birth human/alien creature that is "Ripley's [biological] gift" to the queen alien—the appalling grotesquerie that kills its real mother, the queen, but accepts Ripley. In order to save the crew and the world, Ripley has to both acknowledge and destroy this monster, blood-of-her-blood, that looks at her with human eyes. Its death-scream, a wail like that of a woman in pain, is haunting not just for its sound but for the ambivalence it invokes in Ripley and in the audience: Are we witnessing a victory or a murder? —And that is the true horror of the film, that it forces on the audience as well as the character an inspection of identity, a hall of mirrors showing the monstrousness of human beings.

At the same time, the film does give us a satisfying resolution, for it seems to argue that in all identity is an element of choice: Yes, Ripley has to acknowledge her connection to this alien creature—but she can also betray it without betraying herself, because—unlike her—it has shown itself to be evil from its birth. Yes, we can cringe from what humans have done and still cheer for our favorites, and for the Earth itself, to be saved. Yes, our heroes are *not* fully human, are in some ways frighteningly different—and yet they are, have chosen to be, fully humane. The final triumph is the triumph of a biotech world, the triumph of hybrids and chimeras and semi-organic people over the forces of destruction, both human and alien: the choice to accept the Earth, no matter how foreign it seems ("I'm a stranger here myself," Ripley says of it) because it promises something better than the familiar.—*OVA*

Alligator People, The (1959) [**metamorphosis; scientific manipulation**] (20th Century Fox). *D:* Roy Del Ruth. *S:* Orville H. Hampton and Charles O'Neal. *Cast:* Beverly Garland (Joyce); Richard Crane (Paul); Bruce Bennett (Dr. Lorimer); George Macready (Dr. Sinclair); Lon Chaney, Jr. (Manon).

Transformation from man to animal is usually handled by the mythology of lycanthropy, man morphing into werewolf. However, in the heyday of schlock science fiction produced on a budget during the 1950s, man might find himself changed into many things, even an alligator. Such a silly premise is handled quite seriously in the moody CinemaScope production of *The Alligator People*.

Newly married Paul and Joyce are honeymooning aboard a train when the distraught Paul receives a message and leaves the train, abandoning his blushing bride, leaving her alone to fend for herself.

It seems Paul suffered a horrible, disfiguring car crash and sought experimental treatment in the Louisiana Bayou from Dr. Sinclair—treatment that apparently restored the stud to his former buff status. However, the message states that the experiment has gone awry and that Paul must return for more treatments, thus the reason for abruptly leaving his wife.

Returning to the medical plantation, Paul woefully discovers that his alligator treatments are turning his human skin into scaly alligator skin, creating a hideous humanoid

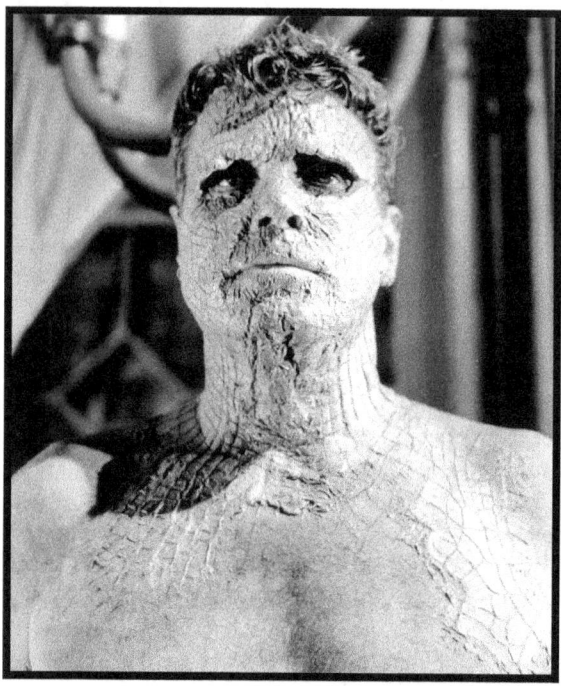

Paul (Richard Crane), trying to find a cure for his scarred body, turns to an experimental treatment which begins to transform him. He forces the doctor to use the full power of his machine and loses his last connection to humanity in *The Alligator People*.

that could not survive in regular society. Much worse, as further treatments continue, he is becoming less and less human and more and more alligator.

Along for the ride is 'gator wrangler Manon, played by Lon Chaney, Jr., a backwoods misfit who lost a hand to the animals (he sports a hook in its place) and constantly screams at the top of his lungs that he will kill any 'gator that he can find. It's the kind of delicious over-the-top performance that Chaney excelled at creating. When Joyce, now using a phony identity, tracks her missing husband to this plantation, Manon is more than a little physically attracted to Beverly Garland's beautiful Joyce and seductively rubs his hook against her face and shoulders and hair. She ultimately screams for her life.

The first pivotal loss-of-identity sequence takes place in the middle of the night when the shadow-cloaked Paul plays sad music in the living room on the piano, attracting Joyce's attention. She cannot see Paul's hideous figure, but she can sense her husband's presence as he performs melancholy music a few feet away. When she approaches the pathetic creature who thinks he is alone, he panics, covers his face, and rushes away—his abrupt, unexplainable behavior again confusing Joyce. The point here is that Paul's body has changed, but his personality remains intact. Because of his

disfigurement, Paul feels it is better for his wife to believe he is dead. So his physical transformation creates a new identity of isolation.

But more change is coming.

Forcing Dr. Sinclair to turn the full power of his x-ray treatments on him in one final chance to bring forth a total cure, Paul is now turned totally into a human alligator, sporting a huge snout and 'gator choppers, losing the last vestiges of his former human identity. Paul has transformed into a savage alligator from the waist up, and now any remainder of the human Paul has been destroyed. His last vain attempt to regain his humanity results in a total loss of identity—his humanity sacrificed in a vile scientific experiment.

The transformation from human to animal is now complete, resulting in the complete loss of human identity and the inevitable loss of life. In the film's final minutes Paul runs amok until he falls and is dragged down into the swamp's quicksand.—*GJS*

Altered States (1980) [**eradication of self; metamorphosis**] (Warner Bros.). *D:* Ken Russell. *S:* Paddy Chayefsky (as Sidney Aaron), Based on the Novel *Altered States* by Paddy Chayefsky. *Cast:* William Hurt (Eddie Jessup); Blair Brown (Emily Jessup); Bob Balaban (Arthur Rosenberg); Charles Haid (Mason Parrish); Miguel Godreau (Primitive Man); Drew Barrymore (Margaret Jessup).

In *Altered States*, Eddie Jessup is looking to find himself and the origin of all things through sensory deprivation, hallucinogenic mushrooms, and whatever else it takes for him to get in touch with his inner primal man—which he ultimately unleashes, losing his identity in the process.

Altered States began life as a Paddy Cheyefsky novel, which he adapted for the screen (with the contractual stipulation that his script remain unaltered) and which was put in the hands of Ken Russell, who was making the painful transition from an auteur who originated his own projects to a director-for-hire (and who was chafing under this loss of identity and power; apparently Arthur Penn had been originally slated to direct, and Russell has claimed that he was the 27th choice). Chayefsky plus Russell, two mavericks who made their reputations on television (albeit two very different kinds: live American drama; BBC biographies), would seem to be a perfect match—Chayefsky had made a career out of elevating ordinary human beings to heroes (e.g., *Marty*), and Russell had made a career out of bringing the celebrated (writers and composers)

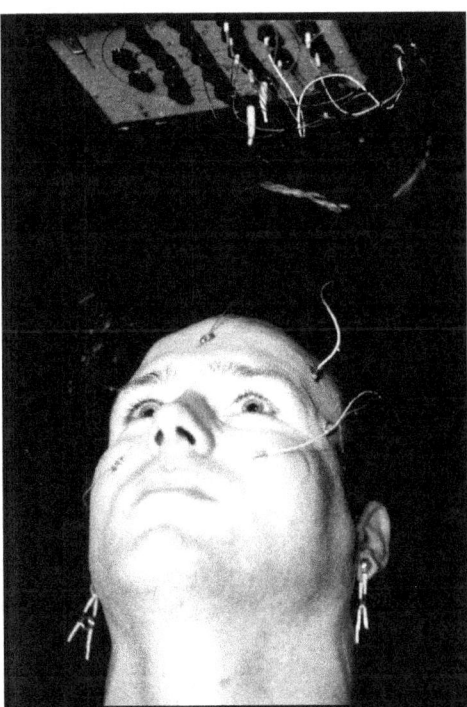

Eddie Jessup (William Hurt) loses himself when he tries to find himself in *Altered States*.

down to Earth. But, alas, it was a clash of idiosyncrasies; Chayefsky so hated Russell's approach that he had his name removed from the credits and replaced by a pseudonym (a fine loss of identity), and Russell—hamstrung by the inviolability of a scenario whose words he couldn't change, had his actors steamroll through pages of dialogue just to get it said and out of the way.

Which is a shame. Because the movie, the product of so much bickering and ill will, is about the triumph of love, and how it can pull us back from and out of the abyss—that it's the only thing that gives us our identity. When Eddie retreats deep into the sensory-deprivation tank, which explodes, inundating him in a "primal soup," it is his estranged ex-wife, Emily, who pulls him back to reality. And, in the climax, when—like Dr. Jekyll, with whose story *Altered States* has several parallels—Eddie finds himself changing without benefit of machines or drugs and infects Emily with the same shape-shifting-into-chaos disease, he fights his way back to humanity, to himself, so he can rescue her, and they regain their identities in a peaceful, naked embrace. (The derrière view of Blair Brown as she kneels, hugging William Hurt on the floor of the Jessups' now-restored-to-normal home, is at once calming and arousing.)

Altered States is by no means the best work that Chayefsky or Russell ever did, but it remains an admirable sub-Jekyll adventure in identity lost and found.—*AFA*

Amanti d'oltretomba, Gli. See ***Nightmare Castle*** (1966).

Angel Heart (1987) [**amnesia**] Carolco International (Tri-Star). *D:* Alan Parker. *S:* Alan Parker, Based on the Novel *Falling Angel* by William Hjortsberg. *Cast:* Mickey Rourke (Harry Angel); Robert De Niro (Louis Cyphre); Lisa Bonet (Epiphany Proudfoot); Charlotte Rampling (Margaret Krusemark); Stoker Pontelieu (Ethan Krusemark); Browning McGhee (Toots Sweet).

A character "finding himself" in a novel or film is usually a good thing. Such is not necessarily the case in a loss-of-identity picture—especially when the protagonist doesn't know what he's going to find, or even that he's looking for himself.

"It will scare you to your very soul," warned the tag-line for this enthralling loss-of-identity classic—an admonition that's not far from wrong. In 1955 New York, small-time private detective Harry Angel meets with a mysterious client named Louis Cyphre. Cyphre wants Angel to locate a singer named Johnny Favorite. "I gave Johnny some help at the beginning of his career," explains the enigmatic Cyphre. Johnny was drafted in 1943 and subsequently "badly injured about the head and face. He had amnesia." Upon his return to the States, Favorite entered a private sanitarium but soon disappeared. Angel's investigations lead him to New Orleans, where he tracks down Johnny's former society girlfriend, Margaret Krusemark, as well as Johnny's illegitimate daughter, a 17-year-old half-black voodoo priestess named Epiphany. Nearly everyone Angel meets turns up dead (usually horribly mutilated), and the private eye fears he's being set up. Angel then learns the whole, horrifying truth, both about his client ("Louis Cyphre"—*Lucifer*) and himself, in the film's powerful identity-lost (and -found) denouement—an ending that once seen is not soon forgotten.

Written and shot in a noirish style, *Angel Heart* is an exquisitely photographed film that often emphasizes both beauty and horror almost simultaneously. The opening credit sequence in which the camera roams a nighttime New York street, for instance,

Angel Heart, **starring Mickey Rourke as P.I. Harry Angel, is perhaps the ultimate loss-of-identity horror.**

is so effectively lit that the scene seems bathed in an eerie blue and silver light, evoking the glittering, dark night of winter (the story takes place in January), and transforming the slush-soaked, dirty street into a landscape of near-abstract beauty. This makes it doubly shocking when the camera comes to rest on a blood-drenched corpse sprawled amongst the refuse and soiled snow. This introductory sequence foreshadows one of *Angel Heart*'s primary themes: Nothing and no one in this film are quite what they first seem, and characters' true identities remain hidden—even from themselves.

After watching Mickey Rourke's intense, quirky, and appealing portrayal, it's difficult to imagine anyone else as Harry Angel. In director Alan Parker's words, Rourke exhibits "something wicked, anarchic, and charming." Disheveled and rumpled, Rourke ingratiates himself with his seedy charisma and unassuming likeability. Small touches, such as when he casually retrieves a lady's hat blown off by the wind or briefly touches the cheek of a small child sitting on the stairs as he wearily passes by, help forge a bond with the viewer so that we become caught up in Harry Angel's plight. Consequently, his frantic, fruitless denial at film's end ("I know who I am!" he shouts over and over with less and less conviction until, finally, he truly *does* know who he is—to his ultimate despair) becomes both horrifying and poignant.

Thanks to a unique and involving story line (perhaps the ultimate loss-of-identity horror), evocative photography, superb acting, and inspired direction, *Angel Heart* remains an innovative, engrossing and artful example of *horror noir*. If there's any justice in the world of cinema criticism, *Angel Heart* is destined to be recognized as a genre classic.—*BMS*

Attack of the Crab Monsters (1958) [**hive mind; alien possession**] American International Pictures. *D:* Roger Corman. *S:* Charles B. Griffith. *Cast:* Richard Garland (Dale Drewer); Pamela Duncan (Martha Hunter); Russell Johnson (Hank Chapman); Mel Welles (Jules Deveroux).

Mel Welles is attacked by a killer crustacean in *Attack of the Crab Monsters*.

Please, no snickering.

Although named one of *The 50 Worst Movies of All Time* and "honored" by *The Golden Turkey Awards* (in books of those titles), in actuality producer/director Roger Corman's *Attack of the Crab Monsters* is a surprisingly imaginative and occasionally creepy sci-fi chiller.

Its premise is risible enough, to be sure: A group of scientists is trapped on a deserted island with a passel of giant, radioactively mutated crabs. (And without a bowl of melted butter in sight!) The film's special effects are indeed laughable, as well. But the script, by longtime Corman collaborator Charles B. Griffith, proves far better than expected from a B-grade exploitation flick, and contains some fascinating ideas.

The best of these—and the one that merits the film's inclusion in this book—is that, as one of the scientists explains: "The crab can eat his victim's brain, absorbing his mind, intact and working." Although the victim's body dies, his personality—his identity—becomes part of the consciousness of the crab-monster. This makes the titular menaces daunting opponents. They are not only larger and stronger than humans, but (since they get more intelligent with each meal) also smarter. Plus, our heroes face the unnerving prospect of squaring off against an enemy capable of telepathically "speaking" to them in the voice of a dead friend.

Wildly original twists like this were Griffith's trademark, and can be found in many of the films he wrote for Corman: *It Conquered the World* (1956), *Not of This Earth* (1957), *Beast from Haunted Cave* (1959), *A Bucket of Blood* (1959), *Little Shop of Horrors* (1960) and *Death Race 2000* (1975). Like those B-movie classics, *Attack of the Crab Monsters*, despite its lowly reputation, proves novel and diverting.

It's certainly not the best film ever made, but it's nowhere near the worst.
—MDC

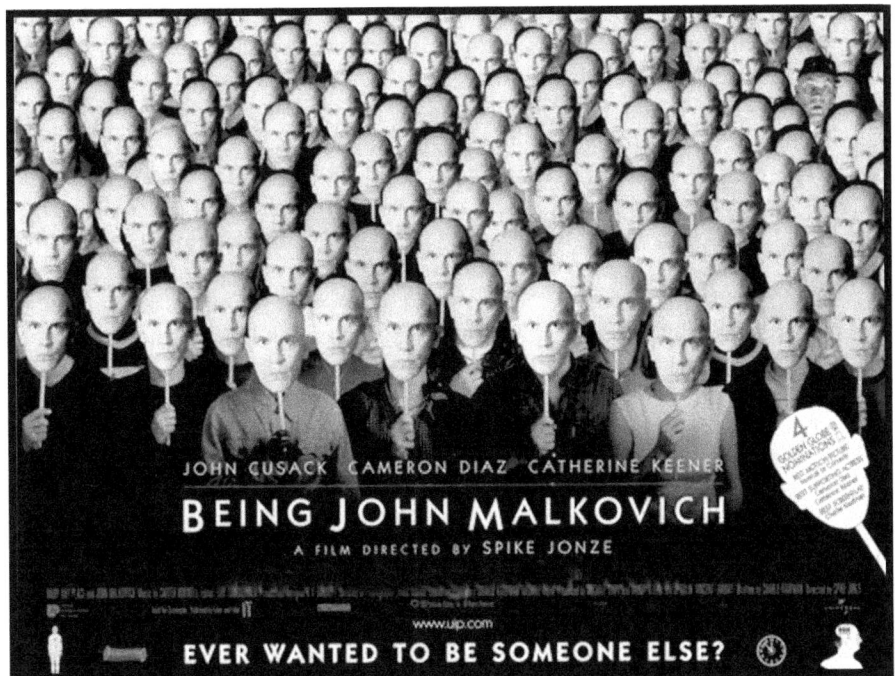

British Quad poster for *Being John Malkovich*

Being John Malkovich (1999) [**erasure of self; possession**] Gramercy Pictures, Propaganda Films, Single Cell Pictures (USA Films). *D:* Spike Jonze. *S:* Charlie Kaufman. *Cast:* John Cusack (Craig Schwartz); John Malkovich (John Malkovich); Cameron Diaz (Lotte Schwartz); Catherine Keener (Maxine Lund).

Being John Malkovich shows how becoming someone else affects three people in particular: Craig, Craig's wife, and John Malkovich.

Craig is a puppeteer because, he says, he likes "the idea of being someone else for a while." He gets the opportunity to *really* be someone else when he discovers a magic chute and finds he's literally able to "get inside actor John Malkovich's head"—to see what Malkovich sees and experience what Malkovich experiences.

At first, Craig is content to just passively inhabit the celebrity's body. Then he moves to active exploitation by selling tickets and letting others experience what it is to be John Malkovich, as if Malkovich is some theme-park ride for those unhappy with their own identities. Finally, his usurpation of Malkovich culminates in his complete possession of the actor, manipulating Malkovich's every move and manipulating others through Malkovich. Possession would seem to be the ultimate act of puppetry: Craig makes Malkovich his puppet and has his puppet "pull the strings" of other puppets. But, despite Malkovich's loss of identity and Craig's supposed control, it turns out that Craig is also a puppet, and has been all along—having been manipulated by a woman, Maxine, from the beginning.

Craig is given to various metaphysical questions—"Am I me? Is Malkovich Malkovich?"—but his interest in these questions of identity evaporates as soon as there's a buck to be made. What does he care, so long as he can further his own career? The film deals most directly with these issues through the character of Craig's wife, Lotte. After her initial experience inside Malkovich's body, she demands to be sent right back in because, for the first time in her life, she says—when she was somebody else—"I knew who I was." Although she may be making a profound philosophical point here, Lotte's character and shifting identity are not quite taken seriously for the rest of the film. (It's a trick of various movies to put a significant and/or moral comment on the action in the mouth of a character who is otherwise regarded as a figure of fun; see Geraldine Chaplin's reporter in *Nashville* [1975] or Sterling Holloway's journalism student in *Picture Snatcher* [1933] with James Cagney.)

Is Malkovich Malkovich? Given the fact that everyone else tries on his identity, it is only dramatically right and fitting that John Malkovich himself should enter the Malkovich portal and experience "a world that no man should see": in one of the funniest and most effective glimpses inside the human ego ever filmed, he's confronted with a world of Malkoviches—he is everyone and no one (loss of identity in a welter of identity). Every actor must feel a similar loss of self inside the multiple people he helps create, and for whom he is so often mistaken.—LJ-C

Beyond, The (*E Tu Vivrai Nel Terrore—L'aldila*) (1981) [**zombification**] Italy: Fulvia Films (Aquarius Releasing, Inc.). *D:* Lucio Fulci. *S:* Dardano Sacchetti, Giorgio Mariuzzo, and Lucio Fulci; story by Dardano Sacchetti. *Cast:* Catriona MacColl [billed as Katherine MacColl] (Liza Merril); David Warbeck (Dr. John McCabe); Cinzia Monreale (Emily); Giovanni De Nava (Joe the plumber).

Many horror movies have featured elucidations about the end of the world, but to date very few match *The Beyond* for its utterly intense, visceral, and brutal interpretation of Judgment Day. Director Lucio Fulci's vision of the apocalypse—as uncompromising as one would expect from a filmmaker of his calibre—features a combination of stomach-churning gore, superlative cinematography, and a well-contrived, dynamic soundtrack. Within this film we witness not only the loss of identity of the unfortunate souls—such as Joe, the ill-fated (and subsequently eyeless) plumber—who are mutilated and transformed into zombies, but also the eradication of the self suffered by several people attempting to outrun Hell itself, as one of its seven gates opens, spilling evil out into the world.

It begins at the turn of the 19th century with a brief consideration of mob mentality and the suppression of individuality that such a group with a single- and bloody-minded purpose can engender, as a collection of torch-wielding Louisiana townsfolk torture and murder an artist, who they suspect is involved with arcane, supernatural practices. Following an intense sequence of systematic violence made all the more sickening by the assailants' almost complete lack of emotion, the artist's corpse is entombed within the walls of the hotel where he resides.

Many years later, Liza Merril inherits the huge, dilapidated hotel, intending to refurbish and reopen it for business. However, her life takes a turn for the worse as she begins to suffer from unfounded fears, initially stemming from the tangibly eerie and foreboding atmosphere within the hotel and the strange disappearances of several of her employees. Although she attempts to shake off her nagging doubts, her fears are then compounded by the appearance of a mysterious blind woman with crystal-gray eyes, who warns her of the mortal dangers lurking within her new home.

At the same time, Liza's friend Dr. John McCabe receives a warning from an architect who suspects that certain markings and structural patterns inside the hotel match the same cryptic blueprints in an antiquated tome, alleged to indicate the location of one of the Seven Gates of Hell. While studying the book, the architect then suffers a bad fall from a library ladder, which completely paralyzes him; in a disturbing sequence, tarantulas eat him alive.

Sadly, these warnings come much too late. Joe's explorations in the basement have already, quite literally, allowed Hell to be let loose upon the Earth. From here the power of darkness

dictates how things go, culminating with the dead in Dr. McCabe's hospital rising, silently clawing their way out of their body bags. Trapped in the midst of the carnage, Liza and McCabe manage to escape the clutches of the undead, but the army of flesh eaters continues to advance inexorably after them.

Trying to outrun the inevitable, they accidentally travel through the basement portal and cross the open boundary from Earth into Hell, to find themselves trapped upon a brooding, desolate landscape covered with human detritus. In the film's distressing conclusion, the two realize that there is no escape from the clutches of Hell and that their souls are damned forever. Finally as the howls of the dead echo all around them, they succumb to the power of evil and turn to face the camera with crystal-gray eyes, standing hand in hand as mindless denizens of the night.—*AJB*

Black Friday (1940) [**body switching; possession**] (Universal). *D:* Arthur Lubin. *S:* Curt Siodmak and Eric Taylor (and, uncredited, Edmund L. Hartmann, Screenplay Construction). *Cast:* Boris Karloff (Dr. Ernest Sovac); Bela Lugosi (Eric Marnay);

Frank Miller (Edmund MacDonald) and Red Cannon/George Kingsley (Stanley Ridges) confront Marnay (Lugosi) as the desk clerk (Jerry Marlowe) looks in *Black Friday*.

Stanley Ridges (Prof. George Kingsley/Red Cannon); Anne Nagel (Sunny Rogers); Anne Gwynne (Jean Sovac); Virginia Brissac (Margaret Kingsley); Edmund MacDonald (Frank Miller); Paul Fix (William Kane).

    The 1940s witnessed a slew of films that mixed horror themes with prominent crime elements. *Black Friday*, one of these curious hybrids, used the additional gimmick of body switching to set its tale of identity confusion in motion.

    When college professor George Kingsley is critically injured in an auto accident, his friend Dr. Ernest Sovac performs an emergency brain transplant to save his life. The donor is the driver of the car that ran down Kingsley, crime boss Red Cannon, who was also injured in the melee. Sovac's intentions are noble at first, but, when he learns that Cannon's stash of stolen money remains hidden, he devises a plan to awaken the dormant criminal memories now residing in Kingsley's new brain. *Black Friday* plays fast and loose with the details regarding the workings of the human mind, even by the relatively primitive standards of 1940. But, like the pulp stories of the day, the film never lets mere facts get in the way of fanciful storytelling.

    As he recovers, Kingsley begins to display some of Cannon's personality traits. Once jovial and mild-mannered, he now flies into a rage for no apparent reason. To spark the Cannon memories, Sovac arranges for Kingsley to visit the New York locale that served as Red's hideout. Kingsley is troubled by the familiar surroundings—he remembers the room numbers of Cannon's adjoining suites and can recall the secret knock used by the hotel's bellboy. Kingsley's disorientation grows until the Cannon personality, spurred on by Sovac's prompting, finally emerges. Like Jekyll and Hyde, George Kingsley is now caught in an identity struggle from within.

For the remainder of the film, Kingsley and Cannon engage in a mental tug of war. Cannon, when in control, tracks down the gang members who betrayed him, ruthlessly murdering each one, including Bela Lugosi, badly miscast as an American crime thug. (The actor, apparently, lost *his* identity in the film, as reports tell us he was initially scheduled to play Sovac and Karloff slated to be Kingsley. Bowing to the wishes of Universal's publicity department, Lugosi suffered another identity loss when he allowed himself to be hypnotized on set by Manley Hall, to make his death scene, locked in a closet, more "realistic.")

Kingsley, when he reemerges from these Cannon bursts, feels ill at ease and longs for his old environs. Each character remains ignorant of the other's actions, save for some vague repressed guilt that troubles Kingsley's conscience. Complicating matters further are Sovac's Svengali-like attempt to keep his patient under control. "I can make you forget you ever were Cannon!" he tells Red at one point, still hopeful that he can manipulate the hoodlum into revealing the location of his secret bounty. The on/off nature of the Kingsley/Cannon transformations is far too extreme to be taken seriously, but it does set up a dramatic finale in which the wail of a police siren triggers Cannon's appearance one final time.

Black Friday contains too much crime and not enough horror to be truly effective. Its gangster elements are a relic of an earlier time, as is the film's cockeyed view of brain transplants as a catalyst for personality confusion. But it is that gray-mattered hackneyed theme that allows the film inclusion in this volume. However, a brisk pace, the presence of Karloff and Lugosi, and an exceptional performance by Stanley Ridges help to overcome these defects. Ridges, in fact, essayed similar roles as the Nazi professor whom Jack Benny impersonates in *To Be or Not To Be* (1942) and as a psychic researcher who becomes possessed by the spirit of an executed killer in *The Phantom Speaks* (1945). Nearly forgotten today, Ridges the actor has become a poster child for loss of identity.—SGT

Black Pit of Dr. M, The (*Misterios de ultratumba*) (1959) [soul transference; possession] Mexico (Joseph Brenner Associates, Inc.). D: Fernando Mendez. S: Ramon Obon. Cast: Gaston Santos (Dr. Jimenez); Rafael Bertrand (Dr. Mazali); Mapita Cortes (Patricia Aldama); Carlos Ancira (Elmer).

Unlike the K. Gordon Murray Mexican movies released directly to television, the seldom seen *Black Pit of Dr. M* enjoyed an actual (if limited) theatrical release in the U.S., mainly on the drive-in circuit, before disappearing. Recently, this Mexican counterpart to Italy's *Black Sunday* (1960), thick with mood and splendid Gothic sets, received its definitive DVD release by CasaNegra with a superb transfer. The movie, no longer lost to us, emerges as an essential statement on loss of identity, in the most spine-tingling way.

Doctors Mazali and Aldama, friends and partners, make a pact: Whoever dies first will return from beyond to allow his colleague to experience the world of the dead, but from the vantage point of the living. Aldama crosses to the other side first, and returns briefly to tell his friend that, on a specific date, at a specific time, he will be confronted

by one door closing and another opening. But he counsels Mazali that it might be best if he rethought his wishes and priorities about discovering the secrets of the dead.

Almost immediately the razor-sharp plot puts the wheels of fate into subtle but inevitable motion. A wild woman in an insane asylum where Mazali works goes berserk and throws acid into the face of orderly Elmer, permanently disfiguring him. Elmer wants revenge and silently stalks the woman until he stabs her with a letter opener (a letter opener found within a case that the deceased Aldama willed to his estranged daughter). Elmer, disgusted with life but now avenged for his mutilation, attempts suicide and is buried quickly in a very, very shallow grave. (Is he even dead?) In the meantime, Mazali happens upon the murder scene, and the mental patient dies in his arms as the door to the room slams shut. When it reopens, people are shocked to find both the dead woman and the murder weapon in the good doctor's possession, so his trial is swift and the outcome inevitable: execution by hanging. Mazali protests his innocence even on the gallows while the noose is tightened around his neck. When the trap is sprung, at the instant of death, his spirit is transferred into the corpse of Elmer, who is now reanimated as a shocking example of the living dead. Mazali's identity has been transferred from his former body into the disfigured body of a rotting corpse, a creature more dead than alive, but who now lives and breathes. The pact between Mazali and Aldama has been fulfilled. Mazali gets his wish to experience death while still being alive, but, as with the twisted irony of "The Monkey's Paw," Mazali should have been careful about what he wished for.

This soul transference is deftly handled; Aldama's estranged daughter and the strange jewelry case willed her by her late father form pivotal pieces of the puzzle. All the divergent plot angles flow nicely together, leading to Mazali's unfair execution and sudden, shockingly unfair resurrection into the body of another horribly mutilated man. As the film twists and turns toward its outrageous conclusion, the audience realizes that Mazali will never return to normalcy and should have heeded Dr. Aldama's subtle hints to jettison the plans to experience death. In this Gothic horror opera of the undead, not only does Mazali experience life from another's body, but he also experiences that new variation of life as a reanimated corpse that crawls its way out of its shallow grave. In the split second that his body drops from the gallows as the rope snaps his neck, this pathetic victim comes to experience life after death in the worst possible way. When it comes to horror and loss of identity, this curiosity-killed-the-cat nightmare becomes haunting and gut wrenching in the best cinematic manner.—*GJS*

Black Room, The (1935) [**twins; impersonation**] (Columbia). *D:* Roy William Neill. *S:* Henry Meyers and Arthur Strawn; story by Arthur Strawn. *Cast:* Boris Karloff (Gregor de Berghman/Anton de Berghman); Marian Marsh (Thea); Robert Allen (Lieutenant Lussan); Thurston Hall (Colonel Hassel); Katherine DeMille (Mashka); John Buckler (Beran); Henry Kolker (de Berghman); Colin Tapley (Lieutenant Hassel).

Casting a popular actor in the role of twins was a popular plot gimmick of the 1930s and 1940s. *The Black Room*, a well-regarded Columbia "B" film from 1935, does justice to the familiar premise and provides a fascinating study of twin brothers whose identities are shaped by a prophetic family curse.

A pronouncement of tragedy clouds the lives of twins Gregor and Anton de Berghman from the moment they enter the world. "Principio et Finem Similia"—"I end as I began," reads the family crest, a testament to the murder of family founder Wolfram by twin brother Brand. According to legend, Gregor is now destined to perish at the hands of Anton in the black room of the family castle, a prediction that will forever throw a shadow of doubt over their relationship.

As the brothers reach adulthood, their temperaments are the opposite of what the murderous prophecy suggests. Anton, the younger, is gentle and compassionate (his paralyzed right arm is symptomatic of his "weaker" personality traits). Gregor, who manages the family estate, has become deceitful and is reviled by the subjects under his rule. In appearance, too, they are dynamically opposed—Gregor is disheveled and slouches angrily; Anton, meanwhile, is well groomed and holds himself with courtly dignity. But the family curse still hangs over their heads.

The yin and yang of their opposing identities convincingly suggest that the two brothers are bound together by the dark ties of fate. When Anton returns after a lengthy

absence, he is shocked to learn that the villagers suspect Gregor's involvement in the disappearance of a number of women from the village.

To appease his subjects, Gregor proposes to relinquish the family title to Anton. But the deal is a ruse—Gregor secretly lures Anton to the forbidden room, where he slays him. Gregor's plan is to assume his brother's identity and continue to enjoy the privileges of the de Berghman family name, including marriage to young Thea Hassel, daughter of a prosperous neighboring family. In the reflective wall of the black room, Gregor imitates Anton's mannerisms, posture, and expressions, adopting the identity that he must now own for the rest of his life. Although Gregor's change of identity is external only, his attempt to "become" Anton recalls Carl Jung's myth of twins who long to be reunited and form a unified whole.

Gregor's attempt, however, is doomed to failure. When Colonel Hassel observes "Anton" signing a document with his immobile hand, he confronts the imposter; Gregor murders him to ensure his silence. As he prepares to be wed to Thea, Gregor tells his servants to get rid of Anton's dog, Thor, an edict that is inconsistent with Anton's sympathetic nature. The deception is finally revealed when Thor attacks his "master" during the wedding ceremony, Gregor's raised right arm giving away the deception. Despite his best efforts to take on the identity of another, Gregor is unable to eradicate his own inner nature. When Gregor attempts to hide in the black room, he falls into the pit where his dead brother lies and is impaled by the knife held in Anton's hand. The curse thus becomes fulfilled—each brother failing to escape the identity that he has been scripted to follow.

Along with a first-rate performance by Boris Karloff, *The Black Room* is given added weight by its constant reminders of human mortality. The inevitability of death renders our individual identities all the more meaningful and poignant. As the story of the de Berghman brothers so aptly reminds us, the theft of that human identity is just as dramatic as the more fantastic tales of genre cinema.—*SGT*

Blade Runner (1982) [**impersonation; scientific manipulation**] (Orion Pictures). *D:* Ridley Scott. *S:* Hampton Fancher and David Peoples, From the Novel *Do Androids Dream of Electric Sheep?* by Philip K. Dick. *Cast:* Harrison Ford (Rick Deckard); Rutger Hauer (Roy Batty); Sean Young (Rachel), M. Emmet Walsh (Bryant); Daryl Hannah (Pris); Joe Turkel (Tyrell), Joanna Cassidy (Zhora).

One of the greatest science fiction films ever made, Ridley Scott's masterpiece confronts the very nature of identity and existence within an incredibly dark and foreboding futuristic cityscape, where the rain never stops. Indeed, one facet of the film's inherent genius is its setting, as the camera follows Rick Deckard, a policeman employed to hunt androids, through a hectic and impersonal environment thronged with thousands of faceless individuals trudging their own paths through the sprawling metropolis. As in any major city, the people caught up within this concrete jungle's complex, unnatural web become emotionally displaced and disempowered, which is clearly one problem Deckard himself struggles with throughout the film.

He is soon sent on the trail of four androids, or replicants—humanoid worker drones constructed by the unscrupulous Tyrell Company for dangerous and laborious tasks. The replicants, developing beyond their operational parameters and seizing an opportunity to attain freedom, escape from their bondage. Initially Deckard approaches his "hunter-killer" task with a dour, dry professionalism, perceiving the replicants as

Deckard (Harrison Ford) and Batty (Rutger Hauer) in the finale are both enemies as well as fellow conspirators in the quest to awaken their separate identities in *Blade Runner*.

mere loose ends in his world of superficial certainties. However, once the hunt begins, he soon meets his first emotional challenge in the replicant Rachel, for whom he develops an attraction. As the pursuit progresses, Deckard is brought back into contact with various aspects of his humanity, perhaps most vividly when he narrowly escapes death at the hands of one of the androids and is nurtured back to health by another.

The film as a whole can be interpreted as an in-depth critique of the impact that the inexorable advance of technology has upon both societal structure and its inherent components—the demystification and dehumanization of the individual and the counter-struggle to reaffirm organic identity. In an ironic twist, Scott utilizes the very products of mechanized and dehumanized society, the replicants, as catalysts in the emotional development of Deckard, initially a shallow and dispassionate protagonist.

Indeed, it's fascinating to note that, as the story unfolds, each android's personality seems to represent an isolated emotion that has been washed out of the denizens of Scott's rainy city. Not that the androids have any hope of fully realizing that emotion—or getting their dehumanized human counterparts to recognize it in them. Except for Deckard. His confrontations with each replicant revive a different facet of his own numbed emotions—most strikingly at the end of the movie, when he finally learns to take pleasure in beauty and is reawakened to love.

Ultimately to take the most from this piece, especially within the context of loss of identity, the viewer must focus primarily upon Deckard's transition throughout the movie. In the beginning, the "blade runner" appears to be nothing more than a languid, uninterested journeyman detective, moving through a joyless existence in the midst of a superficial, technocratic dystopia. However, as the plotline develops and he is drawn into the web of a mystery larger than first perceived, Deckard becomes imbued with a sense of identity and passion, most prominently when he fights with every shred of his being against the replicant Batty in a life-or-death struggle set in a dilapidated, desolate monolith of a building, arguably symbolic of the dark, empty society that has brought them together as both enemies and fellow conspirators in the quest to awaken their separate identities.—*AJB*

Brain Eaters, The (1958) [**alien possession; hive mind**] (American International Pictures). *D:* Bruno Ve Sota. *S:* Gordon Urquhart. *Cast:* Ed Nelson (Dr. Paul Kettering); Alan Frost (Glenn Cameron); Jack Hill (Senator Walter K. Powers); Joanna Lee (Alice Summers); Jody Fair (Elaine Cameron); David Hughes (Dr. Wyler).

This is one that Leonard Nimoy leaves off his résumé—and the special, misspelled ("and Leonard Nemoy") billing he received (in lieu of a decent salary, perhaps?) helps to obscure his identity. The I-Am-Not-(Yet)-Spock actor did his one-day, two-minutes-of-screen-time cameo as a favor to his friend, actor-producer Ed Nelson. "You know," laughed Nelson to interviewer Tom Weaver, "I never paid Leonard for that day. I owe him about 45 dollars..."

Nimoy plays an elderly professor who, complete with long, white beard and hooded robes, is eventually found inside a cone-shaped craft that's come from *inside* the Earth. (The cone's interior was actually producer-star Ed Nelson's *garage*, with some thick fog and a solitary light laid on for atmosphere.) Tiny parasite creatures from the "Carboniferous Age" (200 million years ago) emerge from the "ship" to take over the town of Riverdale, Illinois. By latching onto the necks of citizens, the Brain Eaters are able to control people's minds, linking them to a collective consciousness or "hive mind";

The sheriff (Greigh Phillips) is attacked by *The Brain Eaters*.

when the furry parasites are removed, the hosts die, their minds gone. (This may be the film's most frightening concept: Attempting to free a person's sublimated identity from a controlling alien presence only results in the ultimate loss of identity—death.) Nimoy's character serves as the host leader of the intelligent leeches, explaining that "our social order is pure, innocent," and "we shall force upon Man a life free from strife and turmoil." Opposing said society is scientist Paul Kettering, friend Glenn Cameron, and gruff Senator Walter K. Powers, who's come to Riverside to head the investigation of the mysterious arrival. After the parasites gain control of the telegraph, telephones, and police, the intrepid trio must find a way to halt the invasion themselves.

While the plot may sound suspiciously like *Invasion of the Body Snatchers* (1956 [*q.v.*]), that's where the similarity to that bona fide loss-of-identity classic ends. The non-union, $26,000 *Brain Eaters* is bargain-basement stuff all the way. (Nelson even made the Brain Eaters himself—out of wind-up toy beetles covered in fur scraps, with pipe cleaners for antennae!) In fact, it's actually *sub*-basement, for it's not even up to the level of Roger Corman's similarly-themed, cut-rate (but far more enjoyable) *It Conquered the World* (1956).

The Brain Eaters is so derivative that the film's backers (including Roger Corman) became the target of a $150,000 plagiarism lawsuit filed by science fiction author Robert Heinlein, who maintained that the movie copied his loss-of-identity serial *The Puppet Masters*, which had appeared years earlier in *Galaxy* magazine—making the entire film a case of *stolen* identity. "They stole it," admitted Corman (in Mark Thomas McGee's *Roger Corman*). "No question whatsoever....They changed a few things so it wasn't exactly the same, but it was really obvious that they took it. So I had a meeting with Heinlein and his lawyer. I told them I could probably go to court and fight them, claiming enough had been changed to make it a murky issue, but I knew it was stolen because there were too many points of similarity. We settled for a $5,000 amount because it was such a low-budget picture. Heinlein was a good man."

The Brain Eaters does have its moments, however, such as when two controlled cops—impervious to pain—keep coming at our heroes, who must frantically fire round after round into their bodies until a bullet finally hits a vital spot. And it offers up an unusually grim tone for the time, with sporadic and abrupt violence peppering the proceedings (Cameron watches as his own father, the mayor, must be gunned down), and a rather brutal end for the main protagonist. But, for most of its hour-long running time, *The Brain Eaters* lives *down* to its title.—*BMS*

Brain from Planet Arous, The (1957) [**alien possession**] (Howco International Pictures). *D:* Nathan Juran (as Nathan Hertz). *S:* Ray Buffum. *Cast:* John Agar (Steve March); Joyce Meadows (Sally Fallon); Robert Fuller (Dan Murphy); Thomas Browne Henry (John Fallon); Dale Tate (Prof. Dale Tate/Voices of Gor & Vol).

John Agar, one of 1950s America's iconic science fiction heroes, had slipped from the mainstream when he starred in Howco's B product, *The Brain from Planet Arous*. Actually, the film features *two* alien brains—Vol and Gor—who are at war with one another, just as Agar's character, Steve March, is at war with himself, fighting for his human identity while alien predator Gor uses March's warm, cozy human body as his nesting place. Gor must come out for air a few minutes every evening, and this becomes March's only chance to free himself from this worst-case scenario of alien possession.

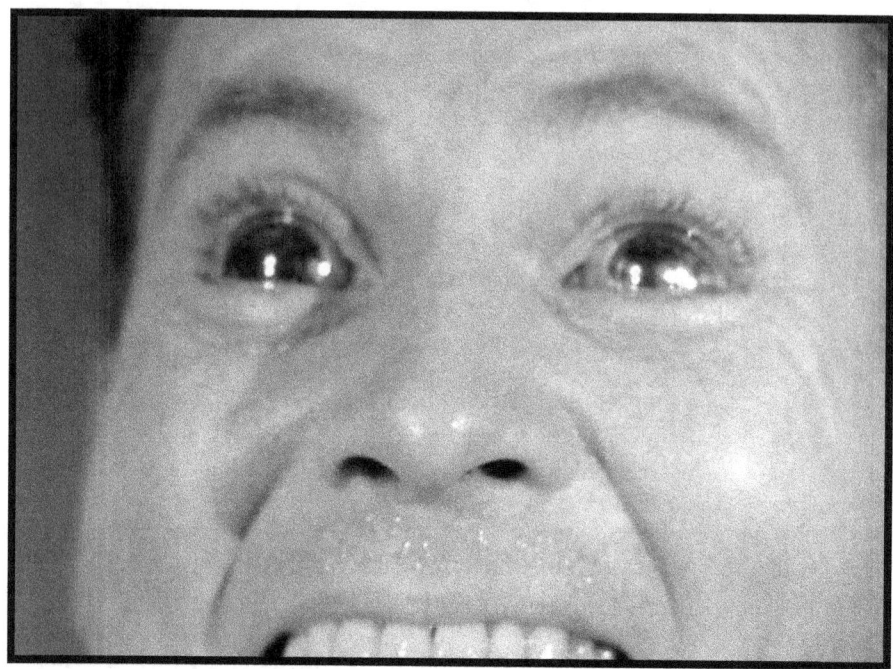

In *The Brain from Planet Arous*, John Agar is a science-fiction Jekyll and Hyde as he loses his identity in three stages.

Regular good guy Steve March is dating the lovely Sally and seems to be hitting things off with her father at their frequent barbeques when he and unfortunate victim-to-be buddy scientist Dan head to the mountains to check out some radioactivity. In moody cavern sequences punctuated with stark photography and eerie music, Dan is destroyed, and evil alien brain Gor quickly possesses March. Within 24 hours March is beginning to cackle like a madman and sport black metallic eyes that can be used to make [model] airplanes [on strings] explode. Gathering military leaders together, March declares his plans for world domination: Surrender or be conquered. Ultimately, the Earth will belong to insane Gor and be ruled by him.

In a strange turn of events, good alien Vol hides within the body of a pet dog, unlike evil Gor, who gets a better host, an actual robust human being. During the final minutes of the film, when Gor momentarily leaves his body for air, March finds a book has been purposely left within easy reach, pointing out the part of Gor's brain that is especially vulnerable—that is, if one happens to possess an axe, which just happens to be handily nearby. Putting two and two together, the transparent Gor (played, in some scenes, by his inflatable balloon double) threatens March, who manages to drive the axe home, killing his alien predator and regaining his humanity.

John Agar, unhappy that his Universal contract had been terminated (he had refused to re-sign because he wanted the Rock Hudson mainstream roles and not the science fiction B leads), is here reduced to giving a performance based upon non-subtle changes from rugged, macho lover to wide-eyed rant-and-rave megalomaniac. Nevertheless, Agar's performance, while lovingly over the top, is ultimately effective because he never winks or plays the role for camp. He makes adolescent audiences believe that this stalwart hero has been totally consumed by an alien criminal who escaped from its prison and now has delusions of conquering the universe. In this science fiction Jekyll-and-Hyde performance, Agar showcases his loss of identity in three stages. First, even when possessed, he mostly plays himself, always cozying up to Joyce Meadows' Sally, always trying to act suave and romantic. However, the wild barking of the dog who knows this isn't March but March-under-the-control-of-alien-Gor, continually disturbs the mood and makes March become atypically snippy and short tempered. Second, we have those sequences where a totally alien-controlled March is in evidence, with those pesky wide eyes and that almost sly smile etched onto his face hinting at the malevolence beneath the surface. Sally seems to be put off and discomfited by her boyfriend's uncharacteristic rants, but he does sound like Steve and look like Steve, so she basically tries to make excuses for his erratic behavior. And the final stage is the balls-out madman from outer space who speaks in platitudes of power and human beings groveling and the world bowing at his feet. It's the stuff from which Golden Turkey Awards are created, and the sequence in which March looks through the Venetian blinds and blows the airplane apart with only his gaze, his body erupting into uncontrolled laughter, shows this other extreme.

What makes *The Brain from Planet Arous* intellectually interesting are the various reactions to alien possession and control. We have Joyce Meadows as the girlfriend, a person quite intimate with the real Steve March, realizing that her man is not himself and is in fact not her man any longer. We have John Agar utterly spent and dejected during those short sequences where Gor momentarily deserts his human host, and he displays power-drunk fits of passion as the Gor-controlled March—as if both human and alien only truly come to life when possessed. Then we have the alien/man truly caught in the middle, one who slyly rants and raves and flashes that devilish smile, yet a man seemingly still controlled by formerly human qualities. In the world of B cinema, the loss of one's human identity doesn't get more nuanced than *The Brain from Planet Arous*.—GJS

Brazil (1985) [regimentation] (Universal). *D:* Terry Gilliam. *S:* Terry Gilliam, Tom Stoppard, and Charles McKeown. *Cast:* Jonathan Pryce (Sam Lowry); Robert De Niro (Archibald "Harry" Tuttle); Katherine Helmond (Mrs. Ida Lowry); Michael Palin (Jack Lint); Kim Greist (Jill Layton); Ian Holm (Kurtzmann); Bob Hoskins (Spoor).

Brazil is a film I first encountered as a child while growing to love horror and science fiction via the well-worn pathways etched out by the Universal black-and-whites, Hammer's Technicolor nightmares, and, of course, a wide array of glorious 1950s science fiction, from *Them* (1955) to *Forbidden Planet* (1957 [*q.v.*]) and far, far beyond. However, although at this early age I enjoyed many of the simpler facets of Terry Gilliam's masterpiece, such as its futuristic setting and technology and enjoyable action sequences, it took many viewings and some serious psychological maturing before I began to grasp the implications of even half of what was actually happening onscreen.

Sam Lowry is the movie's neurotic, bumbling protagonist, tripping and stumbling through a relatively comfortable yet highly regimented and unfulfilling life, in a nondescript desk job offering little satisfaction or opportunity for the spiritual growth he secretly craves. He exists within a society that, in a most Orwellian manner, has shackled its inhabitants within a rigid and unforgiving police state, supported by an impermeable bureaucratic structure. However, away from both the desk and the constant naggings of his superficial, plastic-surgery-obsessed mother, Ida, Lowry also dreams, during which he soars through the clouds on wings and vanquishes his enemies on the battlefield to rescue a woman with whom he has fallen in love.

He soon encounters the first catalyst to a confusing yet briefly liberating identity crisis, when he returns home from a long day's work to discover a serious problem with his air conditioning. Taking the first tentative step toward casting off his sterile identity, he uncharacteristically ignores his usual law-abiding persona and allows maverick plumber Archibald Tuttle to fix the malfunctioning system. Tuttle's appearance sets off a chain of events that begins the evolution of Lowry from whining pen pusher into adventurous, spontaneous rebel. This radical change in him gathers impetus when he purposefully accepts a promotion to gain access to information about Jill, a spiky young woman who bears an incredible resemblance to the one he dreams about.

Convinced that Jill's unwitting entrance into his life has been determined by something greater than coincidence, Lowry determines to meet her at all costs and finally does so while aiding her escape from the clutches of the security forces. Arriving at this point, the protagonist has truly undergone a metamorphosis of personality and outlook, although this marks him, in the eyes of the ruling power, as a deviant malcontent. So, although emancipation briefly gives Lowry the chance to live at least part of his dream, it also unfortunately places him directly in front of the fist of the repressive state apparatus.

Upon incarceration, Lowry suffers brutal and uncompromising punishment, reminiscent of Winston Smith's "healing" at the hands of O'Brien in *1984* [see entry on the 1984 version]. Here, such treatment seems to induce extreme hallucinations with Oedipal implications (within the context of the film's conclusion and not in a strictly Freudian sense), which, after many years, I still don't and won't pretend to fully comprehend. In the face of this torture, Lowry clings fast to his dreams and, at the end, despite his former colleague Jack's ministrations, arguably escapes—from the barren identity fashioned for him by an inflexible society and its machinations—into an alternate world of endless possibilities.—*AJB*

Lowry (Jonathan Pryce) undergoes a metamorphosis of personality and outlook in Terry Gilliam's bizarre cult masterpiece *Brazil*.

Bride of the Gorilla (1951) [**metamorphosis**] Jack Broder Productions (Realart). *D:* Curt Siodmak. *S:* Curt Siodmak. *Cast:* Lon Chaney, Jr. (Commissioner Taro); Barbara Payton (Mrs. Dina Van Gelder); Raymond Burr (Barney Chavez); Tom Conway (Dr. Viet); Paul Cavanagh (Klaus Van Gelder).

A jungle/ape variation on *The Wolf Man* ([*q.v.*] which *Bride* writer-director Curt Siodmak had scripted 10 years earlier), *Bride of the Gorilla* stars Raymond Burr as Barney Chavez, the manager of an Amazonian plantation who kills his boss (with a poisonous snake) and marries the beautiful widow (Barbara Payton). A faithful servant places a curse upon Barney, causing him to transform into a gorilla at inopportune moments and roam the jungle.

Siodmak intended for this monstrous transformation to be strictly a manifestation of the protagonist's *mind* (a sort of self-punishment identity loss brought on by guilt), but the film's moneymen insisted upon a *physical* loss of identity (i.e., they wanted a "real" monster). "It was a marvelous idea," opined Siodmak to interviewer Tom Weaver. "So he's a murderer, but his conscience doesn't permit that, so every time he looks in the mirror he sees an animal. Because an animal can kill without being punished, he's free of guilt. *They* made a gorilla out of it—I didn't even want to show that. *They* called the film *Bride of the Gorilla*; my title was *The Face in the Water*." (Herman Cohen, who served as the film's production assistant, told Weaver, "[Producer] Jack [Broder] wanted an exploitation title, and I came up with *Bride of the Gorilla*.")

Indeed, for most of the film Siodmak shows the ape solely from Barney's point of view (watching the backs of his hands darken and transform into hairy, wrinkled paws; or seeing his animal reflection in water or a mirror), intimating that it's all in Barney's tortured mind. But then, toward the end, full shots of the beast (gorilla-man Steve Calvert in his ape suit) lumbering through the jungle soiled this intriguing idea. And the script

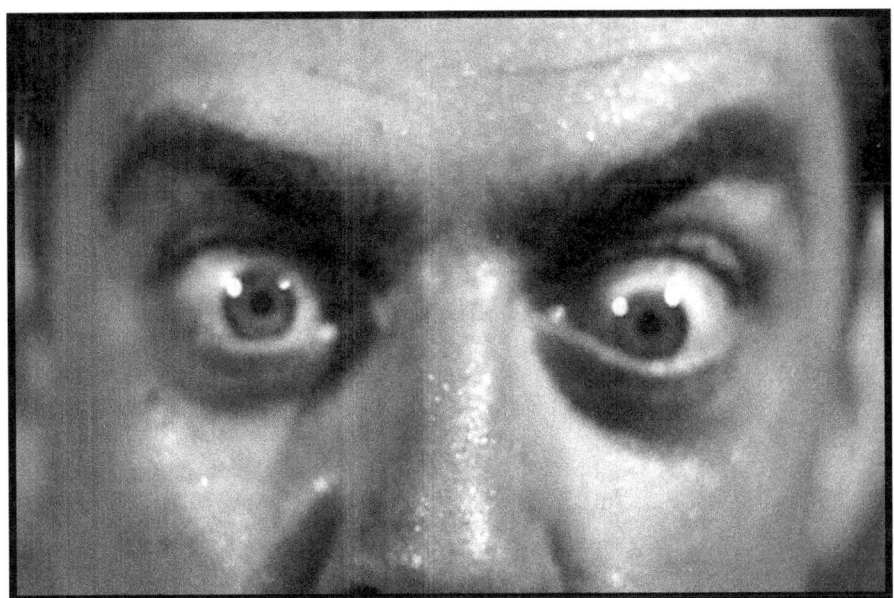

A curse is placed upon Barney (Raymond Burr), causing him to transform into a gorilla in *Bride of the Gorilla*.

fails to play up Barney's feelings of guilt anyway, so Siodmak's "marvelous idea" was really a moot point.

Lon Chaney, Jr., a veteran loss-of-identity sufferer from the Universal *Wolf Man* series [see entries on *Abbott and Costello Meet Frankenstein* (1948), *Frankenstein Meets the Wolf Man* (1943), and *The Wolf Man* (1941) in this volume], here watches Raymond Burr go through his metamorphic paces. Playing a "native" police commissioner, the miscast Chaney's stiff, stilted, and uncomfortable demeanor clashes embarrassingly with the sure-footed, convincing playing of Tom Conway's (as the local doctor/family friend). Chaney's flat tones can't bring to life the often-flowery dialogue ("This is jungle—lush, green, alive with incredible growth, as young as day, as old as time…").

Raymond Burr, on the other hand, brings a raw, almost dangerously elemental edge to his portrayal of the murderous foreman. Yet, when he speaks of the jungle and his newfound senses ("I heard something, something strange and beautiful—a voice, calling me; I couldn't resist going out there"), his tone becomes almost poetic and one can see the genuine longing in his eyes.

Barbara Payton fills her role of tainted heroine well, offering passion—and *compassion*—along with her beauty. Payton's real life, however, proved just as unhappy as her character's. According to a Tom Weaver interview with Herman Cohen, Cohen reflected: "Even in those days, Barbara Payton, who was a gorgeous gal, was one step away from working Sunset Boulevard….Oh, she gave me a great blowjob when she first arrived. I was a young kid, I was scared stiff. She thought she was a cat, and she put whiskers over her eyebrows and on her lips. Drew them on. She thought she was a cat." (Payton reportedly engaged in dressing-room "flings" with both Tom Conway and Woody Strode—who had a bit part as a policeman—while at the same time juggling her ongoing affairs with Franchot Tone and Tom Neal!) Her alternate, "cat people" identity apparently couldn't prevent her ultimate loss of identity: A few years later Payton turned to prostitution and died a destitute, obese alcoholic in 1967 at age 39.

"[*Bride of the Gorilla*] wasn't a bad picture, if I remember," concluded Cohen. With a bit more subtlety in both presentation and acting, it could have become a *good* picture.—*BMS*

Bride of the Incredible Hulk, The (1978) [**dual personality; metamorphosis; hypnotism**] (Universal). *D:* Kenneth Johnson. *S:* Kenneth Johnson; "The Incredible Hulk is a character from the Marvel Comics Group." *Cast:* Bill Bixby (David Banner); Mariette Hartley (Carolyn Fields); Lou Ferrigno (the Hulk); Jack Colvin (Jack McGee); Brian Cullen (Brad); Diane Markoff (The Girl); Duncan Gamble (Mark); Meeno Peluce (The Boy); Rosalind Chao (Receptionist).

"Married," the two-hour second-season premiere of *The Incredible Hulk* television series (derived from the pilot television movie of the same name [*q.v.*]), was released as a feature overseas under the title you see here, *The Bride of the Incredible Hulk*.

Still seeking a cure for his affliction, David Banner travels to Hawaii, hoping that Dr. Carolyn Fields' renowned hypnotherapy techniques will help him gain control of the creature inside him. But Dr. Fields has no time to help Banner; she is dying from an illness similar to Lou Gehrig's disease. Banner reveals his identity and offers his help. Hoping Banner's irradiated blood can strengthen Carolyn's immune system, the two work side by side and fall in love, eventually marrying. But Carolyn dies from her disease just as a hurricane hits the island, and a mournful Banner returns to the eternal road.

As in the pilot film and the series, Banner's loss of identity occurs when he transforms into the Hulk, but the script even more emphatically reminds the audience that the Hulk is, deep down, a part of Banner. In fact, he is a vital part. Carolyn regularly hypnotizes Banner; during their first session, he loses control and metamorphoses into the Hulk—giving Carolyn her first glimpse of the beast within. In their sessions, she has Banner's mind construct traps to incapacitate the creature—nets, vaults, cages, etc. But each time, the Hulk escapes. Banner cannot understand it—even in his own mind, the Hulk is too powerful. But the viewer understands—the Hulk is a part of Banner's makeup and cannot be expunged that easily.

French poster for *The Bride of the Incredible Hulk*

Interestingly, while Banner is falling in love with Carolyn, the Hulk is actually wary of her. When Carolyn first meets the creature, he destroys her living room. She yells "Stop!" and the Hulk turns, fists raised, snarling his defiance. It's a frightening moment, for the normally benevolent Hulk seems poised to hurt an innocent. Later, in bed with Carolyn, Banner has a nightmare and transforms into the Hulk. The Hulk destroys the bedroom and advances menacingly toward Carolyn, all the while twisting the metal bed frame with his massive hands. It's as if the Hulk realizes that Carolyn is helping to rid Banner of the Hulk—and he doesn't want to go. But in the end, the Hulk displays the affection and love that Banner has for Carolyn. Running through the hurricane, he rescues Carolyn, holding her in his arms against the wind and rain. As she dies, she tells David she will miss him. Banner transforms back and finds himself holding his dead wife's body. In a repeat of the pilot's tearjerking finale, Banner has no idea what his wife's last words to him actually were.—*JSM*

Brides of Dracula (1960) [**hypnotism; metamorphosis**] Great Britain (Hammer). *D:* Terence Fisher. *S:* Peter Bryan, Edward Percy, and Jimmy Sangster. *Cast:* Peter Cushing (Dr. Van Helsing); Martita Hunt (Baroness Meinster); Yvonne Monlaur (Marianne); Freda Jackson (Greta); David Peel (Baron Meinster).

Vampires, ungodly creatures of the undead, represent the ultimate supernatural loss of identity. Vampirism's promise of immortality appears to be a boon, something to be coveted. However the vampire's insatiable lust for blood and uncontrollable urge to feed upon the living demonstrates the deadly, darker side.

In *Brides of Dracula* Gina (Andree Melly) threatens her roomate Marianne (Yvonne Monlaur), which clearly demonstrates Gina's loss of human identity.

Hammer's Terence Fisher vampire movies demonstrate this loss-of-identity concept in the Gothic world of the undead. For instance, take Baroness Meinster, the mother of the sordid and diseased Baron Meinster. To protect her son from his bestial urges once he becomes a vampire and predator, she binds him in silver shackles—although she sometimes supplies him with village girls on which to feed. However, once young French teacher Marianne becomes an unwelcome houseguest at the Meinster home, the Baron uses his Byronic good looks and charm to get Marianne to free him from his prison. The now unfettered Baron orders his mother to "come here" and infects her with the curse of the undead. When vampire hunter Dr. Van Helsing arrives at the chateau and finds the Baroness, he realizes she has been vampirized. Her eyes accentuating her fear and disgrace, the normally dominant and powerful Baroness retreats from this stranger, veiling the lower half of her face with a kerchief to hide her fangs, not to deceive Van Helsing but simply because she's ashamed of what she's become. When Van Helsing offers her everlasting peace, a slight smile plays upon her face, and she's able to let her guard down.

Subsequently, Baron Meinster bites Marianne's roommate and fellow student teacher, the sweet Gina, who dies suddenly. Marianne, left alone with her best friend's corpse in a casket locked with chains, screams when the chains magically unlock and fall to the ground. Soon the casket lid rises, pushed open by the undead Gina, who, clad in her burial shroud, rises boldly from her wooden prison. Instead of sweetness, her face has now taken on a savage seductiveness—her pale features contrasting with her red lips, white fangs proudly protruding. Reaching out to give her friend a hug and a promised kiss, Gina advances toward the horrified Marianne. The formerly demure and shy young lady has now become a brazen predator, out for blood. A simple contrast of

Gina as roommate and Gina as vampire demonstrates quite clearly Gina's loss of human identity. She looks basically the same (save for her blood-dry complexion and her animalistic fangs), but her total personality has altered. No longer aware of the mortal human she was, she is now only interested in spreading her cult of the undead to her human comrades.

In each of Terence Fisher's vampire epics, he includes a sequence of the fiendish banshee before staking and afterwards. And such sequences are amazingly mounted and photographed, the after-the-staking sequence always bathing the vampire in light, showing the face no longer anguished, the hair now clean and combed, the mouth closed with no sign of fangs or blood on the lips. During these final seconds, the audience comes to see how the formerly human victim has radically changed because of the curse of the undead. And finally, when true death occurs and the once again human corpse lies at peace, the horrific curse and alteration of vampirism is clearly emphasized. Loss of identity: Human identity becomes undead identity; undead identity becomes human identity once again. No director could demonstrate vampiric loss of identity better than Terence Fisher.—*GJS*

Buck Rogers (1939) [**mind control**] (Universal). *D:* Ford Beebe and Saul A. Goodkind. *S:* Norman S. Hall and Ray Trampe, based on the comic strip by Dick Calkins, based on characters created by Philip Francis Nowlan. *Cast:* Buster Crabbe (Buck Rogers); Constance Moore (Wilma Deering); Jackie Moran (George "Buddy" Wade); Jack Mulhall (Capt. Rankin); Anthony Warde (Killer Kane); Philson Ahn (Prince Tallen); C. Montague Shaw (Prof. Huer).

When I was a kid in the 1950s and saw this serial on television, one episode made an indelible impression on me: the one wherein Buck was "robotomized" by Killer Kane's insidious brain-controlling helmet and became a mindless automaton (Chapter 9: "Bodies without Minds"; the sinister device was apparently called an "amnesia helmet"). Little else remained with me except that particular horror.

The success of Buck Rogers—who was introduced in the 1928 novel *Armageddon 2419 A.D.* and made popular by the comic strip that bore his name (debut: January 7, 1929)—paved the way for other outer-space strips. One of those emulators, *Flash Gordon* (debut: January 7, 1934), surpassed Buck in artistry (no contest between Alex Raymond's and Dick Calkins' illustrations) and in popularity. *Flash Gordon*, in the person of Buster Crabbe, beat *Buck Rogers* to the silver screen by three years. There were already two *Flash Gordon* serials out by the time Universal got around to filming Crabbe as Rogers. Is a Flash by any other name still a Flash? I guess not, since the following year, Universal put Crabbe in another Gordon serial, returning audience favor-

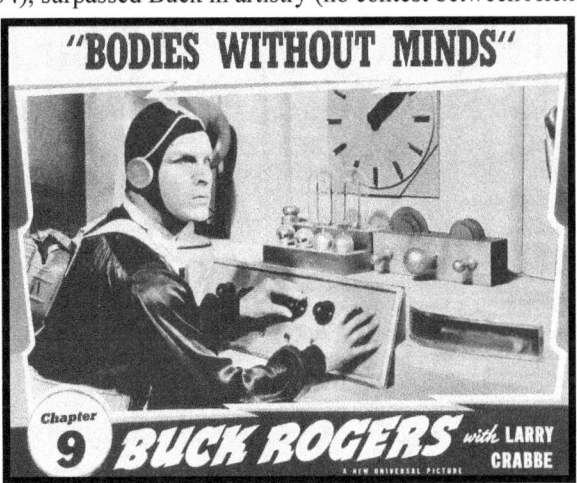

ites Dr. Zarkov, Dale Arden, and Ming the Merciless, who had it all over *Buck Rogers'* Dr. Huer, Wilma Deering, and Killer Kane (except for that automaton thing...).

A couple of years after I saw *Buck Rogers*, a new storyline started in the *Flash Gordon* daily comic strip then appearing in the *Detroit Times*: Flash began to behave strangely; Dale didn't recognize him anymore. Dr. Zarkov explained to her that Flash was *possessed*! This strip marked the first time I had ever encountered this word. I couldn't wait to see what exactly it meant, how Flash had gotten that way, and what was going to happen to him. Unfortunately, the Detroit newspapers went on strike the very next day, and—by the time the long strike was settled—the *Detroit Times* was no more, having been absorbed by the *Detroit News*, which picked up a lot of the *Times'* funnies (but not, if memory serves, *Flash Gordon*; certainly, by that late date, the storyline had ended and another was running, anyway). It was several more years before I learned the meaning of possession—but the *Rogers* serial and *Gordon* strip represented some of my earliest exposure to LOI and greatly impressed me with its power.—*AFA*

Burnt Offerings (1976) [**possession**] Dan Curtis Productions, Inc. (United Artists). *D:* Dan Curtis. *S:* William F. Nolan and Dan Curtis, From the Novel *Burnt Offerings* by Robert Marasco. *Cast:* Karen Black (Marian Rolfe); Oliver Reed (Ben Rolfe); Lee Harcourt Montgomery (David Rolfe); Bette Davis (Aunt Elizabeth); Burgess Meredith (Arnold Allardyce); Eileen Heckart (Roz Allardyce); Dub Taylor (Walker the handyman).

Dan Curtis' movie version of Robert Marasco's novel *Burnt Offerings*, filmed at Dunsmuir House, a 37-room mansion in Oakland, California, tells the story of human beings who are sacrificed to an evil supernatural force which resides within. But instead of being a house haunted by malevolent spirits, the house at 17 Shore Road *is* the evil spirit, which possesses its inhabitants and ultimately kills or absorbs them in order to use each victim's life-force to revitalize itself. When people move in to the house, they do not move out. Instead, the house feeds off of them. Their identities dissolve, and their essences merge with the building and continually refurbish the rooms, revive the dying plants, restart the clocks, and brighten the paint job. Even the rotting shingles slough off to reveal a new roof underneath as the house drains its occupants' energy and disposes of them, leaving only their frozen likenesses in an ornate picture collection silently tended by an unseen "mother" who may or may not really be there.

The latest in a long line of families offered up to the sentient house is the Rolfe family: Marian and Ben, their son David, and Ben's aunt Elizabeth. As the house begins to sap their identities and wills, Marian goes gray and becomes obsessed with caring for the house and the never-seen Mrs. Allardyce, Ben has dreams and visions and abuses David and later Marian at the sinister swimming pool on the estate, and Aunt Elizabeth weakens and dies. Bette Davis' death scene, which anticipates Sylvia Sidney's similar death scene in *Damien—Omen II* (1978) by two years, still gives viewers a jolt as Aunt Elizabeth and Ben are terror-stricken by who or what may be approaching her bedroom door.

Burnt Offerings is one of the most accurate, faithful filmings of a novel ever—until the very end. In the novel, two characters meet their demise in or at the swimming pool, while, for the movie version, Dan Curtis and William F. Nolan devise much gorier, more spectacular finishes. Also, Curtis exchanges Marasco's more nebulous, abstract ending for a cinematic conclusion which is a cross between the climaxes of Alfred Hitchcock's *Psycho* (1960 [*q.v.*]) and Curtis' own *Night of Dark Shadows* (1971 [*q.v.*]). Just as in the latter movie, the characters never should have gone back into the house!—*JDT*

[Editor's Note: While *Burnt Offerings* may not be the greatest horror film ever made, its *Psycho*-inspired finale creates one of the most unforgettable shocks in the annals of loss-of-identity cinema: Marian enters the room harboring the mysterious old lady they've had to care for...Ben comes looking for her and finds—in a shocking shot—not Marian but Marian-as-old-lady (which is enough to send anyone crashing out of the upstairs window to his doom). Karen Black's character's loss of identity here (or the old lady's assumption of Black's *character*'s identity) is nearly as effective as the chilling shot that ends her "Prey" segment in Curtis' more accomplished 1975 television movie, *Trilogy of Terror* (*q.v.*).]

Cabinet of Dr. Caligari, The (*Das Kabinett des Dr. Caligari*) (1919) [hypnotism] Germany (Decla-Bioscop). *D:* Robert Wiene. *S:* Carl Mayer and Hans Janowitz. *Cast:* Werner Krauss (Caligari); Conrad Veidt (Cesare); Lil Dagover (Jane); Friedrich Feher (Francis); Hans von Twardowski (Alan); Rudolf Klein-Rogge (a criminal); Rudolf Lettinger (Dr. Olsen).

The Cabinet of Dr. Caligari, the great-granddaddy of all classic horror films, is also an important early entry in loss-of-identity cinema. The identity issue involves Cesare, a somnambulist, who commits a series of murders while in thrall to sideshow mesmerist Dr. Caligari. In a noteworthy example of an inmate running the asylum, Caligari is then revealed to be the director of a local mental institution whose domination of Cesare recreates the legend of a murderous 11th-century mountebank.

Caligari's use of somnambulism and hypnosis touches upon many identity-based fears. The involuntary crimes that Cesare commits suggest that our moral constraints can be easily surrendered, thus making a mockery of our illusion of self-control. His abduction of Jane, an iconic cinematic episode even at this early date, implies a subconscious expression of sexual violence. Somnambulism itself is given sinister connotations—a blurring of the lines between sleeping and waking, dreaming and reality, even life and death itself. Cesare's corpse-like appearance (skeletal frame attired in black from head to toe) and death-like trance only reinforce the uneasy parallels. In addition, Cesare's psychic ability—he "knows the past and sees the future"—suggests that his human identity has morphed into something dark and preternatural.

Compounding the loss of identity is the use of Expressionism to create visual tableaux that are intentionally surreal. Expressionism, the use of highly stylized production techniques to achieve a unified effect, was a hallmark of the German cinema of this period, but seldom was it utilized to such an exaggerated extent as in *Caligari*. Landscapes are askew, buildings lean at precipitous angles, and painted shadows skulk in every corner—even the town clerk labors away at a desk of comically bizarre proportions. The net effect of this mad imagery is to create a world in which our normal perceptions of reality are clearly out of place. It seems only fitting that Caligari feels at home in a carnival, itself a symbolic distortion of everyday life.

Many of the characters in the film are expressed through parallel relationships, a fact that further clouds the identity issues. Francis and his friend, Alan, both vie for the hand of Jane; Alan's murder subsequently becomes the impetus that draws Francis into the search for the killer. Caligari and Cesare also share a curious duality, both together and individually. Cesare has a double—a dummy that lies in his coffin-like resting place—that provides a convenient alibi for his nocturnal prowling. Significantly, Cesare's backstory is never explained, reinforcing his status as something not quite human. Near film's end, Caligari reveals an obsession with his 11th-century namesake that nearly obscures his own identity. Benign when separated, together Caligari and Cesare forge a deadly partnership—Caligari, the murderer who never soils his hands, and Cesare, the criminal who acts without intent.

In its final act, *Caligari* reveals that the story has been seen through the eyes of Francis, who resides at the asylum as an inmate. Caligari is actually quite sane, and

The nocturnal Cesare (Conrad Veidt) seems something not quite human in *The Cabinet of Dr. Caligari.*

Cesare is the attendant who helps maintain order. Thus, the audience experiences an identity displacement, having been duped into sympathizing with a madman (assuming, of course, that they have not been tipped off by the many clues the film provides). This final revelation puts the film into a new and even more troubling perspective; the "spirits...around us" that haunt one madman early in the film could easily be the shifting identities through which all involved are drawn.

Upon the film's original release, *Caligari*s' groundbreaking style and veiled critique of political authority gave it great cachet among film critics the world over. Though these attributes have faded in importance, the film's influence on the nascent horror genre and its pioneering use of loss-of-identity themes confirm its status as a landmark of early cinema.—*SGT*

Cannibal Virus. See ***Zombies: Creeping Flesh*** (1980).

Captive Wild Woman (1943) [**metamorphosis; scientific manipulation**] (Universal). *D:* Edward Dmytryk. *S:* Henry Sucher and Griffin Jay. *Cast:* John Carradine (Dr. Sigmund Walters); Evelyn Ankers (Beth Colman); Acquanetta (Paula Dupree); Milburn Stone (Fred Mason); Lloyd Corrigan (John Whipple); Fay Helm (Nurse Strand); Paul Fix (Gruen).

Here's a loss-of-identity movie with a twist: Rather than a person losing his or her humanity to overpowering animal traits (such as in *The Wolf Man* [1941 (*q.v.*)], *Bride of the Gorilla* [1951 (*q.v.*)], or even 1931's *Dr. Jekyll and Mr. Hyde* [*q.v.*]), an animal metamorphoses into a human being. While one could argue from an anthropocentric position that the beast is now better off, it remains a significant loss of identity nonetheless (just ask the unhappy Lota, the Panther Girl, from 1933's *Island of Lost Souls*).

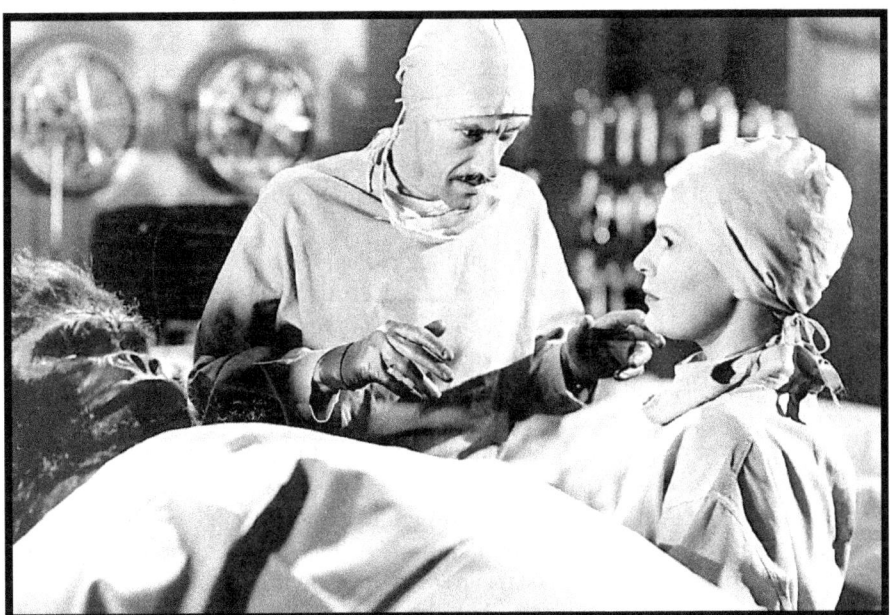

A gorilla, whose fate rests in the hands of mad doctor John Carradine and Fay Helm, is the victim of loss of identity in *Captive Wild Woman*.

"Is she woman or *beast*? Siren or *hate-maddened killer*?" asked the film's trailer. Well, let's find out. John Carradine plays a respected scientist who, through some ambiguous use of "gland extracts," turns a man in an ape suit (Ray "Crash" Corrigan) into the beautiful Acquanetta. He dubs his new creation Paula Dupree and takes her back to visit the circus from which she was stolen. There she proves a "natural," since all the animals seem to fear her. Consequently, animal trainer Fred Mason, unaware that Paula is actually his missing ape, incorporates her into his new and dangerous act—mixing lions and tigers in the same ring. The trouble is, "terrific emotion destroys the new tissue in [Paula's] gland growths," causing her to revert back to a half-simian form. And Fred's fiancée inspires in Paula just such a "terrific emotion" in the form of violent jealousy (a plot point inspired by RKO's *Cat People* [1942 (*q.v.*)], which was itself inspired by *The Wolf Man*).

Not the best of plots, nor the biggest of budgets (much of the time is filled with stock footage of famous lion-tamer Clyde Beatty), but this fun cheapie packs its brief 60-minute running time with plenty of vintage thrills. The film begins with an exciting sequence in which a tiger gets loose on the shipyard docks and is promptly cornered by Fred. From then on it never lets up, alternating thrilling lion- and tiger-taming footage of Beatty from *The Big Cage* (1933) with laboratory chills, presided over by the ever-villainous John Carradine at his subdued best.

Carradine is excellent as the brilliant but amoral scientist, turning in an even-tempered, effective characterization that's a far cry from his many desultory Poverty Row portrayals. Carradine looks downright dapper in his tailored suits and snap-brim hats, and shows a real sparkle in his eye and genuine enthusiasm for his work—to the exclusion of all else, including anything so trivial as morality. When Carradine asks of his protesting nurse, "Why should a single life be considered so important?," his earnest, quizzical expression and serious, questioning tone leave no doubt that he truly cannot fathom her concern.

Milburn Stone (later to achieve modest fame playing "Doc" on television's *Gunsmoke*) as Fred and Evelyn Ankers as his fiancée are solid audience-identification figures, making their characters both approachable and likable. As the titular creature, the exotic Acquanetta (a model-turned-actress inexplicably dubbed the "Venezuelan Volcano"—though she was actually from an Arapaho Indian reservation in Wyoming) looks striking as the gorilla-turned-woman who possesses a strange power over the circus animals. She's not asked to do much more than stand about with an intent look on her beautiful face (though at one point she does manage to effectively convey an ill-controlled rage). This is just as well, since she subsequently proved herself (in films like 1944's *Dead Man's Eyes*) to be an actress of decidedly limited range.

Captive Wild Woman boasts some deft transformation scenes in which Jack Pierce performs his usual top-flight job of turning men (or, in this case, women) into monsters. Via filters to show Acquanetta's face suddenly darken (à la 1931's *Dr. Jekyll and Mr. Hyde*) and effective dissolves (à la *The Wolf Man*), Paula loses her humanity (or, conversely, partially regains her rightful identity) right before our very eyes.

Shaggy in ape form and sexy in human guise (thanks to the dark beauty of the "Venezuelan Volcano"), Paula made for an acceptable Jekyll/Hyde animal update. Sure, *Captive Wild Woman* is horror hokum, but it's exciting, vintage 1940s hokum nonetheless.—*BMS*

Carnival of Souls (1960) [**altered reality; loss of affect**] (Hertz-Lion). *D:* Herk Harvey. *S:* John Clifford. *Cast:* Candace Hilligoss (Mary Henry); Herk Harvey (The Man).

Ambrose Bierce's "An Occurrence at Owl Creek Bridge" contains one of the most justifiably famous endings in short-story history, in which it is revealed that the thrilling, suspenseful escape of condemned Civil War saboteur Peyton Farquhar was nothing more than a split-second fantasy that took place in his mind just before his neck was snapped by the hangman's noose. The story became an acclaimed short film which first aired in America as an episode of *The Twilight Zone*, and it was also pointlessly expanded in a far less memorable installment of *Alfred Hitchcock Presents*. Neither of these adaptations is offered here as a loss-of-identity project; however, the grim punchline of the original story set the stage for a raft of films that qualify as LOI—with Herk Harvey's *Carnival of Souls* setting the remaining standards.

The movie begins with Mary Henry surviving a deadly car crash (or does she?) and follows the somehow strangely altered young woman to a small town where she sees odd things and experiences odd adventures. The revelation that Mary did not actually survive the accident she seemed to walk away from undoubtedly provides an effective conclusion to this eerie tale. But the ending itself, while proven excellent for short films and stories, would not have been enough to sustain a feature film. The midsection of *Carnival of Souls* details the slow, steady disintegration of Mary's status as a member of the land of the living: Quiet moments are shattered by the haunting specter of "The Man" (director Harvey himself), while Mary's attempt to play a church organ (as per her normal occupation) gives way to an uncontrollably "demonic" performance. Mary is no longer who (or what) she believes herself to be.

Mary Henry (Candace Hilligoss) sees odd things after surviving a car crash in *Carnival of Souls*.

When a film plays such games with reality, we can expect that the protagonist will ultimately be revealed to be (a) dead or (b) the owner of an identity that was kept a secret even from himself. Such works can be classified as loss of identity films. I refer to the process of arriving at the answer as "loss of affect"—the loss of the power to have an effect on one's surroundings. The individual's ability fades as she/he gradually comes to realize that she/he no longer has an identity and can no longer influence or even react to events. See *Door to Silence* (1991), *Jacob's Ladder* (1990), *The Jacket* (2005), *The Machinist* (2004), *Secret Window* (2004), and *Soul Survivors* (2001). —SMD

Cat People (1942) [**metamorphosis**] RKO. *D:* Jacques Tourneur. *S:* DeWitt Bodeen. *Cast:* Simone Simon (Irena); Kent Smith (Ollie Reed); Tom Conway (Dr. Judd); Jane Randolph (Alice); Jack Holt (the Commodore).

Simone Simon, in her one pivotal performance, creates a character of cinematic substance that will be remembered for all time. She plays the European Irena, an artist who falls in love with bland good guy Ollie, a man who seems just too ordinary to win the heart and soul of the otherworldly, deeply troubled siren. Seldom has Hollywood created a face and body so sensual, a personality so alluring and sweet—which reveals only the tip of a psychological iceberg that hints at mental illness and depression beneath. From the standpoint of psychological probing, Simon's Irena becomes one of the most complex figures in horror-film history. Her performance is subtle and well crafted.

And her paranoia is based totally around the fear of loss of identity.

Irena (Simone Simon) and the zookeeper (Alec Craig). In *Cat People* (1942), Irena's paranoia is based totally around the fear of loss of identity.

A woman adrift in New York City, whose origins are in a small Serbian village (thus the fear of the gigantic city becomes important), Irena displays her former closeness to nature and to wild animals by her visits to the zoo and her empathy for the caged beasts which she as an artist so tenderly draws. Her daily fear (and the curse of her village) is that, when she becomes aroused (sexually, emotionally), she will transform into a leopard and kill the object of her arousal. It's almost as though her goal in life is to live an emotionless existence of non-commitment because her punishment for feeling deeply is transformation into a savage beast. Curses have never been any darker. Either way her life is a living curse, a living hell. Her identity is circumscribed whether she is the non-emotional human Irena or the vengeful savage beast that will kill without conscience.

Her fear of loss of identity is profound. She enjoys her work, her life, and now her new beau, Ollie, whose love she wants to reciprocate with all her heart. But when the relationship starts to reach the hot-and-sizzling stage, Irena, housing all her insecurities inside, draws away from Ollie. And drab Ollie just does not understand. As her passions are aroused, she fears the cat in her will destroy her husband, so their marriage remains unconsummated. Irena pushes him aside, and Ollie finds solace in his co-worker, Alice, transforming their previous friendship into something more. While Irena is unable to open up emotionally to Ollie, Alice offers him a shoulder to lean on. (The film implicitly suggests an affair.)

Meanwhile, Ollie arranges for Irena to see a psychiatrist, Dr. Judd, and, willing to try anything, she dutifully visits him to try to save her sanity and her marriage. However, the sleazy doctor makes a pass at the vulnerable Irena and thus turns her into the predatory black cat. The aroused beast rips the doctor to pieces.

As with lycanthropy, the only way out is death—hers or someone else's.

Irena cannot live a full life unless she accepts her monstrous ardor and lets the beast within assert itself whenever her passions are stirred—an acceptance she rejects. Conversely, the constant dread of reverting to her bestial alter ego prevents her from having a satisfying life. The fear of transforming into the primitive beast inside, the fear of losing one's humanity to animal instincts, the fear of losing one's identity and harming the one you love is a horrible predicament. And Simone Simon's portrayal of a sexual and vulnerable character crawls under the skin and stays there. With her playfully sensual demeanor punctuated by her French accent, Simon expresses her frustration, her fear, and her depression with just her face and eyes. It is never *what* she says but how she backs away from saying *anything*. Her pain becomes the audience's pain as well. Fear of loss of identity has never been more skillfully created.—*GJS*

Cat People (1982) [**metamorphosis**] RKO/Universal (Universal). *D:* Paul Schrader. *S:* Alan Ormsby, Based on a Story by Dewitt Bodeen. *Cast:* Nastassia Kinski (Irena Gallier); Malcolm McDowell (Paul Gallier); John Heard (Oliver Yates); Annette O'Toole (Alice Perrin); Ruby Dee (Female); Ed Begley, Jr. (Joe Creigh).

The permissive standards of the 1970s and 1980s granted filmmakers the opportunity to rework the classic horror themes of decades past in more graphic terms. Although the results of these cinematic reinventions were decidedly mixed, they occasionally produced moments of interest. The 1982 remake of *Cat People* is one such example. Filled with evocative images that matched the undercurrents of its erotically charged

In the *Cat People* 1982 remake, Irena (Nastassia Kinski) adds the kinky sex element to the mix.

story, the film updated the loss-of-identity theme of the original with echoes of the era's newfound sexual freedoms.

This version of *Cat People* adds a kinky element to the original. Nubile Irena Gallier belongs to an ancient race that once sacrificed its children to the cats of the wild. Legend has it that the souls of the victims grew inside the leopards until they evolved into a species of cat people, hybrids that can only mate with their own kind. Should they dare to have sex with a normal human, they transform into killer panthers [or "black leopards," as the film insists on calling them]: Only by slaying again can they be restored to human form. Horrified by the awakening of her inner beast, Irena spends the film discovering, denying, and finally accepting this new identity that life has thrust upon her.

The sexually charged atmosphere of the times leaves its mark on this adaptation. Irena has moved to New Orleans, traditionally a place of vice and sin, to be with Paul, her brother and prescribed mate. Unable to control his appetites, Paul has led an active sex life, leaving behind a trail of fatal conquests. Meanwhile, Irena, ignorant of her true nature, develops an obsession with zoo curator Oliver Yates—until her subconscious fears become a barrier to their intimacy. Irena's innocence stands in direct contrast to zoo worker Alice Perrin, an experienced "modern" girl who also has eyes for Oliver. Inevitably, Alice becomes Irena's natural rival, setting up slavish recreations of the "bus" and swimming-pool scenes that the original made justly famous. The relationships depicted in this film reflect the dark side of the sexual revolution, in which new roles of gender behaviors were forged without heeding the consequences.

The film uses deliberate stylized imagery to reinforce its primary themes. An elaborate dream sequence takes Irena back to the time of her ancestors' original sin, depicting the transgressions of her forebears in visual terms. Moments in which Irena dons a scarlet cravat or pokes her fingers through a wire-mesh fence call attention to her changing identity. Other images are almost comic in their excess—Paul's solicitation of a ditzy blonde tourist becomes a stylized representation of the cat and the canary. The use of such visuals are sometimes too obvious for the film's own good, but at times the poetry of the camera provides an effective counterpoint for Irena's inner journey.

By the final reel, Irena Gallier is ready to embrace the unknown. Knowing that she can never be Oliver's lover, she instead begs him to kill her. He refuses, prompting her to ask for the next best thing. "Then free me," she pleads, secure in the knowledge that another carnal encounter will transform her back to feral form, presumably forever. Irena's struggle thus results in an uneasy but acceptable truce. Unable to find satisfaction in the real world, she accepts the alternate identity that life has given her. If only cinema's other loss-of-identity tales could be resolved so constructively.—*SGT*

Chinese Ghost Story, A (***Sien nui yau wan***) (1987) [**reincarnation; zombification**] Hong Kong (Cinema City Film Productions). *D:* Siu-Tung Ching. *S:* Kai-Chi Yun, From the Story "Nie Xiaoqian" by Songling Pu. *Cast:* Leslie Cheung (Ning Tsai-Shen); Joey Wong (Nieh Hsiao-Tsing); Ma Wu (Yen Che-Hsia).

In *A Chinese Ghost Story*, a beautiful female ghost serves as man-bait for a tree demon who vampirically feeds on the vitality of men, transforming them into desiccated walking dead, completely deprived of their former identity.

Ning Tsai-Shen, a tax collector, falls in love with this young "woman" while staying in a haunted temple outside of town. Through the help of a Taoist priest who inhabits the temple, Tsai-Shen discovers that the girl is a ghost. But, by the time the young man discovers her identity, she has fallen in love with him and seeks to protect him from her master/mistress, the demon.

In *A Chinese Ghost Story*, the beautiful ghost Nieh Hsiao-Tsing (Joey Wong) is the pawn of powerful demons who force her to entrap living men.

As it happens, she is the demon's unwilling accomplice. When her ashes were buried at the root of a tree, the tree demon captured her and forced her against her will to entrap living men. In the end, Tsai-Shen and the Taoist priest storm hell itself to break the power of the evil spirits and make it possible for her to reincarnate.

Though the men who have their life sucked out of them by the tree demon lose their identity completely, the ghost, Nieh Hsiao-Tsing, still retains her sense of identity—not really a good thing in her Taoist/Buddhist tradition. Her soul should have moved on; it should have lost its identity and journeyed to a new life with a new identity. Instead, she has been trapped by supernatural forces that compel her to do things that are contrary to her former identity's sense of right and wrong. Worse yet, the tree demon is forcing her to marry another demon.

Before Ning Tsai-Shen rescues her, Nieh Hsiao-Tsing is a tragic figure—in the possession of demons, still knowing right from wrong, being forced to do wrong, and falling in love with a pure and good man while being compelled to marry an evil spirit. In the end, her problem is solved by completely losing her identity to reincarnation.

Talk about a loss-of-identity crisis!—*CCS*

Chump at Oxford, A (1940) [**amnesia**] Hal Roach Studios, Inc. (United Artists). *D:* Alfred Goulding. *S:* Charley Rogers, Felix Adler, and Harry Langdon. *Cast:* Stan Laurel (Stan/Lord Paddington); Oliver Hardy (Ollie); Wilfred Lucas (Dean Williams); Forbes Murray (Banker); Frank Baker (Dean's servant); Eddie Borden (Student ghost); Gerald Rogers (Student Johnson); Victor Kendall (Student Cecil); Gerald Fielding (Student Brown); Charlie Hall (Student Hector); Peter Cushing (Student Jones).

Though *A Chump at Oxford*'s LOI (*regaining* of identity, here?) is played for laughs, it's a horror for at least one member of the film: Oliver Hardy. Hardy, used to lording over his pal Stanley (who's even dumber than Hardy is), is more surprised than anyone when a bump on the head from a faulty window frame transforms Laurel (back) into Lord Paddington, boxing champion and hero of Oxford.

The fortuitous metamorphosis allows the duo to be spared the wrath of the student body, out to tar and feather the pair, since the transformed Laurel is now more than a match for them. But Hardy is less than appreciative of Laurel's re-found pugilistic acumen and aristocratic air. When he tries to put Stanley back in his place, he finds himself unceremoniously tossed for a loss along with the rest of the undergrads. Reduced in status to Stanley's valet, addressed as "Fatty" ("Chins up," orders Laurel in a priceless nasty line), Hardy endures in silence until he finally snaps, rebels, and, with much *sturm und drang*, castigates Stanley while packing his belongings and vowing to return to America.

Another fortuitous noggin-bonk from that same *fenêtre-ex-machina* returns Stanley to his former state, much to Oliver's relief and just in time for a happy reunion/ending. This business takes up the last reel of the 63-minute movie. It could easily have been expanded by another 20 minutes—if not for the fact that most Laurel and Hardy Hal Roach features only ran about an hour, and most Laurel and Hardy fans probably couldn't have borne it.

For this episode also generates a level of discomfort on the part of the comedians' audience. *Chump* marks the first and only time we see Laurel so out of character. (Laurel did portray a split personality in the 1925 short, "Dr. Pyckle and Mr. Pride," but that was before he teamed up with Hardy and created his well-known and enduring

In *A Chump at Oxford*, Ollie (Oliver Hardy) has a laugh at the expense of Stan (Stan Laurel), who after a bump on the head thinks he is Lord Paddington.

screen persona.) Even when he was playing Ollie's wife (in "Twice Two" [1933]) or his own son (in "Brats" [1930]), Laurel remained the dim-wit we knew and loved. This totally different aspect is as disquieting to viewers as it is to Hardy—illustrating one of the most disturbing elements of loss of identity: its effect on those familiar with the changed individual—those who are suddenly confronted with a stranger in the guise of the once-known. Thus, fans breathe a sigh of relief when the world is "put right" and Laurel is "normal" again.—*AFA*

Clean Slate (1994) [**amnesia**] (MGM). *D:* Mick Jackson. *S:* Robert King. *Cast*: Dana Carvey (Maurice L. Pogue); Valeria Golino (Sarah Novak/Beth Holly); James Earl Jones (John Dolby); Kevin Pollak (Rosenheim); Michael Gambon (Cornell); Michael Murphy (Dr. Doover); Jayne Brook (Paula); Vyto Ruginis (Hendrix); Olivia d'Abo (Judy).

Sort of a comedic dry run for *Memento* (2000 [*q.v.*]) without the achronological structure, *Clean Slate* tells the tale of Maurice Pogue (Dana Carvey in his first true starring role after being featured on *Saturday Night Live* [1986-1993] and co-starring in the two *Wayne's World* movies [1992 and 1993]), a private detective who suffers from Korsakov's Syndrome—an actual dementia that occurs during the last stages of severe chronic alcoholism, causing memory loss for recent events while leaving long-term memory intact but science fictionalized in the film. Here, this affliction causes him to forget *everything* every time he goes to sleep. This subtle allusion to *Invasion of the Body Snatchers* (1956, 1978 [*q.v.*]) underscores just how much of our identity is *memory*.

In *Clean Slate*, the condition is temporary, brought on, apparently, by severe physical and psychological trauma: Pogue survived the car explosion that killed his lover, Sarah, a woman who was fleeing the mob; Pogue's the only witness against the murderer,

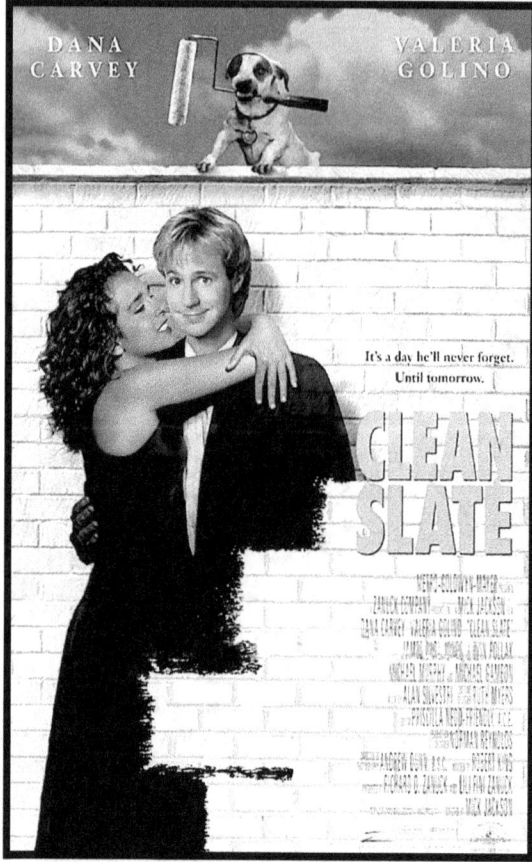

gang boss Cornell; he recorded his testimony before succumbing to Korsakov's Syndrome, but he can't let anyone know about his memory loss until after the trial.

Every night, Pogue thoughtfully provides himself with a tape-recorded message that he can play the next morning to refresh his memory (and, initially, to supply exposition to the viewer); his most important message to himself is "whatever you do, don't answer the door," which is practically the first thing he does. Whisked away by a couple of cops, he ends up at what turns out to be a birthday celebration in his honor and must fake an extemporaneous speech about himself and his comrades (whom he of course doesn't recognize).

Because the film is a comedy, it puts Pogue in a series of situations where his loss of identity renders him at a loss and he must use his wits to recreate and sustain identities where none remain for him. (He mistakes the gang boss for his landlord; he doesn't realize, when his lawyer buddy asks him to find out the identity of his wife's paramour, that he's hunting himself; and he's mistaken for a famous explorer while fleeing from an attacker and manages to turn identity to his advantage.)

Complicating matters is the woman who claims to be the dead Sarah and with whom Pogue falls in love (again) and who, while not the original Sarah, falls in love with the Pogue who doesn't know who he is.

This "resurrected Sarah" is actually Beth Holly, an imposter hired by the other villain of the piece to get Pogue to reveal the whereabouts of the valuable coin—the MacGuffin everyone is after. Of course, she develops scruples and can't go through with the deceit, but it's her posing as his lover and consummating their relationship that ultimately gives Pogue back his memory. (He wakes beside her and recognizes her as "Sarah.")—*AFA*

Clockwork Orange, A (1971) [**scientific manipulation**] (Warner Bros.). *D:* Stanley Kubrick. *S:* Stanley Kubrick, From the Novel *A Clockwork Orange* by Anthony Burgess. *Cast:* Malcolm McDowell (Alexander "Alex" de Large); Patrick Magee (Mr. Alexander); Michael Bates (Chief Guard); Warren Clarke (Dim); John Clive (Stage Actor); Adrienne Corri (Mrs. Alexander).

How do you deal with a monstrous sociopath—a youth with no conscience, only a drive to commit or fantasize about sadistic acts of ultra violence and rape?

Well, in *A Clockwork Orange,* a future British government offers a Pavlovian solution, using aversion therapy to "cure" our working-class antihero, Alex, by making him incapable of violence. The catch is that, in depriving Alex of his ultra-violent identity, the treatment also places him at the mercy of those seeking vengeance; and, by robbing him of moral choice, it robs him of whatever shreds of humanity he possessed.

The "clockwork orange" of the title (indicating a mechanical organism) refers explicitly to Alex's "cure"—making him into an organism which has mechanically predictable responses to violence, sex, and (alas) Beethoven's 9th Symphony (the soundtrack to one of the films shown during his therapy). In becoming this clockwork orange, Alex "ceases to be a wrongdoer," but, as the prison chaplain points out, "he ceases also to be a creature capable of moral choice." He "ceases to be a man." His mechanical responses, in fact, can even be manipulated to force him to attempt suicide—a gambit employed after his release by a writer he savagely wronged.

Has Alex, though, ever been a free agent of moral choice, someone who could transcend social and psycho-genetic programming? In Anthony Burgess' novel, the answer is "yes." Alex's ultra violence turns out to have been a teenage phase, the product of a youth culture that he chooses to abandon in the end. This relatively upbeat ending, though, has no place in Kubrick's film, leaving open the possibility that Alex's

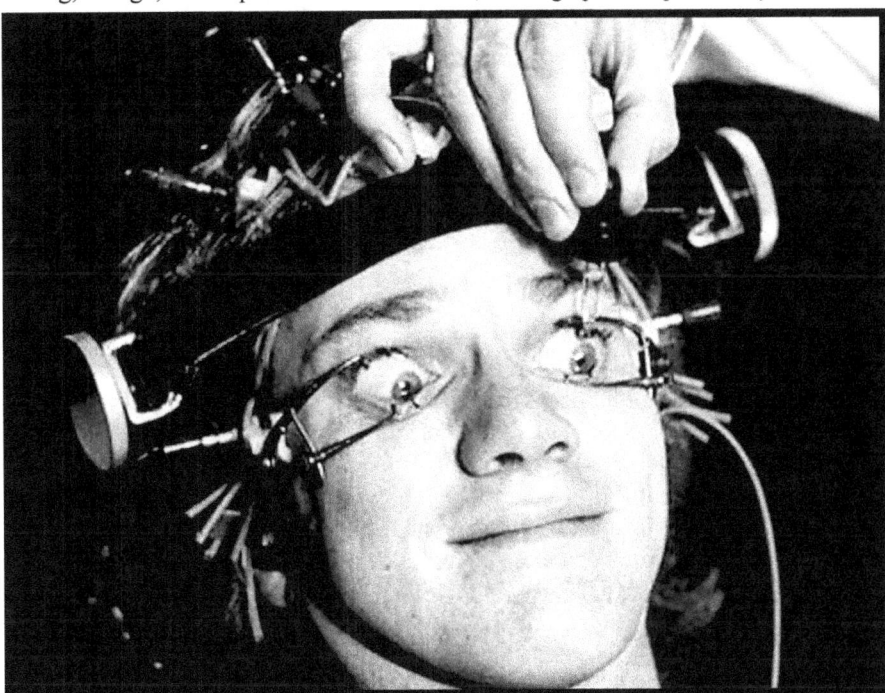

Alex (Malcolm McDowell) undergoes aversion therapy to cure him of his antisocial behavior in *A Clockwork Orange.*

ultra-violent behavior may be encoded into the very chemistry of his psyche—a much more disturbing possibility, implying a determinism different only in substance from the determinism inherent in Alex's treatment.

In the youth culture in which Alex engulfs himself, uniformity is all the rage. Teen boys roam the streets in gangs of four, dressed in identical uniforms, drinking identical orders of "milk-plus," and masking their identities when they make "the surprise visit" on defenseless citizens. But, even within this uniformity, Alex—perhaps because he is his gang's leader—stands out from the rest. He wears the false eyelash; his mask contains the Pinocchio nose; and, even in his sing-song Russified teenage slang, his speech often rises to a perverse sort of poetry.

Kubrick's Alex seems so much more than just a product of his society. Alex is an artist of ultra violence, inspired by some muse that transforms the strains of his beloved Beethoven into a personal soundtrack for violent acts and fantasies. Critics often deem this love of Beethoven to be the boy's single redeeming quality, but Alex twists Beethoven's music into the fabric of an ultra-violent imagination. Beethoven becomes no artistic escape from violence; his music instead becomes integrally entwined in Alex's artistry of violence—implying that violence may be part of the boy's psychological encoding.

Alex's prison experience certainly implies that possibility. Here, separated from society and his droogs, his identity encapsulated in the number 655321, Alex reads the Bible...while relishing the thought of crucifying Christ: "I read all about the scourging and the crowning of thorns. And I could viddy myself helping in, and even taking charge of the tolchoking and the nailing in—being dressed in the height of Roman fashion."

Kubrick's film, thankfully, takes no stand on how Alex became what he is. Except for some flustered questions by Mr. Deltoid (the youth's "Post-Corrective Advisor"), the film never asks whether Alex is a product of nature or nurture or society or some "devil that crawls inside of" him. Alex simply is what he is. And so what is society to do with him? Corrective School has failed. Prison has punished, but also nurtured, his violence. And rewiring his psychological response to violence has proven disastrous. The question remains: Does it matter what suffering may be inflicted on this antisocial sociopath? Does Alex even merit having the inherently human possibility of free choice?

The film argues "yes" by eliciting a paradoxical sympathy for Alex's plight when he becomes the helpless victim. But it argues "yes" with misgivings. After Alex attempts suicide, the government has him deprogrammed and tries to bribe him into helping it wiggle free of public disapproval over the "inhuman cure" that led the boy to desperation. Alex's response to the overture, though, has ominous overtones. When the Minister of the Interior asks if he has made himself clear, Alex replies in the same wording he offered Mr. Deltoid shortly before committing the murder which landed him in prison: The deal is clear "as an unmuddied lake...As clear as an azure sky in summer." Given the wording, we can almost assume that Alex will revert to type. The violent sexual imagery he envisions at the end practically ensures it.

And so Alex regains his ability to commit ultra violence. But does he truly regain an identity, with all the free moral choice human identity implies? Or does he simply revert to another type of programming, driving him inexorably to unleash ultra violence on the society into which the government will release him? Is he, in the end, just a different type of clockwork orange? That single unanswered question makes Alex far more disturbing than all the unsparing depictions of his ultra violence.—*CCS*

Creeping Unknown, The (***Quatermass Xperiment, The***) (1955) [**alien possession; metamorphosis**] (Hammer Film Productions Limited). *D:* Val Guest. *S:* Richard H. Landau, Based on the Teleplay *The Quatermass Experiment* by Nigel Kneale. *Cast:* Brian Donelvy (Prof. Bernard Quatermass); Jack Warner (Inspector Lomax); Margia Dean (Judith Caroon); Richard Wordsworth (Victor Caroon).

Puberty is a terrible thing. For those who went through it, my heart goes out to you. I don't know how it is for girls, but for boys, it's no picnic. There we are, finally figuring out how to be a successful kid. Then, one by one, things happen that drag us screaming into the role of grown man.

Parts of your body go all hairy. There's that growth spurt; your voice changes, then these *desires* start bursting out of nowhere. You never used to think twice about girls, and now you have these all-consuming needs that drive you up the freakin' wall. And that acne! I was lucky. I only had a few pimples burning into my mug, but I knew guys whose faces erupted into an angry wasteland of red volcanoes. It takes a writer the caliber of John Steinbeck in *The Wayward Bus* to truly describe the inhuman compulsion that forces us, against its will to scratch those suckers. There are times when it feels like our entire being is mutating, that we are uncontrollably changing into some kind of... *thing*.

The frightening thing is, we *are*. Inside and out. The physical changes of puberty coincide with adolescence, that time of life when our brain kind of shuts down and we

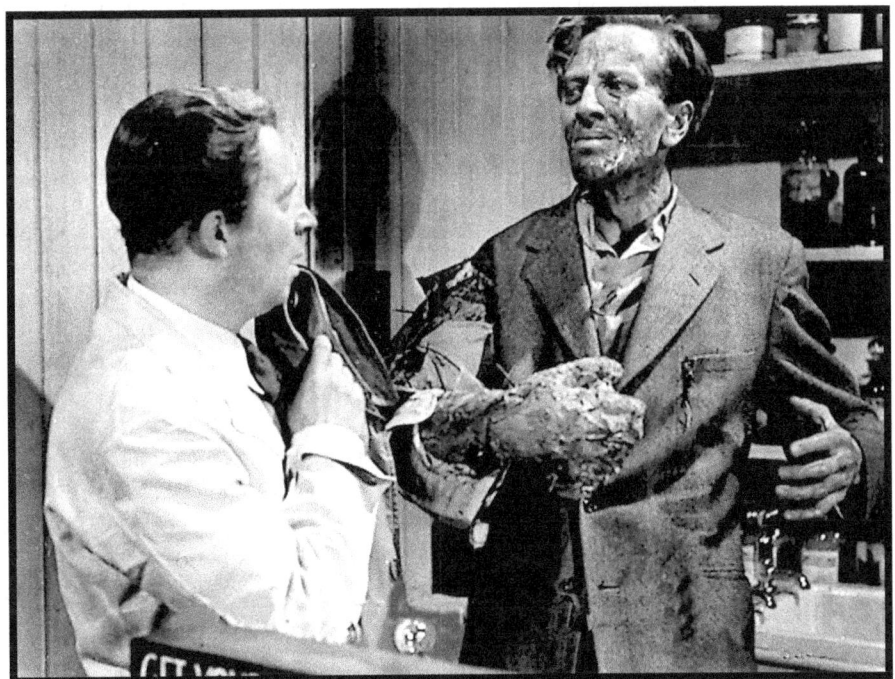

Christie (Harold Lang) is hired by Caroon's wife to help the doomed astronaut Victor Caroon (Richard Woodsworth) escape Quatermass in *The Creeping Unknown.*

spend hours staring blankly off into space as our personality decides just what kind of adult we are going to turn into. For the most part, we don't know what's happening or where it will lead, and, unless we have incredibly communicative parents, it is impossible to talk about. Some people thrive despite the experience; some don't survive, but nobody who went through puberty ever came out the same.

Horror cinema is rife with metamorphoses, full of wolf men and hideous sun demons and Neanderthal men and flies and such. Starting in the 1950s, perhaps inspired by the onslaught of the Baby Boom, a number of films made a deliberate stab at evoking the metamorphosis of adolescence.

Ah yes, behold the horror movies of puberty: *I Was a Teenage Werewolf* (1957 [*q.v.*]). *Fright Night* (1985). *Teen Wolf* (1985). Huge swathes of the oeuvres of the Davids Lynch and Cronenberg. (Who but someone scarred by a brutal adolescence could come up with *Dune* [1984]—or the 1986 remake of *The Fly*?) But there was one movie that really tapped into the experience for me.

In *The Creeping Unknown*, Richard Wordsworth, an almost unknown British character actor, gives an beautiful performance as an astronaut who fights against a malevolent alien intelligence that takes over—and then completely consumes—his body. (Wordsworth is known to horror fans for his performance here and for playing the poor beggar, incarcerated by an evil Marquis, who loses his identity and becomes the rabid prisoner who rapes the servant girl played by Yvonne Romain in *Curse of the Werewolf* [1961 (*q.v.*)]. He was also a descendant of the famous Romantic poet William Wordsworth, who famously wrote, "The child is father to the man.") Now, Wordsworth was too old to explicitly evoke puberty, the way Michael Landon did in *I Was a Teenage Werewolf*. In no way is Richard Wordsworth a symbolic pubescent, but, whether by intent or just dumb luck, the work of Wordsworth, director Val Guest, and screenwrights Richard Landau and Nigel Kneale taps into many of the angsts and agonies we all go through as we leave childhood behind.

For my adolescent self, there was something compelling in the sight of Wordsworth, his skin taking on a ghastly pallor while he sits, staring blankly out into space, deaf to the presence of his worried loved ones. He is silent, as he cannot speak to anyone about what is happening. Or, in Wordsworth's supreme moment, when an inhuman compulsion forces him to smash his bare fist into a potted cactus, his face becomes a mask of anguish as he vainly struggles to hold this unholy need in check.

Ultimately, his entire body dissolves into a shapeless, fungusoidal blob. Well, for most of us, puberty doesn't turn out that bad. But, for a few years, it feels pretty damn close.—*AJL*

Creepshow (1982) [**alien possession; metamorphosis**] Laurel Entertainment/Warner Bros. (Warner Bros.). *D:* George A. Romero. *S:* Stephen King. *Cast:* Hal Holbrook (Professor Henry Northrup); Adrienne Barbeau (Wilma "Billie" Northrup); Fritz Weaver (Professor Dexter Stanley); Leslie Nielsen (Richard Vickers); Ted Danson (Harry Wentworth); E.G. Marshall (Upson Pratt); Viveca Lindfors (Bedelia Grantham); Ed Harris (Hank Blaine); Stephen King (Jordy Verrill).

Back in the early 1980s, maverick indie horror director George A. Romero ventured into the world of full-blown wide-release commercial accessibility. An anthology throwback to EC Comics like *Tales from the Crypt* and the British productions of the same from Amicus Films (*Tales from the Crypt* [1972], *Vault of Horror* [1973]), *Creepshow* boasted an original script from superstar novelist Stephen King.

King also acted in one of the film's five stories, starring in "The Lonesome Death of Jordy Verrell" as the title character, a simple country fellow who witnesses a meteorite crash on his farm. Alas, Jordy's greed and accompanying lack of common sense result in his being somehow affected by an entity that lives inside the meteorite. Much like Lovecraft's "Color Out of Space," the plant-like life-form begins to spread, in time covering every inch of Jordy's farm—and appears well on its way to covering the rest of the world. Even Jordy himself becomes infected, starting with a green patch on his hand—and it isn't long until he is a full-fledged *Swamp Thing* knock-off. His inability to accept his new co-opted existence ends tragically. (Compare the fate of Richard Wordsworth's astronaut in 1956's *The Creeping Unknown* [*q.v.*] and most of the cast in *The Blob* [1958 and 1988].)

Stephen King is a victim of his own creation as Jordy Verrill in *Creepshow*.

There's no purer example of identity loss than in this story. As dim-witted as he is, and as corny as the humor and presentation are (both deliberate decisions on the part of Romero and King), Jordy earns our sympathy as we watch him lose his humanity, inexorably being invaded by the greenery. In the end, he resembles nothing so much as one of the living topiaries from King's novel *The Shining*.

For me, *Creepshow* represented my first paying production job in the film business as a lowly production assistant. One of my duties for a while was to assist in bringing Jordy's tragedy to light. It took a great deal of fluorescent-green spray paint, fake plants, matte paintings, and other special effects to "sell" the concept. Of one thing you can be sure—by the time we finished shooting, we were all very sick of the color green!—*RJT*

Cursed (2005) [**metamorphosis**] (Dimension Films). *D:* Wes Craven. *S:* Kevin Williamson. *Cast:* Christina Ricci (Ellie); Jesse Eisenberg (Jimmy); Joshua Jackson (Jake); Judy Greer (Joanie); Milo Ventimiglia (Bo); Mya (Jenny); Shannon Elizabeth (Becky); Scott Baio (Scott Baio); Craig Kilbourn (Craig Kilbourn).

The much-maligned *Cursed* from Kevin Williamson and Wes Craven, the writing-directing team of *Scream* (1996) and *Scream 2* (1997), is actually a decent addition to werewolf movies and the loss of identity genre—at least in the "unrated director's cut" that I saw on DVD.

Taking a leaf from recent lycanthropy films which bend the myth in different directions, *Cursed* postulates that becoming a werewolf affects our human identity, making

Ellie (Christina Ricci) and Jimmy (Jesse Eisenberg) are wounded by a werewolf and become infected in *Cursed*.

us sexier and bolder—giving us a certain animal magnetism (*cf. Wolf* [1994 (*q.v.*)] and *Ginger Snaps* [2000 (*q.v.*)])—and also argues that we can break the curse by killing the creature who bit us (*cf. Ginger Snaps Back: The Beginning* [2004 (*q.v.*)]).

Orphaned sister and brother Ellie and Jimmy are both wounded in a werewolf attack and begin to exhibit those sexy, bold characteristics mentioned above. In Jimmy's case, these stand him in good stead because they allow him to stand up to Bo, the school bully (and, in the process, get Bo to own up to the truth of *his* identity—that his constant homophobic put-downs of others are a cover for his true, gay tendencies). Ultimately, these attributes help the siblings to sniff out and defeat the lycanthrope(s) in their midst before they can succumb entirely to their darker urges.

As always, Craven treats his characters with respect. His victims have dignity and are never just disposable meat. Thus, when they die (and some of them do), we feel a loss and don't just chalk up their deaths to standard horror-film body count. *Cursed* best illustrates this aspect of Craven's work in a tightly edited four-minute stalking sequence in a parking garage and elevator, involving peripheral character Jenny (a subtle allusion to *The Wolf Man* [1941 (*q.v.*)]?—Mya's Jenny, like Fay Helm's similarly named victim in *The Wolf Man*, is warned about werewolves by a fortune teller—and doesn't escape the beast's claws). Craven has never been one to opt for the cheap downbeat ending so many horror films exploit (except for *Deadly Blessing* [1981] and *A Nightmare on Elm Street* [1984], whose "gotcha" conclusions were imposed upon him), and he doesn't surrender to it here, allowing his protagonists to overcome and to reassert their human identities at the conclusion.—*AFA*

Curse of the Werewolf, The (1960) [**metamorphosis**] Great Britain (Hammer Films). *D:* Terence Fisher. *S:* Anthony Hinds (as John Elder), Based on the Novel *The Were-*

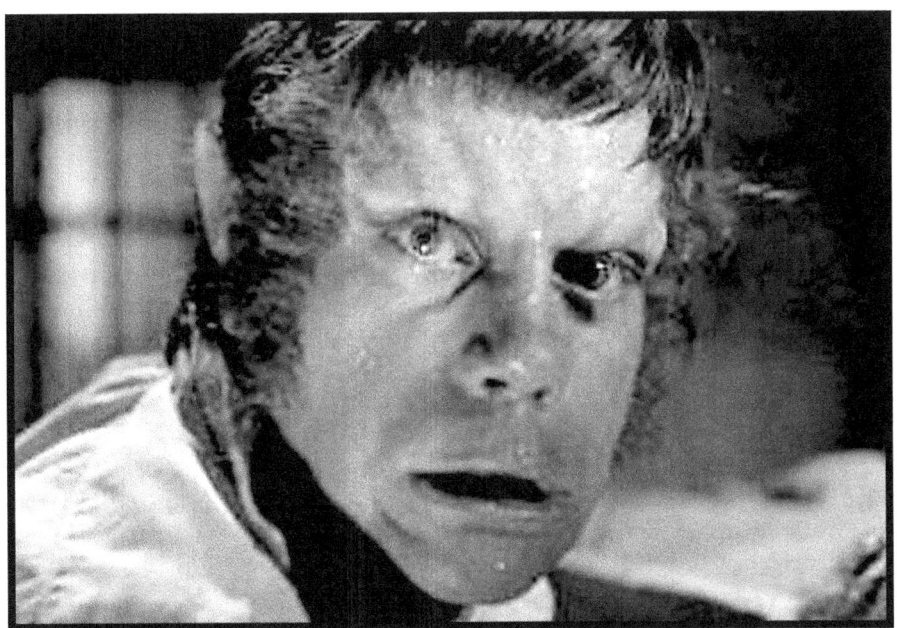

Leon (Oliver Reed) in the grip of transformation. He is a werewolf by birth, rather than from the bite of a werewolf, in *The Curse of the Werewolf*.

wolf of Paris by Guy Endore. *Cast:* Clifford Evans (Professor Carrido); Oliver Reed (Leon); Yvonne Romain (Servant Girl); Catherine Feller (Christina); Anthony Dawson (Marquis); Hira Talfrey (Teresa); Richard Wordsworth (Beggar).

Hammer Films made a name for itself by reinventing the classic monsters first popularized by Universal in the 1930s and 1940s. The best of these adaptations add a unique and compelling spin to the mythos embraced by previous generations of movie-goers. In *The Curse of the Werewolf*, a tragic subtext is incorporated that extends the loss-of-identity elements of Universal's original *Wolf Man* series.

In this reinvention, lycanthrophy is inflicted upon the victim as a spiritual curse. A lengthy backstory depicts the tale of a beggar who offends a Marquis on his wedding night. Imprisoned and forgotten, the beggar reverts to an animal-like state. The years pass. When a deaf servant girl refuses the Marquee's affections, she becomes a cellmate to the beggar, who attacks and rapes her. A hint of the supernatural is dropped too—born on Christmas day, the resulting unwanted child is believed to be an "insult to heaven." As a result, little Leon is at war with himself, forever torn between his human identity and the animal spirit that has entered his body.

As Leon matures, the animal identity within him awakens. The catalyst for this change is a hunting trip, a traditional male rite of passage, during which little Leon observes the death of a squirrel. Moved with pity, he kisses the dead animal—and tastes blood for the first time. Leon then begins to experience "bad dreams" that coincide with his initial transformations and subsequent attacks upon the local livestock. Although unaware of the true nature of his condition, Leon instinctively senses that something peculiar is happening to him. This sequence draws a distinct parallel between Leon's affliction and puberty, a time when all adolescents begin to question their changing identity. [*Cf.* AJT's remarks about same in *The Creeping Unknown* (1955).]

Leon's bestial urges go into remission during his time with a stable surrogate family. But soon he ventures forth into the world. His encounter with a loose woman at a local tavern rouses his sexual urges—and reawakens the animal inside of him. After this, he can remain human during the cycle of the full moon only when he is in the company of the woman who loves him. The contrasting depiction of healthy and destructive carnal impulses further extends the sexual metaphor and illustrates the extent to which his identity remains conflicted. He desires love but remains a slave to his violent urges; these warring factions of Leon's soul are headed toward a tragic resolution.

Although not one of Hammer's most popular films, *The Curse of the Werewolf* has its share of admirers, thanks in part to a fine performance by young Oliver Reed as the doomed Leon. Hammer would soon abandon its ambitious reworking of the classic monsters and settle into a predictable format of endless sequels. Some contend that the studio's identity would never be the same again.—*SGT*

Dark City (1998) [**altered reality**] Mystery Clock Cinema/New Line Cinema (New Line Cinema). *D:* Alex Proyas. *S:* Alex Proyas, Lem Dobbs, and David S. Goyer, From a Story by Alex Proyas. *Cast:* Rufus Sewell (John Murdock); Keifer Sutherland (Dr. Daniel Schreber); Jennifer Connelly (Emma Murdock); Richard O'Brien (Mr. Hand); Ian Richardson (Mr. Book); William Hurt (Inspector Frank Bumstead).

By the end of the 20th century, rampant paranoia and conspiracy fears began to influence our culture's loss-of-identity issues. Cinema reflected this by depicting worlds in which the surface fabric of reality was merely an illusion for a darker universe underneath. *The Matrix* (1999 [*q.v.*]) was by far the most successful of these, but *Dark City*, made a year earlier, also dealt with these issues in a similarly effective manner.

The events of *Dark City* unfold through the eyes of John Murdock. Jolted into consciousness one night, Murdock has no memory of his past life or current identity. Through chance encounters and circumstantial evidence, he realizes that he is wanted for murder. But all is not as it appears to be. He soon discovers that the world as he knows it undergoes an abrupt change each evening at midnight—people fall into an inexplicable slumber and awaken with new lives and new memories. Initially, the loss of identity is personal, but it is soon revealed to have far greater implications.

Dark City **delves into life's big identity questions but provides no answers.**

John Murdock's (Rufus Sewell) world has been one of illusion in *Dark City*.

Eventually, the mystery of *Dark City* is revealed. Murdock's world is indeed an illusion, crafted by aliens who have developed a human colony on an artificial satellite orbiting in space. On this new world, humanity is subject to endless experiments meant to discern the source of our individuality, which the extraterrestrial strangers believe holds the key to their continued survival. Our daily lives are nothing but a series of behavioral games in which our circumstances are dealt out like playing cards until the next day when the slate is wiped clean and the ruse starts all over again. Murdock has somehow developed a resistance to the nightly "imprinting" and shows traces of the alien's ability to "tune"—to alter physical reality through the use of sheer will. His continued existence stands in the way of their experiment and thus becomes a threat to their very existence.

Writer/director Alex Proyas creates a visual style that borrows freely from both 1940s film noir and 1920s German Expressionism. This visual overkill, along with the film's ultra-fantastic premise, threatens to overpower the basic narrative. But the film deserves extra points for taking on some of life's big identity questions. What determines who we are? Are we more than the sum of our memories? And to what extent is life merely an illusion? *Dark City* provides no conclusive answers. The film's hopeful ending, however, suggests that in spite of our circumstances, we do have the ability to reshape our world. For John Murdock, and for us as well, identity is merely a starting point.—*SGT*

Dawn of the Dead (1978) [**zombification**] Laurel Group (United Film Distribution Company). *D*: George A. Romero. *S:* George A. Romero. *Cast:* David Emge (Stephen); Ken Foree (Peter); Scott H Reiniger (Roger); Gaylen Ross (Fran).

This George A. Romero classic, one of the finest horror films ever made, contains everything an action-horror fan could ever want. As in *Night of the Living Dead* (1968 [*q.v.*]), Romero applies the principles of loss of identity to both the survivors and the zombified—but on a much larger scale. *Dawn* is not just about the legions of the dead conquering the planet; Romero cleverly weaves in both subtle and overt features that constitute a scathing attack upon Western consumer culture, which makes it sickeningly ironic that the film would be remade in 2004 to satiate this very culture.

Dawn begins where *Night* left off; the dead continue to rise and seek living human flesh while mankind struggles to mount a concerted response to the rapidly escalating crisis. Caught in the midst of this nightmare of decaying society are the film's four main characters—helicopter pilot and broadcaster Stephen; his girlfriend, television anchorwoman Fran; and SWAT-team members Peter and Roger. Their saga begins in a Philadelphia that, like all major population centers during the zombie pandemic, has become an all-out war zone of chaos, confusion, and paranoia as the armies of the undead march ever onward. Alarmed by the swift decline of social order, the four steal a helicopter to flee to a safer area, which turns out to be a huge mall on the edge of Pittsburgh.

As Romero guides his protagonists across urban and rural war zones, the viewer becomes aware of the widespread disintegration of social and communal values, and the gradual removal of many cohesive facets of collective identity formed by a nation's societal structure. The humans, growing increasingly desperate in their efforts to survive, reject values such as generosity and empathy in favor of more selfish pursuits. Romero expands upon the volatile social microcosm he set within the farmhouse in *Night of the Living Dead* and applies it here on a much larger scale; the result is suitably catastrophic. The loss of societal identity creates disparate groups of humans, some acting at the behest of Uber-admirable leaders, and all of them irrevocably divided in the face of the dead's onslaught.

Instead of maintaining widespread discipline and order, surely the necessary components for combating the threat of several thousand zombies, the human protagonists reject this strategy out of hand. In *Dawn of the Dead*, as the boundaries and conformities placed upon mankind by society are eroded and finally removed (the cumulative effects of which feature in Romero's *Day of the Dead* [1985 (*q.v.*)] and *Land of the Dead* [2005 (*q.v.*)]), many humans value their desires for individuality over the necessity of survival, with often devastating and very bloody results, leading to a larger loss of identity issue: the conflict between environmental and genetic theories of behavior traits and influences.

If society collapsed tomorrow, whether under threat of zombies or terrorism or anything else, would this loss of structure result in a total loss of identity of its populace or simply allow the opportunity for otherwise suppressed aspects of human behavior to surface? Of course, the term "survival of the fittest" (as applied by Herbert Spencer) springs readily to mind here, but Romero repeatedly suggests that embracing such "social Darwinism," far from forging a new identity, offers humanity only oblivion in the face of an overpowering crisis.

In *Dawn*, as the numbers of dead increase enormously, they exhibit paradoxical behavior. Obviously the zombie represents nothing more than a flesh-eating automaton, hunting for its own mindless purposes without awareness of its surroundings or companions. However, in Romero's movies (and the vast majority of subsequent zombie films), the zombies also unwittingly combine their strength in a manner akin to a doddering, clumsy, yet overwhelming army, as their very nature dictates that they congregate en masse at the locations where food can be found. So the fleeing humans, whether traveling as part of a professional army or as individuals living on their wits, usually come into contact with zombies holding a supreme numerical advantage, in the face of which they have little chance of survival. Therefore, despite the efforts of

Dawn of the Dead **features numerous examples of loss of identity, including the blinding materialism which overwhelms the mall-walking zombies.**

gun-toting rednecks, National Guard troops, and other armed groups, the humans' lack of unity and common goals that a tangible mass social structure would provide, coupled with certain people's irrational (yet perhaps understandable) determination to live (or die) by their own rules, allows the zombie plague to swiftly spread across the countryside.

Following some hugely enjoyable gunfights with the hordes of the dead and the execution of a daring plan to block the entrances with trucks (during which Roger is bitten), the mall is secured. From here, the film shifts tone: Within the confines of the mall, the quartet suffers a different form of identity loss, metamorphosing from refugees to landlords. They may have begun life in the mall exhausted and terrified, hiding in a cramped storeroom, eating canned Spam, but now they reside in consummate splendor, indulging themselves in a wide range of luxuries and delicacies. Indeed, all four become ensconced within their private world, seemingly oblivious of the apocalypse raging around them as outside mankind fights for survival. In this respect the film certainly touches a nerve: How many of us haven't hidden ourselves away at one time of crisis or another, or simply obscured rational thought processes by indulging ourselves in consumerist whims?

Ultimately the film features various themes of loss of identity. First, there are the characters, including Roger and Stephen, whose zombification reduces them to mindless meat eaters. Coupled with this is the blinding glare of materialism which completely overwhelms not only the four deserters but also the hundreds of zombies who seem inexorably drawn to the shopping center. Finally, the aforementioned loss of societal identity places the characters in a redefined, almost unbounded world, in a free-for-all against fellow survivors and the ever-growing numbers of ghouls. Romero's vision is bleak indeed.—*AJB*

Day Mars Invaded Earth, The (1963) [**doppelganger**] (20th Century Fox). *D:* Maury Dexter. *S:* Harry Spalding. *Cast:* Kent Taylor (Dr. David Fielding); Marie Windsor (Claire Fielding); William Mims (Dr. Web Spencer); Betty Beall (Judi Fielding); Lowell Brown (Frank Hazard); Gregg Shank (Rocky Fielding); Henrietta Moore (Miss Moore).

The Day Mars Invaded Earth begins with a cheesy robot probe moving across the barren surface of Mars for a few seconds before it stops dead amid a puff of smoke. At a loss to explain it, little knowing that the incident has set off a chain of events that will result in his loss of identity, Cape Canaveral rocket scientist Dr. Fielding heads to an isolated mansion on a huge estate to reunite with his family and try to save his disintegrating marriage. The family members soon begin seeing doppelgangers of themselves and discover these duplicates have been created by the bodiless inhabitants of Mars, who have taken up residence in them. "We have intelligence in the abstract, much like your electricity here," explains Fielding's alien double, elaborating that the Martians used Fielding's probe to "transmit [their] intelligence" to Earth, where they intend to impersonate Fielding and his family in order to halt the exploratory invasion of their planet. Confronting a "twin" who's plotting to supplant you makes for a nightmarish loss-of-identity scenario.

Day generates a creepy ambiance (aided by some surprisingly effective day-for-night photography) as the principals wander about the huge, isolated estate and keep seeing each other in places they simply cannot be. The doppelgangers initially appear more like apparitions than aliens, emerging unexpectedly to simply stare (observing their "hosts" in order to emulate their behavior, we later learn) and exude an air of icy menace. Their terrifying power, however, is revealed when they make a meddlesome family friend spontaneously combust with just a glance and an accompanying high-pitched tone. The dry-ice smoke pouring from the terrified man's clothing (before he's reduced—after a coy cutaway—to a vaguely man-shaped pile of ashes on the flagstones) is cheap but chilling.

The cost-conscious production confines its small cast to mostly a single setting, but this ultimately adds to the general sense of unease and isolation, enhancing the terrifying concept of one's identity being stolen and supplanted by a cold alien intelligence (not to mention the horror of being reduced to ashes in the process!).

Because talk is cheap, producer Robert Lippert's budget dictated that most of the running time be filled with it. The film's lack of action causes it to sag in spots, but those cracks are papered over by its apprehensive atmosphere and likable characters—particularly the often-stiff Kent Taylor, who provides some unexpected animation and warmth as the workaholic Fielding, trying to balance his calling with his family life, and Marie Windsor, both natural and believable as Fielding's long-suffering wife, whose ambivalence about their relationship shines through in her gloomy yet still affectionate interactions. (This marriage-on-the-rocks subplot adds a more adult flavor to the proceedings than that usually found in lower-berth sci-fi/horrors of the time.) And the film's truly terrifying downbeat finale (unusual for a production of the time) makes *The Day Mars Invaded Earth* a day worth remembering and an effective addition to LOI cinema.—*BMS*

Day of the Dead (1985) [**zombification**] Dead Films, Inc./Laurel Entertainment, Inc./Laurel-Day, Inc. (United Film Distribution Company). *D:* George A. Romero. *S:* George A. Romero. *Cast:* Lori Cardille (Sarah); Terry Alexander (John); Joe Pilato (Captain Rhodes); Richard Liberty (Dr. Logan); Howard Sherman (Bub).

George A. Romero's *Dead* series presents the ultimate loss of identity as a worldwide disease wherein former human beings become shells of pestilence and carnage, existing only to wander aimlessly and feed. This loss of identity extends beyond physical death (to which the victims succumb, slaughtered by infectious zombies) to the mindless, soulless existence that follows, when the human beings become what devoured them, returning to life as lethargic, slowly ambulatory creatures with only one goal: to kill other humans and feed on their corpses.

Romero's third entry in the series is the least popular with most fans but perhaps the best of them all. In it, the human survivors, part military regiment and part civilian scientific team, are conducting a zombie-experimentation program that they operate from an underground bunker. (The movie pits the military against the scientists with neither side willing to compromise with the other.) Dr. Logan, aka Frankenstein, conducts ghastly experiments on the living dead to try to control them and restore them to some level of humanity. In the name of protecting the other humans, Logan has the zombies shackled and taken to the research lab, where menial workers spend their time tormenting zombies. These cruel humans, affected by the zombies' savagery, have already lost

Day of the Dead **offers a new slant on loss of identity and asks the question, who suffers the greater loss of identity, zombies or humans?**

their human identity, directing their sadism and cruelty against zombies as though the dead were arcade video games.

Logan has discovered that zombies only need "brains and limbs," that no other organs are necessary. Zombies, working on instinct, crave blood even though they have no stomachs or need to consume nourishment. Logan feels zombies can be domesticated, trained, and thus controlled.

His shining achievement is a zombie he calls Bub, who seems to have some human memories intact. When shown a table with a toothbrush, a razor and a paperback book, Bub is able to mimic the motion of shaving his face—cutting himself, of course, as he carelessly rams the blade back and forth. He picks up the book, flips through the pages, and glares down at the words. Logan declares, "He remembers everything." Also Bub tends to ignore Logan when Logan enters the room—i.e., does not regard him as "lunch." Logan hands him a phone, and Bub carefully picks up the receiver and mimics speaking over the phone. Logan even prompts Bub to try to talk. When Captain Rhodes enters the room, Bub instinctively salutes him. Bub picks up a gun, cocks the mechanism, and shoots at the captain (of course no shells are in the chamber). Bub even listens to music on headphones and reacts with amazement. "It's the bare beginning of socialized behavior, but such behavior must be rewarded!" Logan rewards Bub with the guts and organs of dead military victims that are kept preserved in deep freeze.

In the film's conclusion, as the culmination of his socialized behavior, Bub—armed with a *loaded* pistol this time—stalks and shoots the captain. (The captain's own gun jams.) Wounded and screaming, the captain eggs Bub onward, and Bub shoots him dead center as an army of zombies approaches from the rear and tears Rhodes apart. After the execution, Bub stands solemnly and salutes the captain once more.

Thus, *Day of the Dead* offers a new slant on loss of identity. Human beings are slaughtered and infected and return to life as shells of their former selves—mindless zombies that mimic their former rituals and actions. However, through conditioning and training, such shells can be taught to remember more and more of their past lives, and such training can produce a more docile and controllable zombie. No, the actual return of identity is not possible (zombies are *dead*, after all), but the zombies in many ways can become less savage and cruel than their human captors whose humanity has been compromised by their insensitivity to slaughtering zombies, no longer viewing such creatures as human. After the nonchalant mayhem of shooting zombies in the head for weeks upon weeks, the soldiers find it more difficult to respond to human beings as people. So, by the movie's end, the film asks who suffers most from a loss of identity: zombies or humans? Director/writer Romero seems to imply that human beings have become zombified even before being infected by the living dead. The only few human survivors have helicoptered to a tropical desert island and live apart from society, ready to soak up some rays of sun and have some babies. Time to start a new world of human kindness. (Of course it doesn't work out that way. See *Land of the Dead* [2005].)—GJS

Dead Again (1991) [**amnesia; reincarnation**] Mirage (Paramount). *D*: Kenneth Branagh. *S*: Scott Frank. *Cast:* Kenneth Branagh (Roman Strauss/Mike Church); Emma Thompson (Grace/Margaret Strauss); Derek Jacobi (Franklyn Madson); Andy Garcia (Gray Baker); Lois Hall (Sister Constance); Richard Easton (Father Timothy); Wayne Knight ("Piccolo" Pete Dugan); Robin Williams (Dr. Cozy Carlisle, uncredited).

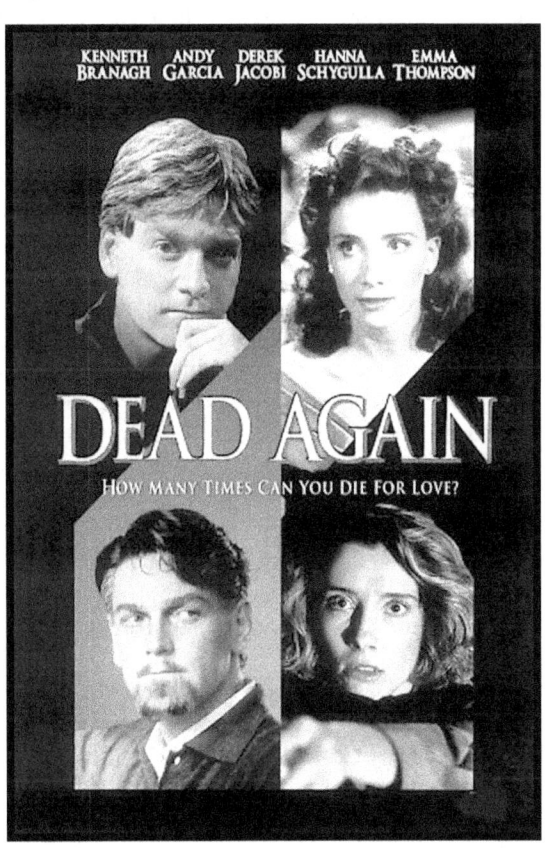

A young woman with amnesia wakes screaming, night after night, from dreams of a decades-old murder; hard-boiled California P.I. Mike Church not only takes her case but also takes her in as she tries to regain her memories—and understand why someone in the present seems to want to kidnap or kill her. As they try to comprehend her nightly fixation with a case that ended before she was born, the two of them are approached by antique dealer Franklyn Madson, who moonlights as a hypnotist capable of leading people "back" into memories of their past lives. He succeeds in getting "Grace" to remember her past life—though not her present one—and the movie cuts between the present day and the story of Roman and Margaret Strauss, he a brilliant foreign composer, she a brilliant pianist, whose marriage was stormy but generally blissful until she was murdered and he was convicted of—and executed for—the crime. (Kenneth Branagh and Emma Thompson play both Mike and Grace and the Strausses.) As Grace's sessions with Madson unearth scenes/memories closer and closer to the murder and as the connections between the present-day characters and their past "selves" become more and more evident, Mike and Grace have to struggle with two questions: What really happened to Margaret and Roman, and—more importantly—will it happen again? Can the two of them control their relationship, or are they nothing more than pawns of the past, doomed to a love that ends in murder?

The cleverest of the several plot twists in this film is the revelation that identity—past or present—isn't always what is seems, and that it's *Mike* who was Margaret in a past life, and Grace who was Roman. But the urgency of solving the movie's mysteries rests in the contemporary characters' fear of discovering themselves to be simply replicants of these long-dead people, their own personalities subsumed, taken over, by what they once were. Can they make things turn out differently, or are they inexorably becoming the people they were? Anyone who's seen the film no doubt remembers the shock with which they heard Mike Church promise Grace, "I would never hurt you, Margaret." And while the film's resolution most satisfyingly answers both of the central questions, the movie leaves us with the lingering, still unnerving remembrance of two people whose lives seem to dissolve into those of people they never knew but may have been.—*OVA*

Dead Next Door, The (1988) [**zombification**] Suburban Tempe & Amsco Studios (Screen Edge). *D:* J.R. Bookwalter. *S:* J.R. Bookwalter. *Cast:* Peter Ferry (Raimi); Bogdan "Don" Pecic (Dr. Moulsson); Michael Grossi (Mercer); Robert Kokal (Reverend Jones).

In zombie movies, one wise old sage or spiritual figure often suggests that the dead have risen to make humanity atone for its sins. Some of the characters in *The Dead Next Door* certainly hold such sentiments, and their loss of rational thought and identity reaches such an extreme that they actually worship the dead and campaign for both national government and local law-enforcement agencies to stop destroying the creatures! Led by Reverend Jones, these protestors riot against the police and armed forces as the zombies attack both factions, resulting in an interesting "triple-threat" confrontation. Jones and his deranged followers reside in a fortified compound in the countryside, entertaining themselves by feeding the hundreds of zombies they have captive with human sacrifices and conducting other strange rituals revering the purity of the undead spirit. And the scary thing is that this concept is actually quite plausible, as humans often follow charismatic leaders like frightened lambs, especially during trying times.

Facing off against these fundamentalist maniacs is the Zombie Squad, a rapidly shrinking number of crack officers hastily put together and equipped to combat the zombie menace. Here "hastily" is the operative word, as the Squad lacks adequate resources and numbers to have a chance of survival, let alone to fulfill its objectives. In the face of the odds, some members of the team display a dogged stoicism whilst others undergo the classic loss of identity from which those on the frontline of the zombie war

Zombies are the focus of *The Dead Next Door*, a low-budget 1980s gorefest.

suffer: loss of confidence in their abilities and training, lack of motivation, and supreme irrationality, which—when manifested in the midst of a zombie pandemic—can only mean trouble. These Squad members crack under the stress, pulling such clever stunts as accidentally putting their hands into zombies' mouths or allowing the creatures to "sneak" up behind them. And, although squad member Raimi in particular seems determined to hold things together within the ranks until the bitter end, the rest of the team adopts an immediate and fatal pragmatism when bitten; for example, in one moment of defeatist altruism, a Squaddie chooses to be eaten by the horde rather than transform into one of them, arguably not the actions of a confident, well-trained soldier, especially in light of the work of the movie's mad scientist, Dr. Moulsson.

In a move away from more traditional zombie science, which often looks to discover a bacterial agent to destroy the undead or for a behavioral method of control, Moulsson's research focuses upon finding a "cure" for the condition. However, the treatment has to be administered to the infected individual *before* death and thus fails miserably to combat the increasing numbers of flesheaters.

Moulsson's work receives the ultimate test when the serum is injected into Mercer, an infected Zombie Squad member who is captured by Jones' cult and paraded at a service in honor of the flesheaters. However, the "cure" fails and, upon reanimation, Mercer promises to rip the doctor to shreds. After fulfilling his promise, Mercer reveals to Raimi that the serum has left his memories and personality intact. So the ill-fated doctor's serum has some effect on the zombified condition: In certain cases, it seems that zombies can retain their former personality, thus negating the total loss of identity from which they usually suffer. Regardless, it still doesn't prevent the feeding impulse, as Mercer imparts this information whilst eating the doctor's tongue, implying that the psychological condition of the zombie doesn't influence its appetite. Here, the creatures, whether mindless or not, still seek warm flesh.—*AJB*

Dead of Night (1945) [**split personality, possession, madness**] Great Britain: Ealing (Universal). *D:* Alberto Cavalcanti, Charles Crichton, Basil Dearden, and Robert Hamer. *S:* John Baines and Angus MacPhail; Additional Dialogue by T.E.B. Clarke, Based on Stories by E.F. Benson (linking story and "Hearse Driver"), John Baines ("The Haunted Mirror" and "The Ventriloquist's Dummy"), Angus MacPhail ("Christmas Party") and H.G. Wells ("Golfing Story"). *Cast:* Mervyn Johns (Walter Craig); Roland Culver (Eliot Foley); Googie Withers (Joan Cortland); Frederick Valk (Dr. van Straaten); Michael Redgrave (Maxwell Frere); Hartley Power (Sylvester Kee); Ralph Michael (Peter Cortland).

The framing story and two of the five tales that make up this famous horror anthology involve loss of identity.

Just what sort of LOI figures in *Dead of Night*'s best-known and most chilling episode is open to question. In "The Ventriloquist's Dummy," ventriloquist Maxwell Frere is convinced his dummy has a life of its own. His conviction may or may not be an example of split personality—following in the footsteps of Eric Von Stroheim's ventriloquist in *The Great Gabbo* (1929) and paving the way for Anthony Hopkins' even more maniacal and homicidal turn in *Magic* (1978). On the other hand, it may be something supernaturally sinister: Hugo, the dummy (whose face is a horrid caricature of the ventriloquist's), may very well be an individual entity in his own right. (How *does* he get from Frere's room to the American ventriloquist Kee's quarters on that fateful night?) Frere may be paranoid, but with good reason: Maybe he's *not* the one making the dummy say he wants to dump Frere for the American ventriloquist; maybe it's the dummy's own idea. And Frere *is* a hollow shell without Hugo: After the dummy's treachery drives Frere to throttle him, Frere ends up practically comatose. When he finally does talk (to the American ventriloquist), it's with the voice (and attitude) of Hugo—he's even filmed so as to resemble the late dummy. (Dare we suggest that his name is an oblique reference to Baudelaire's *"mon semblable, mon frère"* [my double, my brother]?) Thus, like Norman Bates in *Psycho* (1960 [*q.v.*]), Frere has either retreated completely into his alter ego—*or* the spirit of Hugo has now completely possessed his soul. (*Devil Doll* [1964 (*q.v.*)] may have taken its inspiration from this segment.)

"The Haunted Mirror" episode is more clearly and straightforwardly a tale of LOI—possession from the past via an antique mirror. Joan soon-to-be-Cortland buys her fiancé, Peter, the eponymous glass, and it slowly poisons their relationship. At first, all it seems to do, instead of reflecting its contemporary surroundings, is to put Peter in a Victorian setting (a situation that makes him doubt his sanity but which Joan manages to pull him out of. Compare how the "love of a good woman" saves another LOI victim in 1980's *Altered States* [*q.v.*]). Eventually, however, the residual bitterness and jealousy of the 19th-century invalid husband who first owned the mirror and who seems to have leached into its silver is reflected in the current owner, who imagines that he, too, is confined to his room and cuckolded by his wife. Joan only escapes throttling when she smashes the mirror to break the spell. (The later Amicus horror anthology *From Beyond the Grave* [1973] uses the premise of "The Haunted Mirror" for *two* of its segments: one ["The Gate Crasher"] in which a man is possessed by the evil spirit in a mirror and forced to commit murder and another ["The Door"] in which a man purchases an antique portal and finds it opens up onto the era of Charles I.)

The other episodes deal with ghosts ("Christmas Party," "Golfing Story") and premonitions ("Hearse Driver") and so don't figure into this discussion, but the fram-

In the *Dead of Night* segment "The Haunted Mirror," Joan (Googie Withers) must break the mirror to save herself from her husband Peter (Ralph Michael).

ing story is perhaps the most terrifying example of loss of identity in the picture, since it suggests an irrational, uncontrollable, unstoppable descent into madness. In it, architect Walter Craig, when he arrives at Eliot Foley's cottage, instigates the telling of the aforementioned tales by informing everyone about his foreboding sense of *déjà vu*, predicated by a recurring dream he has that always turns ominous and deadly. Importuned by the others—particularly the logical psychiatrist Dr. van Straaten, who tries to rationalize all the weird events as they're related (until he ultimately must admit his involvement in and puzzlement over the Maxwell Frere case)—Craig overstays his welcome and reaches the point of no return—the point at which, as he's told the others, he's compelled to behave murderously. He experiences a loss of identity and loss of control, throttling the psychiatrist (throttling is a recurring activity in this movie), and the narrative spins into a delirious montage/collage/mélange of events and people from the other characters' stories (Hugo the dummy prominent among them). Craig "loses it," and the dream drives him to murder. But what is it about Craig's mind—which is, after all, the engine driving the dream—that transforms this civilized man into a homicidal savage? We don't know, and not knowing the source of loss of identity makes it all the more frightening.

Of course, it *was* all a dream. Craig wakes up in bed at home. We see him. But then he gets the call from Foley, and (over the end credits) dream events begin to unfold in real life this time (unless, of course, Craig is caught in an endless dream loop); Craig is on track to follow a train of somehow determined events; next stop LOI-ville.—*AFA*

Death at Love House (*Shrine of Lorna Love, The*) (1976). [**possession**] Spelling/Goldberg Productions (ABC). *D:* E.W. Swackhamer. *S:* Jim Barnett. *Cast:* Robert Wagner (Joel Gregory, Jr./Joel Gregory, Sr.); Kate Jackson (Donna Gregory); Sylvia Sidney (Clara Josephs); Marianna Hill (Lorna Love [in flashbacks]); Bill Macy (Oscar); Joan Blondell (Marcella Geffenhart); Dorothy Lamour (Denise Christian); John Carradine (Conan Carroll).

Dark Shadows fans consider *Death at Love House* the unofficial remake of *Night of Dark Shadows* (1971 [*q.v.*]). Both films center around a "possessed" husband in the thrall of his artist-forefather's past life and a beautiful "ghost" (and her portrait). Kate Jackson plays the beleaguered wife in *both* films, and each movie has a *Haunted Palace*–like sinister housekeeper.

In this television movie, filmed at the fabulous Harold Lloyd estate in Hollywood, husband-and-wife novelists Donna and Joel Gregory research the life of the legendary 1920s/1930s movie star Lorna Love, whose lover was Joel's father. When the Gregorys move in to Lorna's mansion, Joel loses himself in Lorna's portrait and visions of his father's life with Lorna, who seems to be exerting an influence from beyond (?) the grave. After someone tries to kill her, Donna rescues Joel from his confusion when she discovers that the housekeeper, Mrs. Josephs, is not who she seems to be. Unlike *Night of Dark Shadows*, with its downbeat ending, *Death at Love House* offers—what else?—a Hollywood ending, where identity is not so much lost but just "misplaced" for a while.—*JDT*

Devil Commands, The (1941) [**madness; hypnotism**] (Columbia). *D:* Edward Dmytryk. *S:* Robert Hardy Andrews and Milton Gunzburg. Based on the Novel *The Edge of Running Water* by William Sloan. *Cast:* Boris Karloff (Dr. Blair); Richard Fiske (Dr. Sayles); Amanda Duff (Anne Blair); Anne Revere (Mrs. Walters); Ralph Penney (Karl); Shirley Warde (Helen Blair).

Of the four Boris Karloff "mad doctor" films produced by Columbia from 1939 to 1941, *The Devil Commands* is the best. Additionally, it's a movie that illustrates loss of identity on many different levels. First of all, we have the neatly cut-and-combed Dr. Julian Blair, a quiet and dedicated man of science. He is devoted to his wife and puts his relationship with her above everything else. However, when she is killed in an automobile crash, Blair's hair becomes disheveled and frizzy, signaling far more than a bad hair day. Devastated by his wife's untimely demise, Blair devotes all his scientific energies to contacting her in the afterlife. Cutting himself off from his only daughter, practically becoming a hermit, Blair joins forces with spiritualist Mrs. Walters, who exerts a mesmerizing, Svengali-like influence over the professor. Together, they create a corpse-fueled séance where the bodies of the recently dead are dressed with electronic helmets and body armor to be used as a conduit to contact the dead.

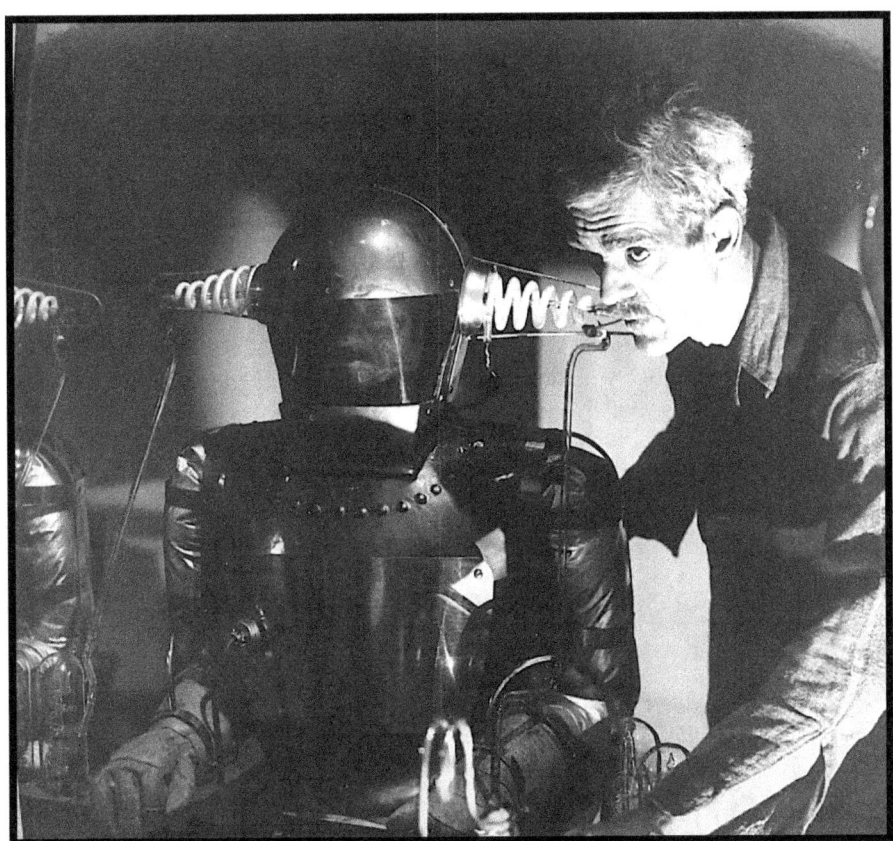

In *The Devil Commands*, the noble scientist (Karloff) becomes the agent of evil by using science for his own needs, not for the good of mankind.

As the film unwinds, we can readily look at Blair's hairdo to immediately understand his obsessive state of mind. Before, Dr. Blair was a quaint, absent-minded, kindly scientist, but after his wife's death, he becomes paranoid, detached, obsessive, and sneaky. This wonderful family man has lost his "grandfatherly" identity, which has been replaced by an unholy, unhealthy, compulsive one where he sells his soul to the devil to transgress into God's domain. (The movie's tag line was "the devil commands…and Karloff obeys!") The otherwise noble, dedicated man of science becomes the agent of evil by harnessing science for his own agenda, not for the good of mankind.

The bulky and obedient Karl, the mentally challenged lab assistant, used to be a regular working-class stiff, a devoted servant to Blair, but his near death from electrocution during one of the experiments reduced the former comic relief into a dull-witted zombie, one who has sacrificed his previous identity to the cause of science (whether he chose that course or not). Once again science has destroyed one kindly and human identity, exchanging it for another more sinister.

The message of *The Devil Commands* is exactly what the title implies. The evil of science, new technology that dares to go too far into the realm of areas better left alone by decent people, seduces and destroys innocents. In this case good-natured Dr. Blair becomes obsessed with contacting his dead wife in the beyond, and he cares not whom he alienates or harms to achieve his cause. Thus, science, through such darkside promises, transforms a benevolent identity into a corrupted one, and the changing hairdo becomes a visual metaphor to illustrate such loss of identity—the "topper" (so to speak) to Boris Karloff's intense and powerful performance as Blair.—*GJS*

Devil Doll (1965) [**hypnotism; soul transference**] Great Britain: Galaworld/Gordon Films (Associated Film Distributing Corp.). *D:* Lindsay Shonteff. *S:* Ronald Kinnoch (as George Barclay) and Charles F. Vetter (as Lance Z. Hargreaves), From an Original Story by Frederick Escreet Smith. *Cast:* Bryant Haliday (the Great Vorelli); William Sylvester (Mark English); Yvonne Romain (Marianne Horn); Frances De Wolff (Dr. Keisling); Sandra Dorne (Magda Gardinas).

Devil Doll offers two variations on the terrors of identity loss. First there's the attendant anxiety arising from hypnosis, with one's will supplanted by that of another; the subject becomes, in effect, a living toy of the hypnotist (who can then make you cluck like a chicken, sing Elvis songs, or perhaps even commit murder). But *Devil Doll* takes this a step further in its more visceral loss-of-identity scenario by presenting the horror of losing one's self so completely that one becomes a *literal* toy—a ventriloquist's doll.

When newspaperman Mark English covers "the Great Vorelli," a mesmerist and ventriloquist whose act has been selling out in London, he determines to get to the bottom of Vorelli's "fakery" (which includes his dummy, Hugo, actually standing up and *walking* across the stage). To this end, Mark enlists the aid of his wealthy socialite girlfriend, Marianne, to serve as a "volunteer" in Vorelli's act. But Vorelli's hypnotic powers are real (and so is Hugo), and the mad mesmerist sets his lascivious sights on hypnotizing Marianne into marrying him. He then plans to place her soul in a doll and abscond with her wealth. But little wooden Hugo, Vorelli's first victim of soul-stealing, has other ideas.

Shot in two weeks in April 1963 at the low-rent Merton Park Studios in London for the paltry sum of $50,000, *Devil Doll* didn't see release until June of 1965, when it went out as support for the straight melodrama *Sylvia*. Though it manages to wring several shudders from its creepy loss-of-identity premise, the movie can't avoid falling into its low-budget trap on occasion.

"The Great Vorelli," for instance, engages in the lamest of hypnotism acts: The big moment comes when he hypnotizes the heroine into thinking she can *dance*—and has an "expert in modern dance" come onstage and do the twist with her (to the vigorous applause of the apparently astounded—and amazingly un-hip—audience).

California-born William Sylvester (from Oakland) offers a general pleasantness but not much presence, though his steady, unassuming "hero," Mark, contrasts nicely with Vorelli's malevolent intensity and dour demeanor. The gorgeous, French-born Yvonne Romain appears rather vapid and makes little impression as Marianne, apart from a strictly decorative one.

Bryant Haliday, on the other hand, carries the film with his rather one-note but highly effective performance as the intense, never-smiling, always smoldering hypnotist, moving—and speaking—slowly and deliberately. His penetrating gaze and unsmiling antagonism make the viewer believe that he can indeed control the wills of others. "The tension between Vorelli and that dummy—it was there—everybody felt it," the hero remarks. Thanks to Haliday's forceful performance, the viewer readily believes it. "Bryant Haliday was chosen to play the lead because he had money in the project," recalled director Lindsay Shonteff in *Shock Express* magazine. "But, in spite of that financial muscle, he was perfect for the role." Indeed he was.

Haliday, an American stage actor who founded the prestigious Brattle Theatre in Cambridge, Massachusetts, made three more British horror movies (all for producer Richard Gordon)—*Curse of the Voodoo* (1965), *The Projected Man* (1966) and *Tower of Evil* (1971). Haliday settled in Paris (he spoke French fluently), and began a long career producing, directing, and acting in French stage and television productions.

The dummy Hugo (played by female circus midget Sadie Corre) generates some genuine chills, with its creepy wooden child-face and slowly shifting eyes. Its measured, awkward advance, as Hugo obeys its "master's" command to walk to the footlights and apologize to the audience for some verbal slight, is nearly as disturbing as its quick lunging with a knife in several deadly (and cleverly edited) sequences. Hugo encapsulates that uneasy fear generated by oversized dolls (especially those of the faux-sentient ventriloquist variety), ratcheted up a notch by the knowledge that this doll is actually a human being caught in the ultimate loss-of-identity trap.—*BMS*

Devils, The (1971) [**possession, regimentation, eradication of self**] Great Britain (Warner Bros.). *D:* Ken Russell. *S:* Ken Russell, From the Novel *The Devils of Loudon* by Aldous Huxley and the play *The Devils* by John Whiting. *Cast:* Oliver Reed (Father Urbain Grandier); Vanessa Redgrave (Sister Jeanne); Dudley Sutton (Baron De Laubardemont); Gemma Jones (Madeleine); Michael Gothard (Father Barré); Christopher Logue (Cardinal Richelieu); Graham Armitage (Louis XIII).

Based on an actual incident in Loudon, France, in the 1630s, Ken Russell's *The Devils* tells a tale of false possession but true loss of identity: citizens bowing before the state's heavy hand, accepting accusations of Satanism to avoid being crushed by the government apparatus. While lacking any supernatural aspects, *The Devils* is as much a horror film as *The Conqueror Worm* (1968) or *Mark of the Devil* (1970), which deal with similar witch hunts in other countries.

To consolidate power, Cardinal Richelieu asks the King's permission to raze the fortifications around cities like Loudon so these towns can't harbor Hugenots or withstand a siege. Louis XIII says okay—*except* for Loudon. He promised the city's late governor, Sainte-Marthe, that he wouldn't disturb even one "teensie-weensie" brick.

During the recent religious war, Sainte-Marthe (a literal saint, apparently) managed to keep his municipality's Catholics and Protestants at peace. His successor, Father Grandier, has rallied the town's integrated militia and invoked Sainte-Marthe to prevent the Cardinal's men from tearing down the battlements. (The gripping scene wherein Grandier confronts the despicable Baron De Laubardemont—warning that, if one brick is dislodged, the Baron will be dead before it hits the ground—is a masterpiece of skillful *mise-en-scène* and editing.)

When sexually frustrated, love-starved hunchback Sister Jeanne of the Angels accuses the priest of possessing her demonically, Laubardemont finds a way to destroy Grandier and thus Loudon. A grotesque "exorcism" fails to purge the Mother Superior. Her charges protest her treatment—and are taken to the woods to be executed as heretics. At the last minute, Father Barré, the exorcist, calculatingly offers the frightened women an out: "Sin can be caught as easily as the plague." Perhaps they're infected like Sister Jeanne. If so, they have an excuse for their conduct. He recites a litany of behavior that they should exhibit: "You will *scream*. You will *blaspheme*. You will *no*

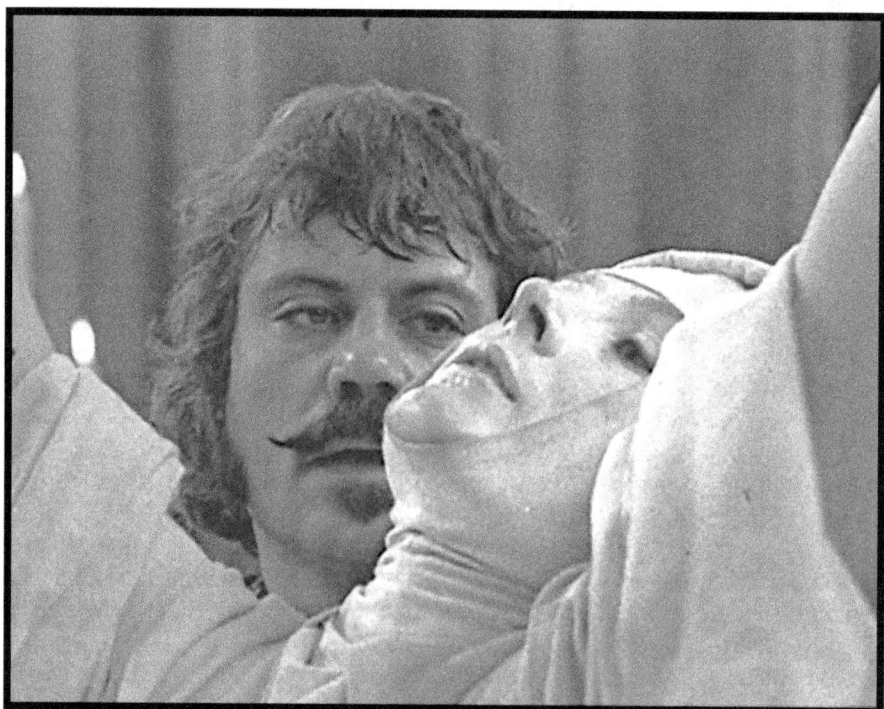

Oliver Reed as Grandier and Vanessa Redgrave as Sister Jeanne in Ken Russell's still-controversial *The Devils*.

longer be responsible for your actions!" The desperate nuns grasp at this opportunity, giddy at the prospect of reprieve, and eagerly embrace his every "suggestion." This "voluntary" relinquishing of identity at the behest of the authorities is more chilling than any actual possession. (And it's not just the nuns' capitulation that illustrates the state's ability to obliterate free will: Laubardemont, acknowledging Barré's power of "persuasion," remarks of the nuns' transformation, "You would not be the *first* to see the light"—and Russell cuts to an archer, crossbow trained on the women, looking pained: He was one of those who, earlier, had helped Grandier defend Loudon, then training his crossbow on Laubardemont.)

The notorious sequences of nuns running wild helped earn *The Devils* its original X rating—the most notorious of notorious sequences being the one where they pull down a massive wooden statue of Christ crucified and crawl all over it, lasciviously licking and rubbing it. This episode, cut before the film's general release, was only recently restored for the DVD. Russell told John Baxter (*Ken Russell/An Appalling Talent*) that this sequence "was really central to the whole thing, intercut as it was with Grandier finding both himself and God in the solitary simplicity of Nature." Having finally seen the segment, I feel the picture worked just as well without it; here, as elsewhere, Russell's editing is so seamless (and the other blasphemies and nudity so plentiful) that one neither misses nor needs the "rape of Christ."

(A perhaps more unfortunate omission—*not* restored on DVD [because the footage no longer exists?]—involves just Sister Jeanne. After Grandier's *auto da fé*, Laubardemont pays her a last "courtesy" call. With the priest dead and the city's walls breached, there's no further need of Jeanne and her nuns. They've lost the lost identities forged for them by the state. The crowds have moved on to other towns, other exorcisms; the nunnery will go back to being an enclosed, ignored order. As consolation, Laubardemont leaves Jeanne with a souvenir: a charred bone fragment from Grandier. The scene in the movie ends here. But there was more—something perversely and poetically fittingly more: Sister Jeanne used the bone to masturbate—achieving the only communion possible with the man she longed for—and damned—from afar.)

At the center of *The Devils* is Grandier—worldly, vain, prone to sleeping with (and sometimes impregnating) the distaff members of his flock. Nevertheless, his sincere effort to carry on Sainte-Marthe's work and keep Loudon independent, a safe haven for Catholic and Protestant alike, puts him on a collision course with the central government. Ironically, just as he comes to spiritual awareness (through the love of a good woman), he's undermined by charges of diabolism, tried, and condemned. He loses everything—position, possessions, freedom, hair (shaved bald and shorn of beard and moustache)—and undergoes excruciating torture before he's forced to crawl to his place of execution and burned at the stake. But, amidst all this loss, he retains a dignity that he never knew he had when his identity was intact.

Loudon, a triumph of art decoration (built of anachronistic white Lego-like bricks), is practically another character in the film—whose identity is destroyed along with Grandier. (As the priest burns, he yells to the crowd watching his face blister, "Don't look at me. Look at your city!"—and the walls' foundations are blown up.) The picture ends with Grandier's widow, Madeleine, leaving the city, trudging through the piles of rubble.— *AFA*

Dr. Jekyll and Mr. Hyde (1920) [**dual personality; metamorphosis**] (Paramount/Artcraft). *D:* John S. Robertson. *S:* Clara S. Beranger, Based on the Novel *The Strange Case of Dr. Jekyll and Mr. Hyde* by Robert Louis Stevenson. *Cast:* John Barrymore (Dr. Jekyll/Mr. Hyde); Brandon Hurst (Sir George Carew); Martha Mansfield (Millicent Carew); Charles Lane (Dr. Richard Lanyon); J. Malcolm Dunn (John Utterson); Cecil Clovelly (Edward Endfield); Nita Naldi (Gina); George Stevens (Poole); Louis Wolheim (Music Hall Proprietor).

John Barrymore as Jekyll (above with Martha Mansfield) and as Hyde (below) in the 1920 silent version of *Dr. Jekyll and Mr. Hyde.*

Dr. Jekyll and Mr. Hyde, one of the most popular titles of the silent era, was adapted for the screen no fewer than 11 times before 1931 (*three* times alone in 1920: this version, the Sheldon Lewis attempt to cash in on this version, and the lost Murnau film, *Der Januskopf*, which, like Murnau's *Nosferatu* [1922], was an unauthorized dramatization of its source material). This film, showcasing John Barrymore in the title role, was the most influential, both for its additions to the plot and for its dramatic handling of the dual-personality subtext.

The film presents Henry Jekyll as a noble doctor of medicine, steadfast in character and saintly in his dedication to helping the poor. Luring Jekyll away from his upright lifestyle is Sir George Carew, a man of the world whose life experiences have included an occasional walk on the wild side. "The only way to get rid of a temptation is to yield to it," declares Carew, introducing a Dorian Gray overtone to Stevenson's original story. The film's opening title warns us that a battle between our good and evil natures wages within us throughout our lives. Carew's credo suggests that those who seek a "good" identity can do so only by suppressing their innermost desires.

Awakened to his base nature, Jekyll yearns for a way to indulge his evil impulses and "yet leave the soul untouched." The solution comes, of course, in the form of the chemicals that transform Jekyll into the leering Mr. Hyde. Freed from moral constraints, Hyde haunts the back alleys of London's Soho district, looking for pleasures to sate his unspeakable appetites. But vice begets more vice, and soon Jekyll finds his life careening out of control. As Hyde, he tramples a child in broad daylight. The transformations also begin to take place on an involuntary basis; in one memorable sequence, Hyde appears as a giant spider that descends upon a sleeping Jekyll and triggers his change of identity. Much too late, Jekyll realizes the addictive nature of evil and the corrupting influence it can wield in our lives. (Is Jekyll Jekyll? Or is Jekyll Hyde?)

Also noteworthy is the film's introduction of two women that reflect Jekyll's dual nature. Millicent Carew, who was given a proper upbringing by Sir George, appeals to Jekyll's higher self. By contrast, music-hall dancer Gina becomes a cosmic soul twin for Hyde's brute instincts. As in later film versions, both women pay a price for their romantic entanglements. Gina, ultimately rejected by Hyde, becomes a physical wreck from the ravages of alcohol and (implied) prostitution. Millicent, too, suffers the pangs of lost love—first, when Jekyll becomes neglectful of her, and, later, when Hyde murders Sir George. Late in the film, Hyde threatens to make the degradation complete when he corners Millicent in Jekyll's laboratory. But the attack fails because Jekyll, aware of the damage that his alter ego could inflict, has planted the seeds for his self-destruction moments before.

Dr. Jekyll and Mr. Hyde has been interpreted both as a cautionary tale against the dangers of drug use and as an admonition against tampering with the laws of nature. The film version also challenges our basic precepts concerning our search for identity. As the opening titles tell us—"What we most want to be, we are." If Henry Jekyll's lesson is an indication, we owe it to ourselves to choose wisely.—*SGT*

Dr. Jekyll and Mr. Hyde (1931) [**dual personality; metamorphosis**] (Paramount). *D:* Rouben Mamoulian. *S:* Samuel Hoffenstein and Percy Heath, Based on the Novel *The Strange Case of Dr. Jekyll and Mr. Hyde* by Robert Louis Stevenson. *Cast:* Fredric March (Dr. Jekyll/Mr. Hyde); Miriam Hopkins (Ivy Pierson); Rose Hobart (Muriel Carew); Holmes Herbert (Dr. Lanyon); Halliwell Hobbes (Brigadier-General Carew); Edgar Norton (Poole).

Loss-of-identity themes featured prominently in the Golden Age horrors of the 1930s. But no film utilized the dramatic possibilities of this device more successfully than Paramount's 1931 production of *Dr. Jekyll and Mr. Hyde*.

In contrast to the influential 1920 John Barrymore version, the motivation for Dr. Henry Jekyll's quest in this adaptation is wholly noble. His goal, which he verbalizes in naïve but enthusiastic tones, is to separate good from evil in the soul of man, thus liberating humanity from its base instincts. After the initial transformation, the immediate reaction for both Jekyll and alter-ego Hyde (portrayed by Fredric March in a theatrical but effective performance) is exhilaration. Hyde's awakening, especially, is portrayed as a type of primal release. He laughs with glee, enjoys the rain, and taunts the landlady like a randy schoolboy, overjoyed at the sensory input that waits at every turn. But soon enough his darker personality traits emerge: Anger, envy, and lust begin to dominate and become stronger with each personality change, until Hyde threatens to subjugate the Jekyll identity entirely.

The awareness of Jekyll and Hyde of their alternate selves adds another layer of complexity to the identity schism. Jekyll spends much of the film in denial regarding Hyde's true nature. Only when Ivy Pierson presents him with evidence of Hyde's monstrous deeds does he finally acknowledge the evil he has wrought. Hyde too is less than comfortable with Jekyll's righteous reputation. He verbally berates the good doctor, mocking Jekyll's concern for Ivy's well being and implying a sexual motivation behind his altruism. Both sides are mortified at the thought that there might be any remnant of the other lurking in the depths of their shared consciousness.

Fredric March as the fiend Hyde and the ill-fated Jekyll in the 1931 *Dr. Jekyll and Mr. Hyde*. March would win an Academy Award for his performance.

The film's female leads also share a paired identity. Muriel Carew is earnestly in love with Henry Jekyll, but she also takes a certain pride in her social status. Her inability to abandon the trappings of her family's patrician lifestyle inadvertently contributes to Jekyll's fall from grace. Ivy Pierson comes from the wrong side of the tracks, but she too dreams of a better life. "Here's hoping that Dr. Jekyll will think of Ivy once in a while," she muses in reaction to Jekyll's show of sympathy. Ivy's idyllic fantasy stands in ugly contrast to the relationship into which Hyde has ensnared her, a brutal bond that inexorably leads her down the road of tragedy.

In another insightful touch, the identity of science itself seems to be up for grabs. As articulated by Jekyll's friend and mentor, Dr. Lanyon, science must respect that there are limits to man's quest for understanding. Jekyll's experiments, Lanyon contends, represent an intrusion into God's dominion, an area that must not be breached. Jekyll, however, expresses a more contemporary mode of thinking. He believes that our reach is limited only by the extent of our knowledge and that there are no arbitrary limits on humankind's innate potential. Given the dramatic flow of the story, Jekyll's point of view hardly gets a fair hearing. But it does provide food for thought, especially in an age where remarkable breakthroughs in medicine and science may be on the near-term horizon.

Rouben Mamoulian's directorial flourishes add immeasurably to the film. Especially effective is the use of diagonal wipes and split screens to introduce character pairs and illustrate parallel situations. These touches, along with fine performances and a script that deftly handles the loss-of-identity issue, make *Dr. Jekyll and Mr. Hyde* a horror film that is both thoughtful and highly entertaining.—SGT

Dr. Jekyll and Mr. Hyde (1941) [**dual personality; metamorphosis**] (Metro Goldwyn Mayer). *D:* Victor Fleming. *S:* John Lee Mahin, Based on the Novel *The Strange Case of Dr. Jekyll and Mr. Hyde* by Robert Louis Stevenson. *Cast:* Spencer Tracy (Henry Jekyll/Edward Hyde); Ingrid Bergman (Ivy Peterson); Lana Turner (Beatrix Emery); Donald Crisp (Sir Charles Emery); Ian Hunter (Dr. John Lanyon); Barton MacLane (Sam Higgins); C. Aubrey Smith (the Bishop); Peter Godfrey (Poole); Sara Allgood (Mrs. Higgins).

Genre cinema flirted with respectability in the 1940s when top-tier Hollywood stars were featured in literate adaptations of classic horror tales. MGM's 1941 remake of *Dr. Jekyll and Mr. Hyde* was one such release. Although the film does little to improve on prior cinematic versions, details were added that lend some curious twists to the story's now familiar loss-of-identity theme.

Religion is used to establish the tone for this film. The opening credits are accompanied by the paean of a church choir, which promptly segues into the image of a Bishop delivering his Sunday sermon. The clergyman, in full self-righteous mode, speaks dismissively of the pleasures of the flesh and longs for a world in which "evil" will not be tolerated in any form. All in the congregation listen approvingly, save for one parishioner who loudly heckles the speaker. (The protestor, who was involved in a recent accident, is written off as a nutcase, but he also provides a very credible voice for the film audience!) Later, Jekyll tells a group of dinner guests, including the

Spencer Tracy, as Edward Hyde in the 1941 *Dr. Jekyll and Mr. Hyde*, is far too restrained to convey the evil of Hyde.

aforementioned Bishop, of his earnest quest to separate good and evil in the human soul. His theories are met with the same dismissive tone that the church crowd had voiced earlier. As depicted in the film, anything that deviates from the small-minded platitudes of traditional faith is considered to be outside the range of acceptable human behavior.

Unfortunately for Jekyll, those platitudes cover just about any form of sexual expression. When he gives his fiancée, Beatrix Emery, the most chaste kiss imaginable, her father objects in overly strident terms. Jekyll's eventual encounter with barmaid Ivy Peterson awakens in him a repressed lust that he does his best to ignore, but which begins to gnaw at his conscience. Troubled by his subconscious desires and distressed by Beatrix' absence, Jekyll then embarks on his obligatory (i.e., story-mandated) quest to resolve his conflicting identities. Almost overlooked in the ensuing mayhem is a brief scene in which Jekyll experiments on various animals in his laboratory—a rabbit quickly turns vicious and a rat suddenly docile, implying that the formula effectively reverses the dominant nature of any organism. Perhaps if Jekyll had thought to try the drug on good-girl Beatrix, his issues of personal identity and sexual frustration could have been worked out in one fell swoop.

MGM's veneer of studio gloss adds little to the basic story. Tracy is too naturalistic to be convincing in a period milieu and far too restrained to impress as a human monster. [Somerset Maugham, observing Tracy's performance on set, famously and cattily remarked, "Which one is he now?"—which can be interpreted as Tracy's failure to differentiate man from monster, *or* as an indication of just how close man and monster are.] One interesting backstory behind the film is Metro's attempt to acquire and then bury the superior Paramount version that was produced a decade earlier. By having the audacity to pose as the ultimate adaptation of Stevenson's venerable thriller, the film only succeeds in confirming its identity as an imposter.—*SGT*

Dr. Jekyll and Sister Hyde (1971) [**dual personality; metamorphosis**] Great Britain (Hammer). *D:* Roy Ward Baker. *S:* Brian Clemens, Based on the Novel *The Strange Case of Dr. Jekyll and Mr. Hyde* by Robert Louis Stevenson. *Cast:* Ralph Bates (Dr. Jekyll): Martine Beswick (Sister Hyde); Gerald Sim (Professor Robertson); Lewis Fiander (Howard); Susan Broderick (Susan).

Robert Louis Stevenson's *The Strange Case of Dr. Jekyll and Mr. Hyde* has inspired countless movie adaptations over the years. England's Hammer Films alone produced no fewer than three screen tellings of the tale. But its final version, 1971's *Dr. Jekyll and Sister Hyde*, remains unlike any other.

Director Rouben Mamoulian's classic *Dr. Jekyll and Mr. Hyde* (1931 [*q.v.*]) introduced the idea that, by transforming into Hyde, the repressed Jekyll liberates his pent-up sexual frustration. Numerous subsequent adaptations had carried forward that story element. In those versions, Hyde represents the darker impulses within Jekyll's soul, which, once freed, threaten to consume the "true" personality of the prim and proper physician.

Director Roy Ward Baker's *Dr. Jekyll and Sister Hyde* adheres to that formula on the surface. But underneath, it's less the story of an identity lost than that of an identity found.

Jekyll experiments with female hormones in hopes of discovering the mythic "Elixir of Life"—the secret of eternal youth. Using himself as a guinea pig, he drinks his potion and is transformed into a physically beautiful, sexually predatory young woman. To his surprise Jekyll discovers he enjoys being a girl, but must begin killing young women to obtain the hormones he needs to formulate his elixir. With each transformation, his female persona grows more powerful (and Martine Beswick as Hyde gets more screen time).

Brian Clemens' screenplay retrofits the classic Jekyll-and-Hyde yarn as an elaborate, not-so-well-masked coming-out story. Jekyll may have been in denial before, but through his experiments he discovers his true sexual identity; his transgender transformations allow his long-denied sexuality to find expression. This much is validated by the film's finale. At the conclusion of previous Jekyll-and-Hyde movies, Hyde is killed and, in death, reverts to his true, noble Jekyll condition. But, in Baker's film, Jekyll—killed in mid-transformation—remains half-man, half-woman.  The message is clear: The female identity was not some monstrous fabrication created by the elixir, but part of Jekyll's real self.—*MDC*

Doctor X (1932) **[madness; metamorphosis]** (First National & Vitaphone Picture). *D*: Michael Curtiz *S*: Robert Tasker and Earl Baldwin (and, uncredited, George Rosener), From the Play *Doctor X* by Howard W. Comstock and Allen C. Miller. *Cast*: Lionel Atwill (Dr. Xavier); Fay Wray (Joan Xavier); Lee Tracy (Lee Taylor); Preston Foster (Dr. Wells); John Wray (Dr. Haines); Harry Beresford (Dr. Duke); Arthur Edmund Carewe (Dr. Rowitz).

Though *Doctor X* has all the trappings of a 1930s old-dark-house murder mystery (and remains one of the best examples of that subgenre), the film qualifies as an early horror classic by nature of its Moon Killer murders, its monstrous serial killer who wears a cloak and skulks in the shadows, its hideous synthetic-flesh sequence, and its mounting body count with victims showing evidence of cannibalization, culminating in a climax of unadulterated horror.

The creepy Michael Curtiz production, using eerie two-strip Technicolor, features superb set pieces, including a haunted mansion overlooking a river by moonlight, the Mott City Morgue with draped corpses and toe tags everywhere, cavernous electrical laboratories, secret rooms with spy holes, and flaming corpses falling down rocky bluffs.

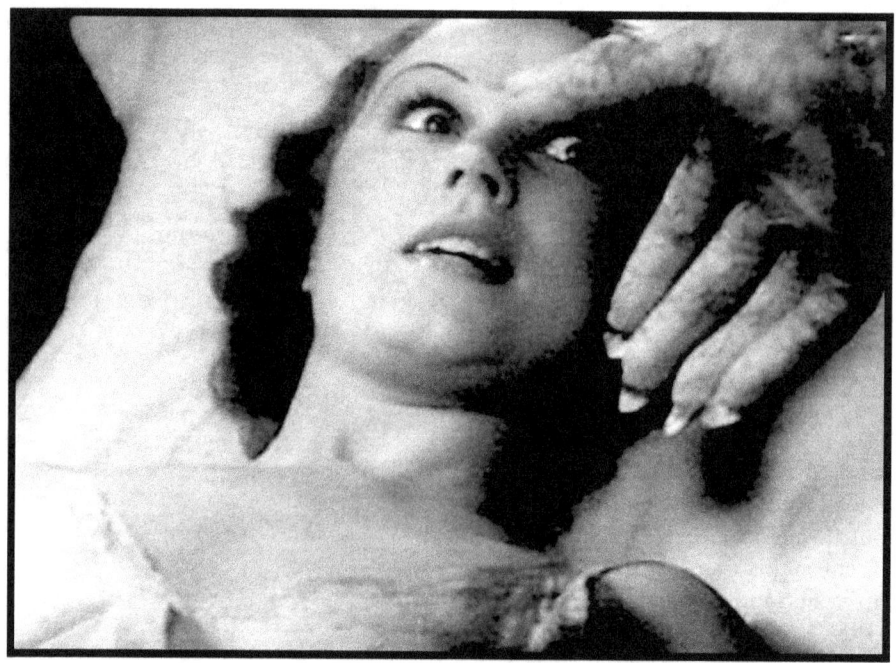

Joan Xavier (Fay Wray) is attacked by the Moon Killer in *Doctor X*.

Lee Tracy as ace reporter Lee Taylor delivers the peppery dialogue with his trademark rapid-fire delivery, and the nicely structured script allows for plenty of red herrings and suspense in determining the identity of the Moon Killer.

But why is *Doctor X* included in a book on loss of identity? Simply stated, the Moon Killer shows the extremes that one human being takes to morph himself into an entity that is radically different from its former self.

When the police inform Dr. Xavier that his Institute of Surgical Research is under investigation because six murder victims were found in close proximity to the building, Xavier—not wishing to attract any negative publicity—asks for 48 hours to discover the identity of the fiend, whom he plans to reveal through scientific tests of his own devising. Examining a murder victim, Xavier deduces that he was strangled by a person with particularly powerful hands but that a scalpel was used to cut into the base of the brain…and that cannibalism was also a factor, as part of the deltoid muscles have been ripped out.

Then the film introduces the surgeons and doctors who work in the institute, and every single man has some quirk or history that potentially connects him to the murderer. Curly-haired Dr. Wells, a student of cannibalism, conducts his personal experiments at the institute at night. Using electricity, Dr. Wells has kept a heart alive in a beaker for three years. But Dr. Wells sports an artificial hand, which immediately rules him out as the strangler. Dr. Haines was shipwrecked with two other men a year ago, their supplies exhausted, and the third survivor disappeared, an obvious victim of cannibalism. Haines' expertise is brain grafting. Dr. Rowitz, Haines' shipwreck-mate, lost one eye and had half his face deeply scarred. Wheelchair-bound Professor Duke assists Rowitz, whose expertise is studying the effects of the moon on human beings. In a sequence very similar to an episode in John Carpenter's *The Thing* (1982 [*q.v.*]), all the scientists, except Wells, are attached to an electrical apparatus that measures excess anxiety via blood pressure, and, as they react to onstage recreations of some of the murders, Dr. Rowitz's gauge boils over. Xavier triumphantly shouts that the device reveals Rowitz to be the murderer. However, Rowitz drops dead, the victim of foul play. Thus, even though he failed the test, his murder explains his excess excitement and proves his innocence (though it does the dead man little good).

In the best case of loss of identity, the actual killer is revealed to be the least obvious, Dr. Wells, who, in a classic sequence, rants about synthetic flesh, breathing heavily under the influence of the full moon, as he reshapes his body by molding actual flesh taken from his murder victims. He recreates his face in the guise of a monstrous, mute pinhead and shapes new, stronger arms and hands to commit the crimes. Electrical apparati spark in the foreground, and chemicals bubble and smoke all around him as he glops the new flesh all over his face and head after restoring his missing hand. In a very literal sense, Wells has transformed his old identity into a synthetic new one, one that allows his bestial urges full expression. With the other scientists chained to their chairs, Wells takes the place of the actor set to play the fiend on the exhibition stage and terrifies Joan Xavier, telling his colleagues the method to his madness. Only reporter Lee Taylor is free to fight the monster, who declares, "There's no use calling for Wells...there isn't any Wells, just a new Wells, one whose name will live forever in the history of science." One loss of identity occurring at the same time a new identity is created. Wells declares he will make a crippled world whole again. But moments later he is torched and pushed backwards through the observatory window to his death. New Wells or old Wells, both are dead.—*GJS*

Donovan's Brain (1953) [**possession**] (United Artists). *D:* Felix Feist. *S:* Felix Feist, adapted by Hugh Brooke From the Novel *Donovan's Brain* by Curt Siodmak. *Cast:* Lew Ayres (Dr. Patrick Cory); Gene Evans (Dr. Frank Schratt); Nancy Davis (Janice Cory); Steven Brodie (Herbie Yocum); Lisa K. Howard (Chloe Donovan); Michael Colgan (Tom Donovan).

Writer Curt Siodmak, who enjoyed a lengthy association with genre films, displayed a notable obsession with loss-of-identity themes. In addition to penning the screenplays for *Black Friday* (1940 [*q.v.*]), *The Wolf Man* (1941 [*q.v.*]), and *I Walked With a Zombie* (1943 [*q.v.*]), Siodmak also wrote the 1943 novel *Donovan's Brain*, adapted for cinema on three separate occasions. The 1953 version comes closest to capturing the book's lurid but intriguing concept of identity-possession-via-disembodied-human-brain.

At a remote western outpost, research scientist Dr. Patrick Cory is attempting to extend the lives of animal brains that have been surgically removed from their bodies. Fate drops a gift into his lap when multi-millionaire Warren Donovan is involved in a nearby plane crash. Donovan's body is brought to Cory's lab in a futile attempt to save his life, and Cory seizes the opportunity to remove the mogul's gray matter and take his research work to the next level. The experiment is a success—Donovan's brain emits a steady stream of alpha waves, confirming the presence of consciousness. Unexpectedly, the brain begins to thrive, growing in size and developing telekinetic powers. Soon, Cory is possessed and unwittingly becomes the vehicle for Donovan to further his unscrupulous business activities.

Initially, Cory embraces the experiment with great zeal. It is his inspiration to use telepathy to communicate with Donovan, prompting him, along with wife Janice and research assistant Dr. Frank Schratt, to dig through news clippings and become familiar with the tycoon's life. Cory is understandably ecstatic after contact is first made and Donovan pens his signature via the scientist's hand. Slowly, however, Cory realizes he has been drawn into a Jekyll-and-Hyde relationship. Donovan begins to dominate his mind for longer intervals. Before long, the scientist is visiting a nearby city to meet with an attorney who is stalling a government investigation into Donovan's taxes. Unable to break free from the brain's controlling influence, Cory also begins to exhibit Donovan's physical traits—he walks with a limp, barks out commands, and shows a preference for the high-priced suits that Donovan favored. Only when the brain is dormant (and apparently sleeping) is Cory's consciousness able to reassert itself.

Although Donovan is interested primarily in financial gain, there is the hint of something evil about his persona. He dominates others with sadistic glee, using money to flaunt his influence. He also reveals an abhorrence to paying taxes that goes well beyond the normal proclivities of the upper class. Disharmonious also are Donovan's family relationships—Cory threatens to have a Donovan heir cut from the will when she speaks disparagingly about her late father. Eventually, Donovan decides that murder is an acceptable strategic option. A news reporter who stumbles onto the story pays with his life when he learns too much. More violence is threatened against Janice and Schratt until fate once again intervenes in the form of a lightning strike that puts Donovan out of commission permanently. Thus the escalating cycle of possession comes to an end, not through human efforts, but via an act of God.

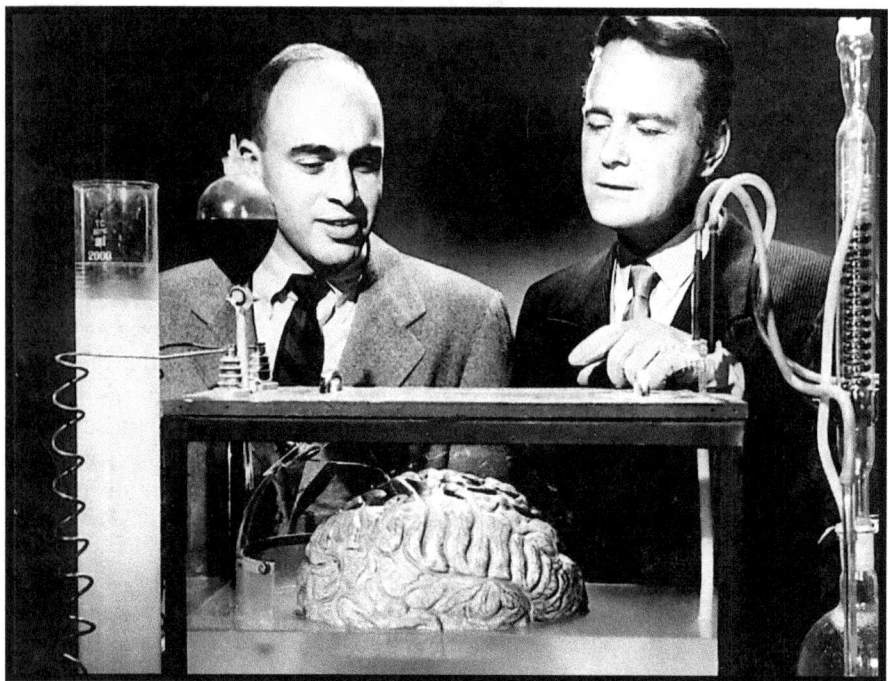

Donovan's Brain **takes the loss-of-identity cinema to a bizarre extreme. Reporter Yocum (Steve Brodie) checks out what's left of Donovan as Dr. Cory (Lew Ayres) watches.**

In the film's closing moments, Donovan suggests that his growing power is limitless. Indeed he has already demonstrated the ability to dominate other personalities; widespread possession appears to be the next logical step. At this point, the story threatens to transcend mere personal loss of identity and begins to invoke the mad fantasies of Nazi world domination. Although seldom screened today, *Donovan's Brain* takes the loss-of-identity cinema to a bizarre and fascinating extreme.—*SGT*

Door to Silence (1991) [**altered reality; loss of affect**] (Filmirage). *D*: Lucio Fulci (as H. Simon Kittay). *S*: Lucio Fulci and Jerry Madison. *Cast:* John Savage (Melvin Devereaux); Sandi Schultz (Mystery Woman); Richard Castleman (Hearse Driver); Jennifer Loeb (Margie); Elizabeth Chugden (Sylvia Devereaux).

Melvin Devereaux knows who he is: a successful businessman and husband in the land of the living. But a near-miss (?) with a hearse at the scene of a New Orleans funeral does more than stop the clock in his car—it marks the end of his "normal" life, as well. Melvin's attempts to return home or to spend some time in a jazz club offer him nothing but surrealism and violence—while a beckoning woman in white and the extremely persistent hearse driver seem to hold the secret of his fate. If Melvin is still a living human being, exactly who is in the casket in the back of the hearse?

Some 30 years after *Carnival of Souls* (1960 [*q.v.*]), there's little room for doubt in this "loss of affect" film. Devereaux becomes less and less effective as the story progresses, his identity dissipating as he comes to have less and less of an effect on his surroundings. Nevertheless, director Lucio Fulci doesn't supply the viewer with the ending he would naturally expect: namely, the "moment of truth" in which Melvin sees himself inside the casket. Instead, the protagonist's furious attempt to pass the hearse and get on with his "life" ends in a (permanently) fatal collision—and the audience is left to decide for itself what really happened.

While *Door to Silence* is not a major loss-of-identity film in itself, the ironic history behind its production deserves to be recounted here. Director Fulci created the film as a project for Filmirage (for producer Joe D'Amato, aka Aristide Massacessi). But between the creation of the film and its release, a Filmirage higher-up declared that the name of Lucio Fulci (auteur of such LOI films as *Zombie* [1979 (*q.v.*)], *The Beyond* [1981 (*q.v.*)], etc.) was no longer marketable and convinced the powers-that-be to substitute the pseudonym "H. Simon Kittay" (an ill-advised play on the

Japanese "Hello Kitty" phenomenon) for the director's signature. This was in addition to the replacement of Fulci's preferred musical soundtrack and the elimination of the director's device of an onscreen chronometer (the film was intended to play in "real time"). All of this may sound like interesting but irrelevant production trivia, but it takes on a new significance in terms of this book project when one notes that *Door to Silence* would turn out to be Fulci's final directorial project. Although his name was once connected to *The Wax Mask* (a film ultimately directed by effects maestro Sergio Stivaletti in 1997), Lucio Fulci passed away due to diabetic complications in 1993. In other words, the black hearse caught up with Fulci shortly after his own identity had been stripped away against his will. At the time of this writing, *Door to Silence* remains officially unreleased in America—but it remains an uncanny epitaph for "the man himself."—*SMD*

Dracula (1931) [**hypnotism**] (Universal). *D:* Tod Browning. *S:* Garret Fort (and, uncredited, Louis Bromfield, Tod Browning, and Louis Stevens); additional dialogue by Dudley Murphey (uncredited). Based on the Play *Dracula* by Hamilton Deane and John Balderston and the Novel *Dracula* by Bram Stoker. *Cast:* Bela Lugosi (Count Dracula); Edward Van Sloan (Prof. Van Helsing); Helen Chandler (Mina Seward); David Manners (Jonathan Harker); Dwight Frye (Renfield); Frances Dade (Lucy Weston).

In *Dracula*, loss of identity is most strongly portrayed by Dwight Frye (right), whose character Renfield begins as a fey, rational Brit and ends up a gibbering lunatic.

Dracula introduced Depression audiences to the modern horror film and Bela Lugosi's Count. (And let's get *his* identity straight: Dracula was Transylvanian and therefore Hungarian—and absolutely *no* relation to the historic Vlad the Impaler of Moldova, a Rumanian folk hero.) Lugosi's vampire introduced viewers to the literal metaphor of the blood-sucking nobleman, who lived off the life of his peasants. Outwardly suave, sophisticated, even charming, he represented the supernatural equivalent of the "Filthy Foreigner originally portrayed by Eric von Stroheim," as Robert Bloch once so succinctly put it, adding, "Von Stroheim kissed hands, and Lugosi bit necks"—but the results were the same. Lugosi's Dracula showed us how a seductive evil could rob easily duped innocents of their souls.

The women that Dracula gravitates to are all innocent (i.e., all *virgins*) and fairly colorless. (Mina *is* initially spirited enough to mock his stentorian tone—"It reminds me of the broken battlements—of my own castle—in Transylvania!"—thus making actress Helen Chandler the first of many filmic Lugosi impersonators.) Once vampirized, they become hollow shells, vacant, staring things—like Dracula's three brides (and like Mina, once she's under his influence)—which suggests that the undead Continental seducer is quite a necrophile; he likes it when they just lie there and take it.

Loss of identity is most strongly portrayed in *Dracula* by Dwight Frye, whose Renfield begins the film as a fey, rational Brit and ends as a gibbering lunatic, his mad replacement personality a minor reflection of the strong-willed vampire who holds him in thrall. Just how Dracula gained his power over Renfield and how he holds him in thrall is never adequately explained in the movie; David J. Skal, in *V Is for Vampire*, suggests that it's *amore*: "Renfield's unrequited love for Dracula becomes the only compelling story line; the heterosexual hero and heroine are bloodless ghosts by comparison." Renfield occasionally regains the remnants of his former identity and, in his few lucid moments, warns the protagonists about the vampire, despairs of the deeds he's been forced to do, and fears dying with blood on his hands—but he does, by Dracula's hand (suggesting that the tragedy in *Dracula*, if there is any, is Renfield's).—*AFA*

Empire Strikes Back, The. See *Star Wars: Episode V – The Empire Strikes Back* (1980).

Enemy from Space (*Quatermass II*) (1957) [**hive mind; alien possession**] Great Britain: Hammer Film Productions (United Artists). *D:* Val Guest. *S:* Nigel Kneale and Val Guest, From the Teleplay *Quatermass II* by Nigel Kneale. *Cast:* Brian Donlevy (Professor Quatermass); John Longden (Lomax); Sydney James (Jimmy); Bryan Forbes (Marsh); Tom Chatto (Broadhead).

Few science fiction movies are more cerebral than the quartet that forms Nigel Kneal's Quatermass series, the first two of which were released in America in the mid-1950s, starring American actor Brian Donlevy as rocket scientist Professor Quatermass. [For commentary on the other, see *Creeping Unknown, The* (1955). For commentary on the third in the series, see *Five Million Years to Earth* (1968).]

The second feature film, *Enemy from Space*, a taut science fiction thriller of the most paranoiac kind, explores the theme of loss of identity through alien possession in a very specific manner. This LOI is very subtle and devious. In this Val Guest–directed thriller, aliens take possession of human beings through the use of meteorites that expel

Enemy from Space abounds with sequences that illustrate a hive-like societal cohesion.

a gas that burns upon contact, searing the alien consciousness into the unsuspecting human flesh and merging that human into the collective alien consciousness. The humans possessed by this alien life form still look exactly the same; however, they have a burn mark somewhere on their body showing the point of infiltration. Once possessed, the former human beings still seem to remember their previous identity, yet the possessed now have as their goal the proliferation and propagation of the alien cause. Like the gigantic alien blobs sustained in huge industrial domes, each amoeba cell united with all the other amoeba cells to create one huge monster blob, these aliens in human shells share one common goal, one group consciousness. Once humans become possessed, they're overcome by a hive-like mentality; they live and breathe to further the cause of the alien essence without regard to individual wishes or needs. So, metaphorically, the individual becomes absorbed by the alien blob and lives only for the good of the group; the blobs-in-domes are the emblem of this absorption of identity.

The film abounds with sequences that illustrate this hive-like societal cohesion. In one key episode, a meteorite shower bombards a local pub. A barmaid, fascinated by the hot rocks falling at her feet, bends down to pick one up, despite Quatermass' warning to leave it alone. The brazen Cockney beauty is unaware of the imminent danger, and the meteorite explodes and releases its gas, the burning mark of alien possession appearing on her flesh within seconds. Quatermass realizes it is now too late to help her. A few minutes later, the military police/alien army arrives to gather up the stones. (The military men, dressed in gas masks and full riot gear, look like insects, furthering the hive-mentality imagery.) A reporter hiding behind the pub's bar is phoning in his story, and not being very careful to hide the fact. Discovering the reporter, the alien-controlled militia shoots him to death before he can say another word.

In another sequence Quatermass is among a group of people touring the alien facility (the visitors think it is only a top-secret government-sponsored military base) when one man disappears from the rest of the tour. (Their guide, while pretending that guests have total access to the grounds and can go where they please, has been closely monitoring their movements, steering them in the direction he chooses.) Breaking away from the rest, Quatermass goes outside and hears a hideous scream coming from the top of one of the domes. Howling in agony, the missing politico, covered in burning, corrosive material that eats at his flesh, stumbles down the winding stairs that lead to the bottom, and dies within a few feet of Quatermass, pleading all the time for Quatermass *not* to touch him. It appears that the synthetic food engineered for the alien blob creatures consumes the inquisitive investigator.

The paranoiac air gets thicker when Inspector Lomax, working closely with Quatermass in his investigation, is about to go to his superior to share his theory of alien infiltration in high government places when he eyes the burn scar on his supervisor's hand, alerting him to the fact that even the government and the police have already been compromised and he must be careful about whom he approaches for help.

Enemy from Space illustrates our fears of alien infiltration at the highest levels: our government and the military, those protective agencies we tend to trust implicitly. Those sacred institutions that supposedly protect the individual members of society have now become part of the dreaded alien hive, and those in charge might now be part of the alien invasion. The theme of loss of identity applies not only to the sacrifice of the individual but also the sacrifice of those trusted social institutions that are being infiltrated. Seldom do science fiction movies get more thoughtful or chilling than *Enemy from Space*.—GJS

Eternal Sunshine of the Spotless Mind (2004) [**amnesia; erasure of self**] Anonymous Content, Focus Features, This Is That Productions (Focus Features). *D:* Michael Gondry. *S:* Charlie Kaufman; Story by Michael Gondry and Pierre Bismuth. *Cast:* Jim Carrey (Joel Barish); Kate Winslet (Clementine Kruczynski); Elijah Wood (Patrick); Kirsten Dunst (Mary); Tom Wilkinson (Dr. Howard Mierzwiak).

"Would you erase me?" asked the film's tagline, a tagline intended to provoke conversation among lovers, for *Eternal Sunshine of the Spotless Mind* busily pretends to be all about love—how it can hurt, and what we'd go through to keep or regain it.

What this film doesn't quite ask is, "What would erasing me do to you?" Without memory, there can be no identity; without the past, there is little point in the present. No film has shown the crumbling of identity quite so literally as this one does—the characters dash from one section of protagonist Joel's brain to another, with people disappearing around them and cars dropping from the sky as they try to save not only Joel's memories of Clementine but, we suspect, the very Joel

who knew her. The identity loss inherent in memory loss is hinted at in scenes like the one in which Joel re-enters the office of Lacuna, Inc., where Dr. Mierzwiak performs his selective-memory erasures, and sees himself being treated there. His outburst of confusion is not "What's happening?" but "What am I?"

Mary, Dr. Mierzwiak's assistant, whose affair with her married boss was erased, learns of this brain spot-cleaning, and in retaliation steals Lacuna's records and mails them to its presently clueless clients. Through its effect on Mary, Lacuna's memory-erasure process proves to be both impermanent and harmful, much like humanity's old-fashioned, psychological defense mechanisms for dealing with pain. Given this, and given the importance of personal history in its script, *Eternal Sunshine* seems to raise and then duck some weighty questions of identity. In the framing scenes when Joel and Clementine meet on the Montauk train as if for the first time, they are still very much the same two people they were before their forgotten, or almost-forgotten, relationship happened. In the end, *Eternal Sunshine* suggests that it is possible to step in the same river twice, arguing with cockeyed optimism against directors like Wong Kar-Wai (*Chungking Express* [1994], *2046* [2004]) and the notion of the missed moment.—LJ-C

E Tu Vivrai Nel Terrore—L'aldila. See *Beyond, The* (1981).

Exorcist, The (1973) [**possession**] (Warner Bros.). *D:* William Freidkin. *S:* William Peter Blatty, From his Novel *The Exorcist*. *Cast:* Ellen Burstyn (Chris MacNeil); Linda Blair (Regan MacNeil); Jason Miller (Father Damien Karras); Max Von Sydow (Father Lankester Merrin); Lee J. Cobb (Inspector William Kinderman); Jack MacGowran (Burke Dennings); Mercedes McCambridge (demonic voice of Regan, uncredited).

The quintessential cinematic example of demonic possession (all subsequent possession films are pale imitations) is also the most horrifying portrait of the individual's loss of self.

One of the purest examples of terror is the horrifying awareness that someone we know is *no longer* the person we know. Imagine sitting alone at night with your sibling, your parent, your spouse—and having him/her turn and look at you with eyes you don't recognize as s/he chuckles in a guttural, malevolent voice. This nightmare scenario is played out to a T in *The Exorcist*, wherein a young girl on the cusp of adolescence gradually and then more terribly becomes something unrecognizable, unholy, and wholly frightening to those around her who thought they knew her. For me, more than anything else, *that voice*—supplied by Oscar-winning actress Mercedes McCambridge—frightens as much as, if not more than, the girl's actions and appearance, though her ever-changing appearance re-inspires fear every time.

Fear of the shape-shifting, ever-more-frightening, no-longer-identifiable girl in *The Exorcist*—fear of seeing what's become of her now and what she'll do next—is why *The Exorcist* contains some of the scariest moments ever put on film.

For *The Exorcist* (and *Alien* [1979], too, for that matter) keeps its monster in constant flux. Every time we see the possessed girl, she looks progressively worse; the monster's face is never "fixed," and we're scared each time because we don't know what worse to expect. Then, too, besides all the demonic *sturm und drang*, the picture employs clever camera tricks to scare us. After one particularly harrowing episode in the bedroom, the following scene offers nothing more than the mother coming in to check on the fitfully sleeping girl: She enters; she goes out. But, all the while, the camera is placed *inside that goddam bedroom!*—about at the spot where the window (through which film director Burke Dennings jumped—or was thrown) would be. We in the audience are saying, "C'mon, just get out of there! Get out! Before something happens!" Nothing does—but we don't know that, and the anxiety is palpable. (Compare the same effective camera placement in *The Uninvited* [1944 (*q.v.*)], when, after the séance, the heroes go up to check out the "cold room." "It's still as rotten and clammy as ever," they conclude. They're standing on the threshold of that clammy room; we—the viewers—are *in* that room: The camera is placed there and shooting them from that vantage point.)

***The Exorcist* (featuring Max Von Sydow and Linda Blair) is the quintessential cinematic example of demonic possession and a horrifying portrait of the individual's loss of self.**

Loss of Identity in the Horror Film

By 1973, horror films were beginning to employ the downbeat, anti-climactic ending of Evil Triumphant, so I waited in dread during the closing moments of the movie (when a dispossessed Regan sees the priest's collar and instinctively embraces him) for the shot—for the shock—that never came: the flash of yellow in her eyes—or *something*—that would indicate that she was still not herself and the demon dwelt within her. Thank God we were spared that moment; otherwise, I don't think I could have endured it. (As it was, I did not sleep a wink that night—and I was 25 years old! This reaction may be difficult to grasp for those who've grown up seeing dozens of imitations and caricatures of pea-soup-vomiting, head-spinning possessees, but anyone who lived through the *Exorcist* phenomenon—and anyone who approaches the film today with a non-*Mystery Science Theatre* attitude—knows *exactly* what I mean.)

Shortly after I saw the movie, I met a child psychologist, who claimed that *The Exorcist* was a perfect metaphor for a disaffected condition that she had seen and treated in children. I can't comment on the film's clinical nature, but I do know that, when my older daughter was about four and in the throes of a high fever which distorted her voice and caused her to hallucinate, I saw my wife experience something of the same profound fear that Chris MacNeil exhibited toward her own child in *The Exorcist*.—AFA

Eyes Without a Face (***The Horror Chamber of Dr. Faustus***; ***Les Yeux sans visage***) **(1960) [disfigurement/medical intervention]** France (Lopert Pictures). *D*: Georges Franju. *S*: Adaptation by Pierre Boileau, Thomas Narcejac, Jean Redon, and Claude Sautet; Dialogue by Pierre Gascar; From the Novel *Les Yeux sans visage* by Jean Redon. *Cast*: Pierre Brasseur (Dr. Genessier); Alida Valli (Louise); Edith Scob (Chrisiane Genessier); Juliette Mayniel (Edna).

Four years ago, young Christiane was disfigured in a fiery car crash (the driver of the car was her father, the eminent surgeon Dr. Genessier). Now she lives a reclusive life, imprisoned—by her own volition—in her father's elegant villa. With her face destroyed, Christiane lives in an environment devoid of mirrors, forced to wear a hard, expressionless mask that approximates her former beauty. Only her penetrating, beautiful sad eyes reflect her depression and sorrow. The stylish shimmery gowns she wears give the waif a ghostly and otherworldly presence, and she languishes away on her divan thinking about the life she might have had, wishing now that she were blind or dead. Egocentric Dr. Genessier has attempted multiple face transplants, but all have failed. Trying to renew the young woman's hope, Genessier's mistress, Louise, tells Christiane that she, Louise, had her face successfully restored by Genessier—but doesn't mention that she was never as badly disfigured as Christiane.

When Louise lures the latest young lovely, a girl named Edna, to the villa under pretense of renting her a room, Christiane hovers on the staircase overhead as the unconscious girl is carried awkwardly to the makeshift operating room behind the garage. Christiane sneaks into the operating room while Genessier's dogs in the nearby kennel raise a ruckus. Inside the operating theater, the victim, beautifully draped under the sheets, is strapped to the table, unconscious. Christiane takes off her mask and fondles her new potential face, stirring the victim back to consciousness, the bound victim screaming as she sees the disfigured girl's visage in semi-darkness. In the next sequence, the surgeon removes the victim's face in one piece, and the transplant is performed. Edna is meanwhile imprisoned in the house but fed and cared for. However, the college

In *Eyes Without a Face*, **Christiane (Edith Scob) lacks an identity.**

student, now without a face, jumps to her death from a top-floor window. At the dinner table, Genessier rants about how he knew he would succeed and tells his daughter that she can start her life over again. Though Christiane's new face might be radiant, her eyes remain sad as she tells her father she needs to come back to life for her family and friends who now think she is dead, since Genessier staged a grand funeral, pretending one of his female victims found in the river was actually Christiane. The doctor advises Christiane to first start by taking a long trip and then he will prepare new papers for her, as she decides upon a new name. "A new face, a new identity," Genessier tells her; "you're more beautiful than ever." Louise tells her there's something angelic about her now. Christiane says that, when she looks in the mirror, she feels she is looking at someone who looks like her…from the Beyond!

Before leaving, Genessier examines his daughter's face with some concern, but not enough to alarm her. Outside, the doctor tells Louise he failed, and, in a dramatic series of time-dated still photographs, the audience experiences the deterioration of the translated face and its ultimate rejection. Though her father remains committed to giving her yet another face, Christiane has reached a point where she feels the dead should stay dead, and she wants to actually die—she is tired of being her father's human guinea pig.

The theme of loss of identity is an essential one in *Eyes Without a Face*, for the human face establishes the human identity, and this is what Christiane lacks. When the approximation of a beautiful face is created via a mask, something profound remains missing. Even after her face transplant Christiane knows the face she sees in the mirror is not her face, not her identity, but the face of an innocent victim. And her father tells her most definitely that a new face means a new identity—that she can never return to being the former Christiane, now symbolically dead and buried. Even if the new face could somehow look like the old one, Christiane's identity has been irrevocably changed, irrevocably lost.

The image of Christiane in her light-colored gown, flowing up or down the stairs, her face motionless but her eyes radiating profound depression, becomes a vision of a personality lost or caught between two worlds. When Christiane finally cuts free the last innocent victim and stabs Louise in the neck (at exactly the point where her facial transplant ended), she is cutting herself free, cutting away the cheating flesh, the illusion of the person she has become. After freeing the innocent victim, Christiane then unchains the hounds in the kennel, those animal victims on whom Geniessier experimented, and, in their liberation, the dogs rip the doctor to shreds. Christiane, or whoever she has become, is now free—literally free—of any specific identity. One of the now-uncaged fluttering doves lights on her arm as Christiane walks trancelike into the dark night and the end title comes up.

Christiane had been imprisoned by her illusory identity, by her attempt to cling to an identity long lost—by her shimmering gowns and ivory-white mask. Only when she accepts that her previous self is dead to the world does she have the courage to free the innocent victims and embrace her non-identity. For Christiane Genessier, her loss of identity is ultimately liberating; Christiane finally becomes a whole person once again only by destroying her former identity.—*GJS*

Faceless Monster, The. See **Nightmare Castle** (1966).

Face/Off (1997) [**disfigurement/medical intervention**] (Paramount). *D:* John Woo. *S:* Mike Werb and Michael Colleary. *Cast:* John Travolta (Sean Archer/Castor Troy in disguise); Nicolas Cage (Castor Troy/Sean Archer in disguise); Joan Allen (Eve Archer); Gina Gershon (Sasha Hassler); Dominique Swain (Jamie Archer); Alessandro Nivola (Pollux Troy); Nick Cassavetes (Dietrich Hassler); Harve Presnell (Victor Lazarro).

In November 2005, a French woman received a successful face transplant, but *Face/Off*—hyperkinetic Hong-Kong–action director John Woo's most successful and satisfying American film to date (2007)—takes a science fictional approach to the procedure, à la 1959's *Eyes without a Face* (*q.v.*; the doves in this picture may be an allusion/homage to the birds in that earlier face-transplant film).

The film's first 20 minutes play like a compressed action picture: FBI agent Sean Archer survives master assassin Castor Troy's attack but sees his six-year-old son killed in his place. He drives himself and his agency hard for six years and finally captures Troy and his gang in a spectacular action sequence. A conventional movie would have expanded these two reels into 10 and ended here, with Troy (brain)dead and Archer vowing to take a desk job, attend counseling, and spend more time with his wife and their mixed-up teenage daughter.

But *Face/Off* has something else on its mind, so it introduces a MacGuffin—a doomsday bomb that Troy set to explode in a few days, the whereabouts of which Archer must somehow glean from Troy's incarcerated brother, Pollux, by going undercover and literally becoming the man he hates. This transformation is achieved not through makeup, disguise, or normal plastic surgery, but by giving Archer the actual face (and, through electronic means, the voice) of his arch-enemy. Then, in a further contrivance, the comatose, faceless Castor awakens, steals Archer's stored-for-safekeeping countenance, and murders the only people who knew that the current "Castor" is really Archer. (Shades of Fritz Lang's *Beyond a Reasonable Doubt* [1956] and other films noir featuring a hero going undercover in prison and losing his only contact on the outside.)

The visage-altering premise is a little like *First Yank into Tokyo* (1945 [*q.v.*])—although, unlike the poor unfortunate first Yank, Archer is reassured that the face-lifting procedure is completely reversible, so he can eventually return to himself. And *Face/Off* echoes another LOI film, *The Raven* (1935 [*q.v.*]): Compare the scene where Archer wakes up with Castor's face, sees "himself" in the mirror, and smashes the glass to Bateman's reaction after Dr. Vollin's purposely botched surgery transforms him into a monster.

In prison, "Castor"/Archer is almost immediately caught up in a fight, and—both to survive and prove he's the real Castor—he reacts as Castor would and then proclaims, "*I am Castor Troy!*" A convinced Pollux happily spills the beans about the bomb, but "Castor"/Archer can't use the knowledge to get out of jail free for he's soon paid a visit by "Sean Archer." Castor-in-Sean's-clothing taunts him ("I torched all the evidence that proves you're you"), leaves him to rot, releases Pollux because Pollux "coöperates" and reveals the bomb's location, and heroically "disarms" it (typing in a code *he* programmed), all to give credence to and pour greater glory on his Archer identity.

Thus, while the MacGuffin does some peripheral plot and character duty, it's really immaterial to the story, which only wants to put each antagonist in the other's shoes—a circumstance that's agony for Archer, and not just because he's in jail but because, to escape, he must practice the methods of his nemesis (methods he knows only too well, having made this man his life's study for six years) and take up with his nemesis' partners—people whom he equally despises (but, in the process, comes to understand in a way he couldn't before).

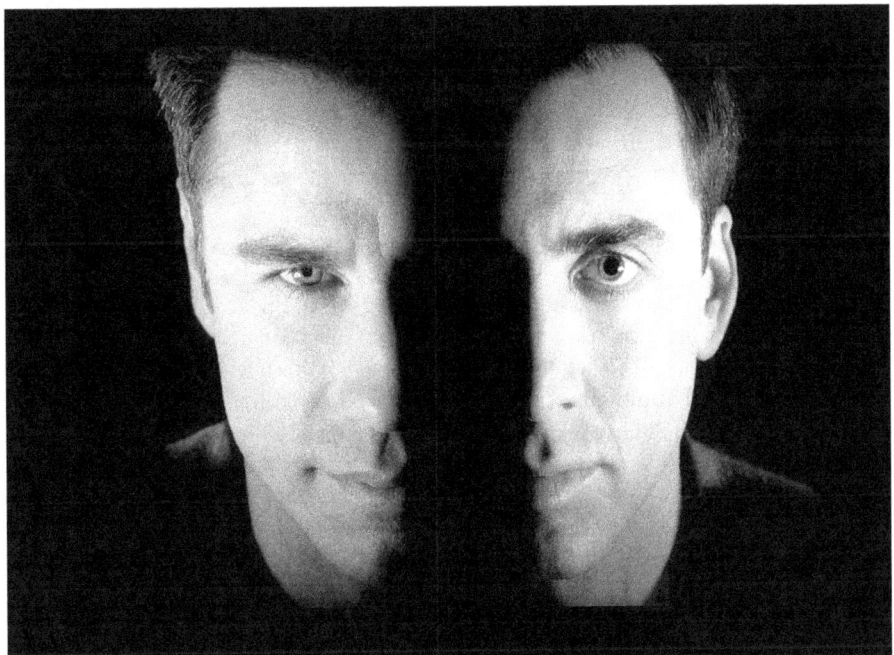

Confusion and loss of identity reign supreme in John Woo's *Face/Off* starring John Travolta and Nicholas Cage as hero and villain who switch faces and identities.

Sasha, Castor's gun-toting mistress, has a son (the same age now as the boy Sean lost then), and she tells "Castor"/Archer that the child is his. "Castor"/Archer, having just downed a drug cocktail to fit in with Castor's "high"-minded cohorts, has been having another identity crisis, speaking to his mirror reflection ("I'm not me. I'm *me*: …Castor—Archer," he says in a confusion of identities), but Sasha's revelation helps to sober him up quickly. He promises her that he'll make sure Sean Archer leaves her and her son alone. Later, when she wonders about his changed attitude, he explains, "I'm not the same person you knew." In the end, when Sasha is mortally wounded, he vows to look out for her son.

"Archer"/Castor initially has an easier time of it. True, as he drives through the suburban neighborhood to "his" family home, he mutters, "I may never get a hard-on again," but that changes pretty fast when he sees "his" wife, Eve. She's happy, too, since this Sean suffers none of the psychological impotence of the real one! It's hard to say if "Archer"/Castor is at all touched by their visit to their dead son's grave. Is he merely annoyed by Eve's outburst of grief or does he feel guilt for the tragedy and pain he caused? (At the climax, he defends himself—more or less—to the real Sean: "Your son was an accident. I wanted to kill *you*. But you took it so personal.") What *is* clear is that Castor's Archer gets through to Sean's rebellious teenage daughter in a way the real Sean never could. After saving her from date rape, he speaks some home truths to her, telling her she hasn't been the same since her little brother died and accusing her, with her steady stream of goth/punk/etc. guises, of "hiding behind someone else's face." (That rather unsubtle irony is followed by a subtler one: He gives her a knife to defend herself against the next guy who harasses her; that guy turns out to be him, and she follows his advice, to his misfortune.)

The confusion of identities is compounded throughout the film. (And for us viewers—especially if you, like me, don't particularly like Nicolas Cage and are happy to see John Travolta playing a good guy and then have to "readjust" to Cage playing Travolta-as-Cage, and vice-versa.) After "Castor"/Archer escapes from jail, he telephones "himself." When Troy answers with "Archer," he says, "Well, if you're Sean Archer, I guess I'm Castor Troy." At one point, the pair faces off yet again, on either side of a mirrored wall, pointing a gun at "his" reflection.

Archer finally gets to reassert himself, even in Castor's body, when he explains to his wife the sequence of events and skewed logic leading up to his current predicament. "I know it's a crazy story," he admits—something we in the audience have probably been thinking all along, so, if we don't read some of this on a metaphorical level, it can seem pretty ludicrous. (The fact that his blood type remains unchanged and is different from Castor's is what ultimately convinces Eve and saves him.) In the end, the two men have it out; and Archer wins by, essentially, killing "himself," the man obsessed with and ruined by Castor Troy—the man who *allowed* himself to be obsessed with and ruined by Castor Troy—and, after eventually getting his old face back (i.e., regaining his identity), he's both able to let go of the crippling memory of his son's fateful killing *and* to take in Sasha and Castor's boy, who, in many ways, *is* his son.—*AFA*

Fearless Vampire Killers, or Pardon Me, But Your Teeth Are in My Neck, The (1967) [**hypnotism**] Great Britain (MGM). *D:* Roman Polanski. *S:* Gérard Brach and Roman Polanski. *Cast:* Jack MacGowran (Professor Abronsius); Roman Polanski

(Alfie); Ferdy Mayne (Count Von Krolock); Sharon Tate (Sarah); Alfie Bass (Shagal, the innkeeper).

Sexual surrender has been part of the vampire film ever since Lugosi donned his cape for *Dracula* (1931 [*q.v.*]). Sexual anticipation (on the victim's part) has been part of the vampire film since Christopher Lee paid his first nocturnal visit in *Horror of Dracula* (1958 [*q.v.*]). But actual sexual climax—the vampire bite as orgasm-inducing penetration—came later. As far as I know, loss-of-identity as sexual surrender—the rendering explicit of the predatory sexual nature of the vampire attack—originated in the genre milestone *The Fearless Vampire Killers*.

Leave it to Roman Polanski—who'd already given us a portrait of a repressed woman sinking into sexual madness with *Repulsion* (1965)—to depict oral rape and make it disturbingly erotic. He sets up the vampire's attack on the innkeeper's daughter by diverting us with humor—first the *double entendre* misunderstanding between the young inept protagonist, Alfie (who doesn't know what it's all about) and the girl with whom he's smitten. An earlier scene established that Sarah likes to bathe and that Alfie and Professor Abronsius' rooms are the only ones with access to a tub. But it's easy for the viewer to forget those minor details, as Alfie does when Sarah, in her shift, "comes on" to him, explaining how she adores "it," that she "got into the habit of it at school," that it's "good for your hair; once a day, at the very least," hoping he doesn't mind if she has a "quick one"—and then slips past him into the closet that contains the tub.

Alfie is left to fetch her some hot water and then to stand outside the door, where his gentlemanliness prevents him from doing a Norman Bates and spying through the keyhole. The vampire, on the other hand, has no such scruples. In a masterful, wordless sequence lasting about 90 seconds—Polanski gives us Sarah, luxuriating in her bath, sponging her shoulders and neck, then pans up to the snow-covered skylight, cleared by Count Von Krolock's hand, so he can get an eyeful of the bathing beauty. Cut to Alfie, fighting the same urge to look. Sarah

Loss of Identity in the Horror Film

notices something wrong: snowflakes mingling with the suds. She looks—up—to see the Count descending, floating down through the now-open window, bending over her, using his hand to muffle any screams before she can utter them, biting her neck. She thrashes about, splashing water—and then her expression changes, from harsh struggle to ecstatic surrender. (Poor Sharon Tate, who died much too early—murdered by a real-life maniac—shows that she is excellent at pantomime because she really "sells" Sarah's seduction.) Alfie, drawn by the watery commotion, sneaks a concerned peek—and sees the vampire, mouth bloodied. Roman Polanski, as Alfie, does a Lou Costello from *Abbott and Costello Meet Frankenstein* (1948 [*q.v.*]), unable to speak, acting out "vampire" for Professor Abronsius. By the time the Professor understands and opens the door, the Count and Sarah are gone; leaving a fluttering trail of snowflakes and a red smear on the once virginal soap suds. Only a minute and a half of film; it always seemed so much longer, and it's stayed with me ever since.

The rest of the movie contains several amusing comic bits but doesn't explore Sarah's loss of identity in any depth. When Alfie finds her at the Count's castle, she's perhaps under the vampire's power but sounds like the same innocent she was at the inn—happy to go along with whatever plans Von Krolock has for her, as long as she can take a bath and dress nicely. I'm not sure that Polanski meant to portray Sarah as a shallow girl with not much identity to lose, but that's how she comes off. She does figure prominently in the ironic ending, when she and the heroes have successfully eluded the vampires in a one-horse open sleigh, Professor Abronsius driving, Alfie cradling a swooning Sarah in the back. Having succumbed completely to the vampire's bite, she awakens—now totally devoid of any human personality—and reenacts her oral rape, only this time with herself as the aggressor and poor Alfie as the victim, while the narrator (is it Von Kroloch?) informs us that Professor Abronsius, who had come to Transylvania to exterminate vampirism, became the unwitting instrument for spreading it throughout Europe.

The Fearless Vampire Killers has identity problems of its own. Polanski thought it lost its identity in America due to interference from executive producer Martin Ransohoff, who edited the director's 107-minute cut to 98 minutes for U.S. audiences, dubbed in a different voice for Polanski's character, and added a "Professor and Alfie vs. the Vampire" pre-credit cartoon (echoes again of *Abbott and Costello Meet Frankenstein*—and *Creature from the Haunted Sea* [1961], for that matter!). Today, Polanski's cut has been restored, but it's my painful duty to report that Ransohoff's version actually plays better. My impression may be colored by the fact that, for years, the shortened version is the one I saw, and maybe I got used to it. But, now that I'm in possession of a DVD that lacks the pre-credit cartoon that I always liked and adds 10 minutes of mostly inconsequential footage, I am struck by what a difference a reel makes (and wishing my DVD contained *both* versions). Polanski's assured bravura scenes are still there (like the aforementioned abduction and Alfie's encounter with the Count's fey, obviously gay vampire son), but the pace is considerably slower (the movie seems much *longer* than 107 minutes now). While it's nice to have Polanski speaking in his own voice, I do not understand why other sounds have been erased from or were never on this soundtrack. Specifically, when the frozen and feasted-upon body of Shagal is returned to the inn, the Professor examines the corpsicle, spinning it around on a table, revealing bites on the neck, on the wrist, on the ankle. At each new revelation of bloodsucking, Abronsius (in the American version) lets out an "Ah-HA!" or "Um-HMM!" These comic verbal confirmations of the skin puncturing are what made the scene so funny for me. I was mightily disappointed to find them lacking in the supposed "official" version (though it's possible they were supposed to be there but somehow got lost when the version was "restored"). Anyway, for me, *Fearless Vampire Killers*' reclamation of its original identity is *my* loss.—*AFA*

Fifth Element, The (1997) [**amnesia**] (Columbia). *D:* Luc Besson. *S:* Luc Besson. *Cast:* Bruce Willis (Korben Dallas); Milla Jovovich (Leeloo); Gary Oldman (Jean-Baptiste Emanuel Zorg); Chris Tucker (Ruby Rhod).

After *Alien* (1979) blew box-office returns into the outer galaxies, silver-screen sci-fi became Western noirs filled with pitch-black darkness oozing from pedestrian screenplays and obscuring their over-used special effects, which audiences could hardly see. And, if viewers were looking for even one happy-go-lucky cheerful resident of the future—well, we were pretty much out of luck.

Ah, but happily along came a little-hyped but big-, big-budgeted ($90 mil) sci-fi gem from the mind of a French teenaged wannabe filmmaker, Luc Besson. He had to wait 22 years to bring his vision to life, but, boy, was it worth the wait!

The Fifth Element is a silly, heart-pumping, breathtaking visual feast from start to finish. Besson uses colors as effectively as the best Technicolor experts of the past. And the film is a masterwork that should be studied by anyone considering a career in film editing—Sylvie Landra's work is just brilliant.

We'll try to simplify the plot as much as possible for *Element*al virgins…every 5,000 years a doorway opens between dimensions, and an evil force emerges to destroy the universe. But there is a weapon composed of five elements that is the only thing that can defeat the darkness. The weapons are guarded by a race of good aliens who had at

Fog (Lee Evans) and Father Vito Cornelius (Ian Holm) desperately try to save the world by using the fifth element Leeloo (Milla Jovovich) in *The Fifth Element*.

one time kept them safe on the Earth with a brotherhood of priests as their guardians. But a race of bad-guy aliens learned of their location and tried to steal the weapons.

Fast-forward to NYC in the year 2259. Cynical cabbie Korben Dallas thinks he's been blessed from the heavens when exotic red-headed beauty Leeloo literally drops into his flying cab. Leeloo has survived an alien attack, sort of. The bad-guy aliens blew up the spaceship she was traveling on. Power-mad politicos resurrected her, and she managed to escape them by falling out of a skyscraper into Korben's cab. The beauty has no memory and cannot communicate.

Leeloo, the fifth element, along with earth, air, water, and fire, is the only thing that can save the universe from complete annihilation. Leeloo is the element *life*, who, together with the other four elements, can combine to create a light the drives away the darkness. But Leeloo has no identity; she knows no emotions and has no memories.

With help from an odd assortment of unlikely heroes (including the flamboyant Ruby Rhod, played by Chris Tucker in an over-the-top but hilarious performance), Korben is able to travel off world, find the missing elemental stones and head back to Earth to activate the five elements. En route, Leeloo finishes her education (everything from W to Z) via video encyclopedias. But, as Leeloo begins to slowly find her identity, she also mournfully discovers the horrors mankind can inflict upon itself and others as she watches video images of the mass murder and mayhem of several world wars.

The tension rises as Korben Dallas and company activate the elements and he leads Leeloo into the center. Fully conscious of herself and the world around her, she refuses to save what she now considers an unworthy universe. Dallas tries to convince her of the good in the world and finally wins her over with his osculatory declaration of love. That must be some kiss!—because she is convinced, and a beam of light bursts from her to destroy the darkness, making the universe safe for another 5,000 years.

The Fifth Element isn't a deep Freudian art-house special. The story is a brilliantly colorful contrast of black and white. Good vs. evil. Love vs. hate. Peace vs. war. Leeloo finds her identity only to almost lose it again when she discovers the horrors humans can inflict upon one another. And, as in any good old-fashioned morality tale, she manages to see (and become) the light by giving love and by being loved. Of course, most old-fashioned morality tales don't conclude with a hot sweaty love scene to cinch the deal.—*SAS*

Fight Club (1999) [**split personality**] (20th Century Fox). *D:* David Fincher. *S:* Jim Uhls, From the Novel *Fight Club* by Chuck Palahniuk. *Cast:* Brad Pitt (Tyler Durden); Edward Norton (the Narrator); Helena Bonham Carter (Marla Singer); Meat Loaf (Robert "Bob" Paulson).

One of the true cult classics of the 1990s, David Fincher's *Fight Club* is a film with a lot to say. Indeed, it is a hodgepodge of ideas, a satire of materialism, gender roles, and modern life in general. Among the most interesting ideas contained within the film is its "big twist" revelation: Our protagonists, the Narrator (Edward Norton) and his charismatic pal Tyler Durden (Brad Pitt), are actually the same person. Thus everything we have seen Tyler do has, in reality, been done by the Narrator, who clearly suffers from an acute case of split-personality disorder.

What is most intriguing about this twist is that it reveals the depths of self-loathing to which the Narrator (never accurately named, neither in the film nor in the book,

Tyler Durden (Brad Pitt) and the Narrator (Edward Norton) are actually the same person in *Fight Club*.

although he uses various aliases) has sunk. Bitter and depressed over his empty, loveless, meaningless life, the Narrator has in a sense given birth to a new, ostensibly better, self—as "Tyler" explains, "All the ways you wish you could be, that's me. I look like you wanna look; I fuck like you wanna fuck; I am smart, capable, and, most importantly, I am free in all the ways that you are not." Thus *Fight Club* presents a very interesting variation on the theme of identity loss: We have a protagonist who (subconsciously, at least) willfully abandons his identity to replace it with a theoretically better one. This conceit is quite different from that found in traditional LOI standards like *Invaders from Mars* (1953, 1986 [*qq.v.*]) or *Invasion of the Body Snatchers* (1956, 1978 [*qq.v.*]), films in which the subversion of the self is portrayed as an unconditionally negative development. Traditional LOI films mourn those elements of "normal" life lost—family, friendship, freedom of individual choice—when protagonists have their personalities overwritten by outside forces. *Fight Club* suggests that the accoutrements of normal life—the material wealth of modern existence—are the source of the discontent that makes the Narrator's new personality so attractive.

As in Chuck Palahniuk's source novel, Fincher's film climaxes with the Narrator desperately trying to stop the underground revolution he (in his Tyler persona) has initiated. The Narrator winds up literally engaged in mortal combat with himself, a struggle that symbolizes the dueling personalities in his mind. In both the film and the novel the Narrator winds up shooting himself in the head, somehow not inflicting a fatal wound yet "killing" Tyler Durden. However, the destruction of the Tyler personality does not result in a happy ending for the Narrator. In the film he apparently dies as the skyscrapers his henchmen have wired with explosives blow up; in the novel he winds up incarcerated in a mental hospital staffed by "Durdenites" already plotting his release and return to power. In both cinematic and print forms, *Fight Club* concludes with the same message: Once identity has been sublimated, even a complete restoration of self cannot undo "collateral damage" to the protagonist. In this context *Fight Club* complies with the lesson of traditional LOI films—whatever faults we may demonstrate, our "real" personalities are infinitely preferable to the "unreal" personalities foisted upon us.—*JML*

First Man into Space (1959) **[metamorphosis]** Anglo Amalgamated (MGM). *D:* Robert Day. *S:* John C. Cooper and Charles F. Vetter (as Lance Z. Hargreaves). *Cast:* Marshall Thompson (Commander Charles Prescott); Marla Landi (Tia Wellington); Robert Ayres (Captain Ben Richards); Bill Edward (Lieutenant Dan Prescott); Bill Nagy (Asst. Chief Wilson); Carl Jaffe (Dr. Petersen).

Hotshot military test pilot Dan Prescott disobeys orders and takes his experimental "rocket-plane" too high, leaving Earth's atmosphere to become the film's title character. ("Who's gonna forget the first man into space?" he recklessly reasons, trying to forge a memorable identity for himself—and ironically initiating his eradication of self.) Dan encounters a cloud of "meteorite dust" that damages his ship and sends him spinning back to Earth. Oh, and his exposed head and space-suited body become coated with a hideous "space crust." (Compare the LOI fate of astronaut Victor Caroon in 1955's *The Creeping Unknown* [*q.v.*].) The man/monster, now needing blood to survive, goes on a killing spree, pursued by his mission commander—and brother—Charles, who tries to track him down while they still recognize each other, while some of Dan's human identity is still intact. "It's incredible to think of your [own] brother as a blood-drinking monster," ponders Charles in one of the film's lamer loss-of-identity lines—matched by his later postulation, "If he can still drive a car, he still retains some intelligence; he's not all monster."

Saddled with a bulky costume and immobile mask, actor Bill Edwards not only had to impart menace but somehow suggest the horror and self-loathing that becoming a hideous bloodsucking monster would bring. Such a metamorphosis has not only subsumed Dan's identity, it has completely separated him from the rest of humanity; and Edwards, via body language, manages to effectively convey the agony of such a terrible fate.

Director Robert Day was less than enthusiastic about his movie's menace. "I thought it was dumb. My feeling at the time was, I thought that somebody could come back out of space with an aberrated mind, rather than the costume. I put that idea forward, but most of the people involved wanted the horror. Which I thought was almost a caricature." [*Cf.* Curt Siodmak's remarks about *Bride of the Gorilla* (1951), in that entry.]

Despite his dislike of the "horror" material, Day handled his hated monster well. It's first seen only as a menacing shadow on a wall (with heavy, strangled breathing on the soundtrack). Low-angle shots and darkened hallways generate a real sense of horror as the man-monster breaks into a blood bank. When Day finally exposes the creature to full view, it comes with a sudden, brief shot of the horrific face bursting forth from some bushes, making for a startling and memorable moment.

Oddly, MGM tried to alter *First Man*'s identity, downplaying the movie's horror angle in its advertising (there's no *hint* of a monster in any of the film's posters, for instance). "MGM thought it would have more appeal to a general audience and that it

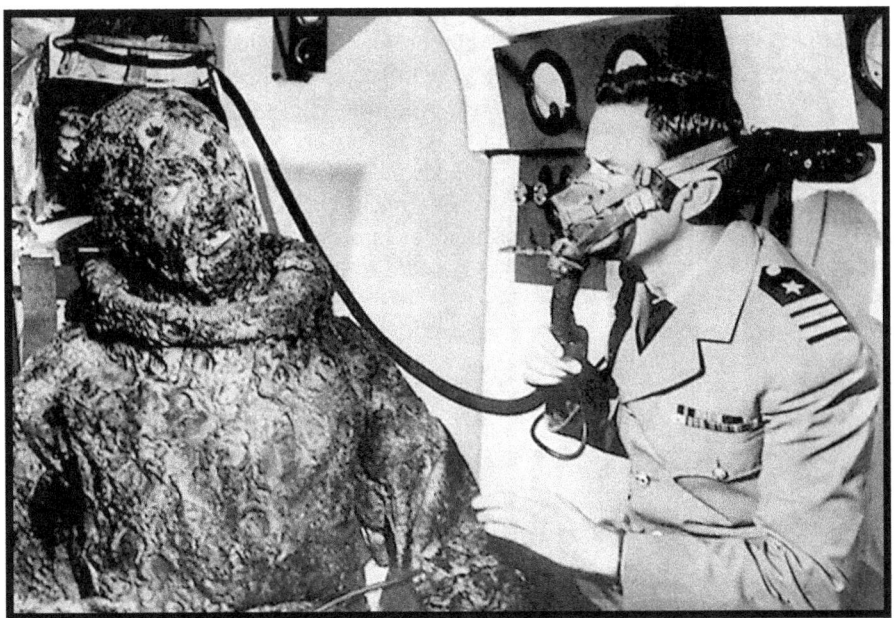

Hotshot astronaut Dan Prescott (Bill Edward) is examined by his brother Charles Prescott (Marshall Thompson) in *First Man Into Space.*

could play much more widely than a horror picture might," explained executive-producer Richard Gordon, "so they decided to play up the science fiction rather than the horror or monster angles."

But it's those very "horror" and "monster" angles that make *First Man into Space* memorable—and watchable—today.—*BMS*

First Yank Into Tokyo (1945) [**disfigurement/medical intervention**] (RKO Radio Pictures Inc.). *D:* Gordon Douglas. *S:* J. Robert Bren, Story by Gladys Atwater. *Cast:* Tom Neal (Steve Ross); Barbara Hale (Abby Drake); Marc Cramer (Lewis Jardine); Richard Loo (Hideko Okanura); Keye Luke (Haan-Soo); Leonard Strong (Major Nogira).

First Yank Into Tokyo begins as an ordinary WWII action film. Tom Neal (*Detour* [1945]) stars as Steve Ross, a soldier who lost his reason for living when the love of his life, nurse Abby Drake, is reported killed by the Japanese. He volunteers for a suicide mission to infiltrate a Tokyo POW camp where an American prisoner possesses an essential secret of the nascent atomic bomb (!). With the help of a little plastic surgery, Ross will pass himself off as a Japanese soldier. [The plot seems to be a reversal of Monogram's 1942 film, *Black Dragons*, wherein Bela Lugosi plays a Nazi scientist who transforms a half-dozen Japanese into Caucasians.]

So far, so far-fetched—but, as WWII Hollywood goes, not totally unreasonable. Until the moment when Ross is informed, "Once your features are changed, *they can never be changed back*. You will carry the face of a Jap all of your life." In one fell swoop, the film goes from action thriller to absolute horror noir, and Steve Ross goes from moody soldier to doomed existential figure wearing what the film treats as the face of pure evil.

For the Japanese are evil in this movie, as Abby herself says. "You Japs couldn't change. You're all alike. You ought to be put in cages." Yes, even when Ross discovers Abby still living—in the very prison camp he must infiltrate—he knows there can be no future for their love. "Every time she'd look at me, I'd remind her of the other Japs on Bataan and Corregidor." The only peace for him will lie in an open grave.

Words fail to do justice to the sheer weirdness of *First Yank Into Tokyo*, so I'll just stop here and hope that I've tempted readers into tracking it down next time it plays on television. Make no mistake; *First Yank* is a horror movie as much as *Frankenstein* (1931) ever was. It was completed after the atomic bombing of Hiroshima, and the film's efforts to incorporate the super-bomb into the plot of *First Yank* give its pulp surrealism a kind of apocalyptic zing unique to popcorn movies of the Second World War.—*AJL*

Five Million Years to Earth (*Quatermass and the Pit*) (1967) [alien possession] Great Britain (Hammer Films). *D:* Roy Ward Baker. *S:* Nigel Kneale, From his Teleplay *Quatermass and the Pit. Cast:* James Donald (Dr. Roney); Andrew Keir (Prof. Quatermass); Barbara Shelley (Barbara Judd); Julian Glover (Col. Breen); Duncan Lamont (Sladden); Bryan Marshall (Capt. Potter).

Unlike their American cousins, British science fiction films of the 1950s and 1960s remained faithful to the cerebral roots of their source material. *Five Million Years to Earth*, the third film based on Nigel Kneale's successful BBC Quatermass teleplays, performed the heady task of balancing mythic elements with the loss-of-identity attributes commonly found in alien-possession films.

The central conceit behind *Five Million Years to Earth* is a bold one—a dying race from Mars established a colony by proxy on our planet some five thousand millennia ago. Selective breeding and other techniques were used to genetically alter abducted humanoids, a process that resulted in new faculties both mental and physical. Via this method, the inhabitants of our interplanetary neighbor lived on through the new man. The loss of identity depicted by the film thus has its roots in a cataclysmic event that affected our entire species.

The apparent success of the Martian plan has left humankind with a fearful race memory. As revealed by the research team of Prof. Quatermass, Dr. Roney, and Barbara Judd, the Martian ability to manipulate thought and action subsequently became a source

Quatermass (Andrew Keir), Barbara Judd (Barbara Shelley), and Dr. Roney (James Donald) are the only hope for the human race in *Five Million Years to Earth.*

for worldwide religious myth. Subconscious recollections of violent hive purges on the Red Planet were manifested in an instinctive fear of the "horned devils" and "hideous dwarfs" (references to the Martian's diminutive, arthropod-like appearance). Ancient tales of weird occurrences near a buried landing site, recorded in ancient writings, were passed down through the generations and became firmly entrenched in folklore. Even more troubling is the revelation that the sadistic Martian tendencies live on in us today: When an unearthed Martian craft is disturbed and the ship's inert energy is released, the residents in the surrounding area succumb to a trance-like state, instinctively seeking to destroy any "mutations" who deviate from the social norm. Only through the heroic actions of Quatermass, Roney, and Judd is our planet spared the awakening of the dormant Martian influence, presumably on a massive scale.

Although the name Quatermass was a phenomenon in England, it meant nothing in the United States, a fact that hampered the film's international box-office prospects. As a result, *Five Million Years to Earth* garnered little attention, a sad fate for such an intelligent and thought-provoking movie. Within a decade, the identity of cinema science fiction itself would undergo a dramatic shift in light of *Star Wars*' (*q.v.*) unprecedented success in 1977. Thought-based sci-fi films would soon become a thing of the past. But, although it was a late entry in the cycle, *Five Million Years to Earth* was a standout among the many space-based loss-of-identity films.—*SGT*

Forbidden Planet (1956) [alien possession] (MGM). *D:* Fred McLeod Wilcox. *S:* Cyril Hume; Story by Irving Block and Allen Adler, From William Shakespeare's Play *The Tempest* (uncredited). *Cast:* Walter Pidgeon (Dr. Morbius); Anne Francis (Altaira);

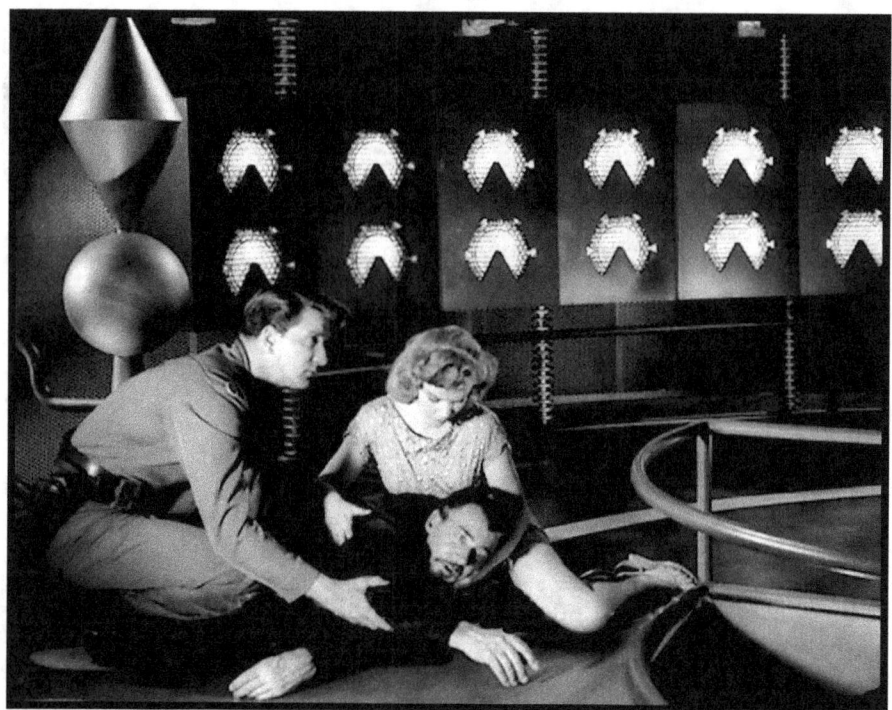

Commander Adams (Leslie Nielson) and Altaira (Anne Francis) are unable to save Morbius (Walter Pidgeon) from his psyche in *Forbidden Planet.*

Leslie Nielson (Commander Adams); Jack Kelly (Lt. Jerry Farman); Warren Stevens (Lt. "Doc" Ostrow); Richard Anderson (Chief Engineer Quinn); Earl Holliman (Cook); Marvin Miller (voice of Robby the Robot); James Drury (Crewman Joe Strong).

The big-budget, supremely satisfying *Forbidden Planet* contains some big ideas, too. Not only does it transplant Shakespeare's *The Tempest* to outer space, but it offers a Jungian-cum-Freudian gloss on the play and twist on the theme of loss of identity. One modern interpretation of *The Tempest*'s Prospero-Ariel-Caliban trio maintains that they represent the superego, ego, and id, and the movie embraces this analysis: Morbius, the Prospero figure, is essentially a magician who's mastered some of the secrets of the Krell, the ancient race that inhabited his adopted planet Altair IV. His Ariel (good fairy) and Caliban (evil creature) take the solid incarnation of Robby the Robot and the intangible figure of the "id monster," a manifestation of his own unconscious desires.

Here's where the film yokes this Freudian trinity to the Jungian idea of the collective unconscious: The super-intelligent Krell, who created a vast underground network of machinery that supplies power in perpetuity to the planet, were at one time on the verge of implementing their greatest accomplishment—the ability to use mere thought to achieve their every desire. But something destroyed them. (We later learn that, while they slept, their marvelous machines gave form and action to the unchecked, unconscious evil buried in their psyches, and they were done in by these usually suppressed, malign thoughts.)

Morbius feels at home on this planet (unlike his shipmates on the original expedition to Altair IV, who didn't—and died trying to leave). In fact, he has managed, through a Krell-machine "brain boost," to "go native"—become Krell enough to understand something of their science and language, build marvels like Robby, and make a good life for himself and his daughter Altaira (born on the planet and who, like *The Tempest*'s Miranda, has known no man other than her father). Morbius doesn't realize that he's also inherited the Krell ability to materialize his darker thoughts (which caused the deaths of his colleagues who opposed him two decades ago and now threatens the starship crew that's come to fetch him).

In the pulse-pounding conclusion, Commander Adams, the man who's won Altaira's heart (and therefore roused an even more disturbing, possessive, and undoubtedly incestuous demon of Morbius' mind), finally gets the scientist to realize the awful truth: that *he* has given rise to the unseen force, that the thing which is using the boundless power of the Krell to melt the seemingly impenetrable doors behind which they're hiding is Morbius himself.

As in other loss-of-identity tales, *Forbidden Planet* illustrates a Jekyll/Hyde-like split between a basically decent person and his baser instincts, which—the film postulates—are a part of even the most noble of us (human or alien). However, this Jekyll is allowed to confront his Hyde directly. Before the terrible creature that is the twisted piece of Morbius' soul can burst through the barrier and claim not only Adams but Altaira, Morbius renounces it, consciously denies it—thus saving his daughter but precipitating his own demise (an action akin to Prospero breaking his staff and renouncing magic in *The Tempest*—or to Dorian Gray plunging the dagger into the heart of his portrait; of course, as an eight year old, viewing the film during its first run, *I* didn't see any of this because the suspense was too much for me, and I closed my eyes at the crucial moment).

This quintessential 1950s space opera, the prototype for *Star Trek* (as Gene Roddenberry eventually admitted), is also essential for understanding that 1960s supernatural hit, *The Birds* (1963), in which there's seemingly no reason for our feathered friends' vicious attacks, until we realize that the mother's feelings toward her son's romantic interests have unleashed the uncontainable avian fury (a not-so-far-fetched explanation, considering that *Birds*' director, Alfred Hitchcock, was a cinematic Freudian par excellence).—*AFA*

Frankenstein Meets the Wolf Man (1943) [**metamorphosis**] (Universal). *D:* Roy William Neill. *S:* Curt Siodmak. *Cast:* Lon Chaney, Jr. (Lawrence Talbot); Ilona Massey (Baroness Elsa Frankenstein); Patric Knowles (Dr. Frank Mannering); Lionel Atwill (Mayor); Bela Lugosi (the Frankenstein Monster); Maria Ouspenskaya (Maleva); Dennis Hoey (Inspector Owen); Don Barclay (Franzec); Rex Evans (Vazec); Dwight Frye (Rudi).

Frankenstein Meets the Wolf Man was a financial success for Universal because audiences were excited about seeing two of their favorite monsters together in one picture. Billed as "the Battle of the Century," the picture was a follow-up to *The Wolf Man* (1941 [*q.v.*]), while also carrying over characters and plot threads from *The Ghost of Frankenstein* (1942).

The film opens with two grave robbers disturbing the resting place of Lawrence Talbot, the Wolf Man. The full moon brings Larry back to life, and he kills one of the crooks. (This opening is arguably Universal horror at its very best—it is the most atmospheric and perhaps the scariest scene from any of the studio's classic fright flicks.) When Larry is subsequently confined to a hospital, neither the police nor Talbot's physician,

Dr. Mannering, believes that Talbot is who he claims to be, telling him that Larry Talbot died years earlier. Talbot again transforms into a werewolf and breaks free, escaping to the countryside. Knowing that only death will free him from his curse, he seeks the aid of Maleva the Gypsy woman—the mother of Bela, the werewolf who bit Larry in the original *Wolf Man* film. Maleva tells Larry that the great scientist Dr. Frankenstein can help him find eternal rest, but when they reach the ruins of Frankenstein's home, they learn the doctor is dead. Talbot discovers the Frankenstein Monster frozen in ice and thaws him out, hoping the creature knows the location of the doctor's notes. Talbot also pretends to be interested in purchasing the land in order to meet Frankenstein's daughter, Elsa. But Dr. Mannering throws a wrench in the works when he arrives in town, having pursued Talbot across Europe. Using Frankenstein's notes, he attempts to help Talbot but instead becomes obsessed with seeing the Monster at full power. Talbot transforms into the Wolf Man and battles the Monster; they are both swept away when an angry villager blows up the dam.

Frankenstein Meets the Wolf Man is definitely more interested in Lawrence Talbot's plight than in the story of the Frankenstein Monster (who was on his way to becoming a prop in these films—just as Boris Karloff had predicted). As a result, the film emphasizes Talbot's lycanthropy and his loss of identity; when Talbot transforms into the Wolf Man, he loses all intelligence, reason, and control. He becomes a savage animal, a killing machine. The audience feels great sympathy for Talbot; he has no control over what happens to him, and he does not want the transformation to occur. And Chaney plays the role to perfection.

In this film, Talbot's loss of identity makes his life unbearable, and he seeks the ultimate solution—he wants to die. In most horror films that deal with loss of identity, the character who loses his identity through metamorphosis or alien control usually dies—it is the expected conclusion. But seldom does the character actively seek his own demise. Talbot is obsessed with his own death. This mania becomes overly evident during the village's Festival of the New Wine. When the singer belting out the song "Faro-La, Faro-Li" mentions living eternally, Talbot snaps. He grabs the man and demands to know why he would say something like that. Poor Larry is already cursed with eternal life and eternal torment—countless nights of losing himself to the beast within. He just doesn't have the strength to go on. Lon Chaney, Jr. may not have been the most gifted actor to make his mark in the horror genre, but it's near impossible not to feel for him and his plight as Lawrence Talbot. The Wolf Man was Chaney's baby for good reason. This character who frequently lost his identity gave Chaney his primary identity as an actor.

Interestingly, a loss of identity seemed to play out on the other side of the cameras in *Frankenstein Meets the Wolf Man*. Every horror fan knows Bela Lugosi turned down the role of the Monster in the 1931 *Frankenstein*. At the time, it seemed like a good choice. Ten years later, Lugosi was hard up for work and had no option but to accept the role he had originally refused. Still, Lugosi gave his all to every part he took, and he did so again with the Monster. In the original script and as it was originally filmed, the Monster *spoke* but was blind. (He had, after all, been given Ygor's brain in *Ghost of Frankenstein*—Ygor being played by Lugosi. He had even spoken in Lugosi's Ygor voice at the end of that film—when he became blind because Ygor's blood type didn't match the Monster's.) His evil grin just before the climax of *Frankenstein Meets the*

***Frankenstein Meets the Wolf Man*, starring Lon Chaney, Jr., emphasizes Larry Talbot's lycanthropy and his loss of identity rather than focusing on the Frankenstein Monster.**

Wolf Man was *supposed* to be the acknowledgment of his restored sight. Lugosi played the Monster as if he were blind and dutifully recited his lines. However, the studio felt the effect did not work and cut out all of the Monster's dialogue, as well as any reference to his blindness. As a result, Lugosi comes off unfavorably, and his performance has been criticized over the years as one of the genre's worst. In a way, the Monster's identity was yanked out from under him, as was Lugosi's. Still, as my good friend director/producer Kent Hagen recently reminded me, Lugosi's Monster was the first one that many a young fan encountered (thanks to television's *Shock Theater*), and it remains the interpretation that they recall with fondness. I hope that's a consolation for Lugosi—savvy horror fans can always see through identity loss.—*JSM*

[Identity vindicated? Glenn Strange always claimed that Boris Karloff taught him how to play the Monster when they appeared as Monster and mad scientist, respectively, in *House of Frankenstein* (1944). But the jerky walk with arms outstretched that Strange effected in his three turns as the Monster was pure Lugosi from *this* film.]

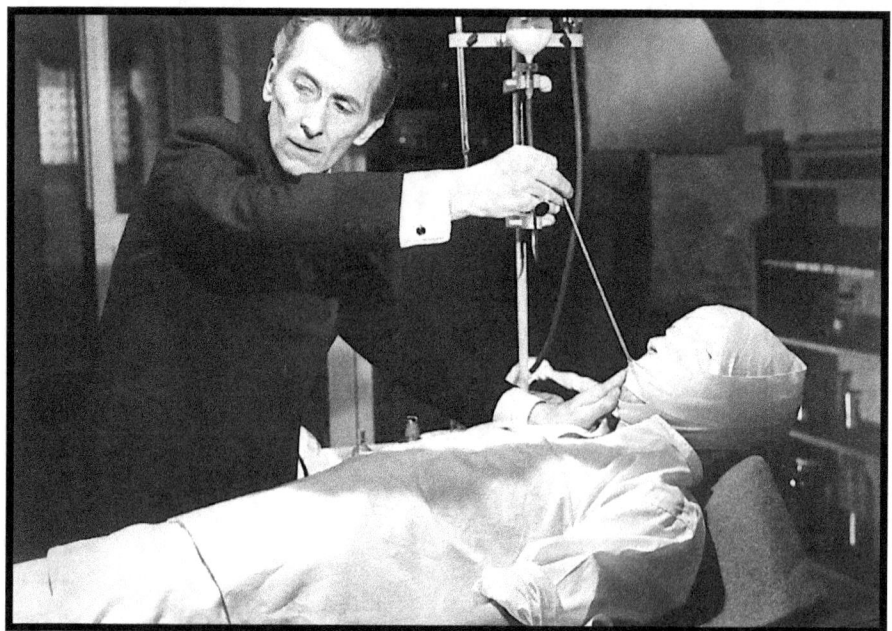

In *Frankenstein Must Be Destroyed*, Dr. Brandt's identity is defined by how others perceive him after Frankenstein (Peter Cushing) transplants Brandt's brain into a different body.

Frankenstein Must Be Destroyed (1969) [**brain switching**] Great Britain (Hammer). *D*: Terence Fisher. *S*: Bert Batt; Story by Anthony Nelson Keys. *Cast*: Peter Cushing (Baron Victor Frankenstein); Simon Ward (Karl Holst); Veronica Carlson (Anna Spengler); Freddie Jones (Professor Richter); George Pravda (Dr. Brandt); Maxine Audley (Ella Brandt); Thorley Walters (Inspector Frisch).

The fifth entry in the series of Frankenstein movies produced by England's legendary Hammer Film Productions contains one of the more effective presentations of identity loss in fantasy cinema. Baron Frankenstein needs the help of fellow mad scientist Dr. Brandt, who is incarcerated in an asylum. Unfortunately Dr. Brandt dies during a breakout attempt, so the Baron preserves his colleague's brain in the body of Prof. Richter. His sanity restored but his appearance drastically altered, Brandt/Richter visits his grieving wife, Ella, who rejects him in horror.

Masterfully directed by Terence Fisher, the sequence works primarily because Freddie Jones and Maxine Audley, as Professor and Mrs. Richter, portray their characters' dilemmas sensitively and realistically. The scientist initially hides behind a dressing screen; he tries to prepare Ella for the shock, speaking tenderly and quietly. The look of horror and dejection on Jones' face says it all: Brandt still thinks of himself as Brandt, feeling and thinking as always—but he is not himself. Seeing is believing; our identities are defined largely by how others perceive us (literally and figuratively). Ella's inability to accept her beloved husband's physical changes precludes any resumption of their previous domestic relationship.

The idea of a transplanted brain unable to reconcile itself to its new body is quickly abandoned, and the reunion of the Brandts may be too subtle, given the film's many more graphic scenes of horror. Nevertheless, *Frankenstein Must Be Destroyed* is enriched by this unsettling portrayal of loss of identity.—*JML*

Geung si sin sang. See **Mr. Vampire** (1985).

Ghidrah, the Three-Headed Monster (*San daikaijû: Chikyu saidai no kessen*) (1964) [**mind control**] Japan (Toho). *D:* Ishirô Honda. *S:* Shinichi Sekizawa. *Cast:* Yosuke Natsuki (Detective Shindo); Yuriko Hoshi (Naoko Shindo); Hiroshi Koizumi (Professor Miura); Akiko Wakabayashi (Mas Selina Salno, Princess of Sergina); Emi Ito (Shobijin [Twin Fairy]); Yûmi Ito (Shobijin [Twin Fairy]); Takashi Shimura (Dr. Tsukamoto).

Wouldn't it be great if we had a self-preservation instinct that would get us off a plane just moments before it exploded, and even give us prophetic abilities to help save Earth from extinction? In *Ghidrah, the Three-Headed Monster*, Princess Salno has just that. The self-preservation instinct comes from an ancestor who escaped Venus on the day it was destroyed by the gravity-beam breath of King Ghidrah. When the Venusian instinct kicks in, though, the Princess retains no memory of her Earthling identity. She becomes a nameless Venusian, walking in a hypnotic trance, accurately preaching catastrophe to the people of Japan.

The catastrophe, of course, is all about giant monsters. Rodan will emerge from a volcano. Godzilla will emerge from the ocean. And Ghidrah will emerge…to make Earth a "dead planet," just as he made Venus 5,000 years ago. Well, the monsters do emerge as the Venusian prophetess prophesied, and Rodan and Godzilla naturally rumble, while Ghidrah ravages Earth. It's all enough to convince the Twin Fairies from Infant Island to call on the baby Mothra for help! Maybe Mothra can persuade (or shame) Godzilla and Rodan to stop fighting each other and team up to fight Ghidrah.

Princess Salno (Akiko Wakabayashi), Naoko Shindo (Yuriko Hoshi), Detective Shindo (Yosuke Natsuki), and Dr. Tsukamoto (Takashi Shimura) try to save the world in *Ghidrah*.

And so *Ghidrah* becomes a movie full of firsts: It features the first Toho Giant Monster Rally, with several of its giant "stars" battling it out. It features the first cooperation between the Earth monsters (Godzilla, Mothra, and Rodan) against a space monster (Ghidrah)—transforming the Earth monsters into Earth protectors so fully that between *Ghidrah* (1964) and *Mechogodzilla* (1975), Godzilla will stomp Tokyo only at the prompting of alien mind control (except, of course, when stomping Tokyo becomes unavoidable in order to protect the Earth).

And that brings us to the topic of alien mind control. *Ghidrah* introduces aliens (and alien mind control) to the Godzilla series. In *Ghidrah*, the mind control is exerted not by an external force, as it will be in later Godzilla movies. Rather, it is part of the Princess' genetic structure. As her Venusian persona tells the doctor who examines her: "When this Earthling was in danger, her latent abilities awoke within her. This instinct [which foretells the future] is part of a greater self-preservation reaction." In other words, when the Princess faced assassination, the alien part of her mind took over, prompting her to walk out of an airplane, and presumably allowing her to survive the fall into the ocean. While the American version (which substitutes "Martian" for Venusian") uses the voices of flying-saucer people to prompt her to leave the plane, the original Japanese version places the prompting clearly within her own mind.

The assassination attempt, curiously enough, coincides with Ghidrah's meteoric arrival on Earth. Would the Princess have reverted to the Venusian with Ghidrah's arrival alone? Or did she need the assassination plot to make her recognize the impending threat posed by Ghidrah, destroyer of Venus? Whatever the case, the alien part of her mind places the Princess in a prophetic trance so long as necessary to protect her life—and Earth's life—from assassins and giant monsters.

In the end, she reverts to the Princess when a bullet grazes her forehead. But given that Shindo, her Japanese bodyguard, also sustains light wounds during the gun battle, the Princess' return to her human identity—and thus to the human emotion that will cause her to bind Shindo's wound—may be the more necessary part of self-preservation. Regardless, she reverts from Venusian to Princess only moments before her assassin dies and the Earth monsters send Ghidrah packing back into space.

In *Ghidrah, the Three-Headed Monster*, loss of human identity is not really such a bad thing. It proves a tad embarrassing for the Princess, who asks in the end if she really called herself a Venusian. But it also saves her life, and better yet, helps save the Earth.—*CCS*

Ghost Breakers, The (1940) [voodoo] (Paramount). *D:* George Marshall. *S:* Walter de Leon, Based on the Play *The Ghost Breaker* by Paul Dickey and Charles W. Goddard. *Cast:* Bob Hope (Lawrence Lawrence); Paulette Goddard (Mary Carter); Richard Carlson (Geoff Montgomery); Paul Lukas (Parada); Willie Best (Alex); Pedro De Cordoba (Havez); Virginia Brissac (Mother Zombie); Noble Johnson (The Zombie); Anthony Quinn (Ramon and Francisco Mederos); Tom Dugan (Raspy Kelly); Paul Fix (Frenchy Duval); Lloyd Corrigan (Martin).

The Ghost Breakers was the second of two consecutive horror comedies Bob Hope made with Paulette Goddard (the other being 1939's *The Cat and the Canary*). These films made Hope a movie star and established his character of the "brave coward"—the nervous wisecracker who saves the day in spite of himself—which he would use in many of his subsequent movies. Basically an old-dark-house comedy based on a popu-

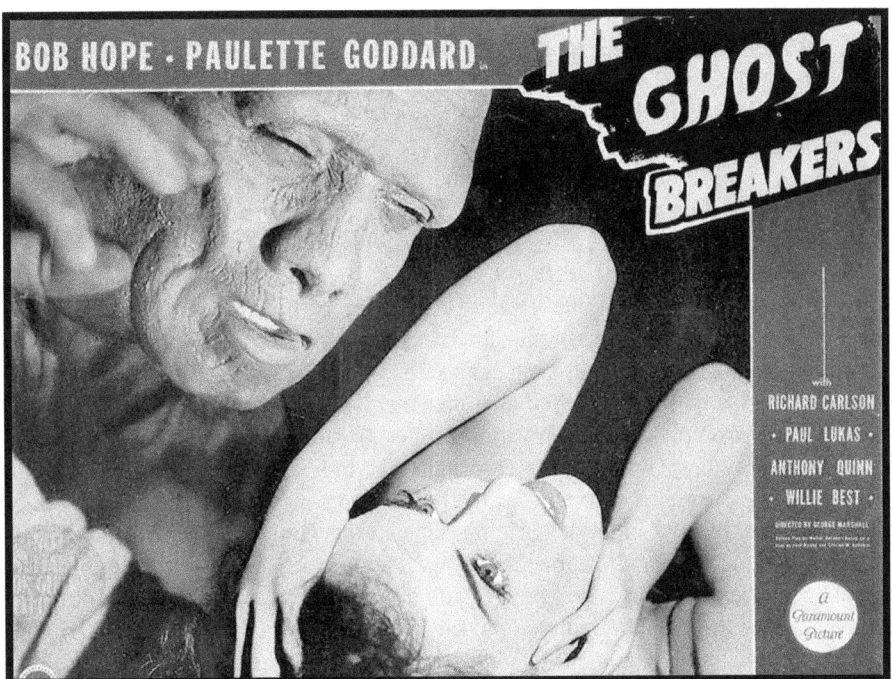

In *The Ghost Breakers* lobby card, Mary Carter (Paulette Goddard) is threatened by a zombie (Noble Johnson).

lar Broadway play, *The Ghost Breakers* follows radio announcer Lawrence Lawrence, who mistakenly assumes he has murdered a gangster. Hiding out in the hotel room of beautiful Mary Carter, Lawrence is accidentally sent with her baggage to a ship heading for Cuba, where Mary has inherited a haunted castle on Black Island. Falling for Mary, Larry and his valet, Alex, pose as "ghost breakers" and offer to help expose the spooks. Most of the ghostly goings-on are proved to be fake, but the three are briefly menaced by a real zombie who lives on the island with his voodoo-practicing mother.

The zombie is *The Ghost Breakers*' loss-of-identity connection. Though he does not appear until about halfway into the film, he is talked about on the ship to Cuba. Mary's friend Geoff explains, "A zombie has no will of its own. You see them sometimes, walking around blindly with dead eyes, following orders and not knowing what they do, not caring." To which Larry replies, "You mean like Democrats."

The zombie in the film is used too briefly to make any real comment on the theme of loss of identity. The audience learns nothing about who he was when he was alive, so there is no way to comment on or examine the change that occurred when he became undead. Still, one of his appearances is the most frightening zombie scene in classic horror cinema (and perhaps one of the most overall unnerving sequences of any classic horror film). Larry and Alex peer through the window of the old caretaker's cabin and spy the zombie lying on his bed. Well-lit and making excellent use of shadows, the scene has the two staring through slots in the shade. The zombie's eyes dart over to look at them; then, ever so slowly, the creature turns his rotting, ugly face toward the window and stares at the pair. A simple turn of the head creates almost unbearable tension and unease.—*JSM*

Ginger Snaps (2000) [**metamorphosis**] (Lions Gate Films). *D:* John Fawcett. *S:* Karen Walton, From a Story by Karen Walton and John Fawcett. *Cast:* Emily Perkins (Brigitte "B" Fitzgerald); Katharine Isabelle (Ginger Fitzgerald); Kris Lemche (Sam); Mimi Rogers (Pamela Fitzgerald); Jesse Moss (Jason McCardy); Danielle Hampton (Trina Sinclair).

As its tagline, "They don't call it 'the curse' for nothing," makes clear, *Ginger Snaps* deals head on with the issue of puberty and transformation (*cf. The Creeping Unknown* [1955 (*q.v.*)] and *I Was a Teenage Werewolf* [1957 (*q.v.*)]—not to mention the comic treatment of same in *Teen Wolf* [1985]).

Siblings Ginger and Brigitte, 16 and 15 respectively (but in the same grade because Brigitte was double promoted), physically "late bloomers," are very close. They've made a pact—together forever, them against the world—and their perhaps not entirely unhealthy contempt for their suburban milieu manifests itself in morbid rebellion (e.g., a school project depicting each in various grotesque suicide-murder scenes).

On the day that Ginger first menstruates (the movie, like the sisters, mocks the well-meaning counselor who advises the pair not to worry about "so much blood"), she is attacked by a lycanthrope (Brigitte suggests that Ginger's bleeding attracted it), and her metamorphosis into something other than the girl she was becomes anything but metaphorical. She discovers boys—with a vengeance (pun intended)—and metes out vengeance to Trina, the snotty popular-girl classmate who bullied her and Brigitte. Except for an annoying amount of stubborn hair growth (she has to shave more than just her legs) and the appearance of a proto-tail at her coccyx (she has to tape it to her leg), the developing lycanthrope's new life is great. (In this film, werewolves don't change back and forth during the full moon or at will but gradually lose their human identity until they evolve, permanently, into something lupine.) Brigitte watches her

Sam (Kris Lemche) is at the mercy of the fully morphed Ginger in *Ginger Snaps*.

sister's transformation with dismay, trying on the one hand (with the help of Sam, the sympathetic local high-school dope dealer) to stave off and even reverse the effects of Ginger's change, and on the other hand, attempting to preserve the bond between them—even going so far as to mingle her blood with Ginger's in an effort to keep the pair together and equal.

But it doesn't work out. Ginger succumbs more and more to her animal instincts, while Brigitte fights against hers, and—in the end—after the fully transmogrified Ginger viciously murders Sam, Brigitte discovers that she cannot be like her sister. (Brigitte gags when, as an act of wolfish solidarity, she tries to join her sister in lapping up the spilled blood of this boy for whom she cared.) Asserting her independence, individuality, and humanity, Brigitte fights back against her ferocious no-longer-sister before the inhuman Ginger can kill her. Brigitte permanently severs their relationship—with a knife (though she can't quite leave the corpse...not until *Ginger Snaps: Unleashed* [2004 (*q.v.*)] does she finally let go).—*AFA*

Ginger Snaps Back: The Beginning (2004) [**metamorphosis**] (Lions Gate Films). *D:* Brett Sullivan. *S:* Megan Martin, Based on Characters created by Karen Walton. *Cast:* Katharine Isabelle (Ginger Fitzgerald); Emily Perkins (Brigitte Fitzgerald); Nathaniel Arcand (the Hunter/the Indian); JR Bourne (James); Hugh Dillon (Reverend Gilbert); Adrien Dorval (Seamus); Brendan Fletcher (Finn); David La Haye (Claude).

This film provides a novel setting for a werewolf movie—a fort in the Canadian north woods in the 1800s, under siege by a tribe of werewolves. There's a bit of *The Thing* (1982 [*q.v.*]) here, wherein no one can be sure that his neighbor is not infected

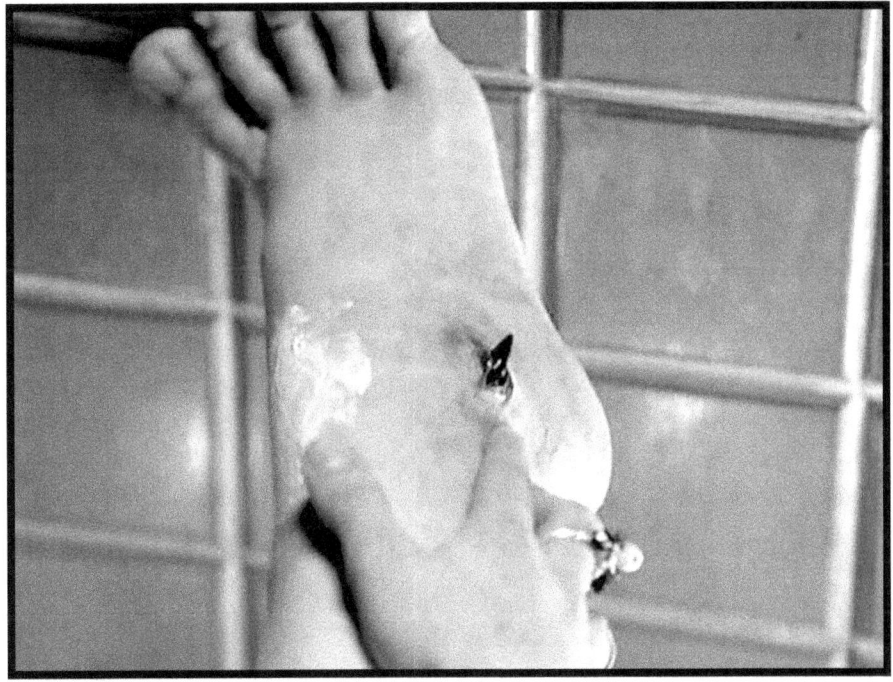

Ginger (Katharine Isabelle) begins her transformation into a werewolf in *Ginger Snaps*.

by the curse of lycanthropy. (There's even a "test," as in *The Thing*, to determine if a seeming human is en route to becoming something other.)

As in the other films in this series, there is more character development here than in a dozen run-of-the-mill horror films (e.g., consider the fort's commander, who goes to great lengths to conceal the fact that his young son is alive but infected, then ultimately shoots the boy himself before the others can do it; or the relationship between a pair of brothers, which forms an interesting contrast/parallel to the two protagonist sisters, Ginger and Brigitte). The film is best read as a companion piece to/alternate take on the original (*Ginger Snaps* [2001 (*q.v.*)]). In that movie, the two sisters pledged undying fealty to each other—until Brigitte's inherent humanity caused her to reject her sister's lycanthropy and turn against the beast that Ginger had become. Here, however, when there's a choice between her sister and the male (the Hunter) who comes between them, Brigitte makes the exact opposite choice, disposing of the man and throwing in her lot with her sibling. This sequel, therefore, enhances the (qualified, some would say) triumph at the end of the first film, wherein Brigitte breaks the nearly 200-year hold that has, in one form or another (human or lycanthrope), carried through the generations.—*AFA*

Brigitte (Emily Perkins) winds up in rehab after fleeing a werewolf who wants to mate with her in *Ginger Snaps: Unleashed.*

Ginger Snaps: Unleashed (2004) [**metamorphosis**] (Lions Gate Films). *D:* Grant Harvey. *S:* Stephen Massicotte and Christina Ray. *Cast:* Emily Perkins (Brigitte); Tatiana Maslany (Ghost); Eric Johnson (Tyler); Janet Kidder (Alice Severson); Brendan Fletcher (Jeremy); Katharine Isabelle (Ginger).

Perhaps the best of the series (despite its decidedly downbeat conclusion), this sequel to *Ginger Snaps* (2001 [*q.v.*]) follows Brigitte, who voluntarily infected herself with her sister Ginger's lycanthropy in the first installment, as she flees from an unknown werewolf who wants to mate with her (shades of *Cat People* [1982 (*q.v.*)]) while she tries to maintain her identity through regular (painful) injections of wolfsbane. Injured after her latest escape from her hirsute would-be lover, she ends up in a hospital for addicts, where her medication is kept from her and where she has to deal with Tyler, the orderly who'll supply her with fixes from her stash, for a price; Ghost, a gabby little girl whose horribly burned grandmother is a patient and who seems to sense Brigitte's lupine nature; and that lupine nature itself, which she continues to fight against (e.g., by lopping off the pointed portion of an ear when it appears) and which calls to her in the imagined person of Ginger, who periodically appears to Brigitte and tells her to give in to it.

As in the previous film, Brigitte has to resist the temptation that is represented by her sister, or the ghost of her sister (that imaginary voice in her head). She succeeds in leaving that ghost behind, but in the process, leaves herself open to the machinations of that other Ghost, who has her own agenda for Brigitte and who prevents Brigitte from avoiding her hairy fate.

As with the other *Ginger Snaps* movies, this one features well-developed characters rather than stereotypes. Even Tyler, who seems to be (and pretty much is) such a slimeball, has more depth than the standard horror-film slimeball. Much as Brigitte loses her identity, he loses his life because they both mistakenly interpret Ghost's true identity and intentions.—*AFA*

Goodbye, Charlie (1964) [**gender confusion; reincarnation**] Venice Production (20th Century Fox). *D:* Vincente Minnelli. *S:* Harry Kurnitz, From the Play *Goodbye, Charlie* by George Axelrod. *Cast:* Tony Curtis (George Tracy); Debbie Reynolds (Charlie Sorel/Virginia Mason); Pat Boone (Bruce Minton III); Joanna Barnes (Janie Highland); Ellen Burstyn [as Ellen MacRae] (Frannie Saltzman); Laura Devon (Rusty Sartori); Roger C. Caramel (Inspector); Walter Matthau (Sir Leopold Sartori).

One of the most frightening things about sexual identity is that, for the most part, you don't choose it. It chooses you. Somehow, as you're growing up, the chemicals that slosh around inside your body are taking their sweet time while they make up their minds as to just what sexual orientation they are going to foist upon you.

I can remember the summer day when the daughter of one of my Boy Scout leaders climbed out of the Andover Swimming Pool's diving area while wearing a blue, one-piece bathing suit. My scrawny frame became suddenly paralyzed, able to do nothing but stare at her in gaping, trembling enthrallment, and, had there been any question, from that moment on my sexual orientation was etched in stone.

It is scary to be so at the mercy of such an irrational, biological force. But, if we want to think of something *really* scary, given the unbelievably complex machinery of humanity, what is to stop everything from changing if some of those chemicals somehow get out of whack?

That is the fear at the heart of the romantic comedy *Goodbye, Charlie*, Vincente Minnelli's 1964 film adaptation of a Broadway stageplay by George Axelrod.

The Charlie of the title, a womanizer who has been murdered by one of the many husbands he's cuckolded, finds himself returned to life in the body of a full-grown woman.

The film takes up most of its running time getting the newly female Charlie to understand her predicament, explain it all to Charlie's best friend George, and attempt to make a living, having been flung into the world without so much as a driver's license. But underneath this fairly undemanding Hollywood star vehicle lurks a disturbing proposition: that gender behavior is not solely determined by culture and upbringing,

The womanizing Charlie (Debbie Reynolds) checks himself out in the mirror after being reincarnated as a beautiful woman in *Goodbye, Charlie*.

it is predominantly a question of biology. For the most part the film pussy-foots around the issue. Until one scene.

When George threatens to walk out and leave Charlie to face the world alone, Charlie becomes overwhelmed by stress, and behaves for the first time in a way the male Charlie never would. She becomes emotional and begins to cry. There is something alternately terrifying and intriguing in seeing Charlie giving over to emotions s/he had always kept at bay (Debbie Reynolds as female Charlie does a great job conveying the emotional tsunami overwhelming Charlie). But wait; the scene is not over yet. George automatically reacts as he would when confronted by any emotional female, and calms Charlie down, wiping her tears away with soft words and caresses. Charlie responds to George's soothing manner, and is soon lying exhausted in his arms. Then George realizes where he is and becomes completely freaked out to see how physically intimate he has just been with a person he knows to be a man. Charlie, however, feeling comforted and secure, doesn't seem hostile to what has happened or averse to where it might lead.

And where does this lead? How might Charlie reconcile her masculine upbringing with her emerging feminine nature? What would she wear? Who would she date? Well, there are all sorts of interesting possibilities, but thanks to the Production Code, a 1964 feature film is going to avoid every one of them. (Twenty-seven years later, the Blake Edwards comedy *Switch* [1991] wouldn't do much better.) So Charlie ends up dead. Worse than dead, she ends up…well, let's just say that after what she's gone through, the punishment seems unnecessarily cruel. [*Editors spoiler:* It shouldn't happen to a dog! Shades of Francis, the talking mule, or Mr. Ed: S/he comes back as a horse!]

In those days writers could go a little farther on Broadway, and playwright George Axelrod was no stranger to dramatizing the conflict of sexual versus social identity, as witness his screenplays for *The Seven Year Itch* (1955) and *How to Murder Your Wife* (1965). His Broadway stageplay posits that the love of men and the love of women are two different things, and neither will quite understand what love means to the other. Axelrod's Charlie has a talent for making women fall in love with him without ever falling in love himself. The play treats his exploitation of this talent as Charlie's greatest sin, and Axelrod's entire gender-bending premise is intended to teach Charlie this concept of what love means to a woman.

At the play's conclusion, reincarnated Charlie does indeed come to understand. Having become emotionally dependent upon George, she finds that she has fallen in love with the one man who, due to his identity as a heterosexual male and awareness of Charlie's past life, can never reciprocate. Charlie experiences a moment of grace, and begs God for a miracle, that George forget everything he knew of Charlie's past identity. The miracle occurs, and George is introduced, as if for the first time, to a woman whom we recognize as Charlie, but who, according to the stage directions: "you would never guess…had ever been anything except what she seems to be: a very pretty girl." The final line of the play is the title of both play and film. It is spoken by the girl, and, in a rather disturbing finale, it is a final bidding of farewell to the masculine identity of the person known as Charlie.—*AJL*

Gorgon, The (1964) [**amnesia; metamorphosis**] Great Britain (Hammer Films). *D:* Terence Fisher. *S:* John Gilling and Anthony Hinds (as John Elder), Story by J. Llewellyn Devine. *Cast:* Peter Cushing (Dr. Namaroff); Christopher Lee (Prof. Meister); Barbara Shelley (Carla); Richard Pasco (Paul); Michael Goodliffe (Prof. Heitz); Patrick Troughton (Kanof).

Hammer attempted on numerous occasions to establish an original horror mythology for the screen. *The Gorgon*, one of their many failed but interesting efforts, incorporates a liberal dose of loss-of-identity components into a plot that walks the tightrope between standard melodrama and Gothic horror.

The first half of the film focuses on the strange events taking place in Vandorf, a small European village, in the early 1910s. Over a period of years, countless people have been found dead, their bodies petrified to solid stone. Rumors persist that the spirit of Magera, one of the legendary Gorgon sisters, has returned to take on human form. Despite the bizarre condition of the victims, resident physician Dr. Namaroff has managed to convince local authorities that the deaths are no cause for alarm. The rash of murders and the general atmosphere of superstition conspire to keep the populace in a state of tight-lipped fear, unwilling to face the question—who or what is the Gorgon?

Prof. Meister (Christopher Lee) confronts Dr. Namaroff (Peter Cushing) as the Gorgon makes her appearance in *The Gorgon*.

As the suspects dwindle in number, the finger of suspicion points to Carla Hoffman, Namaroff's trusted nurse. An amnesia victim who was entrusted to the doctor's care years before, Carla was apparently "cured" but still suffers from occasional blackouts. "What happens during those times?" she asks Namaroff, her eyes suggesting that she knows the worst to be true. No explanation is ever given for the root cause of Carla's affliction. Whether an act of God or a simple twist of fate, the implication is made that spirits from beyond could compromise our identity anywhere and at any time.

Like many loss-of-identity films, *The Gorgon* ends on a decidedly downbeat note. Most of the principals are dead, love lies vanquished, and evil has been battled to an uneasy standoff. Perhaps the only real lesson to take from the film is the realization that Namaroff's well-intended acts of deception contributed greatly to the tragedy. Only by being honest with ourselves can we hope to save ourselves from a life of illusion—which (the film implies) is the greatest loss of identity of all.—*SGT*

Gothika (2003) [**madness; possession**] Dark Castle Entertainment (Warner Bros.). *D:* Matthieu Kassovitz, Thom Oliphant (added scenes). *S:* Sebastian Guttierez. *Cast:* Halle Berry (Dr. Miranda Grey); Robert Downey, Jr. (Pete Graham); Charles S. Dutton (Dr. Douglas Grey); Penelope Cruz (Chloe).

Dr. Miranda Grey works with her husband Douglas in an isolated women's penitentiary/asylum. Her daily routine consists of counseling and treating those who have been determined to be criminally insane—until one fateful evening in which she begins her usual drive home during a violent thunderstorm. The next thing Dr. Grey knows, she's an inmate in her own workplace—and she stands accused of axing her husband to death.

As a mystery thriller, *Gothika* would seem to have little to do with the theme of loss of identity—wouldn't this setup simply qualify as a loss of memory? And meanwhile, though Miranda desperately seeks an alternate solution for the crime, it becomes quite clear that she did, indeed, wield the axe that dismembered Douglas. However, the supernatural gets involved in the story as well, raising a different question. Did Miranda kill Douglas in the throes of temporary insanity when she learned of an unspeakable crime of his own? Or was she actually possessed by a vengeful spirit (and thus truly not herself) when she did the deed?

The ghostly apparitions seen throughout the film (not to mention the "I see dead people" epilogue)

would seem to favor the latter explanation, but narrative coherency isn't exactly *Gothika*'s strong point (performances and production design carry the show in this case). Loss of identity is unquestionably addressed (the asylum setting alone puts the film in contention for coverage here), but in this film, it's just as easily dismissed.
—SMD

Grip of the Strangler. See **Haunted Strangler, The** (1958).

Groundhog Day (1993) [**altered reality**] (Columbia). *D:* Harold Ramis. *S:* Harold Ramis and Danny Rubin, Story by Danny Rubin. *Cast:* Bill Murray (Phil Connors); Andie MacDowell (Rita); Chris Elliott (Larry); Stephen Tobolowsky (Ned Ryerson); Brian Doyle-Murray (Buster Green); Marita Geraghty (Nancy Taylor).

Groundhog Day is the odd movie in which loss of identity signals redemption, not damnation. In it, weatherman Phil Connors must relive the same day—Groundhog Day, in Punxatawny, PA—over and over and over again, until he finally gets it right.

But he has one problem, a big problem. So long as he—the cynical, manipulative, egotistical, selfish scumbag who wants to be *anywhere else*—remains, Phil has no chance of ever getting it right. In order to move forward, he can't simply change his behavior. The entire DNA of his identity must be re-written, and this proves no easy task.

Initially, it is not identity that Phil loses, but the movement of time. He is kicked loose from linear time—stuck in a timeloop—and stuck, repetitive day after repetitive day, in his hellish identity. After some initial panic, Phil settles in to the repetition, even relishing it, because it lets him behave as wildly as he wishes, with no consequences. There never is a morning after. He wakes up again and again, on the same morning he woke up on the day before, with no social record of his actions from any day before. He can drive recklessly, rob armored cars, go to jail, sleep with an endless string of women...and nobody besides Phil himself will ever know. He can literally live like there's no tomorrow because, in Phil's timeloop, there never *is* any tomorrow.

Though the film gives no clear sense of just how long Phil is stuck in this single day, screenwriter Danny Rubin originally conceived of Phil reliving February 2 for thousands of years—a not unreasonable estimate. So let's say, for arguments' sake, that Phil's reckless period lasts, oh, 18,262 February 2nds (50 years). Eventually, Phil grows tired of reckless living, and moves on...to selfish manipulation of Rita, his buoyant producer and true love interest.

Since Phil apparently has an eternity of opportunity to perfect his knowledge of Rita, he uses each Groundhog Day to learn more about her, with the purpose of creating the "perfect line" so that she will sleep with him. He learns her favorite drink, her favorite toast, her favorite poetry. Heck, he even learns French! But his too-perfect knowledge always hits a snag, and he ultimately ends up with a slap in the face. Unable to manipulate Rita into sleeping with him, Phil despairs and starts killing himself (and even the groundhog) in the effort to kill the endless repetitions of Groundhog Days.

Phil has gone as far as the identity he came to Punxatawny with can take him. All it has done is lead him to despair and land him in the morgue—dozens and dozens of times. Ironically, this despair signals the beginning of his redemption. At first, he tries to kill his identity by killing his body. But, as that strategy fails, he starts learning to live where he is and to develop interest in (and ultimately great affection for) the "hicks" of Punxatawny. And a new identity begins, haltingly, to emerge.

Studio publicity poster for *Groundhog Day* featuring Bill Murray and Andie MacDowell

Sure, for a time he's still trying to escape. But as he lets go of his desire to manipulate Rita, and begins to interest himself in people outside himself, he becomes a positive force in the community. He studies medicine, becomes an accomplished pianist, saves lives, changes tires, brings people joy. And, finally, he becomes fully content...*in* the endlessly repetitive moment.

Director Harold Ramis has received mail from Buddhists, Jesuits, and Fundamentalists all saying that this film speaks on some level to what they believe. For the Buddhist, it would be about the death of ego. For the Christian, it would be about dying to self in order to be reborn (in God). But no matter what perspective the viewer takes, it is clear that the Phil Connors who comes to Punxatawny to provide Groundhog Day coverage for Pittsburgh news truly does die. The cynic becomes fully engaged with life. The grasper and manipulator lets go of all his expectations. The snide humorist becomes the affirming friend. He has let go of his ego. And he has been reborn...into a world in which Punxatawny is "Beautiful!"

This new Phil does not need to manipulate Rita for her to love him. He simply needs to be himself. And this new Phil does not need to manipulate his way out of Groundhog Day. Groundhog Day simply, finally, releases him.—*CCS*

[*Editor's two cents:* I always had the impression that Phil lived through 365—or one year's worth of February 2nds. Can't point to any internal evidence except for the symmetry of such a situation: the spell "broken" once Groundhog Day "officially" comes around again. ...I know; I know: Why should redemption be symmetrical?]

Handmaid's Tale, The (1990) [**regimentation**] Bioskop Film/Cinetudes Films/Master Partners/Odyssey (Cinecom International). *D:* Volker Schlöndorff. *S*: Harold Pinter, From the Novel *The Handmaid's Tale* by Margaret Atwood. *Cast:* Natasha Richardson (Kate/Offred); Faye Dunaway (Serena Joy); Aidan Quinn (Nick); Elizabeth McGovern (Moira); Victoria Tennant (Aunt Lydia); Robert Duvall (Commander).

A somewhat faithful adaptation of Margaret Atwood's dystopia, *The Handmaid's Tale* depicts the future of what was the U.S. but is now the Republic of Gilead, a eugenics-obsessed theocracy that has shipped off or killed all non-white people and most dissenters (of any race) and has turned women into chattel. In Gilead, women exist in one of three categories: They are either "Wives," "Marthas" (servants), or "Handmaids," a position based on Hagar's in the Bible, where unmarried or otherwise inappropriate but fertile women are brought into well-off couple's houses in order that the husband might get a child off them—they are, quite literally, body servants. It is a truly horrific vision of a future in which religious discourse of dehumanization has taken over society—frightening not just for the absolute repression and erasure of women (in particular) as humans and individuals, but because it's a future that's not so hard to believe, especially in the second four years of the George W. Bush administration.

Kate, who was caught trying to escape Gilead with her husband and daughter, is forced into a new life as a Handmaid, and it is through her story that we're introduced to this new country, whose main purpose seems to be to destroy personal identity and transform its women in particular into objects. The truck that carries Kate and her fellows to the Red Center, the boot camp for future Handmaids, is a former cattle car, on whose side the word "livestock" has been crossed out and replaced with "116." The

In *The Handmaid's Tale*, women are chattel and forced into being either wives, servants, or handmaids, women forced to bear children for wealthy couples.

Red Center itself is a brain-washing camp in which the women are taught to repeat certain key phrases (e.g., "May the Lord Open"), to repent for their past lives, to blame themselves for rape, and to recognize and appreciate that, while in the past, they had "freedom to," they now have "freedom from." That is, in the past they were people with the agency to run risks; in the present they are possessions, sheltered from their own and others' actions. And, although the women whisper their names to one another in the Red Center dormitory at night, these names are not brought into their new lives: Their identifiers are their red cloaks (symbol of their "profession"), their permanently affixed barcode bracelets, which guards, like check-out clerks, scan at each check-point, and their new names as possessions: Kate, for example, becomes "Offred," the Handmaid of a Commander whose first name is Fred.

At the base of the horrors of this society (public hangings of dissidents or "spies," guards with guns, required escorts, restricted travel) and of Kate's situation (forced, ceremonial sex with the Commander, the dislike and suspicion of his wife and the Marthas, the "rights" and life of a slave) is the destruction of humanity and individuality, and the struggle to maintain identity. While men, provided they are of a certain rank, are allowed a degree of personality, all women have been reduced to their functions, and color-coded to match them (red for Handmaids, blue for Wives, brown for Marthas); we see that even the hostile and complicit Commander's Wife was once a television evangelical star with a name, Serena Joy. And Kate, while struggling to find some way out of this life, also deals with the horror of knowing that her daughter has been taken in by another Commander's family, no doubt to be brainwashed into forgetting or reviling her mother and her past. The ultimate taboo that the Commander coerces/bribes Kate into for his titillation is not a perverse sex act but an act even more unnatural in this society: playing Scrabble—and, in doing so, suggesting that Kate is a being of intelligence. Nonetheless, even the Commander believes this to be no more than an arousing pretense; the man Kate is drawn to is Nick, the chauffeur, who seems to view her as a fellow human being, and who reveals himself to be part of the underground.

Although the film's ending—Kate's catalyst for escape being her discovery that she's pregnant by Nick—seems to miss the point, it nevertheless gives us hope for a different future, with Kate, heavily pregnant, in a safe place in the mountains, waiting for the time when she can rescue/reclaim her daughter: "I *will* find her. She *will* remember me," Kate concludes—a hope that seems to embody the potential for all women, for *each* woman in Gilead, to be remembered, reconstructed, returned to her own identity.—*OVA*

Haunted Palace, The (1963) [**possession**] (American International Pictures). *D:* Roger Corman. *S:* Charles Beaumont; additional dialogue by Francis Ford Coppola (uncredited), Based on the Story "The Case of Charles Dexter Ward" by H.P. Lovecraft. *Cast:* Vincent Price (Charles Dexter Ward/Joseph Curwen); Debra Paget (Ann Ward); Leo Gordon (Edgar Weeden/Ezra Weeden); Lon Chaney, Jr. (Simon Orne); Elisha Cook, Jr. (Gideon Smith/Micah Smith).

This film, the fifth in American International's series of Poe/Price/Corman collaborations, takes its title from Poe but little else. It is instead a relatively faithful adaptation of H.P. Lovecraft's "The Case of Charles Dexter Ward." Scripted by Charles Beaumont, *The Haunted Palace* tells a now-familiar tale of a good man, Charles Dexter Ward (Vincent Price), possessed by the spirit of an evil one—his own ancestor, war-

Ann Ward (Debra Paget) comforts Charles Dexter Ward (Vincent Price), who is possessed by his evil ancestor in *The Haunted Palace*.

lock Joseph Curwen (also Price). After being burned at the stake 110 years earlier, the sorcerous Curwen uses his bewitched descendant to seek retribution upon the offspring of his executioners. As so often happens in an American International Pictures thriller, a flaming finale—indeed the same stock footage used by the company over and over again—brings the proceedings to a close. However, this time the film ends on a downbeat note, suggesting that the wicked Curwen has triumphed after all.

Loss of identity is the most disturbing aspect of possession stories, at least if a film has infused its audience with sufficient sympathy for the protagonist. Although not generally classed among Price's better Gothic efforts, *The Haunted Palace* does offer the actor an opportunity to essay a sort of Jekyll/Hyde role, and he does not disappoint; he convincingly conveys the villainy of Curwen and the nobility of Ward, and the transference of personalities is demonstrated subtly, almost tragically. Indeed few other films have captured the Lovecraftian mood of inevitable fatality laced throughout the writer's best stories—but then few other Lovecraft-inspired films benefit from actors of Price's range and dedication. Often criticized (or praised) for playing his horror parts with his tongue firmly in his cheek, here Price takes both Curwen and Ward very seriously.

Overall, *The Haunted Palace* is a minor but engaging exercise in LOI weirdness. Horror fans will note the presence of genre veterans Debra Paget, Lon Chaney, and Elisha Cook in supporting roles. An amusing footnote: According to James Robert Parish and Steven Whitney's *Vincent Price Unmasked* (pp. 117-118), the film performed reasonably well in America but was a smash in Australia, where Lovecraft fans apparently dwell in tremendous numbers.—*JML*

James Rankin (Boris Karloff) unearths the grave of the Haymarket Strangler and goes on a murderous rampage in *The Haunted Strangler*.

***Haunted Strangler, The** (**Grip of the Strangler**)* (1958) [**dual personality**] Great Britain: Amalgamated Productions (MGM). *D:* Robert Day. *S:* Jan Read and John C. Cooper, From an Original Story, "Stranglehold," by Jan Read. *Cast*: Boris Karloff (James Rankin); Anthony Dawson (Supt. Burke); Derek Birch (Hospital Supervisor); Dorothy Gordon (Hannah); Elizabeth Allan (Barbara Rankin); Diane Aubrey (Lily); Tim Turner (Dr. McColl); Jean Kent (Cora); Vera Day (Pearl).

The Jekyll/Hyde duality has proven to be one of the most durable mythologies in loss-of-identity cinema. An interesting variation can be found in 1958's *The Haunted Strangler*, which stars Boris Karloff as a social reformer whose investigation into a decades-old murder case yields much more than he expected.

Boris Karloff essays the role of James Rankin, a novelist who has dedicated his career to improving Britain's outmoded criminal-justice system. His latest quest is an investigation into the mystery of the Haymarket Strangler, a serial killer who murdered five women in a manner akin to Jack the Ripper. The finger of suspicion pointed to John Styles, a one-armed man who was hanged for the crime, but Rankin is convinced the truth lies elsewhere. "If Styles had had an adequate defense, he never would have hanged," asserts Rankin, who believes instead that Dr. Tennet, the attending surgeon at Style's autopsy, was the guilty party. But Tennet's sudden departure and the disappearance of his surgical knife, a possible murder weapon, fail to convince the authorities, and the case remains closed.

Following a hunch, Rankin unearths Styles' grave and finds the missing scalpel. Suddenly, the unexpected occurs—Rankin's body and face contort in a manner similar to the Haymarket Strangler, and he embarks on a murderous rampage. Eventually, it is revealed that Rankin and Tennet are one and the same. Rescued from an asylum years before by a nurse who pitied and fell in love with him, Tennet has been living under an assumed identity, his murderous impulses held in check until the memory of his past life is reawakened.

The film does not provide a detailed explanation of Rankin's disorder. Dr. McColl, Rankin's young assistant, theorizes that his mentor was possessed of a dual personality, and that the knife was needed to make the transformation complete. Early in the story, a minor parallel is drawn between the Haymarket Strangler and Saucy Jack, although little is done with this analogy. There also remains the slight hint that the knife acts as a sort of spiritual talisman. In the final reel, Rankin dies trying to return the surgical knife to its earthly refuge. "Those faces, they haunt me," he says sadly as he struggles to reconcile the puzzle of his conflicting identities.

Karloff has an actor's field day in the role of Rankin, giving a performance that runs the gamut from concerned do-gooder to raving lunatic. It's not the actor's subtlest work, but it is colorful, and it serves the film well. While no classic, *The Haunted Strangler* is a well-crafted and sadly overlooked film that explores how loss of identity can leave a long and formidable shadow over our lives.—*SGT*

Haute tension. See *High Tension.*

High Tension (*Haute tension*) (2003) [**split personality**] France: Alexandre Film (Europa Corp.). *D:* Alexandre Aja. *S:* Alexandre Aja and Grégory Levasseur. *Cast:* Cécile De France (Marie); Maïwenn Le Besco (Alexia); Philippe Nahon (the Killer); Franck Khalfoun (Jimmy); Andrei Finti (Alex's Father); Oana Pellea (Alex's Mother).

Ah, those French. They begin this film (made in 2003 but not released theatrically in the U.S. until 2005) with a Gallic *homage* to the likes of *Halloween* (1978) and *The Texas Chainsaw Massacre* (1974), but they can't leave it there, introducing a loss of identitity that effectively destroys the picture's identity.

It's okay to use a little misdisrection when you're telling the tale of a repressed lesbian who's so disassociated that she has to invent a killer (who—deliberately, it seems to me—the filmmakers style as a Lon Chaney, Jr. look-alike) so she can dispose of her would-be lover's family because they are (in her mind) an impediment to true happiness with the object of her affections, whom she (as the non-existent killer) kidnaps—just so that she (as

Marie (Cécile De France) is the confused killer and frightened victim in *High Tension.*

herself) can somehow rescue her *petite amie* from herself. (I guess the "dream" she relates at the beginning is supposed to be a giveaway, as are her longing looks at her friend and her odd inaction when the killer first strikes, but the movie—in an unfair bit—introduces the killer in a separate scene when the young women are on their way to Alex's parents' farm, so he seems to be external to the pair.)

And then there's that business of the truck the killer drives. It can't be a figment of Marie's imagination, but then where does it come from? At one point the killer in his truck is chasing Marie in a car, so she's apparently vehicularly schizophrenic as well. The killer causes Marie's vehicle to overturn, and she suffers cuts, abrasions, and contusions, all painfully with her when it's revealed that she must never have had this accident because *she* is the killer.

What could have been a straight-forward slasher film is skewed (and screwed) by this illogical loss-of-identity gambit that raises more questions than it has the ability to answer.—*AFA*

Horror Chamber of Dr. Faustus, The. See ***Eyes Without a Face*** (1960).

Horror of Dracula (1958) [**hypnotism; metamorphosis**] Great Britain (Hammer Films). *D:* Terence Fisher. *S:* Jimmy Sangster, From the Novel *Dracula* by Bram Stoker. *Cast:* Christopher Lee (Dracula); Peter Cushing (Van Helsing); Melissa Stribling (Mina); Michael Gough (Arthur Holmwood); Carol Marsh (Lucy); Janina Faye (Tania).

It takes no great exercise of mind to discuss loss of identity in a watershed film like *Horror of Dracula.* Some horror may remain buried in our subconscious, but one

Dracula (Christopher Lee) puts another victim under his spell in *Horror of Dracula.*

needn't dig too deeply in this film before confronting a variety of fears—including those that fall within the scope of this book.

The production team on this film made a conscious decision to streamline the source material while at the same time holding tight to the core conflicts and situations from Stoker's novel. In a nutshell, Dracula clashes head-on with the rigid moral codes and behaviors of what—despite being ostensibly set on the Continent—is a thinly veiled Victorian England. He threatens the male-dominated order of things by striking and subverting that which is held most sacred—"good" women—be they unmarried virgins or dutiful wives.

Dracula demonstrates hypnotic power before ever setting tooth to neck. And once that particular act of penetration occurs, the world turns upside down. Lucy Holmwood is the first to fall victim to Dracula's advances. In life she is a sweet virginal girl, betrothed to the late Jonathan Harker (Dracula's first victim in the film and the reason he descends on the Holmwood family with a vengeful bloodlust). In un-death, however, she is quite different—an amoral parasite who cowers from the cross, attempts to feed on an innocent child, and even makes incestuous advances to her brother.

When Mina Holmwood falls under the same spell, she becomes even more dangerous. She carries on a clandestine affair with her "lover," Dracula, defiling her own house by providing the vampire shelter—not to mention effectively cuckolding her husband. Which brings a thought to mind...

In the case of Mina, I wonder how much of her identity was lost by Dracula's kiss—in fact, I wonder if in actuality she didn't finally embrace her true self. Her husband Arthur is a cold prig. It's rather hard to imagine him ever being much of a player in the bedroom—an assumption made all the more easy to embrace considering the couple are obviously nearing middle-age yet have no children.

And, in the end, I believe it is Arthur Holmwood who, though not a direct recipient of Dracula's powers of will, is nonetheless a victim as well. Once the well-respected, pompous, regally aloof landed gentry filled with self-satisfaction, he is ultimately an impotent, effete cuckold—a point driven home every time we gaze into Mina's eyes, dripping with post-orgasmic satisfaction, courtesy of a living dead man.—*RJT*

Hour of the Wolf (*Vargtimmen*) (1968) [**altered reality; eradication of self**] Sweden: Svensk Filmindustri (Lopert Pictures Corporation). *D:* Ingmar Bergman. *S:* Ingmar Bergman. *Cast:* Max Von Sydow (Johan Borg); Liv Ullman (Alma Borg); Erland Josephson (Baron Von Merken); Ingrid Thulin (Veronica Vogler).

Director Ingmar Bergman's searing, enigmatic *Persona* (1966) stands as the finest cinematic meditation on the search for, meaning of, and destruction of identity. Yet, even after *Persona*, Bergman remained fixated on the idea of LOI, and the theme recurred in his next several films, including *Shame* (1968), *The Rite* (1969), and *The Passion of Anna* (1970). But it resurfaces most prominently in *Hour of the Wolf* (1968), which also happens to be the closest thing Bergman ever made to a horror film (although the director was greatly influenced by German Expressionism and many of his pictures include supernatural elements).

Bergman was never known for creating lighthearted entertainments, but the films he made from 1966 through 1970 are the darkest, most difficult and disorienting of his career. *Hour of the Wolf*, while not as stylistically radical as *Persona*, remains a me-

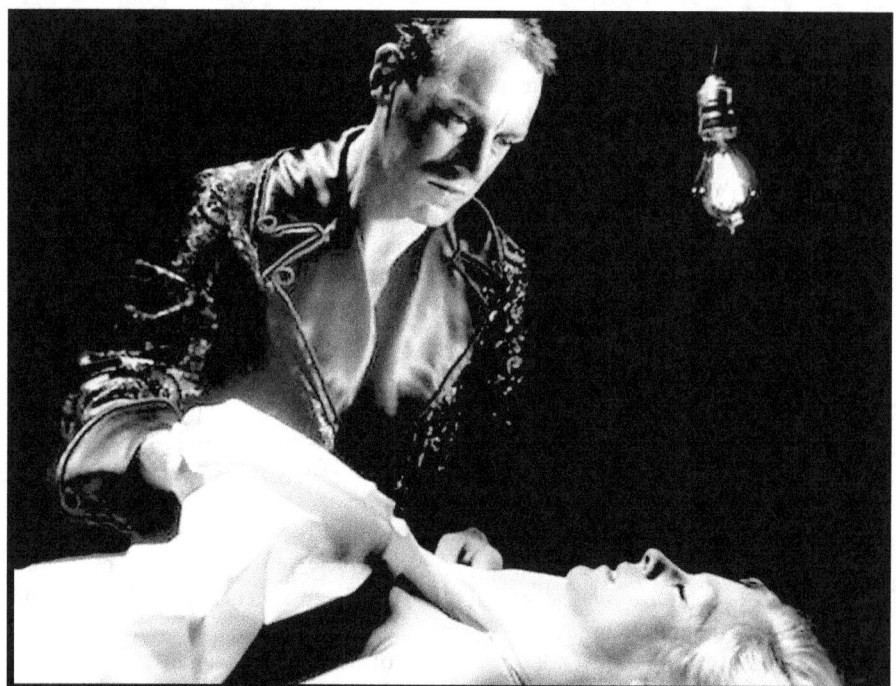

Johan Borg (Max Von Sydow) is enticed by the naked corpse of his old lover Veronica Volger (Ingrid Thulin) in *Hour of the Wolf*.

thodically paced, disturbing picture whose narrative jumps back and forth between the "real" world and the realm of nightmares, leaving it to the audience to sort out which is which and to decide what it all means.

Artist Johan Borg and his young wife Alma move to a secluded island, where Johan spends his days painting and his nights wrestling with irrational (?) fears. Early on, Alma asks if Johan believes that two people begin to resemble one another if they live together long enough. Clearly she believes this, and, as the story progresses, she begins to fear that her love for Johan is drawing her inexorably into her husband's troubled mind; her meek identity is being subsumed by his powerful, disturbed one.

Johan shows Alma sketches of the "monsters" he believes inhabit their island—"spider men," "the bird man," "the cackling woman." Then Alma begins reading her husband's diary, and finds herself plunged into his world, actually seeing the characters her husband sketched. Things get even weirder when the Borgs accept a dinner invitation from the vaguely vampiric Baron Von Merken. In the film's surreal final sequence, set in and around Castle Von Merken, Bergman employs horror iconography—including a *Wolf Man*–like forest of twisted, leafless trees—to arresting and unsettling effect.

What is real and what is delusion? Did Johan really murder a young boy (as we see in a dreamlike flashback sequence)? Are the Von Merkens vampires? Ghosts? Or just really strange neighbors? (In his book, *Images*, Bergman refers to them as "demons.") Do the Von Merkens even exist, or are they figments of Johan's (and Alma's) imagination? The film's conclusion is equally ambiguous. Has Alma entered Johan's madness? And, since Alma is narrating the story herself, how valid is this bizarre narrative? Could it be merely the ravings of a madwoman?

Like *Persona, Hour of the Wolf* refuses to answer the many questions it poses. The pleasure of the film—above and beyond Bergman's haunting imagery, Sven Nykvist's gorgeous black-and-white cinematography, and the superb performances of Von Sydow and especially Ullman—lies in pondering its riddles. Clear-cut answers would spoil the fun.—*MDC*

House of Dark Shadows (1970) [**hypnotism**] (MGM). *D:* Dan Curtis. *S:* Sam Hall and Gordon Russell. *Cast:* Jonathan Frid (Barnabas Collins); Grayson Hall (Dr. Julia Hoffman); John Karlen (Willie Loomis); Kathryn Leigh Scott (Maggie Evans); Roger Davis (Jeff Clark); Nancy Barrett (Carolyn Stoddard); Thayer David (Prof. T. Eliot Stokes); Joan Bennett (Elizabeth Collins Stoddard).

In some ways more like a Hammer horror movie than its television antecedent, *House of Dark Shadows* is the 1970 theatrical version of ABC-TV's daytime serial *Dark Shadows* (1966-1971). The film is a bloodier, more violent retelling of the television show's 1967 storyline, in which Willie Loomis releases the 18th-century vampire Barnabas Collins from his chained coffin. Barnabas preys on the residents of Collinsport, Maine, and mesmerizes Maggie, who bears an uncanny resemblance to his lost 1790s love Josette du Pres.

With its change of venue from the familiar television sets to the Lyndhurst mansion, its emphasis on excessive blood and gore (by 1970 standards), and its portrayal of Barnabas Collins as pure evil instead of tragic and conflicted, *House of Dark Shadows* represented to many *Dark Shadows* fans a loss of identity on the part of the television show, which had spotlighted Gothic mystery and doomed romance over violence and body counts. Director Dan Curtis, obviously influenced by Hammer horror and wanting to top his tamer television show, chose to depict Barnabas according to Curtis' original vision of the character. (*Dark Shadows* fans soon grew accustomed to such shifts in tone and identity as the television show's tragic hero Barnabas became a romantic hero in Dan Ross' *Dark Shadows* novel series, almost a superhero in Gold Key's comic-book series, a teen idol in *16* and *Tiger Beat,* and a ruthless villain in *House of Dark Shadows*.) In the film, Barnabas vampirizes Carolyn, Stokes, and Roger, and he strangles to death several other characters, including Julia, who seeks to cure his vampiric condition.

As in almost all vampire films, the idea of loss of identity manifests itself in the dehumanization of the vampire's victims. Willie becomes Barnabas' Renfield, and even Jeff briefly falls under Barnabas' hypnotic thrall. Carolyn becomes Barnabas' slave before and after her death, and her bite enslaves her fiancé, Todd. In all cases, the victims' identities and wills disintegrate under the vampire's irresistible influence.

However, *House of Dark Shadows* is really about Barnabas' attempt to *regain* his identity more than 170 years after he lost it ("when they put this curse on me," he cryptically explains). When this man of the 1790s is released into the world of 1970, he seeks to reconnect with who he was by introducing himself to his "relatives" (actually, his family's distant descendants), taking up residence in "the Old House" (the now-dilapidated ancestral home where he used to live), and making over Maggie into his long-lost bride-to-be Josette.

Julia aids Barnabas in his quest to regain his identity when she briefly returns him to normalcy. The plan goes awry, and what follows is a *total* loss of identity as Barnabas ages rapidly and displays Dick Smith's old-age makeup design, which would be seen again on Dustin Hoffman in Arthur Penn's *Little Big Man* (1970). Perhaps the only sympathetic aspect of this bloodsucker is his misguided but earnest search for identity and love in the modern world, a quest shared by Boris Karloff's Ardath Bey before him [see entry on *The Mummy* (1932)] and both Jack Palance's and Gary Oldman's Dracula after him. This twice-told unchaining-of-Barnabas storyline would be told yet again in Dan Curtis' 1991 and never-aired 2004 television reprises of *Dark Shadows*. *Night of Dark Shadows* (*q.v.*), his 1971 cinematic follow-up to *House of Dark Shadows*, foregoes vampires for ghosts and a different kind of loss-of-identity tale as Quentin Collins becomes possessed by the spirit of his ancestor.—*JDT*

Howling, The (1981) [**metamorphosis**] (AVCO Embassy Pictures). *D:* Joe Dante. *S:* John Sayles and Terence H. Winkless, Based on the Novel *The Howling* by Gary Brandner. *Cast:* Dee Wallace (Karen White); Christopher Stone (R. William [Bill] Neill); Patrick Macnee (Dr. George Waggner); Belinda Belaski (Terry Fisher); Dennis Dugan (Chris); Kevin McCarthy (Fred Francis); Slim Pickens (Sheriff Sam Newfield); John Carradine (Erle Kenton); Dick Miller (bookstore owner); Robert Picardo (Eddie Quist); Elizabeth Brooks (Marsha Quist).

The Howling—the second greatest werewolf movie after *The Wolf Man* (1941 [*q.v.*])—was the first to depict werewolves as shape-shifters, able to transform into animals at will, full moon or no, and the first to show the animal aspect as an extrapolation of the human personality (an idea elaborated upon and refined in *Wolf* (1994 [*q.v.*]).

Among *The Howling*'s many werewolves, one is in the traditional Larry Talbot mold: Bill Neill, husband of reporter Karen White, is the victim of a lycanthrope's bite and, under the influence of the moon (or maybe it's lust) changes into lupine form (so he can have savage sex with werewolf Marsha Quist—a consummation he, as a human male, seemed to devoutly wish for, though not necessarily like this). He suffers all the torments of the good condemned to be bad—but gets no understanding from his spouse, who's understandably ticked off when she correctly reads the scratch marks on his back. She accuses him of carrying on with Marsha, and he strikes her (the beastliness of his new nature spilling over into his human identity). As Karen prepares to walk out on him, an immediately repentant Bill pleads, "You don't know what it's like," to which she replies, "I don't want to know!"—ironic foreshadowing, considering her

Bill Neill (Christopher Stone), the victim of a werewolf's bite, transforms under the full moon in *The Howling*.

ultimate fate: Later, she's bitten by her werewolf husband, whom she kills (in perhaps an oblique, ironic reference to *House of Frankenstein* [1944], wherein Larry Talbot's lycanthrope is killed by one who "loves enough to understand"), and she learns what it's like, inheriting the curse from him.

Critics have complained about the "Pekingese-like" werewolf that Karen becomes on camera at the end of the film, when she transforms in order to alert her viewing audience (and the world) to the werewolf danger in their midst, just before her producer friend, Chris, puts her down with a silver bullet, but—since the movie postulates that people can retain something of their identity even when they lose themselves to the beast within, it makes sense that her beast should be more puppy dog than wolf.

Indeed, Dr. George Waggner, a "closet lycanthrope" himself, insists that being a werewolf is a "gift" which humanity can use to positive ends, and he's spent his life trying to get others like him to repress the destructive side of their nature and embrace the positive—an effort that ultimately fails when his followers at the Colony (his retreat for werewolves) give over to their dark side (represented most darkly by the Charles Manson–like Eddie Quist, who's a lousy human being to begin with and therefore even worse as a werewolf). The rebels tell Dr. Waggner that suppression of total werewolf identity isn't natural; "We should have stuck with the old ways," says Erle Kenton. "Raising cattle for our feed! Where's the life in that?" Charlie Barton argues, "*Humans* are our cattle," and Erle elaborates: "Humans are our *prey*. You can't tame what's meant to be wild, doc," he adds, as justification for ceasing to try. (Thus, poor Waggner essentially commits suicide—forcing Chris to shoot him and regarding death as a gift when the bullet puts him out of his disillusioned misery.)

Director Joe Dante and scripter John Sayles, who collaborated so successfully on *Piranha* (1978), surpass themselves here, jettisoning the source novel in favor of an excellently crafted, multi-layered story dealing with themes of appearance vs. reality (media vs. life) and, of course, issues of identity among its Altman-sized cast, all of whom are individuated even if (or perhaps because) so many of them are named after directors of werewolf movies, reinforcing their identities even in the loss. Fittingly, George Waggner shares his name with the director of that most seminal werewolf picture, *The Wolf Man*; Bill O'Neill is the namesake of Roy William Neill, who helmed the defining appearance of Larry Talbot (*Frankenstein Meets the Wolf Man* [1943 (*q.v.*)]), suffering and searching for relief from his agony. And, in a double in-joke due to casting, Erle Kenton recalls Erle C. Kenton, auteur of both *House of Frankenstein* and *House of Dracula* (1945), which featured the Wolf Man and also Dracula, who was played by the actor who portrays Erle, John Carradine. (I'll leave you to draw your own conclusions about the significance of characters like sympathetic lycanthropy victim Terry Fisher [Terence Fisher, *Curse of the Werewolf* (1961 [*q.v.*]), extraneous Stu Walker [Stuart Walker, *Werewolf of London* (1935)], annoying television exec Fred Francis [Freddie Francis, *Legend of the Werewolf* (1975)], and the various werewolves in human clothing, Sam Newfield [Sam Newfield/Newfeld, *The Mad Monster* (1942)], Charlie Barton [Charles Barton, *Abbott and Costello Meet Frankenstein* (1948 [*q.v.*]), Jerry Warren [Jerry Warren, *Face of the Screaming Werewolf* (1964)], and Lew Landers [Lew Landers, *Return of the Vampire* (1944)]. I can't do *every*thing.)—*AFA*

Hulk (2003) [**dual personality; metamorphosis**] (Universal). *D:* Ang Lee. *S:* John Turman, Michael France, and James Schamus, story by James Schamus, Based on the Marvel Comic Book Character created by Stan Lee and Jack Kirby. *Cast:* Eric Bana (Bruce Banner); Jennifer Connelly (Betty Ross); Sam Eliott (Ross); Josh Lucas (Talbot); Nick Nolte (Father); Paul Kersey (Young David Banner); Cara Buono (Edith Banner); Todd Tesen (Young Ross).

In 2003, Universal released the big-budget summer-event film *Hulk*, which was supposed to return to the character's comic-book roots. But director Ang Lee, neither a regular reader of the comic book nor viewer of the 1970s television series, instead gave us an entirely new origin for the Hulk and ultimately a disappointing film. Bruce Banner's mad-scientist father experimented with his body chemistry when he was a child. After being exposed to gamma radiation, Bruce now finds himself transformed into a CGI Hulk whenever he becomes angry. The army tries to contain him, and a rival scientist tries to exploit him while his maniac father repeats the process on himself and becomes a twisted version of the comic-book villain the Absorbing Man.

But the audience never really cares about Eric Bana's Bruce Banner the way they cared for Bill Bixby's David Banner. It's not the actor's fault; he's just not given a lot to work with. The film tells us that Bruce always kept his emotions in check and the reason his girlfriend Betty Ross broke up with him at the start of the picture was because Banner was so bland and uncaring. This idea works against the film—the audience has no sympathy for a guy with no emotions. Transforming into the Hulk is the only time Banner actually comes alive. Sure, the loss of identity is there—Banner has no control over the Hulk, and he does not want to become the Hulk for fear of what he will do. (The old line from the television series "Don't make me angry; you wouldn't like me when I'm angry" comes into play once more.) But the movie spends too much time

After being exposed to gamma radiation, Bruce Banner transforms into *The Hulk* whenever he becomes angry.

on the machinations of bad daddy David Banner rather than on actually developing Bruce's character. More sympathy for that character would have allowed for a deeper exploration of the loss-of-identity theme. If he had an identity to lose, we could have sympathized more when he lost it.

I'll take Lou Ferrigno's monster over the CGI Hulk and Bill Bixby over Eric Bana any day—as well as that classic white-eye effect and the "Lonely Man" theme composed by Joseph Harnell. Week after week, the television series just did it better. (See *Incredible Hulk, The* [1977] and *Bride of the Incredible Hulk, The* [1978].)—*JSM*

Hypnotic Eye, The (1960) [**hypnotism**] (Allied Artists Pictures Corporation). *D:* George Blair. *S:* Gitta Woodfield and William Read Woodfield. *Cast:* Jacques Bergerac (Desmond); Allison Hayes (Justine); Marcia Henderson (Marcia Blaine); Merry Anders (Dodie Wilson); Jimmy Lydon (Emergency Doctor).

On the back pages of comic books, when I was a kid, Norman Rockwell was looking for people who liked to draw and Charles Atlas wanted to twist me into a he-man using dynamic tension. Then there were these other advertisements asking "Do you realize the power that hypnosis will give you? With the magic power of hypnosis, you can hypnotize at a glance, make people obey your commands, etc." Another exhorted me to "Develop your hidden hypnotic powers to control the minds and bodies of men and women," offering to provide me with a "Whirling hypno-coin" to do it. Yet another offered the power to "Hypnotize with Your Own TV!" which illustrated the suggestion with a drawing of a sexily built young lady luxuriously stretching her arms in front of her while she begins doing...I'm not sure what. But, if I thought about it for a minute, I'm sure I could have come up with a few suggestions.

The guys who put together the 1960 B-movie *The Hypnotic Eye* have given the idea a lot of thought. And the result is one sleazy, unhealthy little film designed to ap-

peal to our baser nature. This is surprising, considering that the film sprang from the squeaky-clean imaginations of co-writer William Read Woodfield, who would go on to write virtually every one of my favorite episodes of *Voyage to the Bottom of the Sea*, and director George Blair, whose main claim to fame are episodes of the 1950s *Adventures of Superman*.

Basically there's this evil hypnotist who puts volunteers into trances as part of his nightclub act. For resistant subjects, he's got this electrical doohickey called "the Hypnotic Eye," and, when he flashes it at you, even the most unwilling subject immediately falls into a hypnotic trance. If the volunteer is really pretty, he'll whisper hypnotic suggestions into her ear when no one's looking and make her go out on dates with him and stuff. Back in high school, I definitely could have used that.

So that's the basic plot, which obviously exploits our fear of loss of volition. But it's got this one scene that takes its exploration of the loss of identity up into the stratosphere. You see, there's this spunky girl who is trying to link the hypnotist to a series of mutilations of beautiful women. So at his show she volunteers to be one of his subjects. But she doesn't really let herself get hypnotized, see? And when he hypnotically suggests she come back to his dressing room after the show, she willingly does so, with her detective boyfriend tagging along outside.

Okay, that's the set-up. Now here's the big scene. The hypnotist is changing in the bathroom. While he dresses, he talks to the spunky girl in the other room, giving her hypnotic instructions to deepen her trance. Only, the girl's not hypnotized, remember? She's not helpless at all. In fact, while he's talking away, she's rifling through his things looking for evidence to use against him in a court of law.

And that's when it happens. The hypnotist is talking away hypnotically, and she is searching frantically, and she opens this little container. Only it's not full of evidence, it's full of *the Hypnotic Eye*!

The girl can feel its mesmerizing power, and she starts to look away before it can hypnotize her. Only, she can't quite look away. Against her will, her eyes move back toward the Eye. And as the hypnotist's soothing voice continues talking, she cannot help falling under his spell. There is a primal power in this scene that movies with a dozen times its budget fail to match. I can remember watching, with my breath coming in shallow gasps, fascinated as I witnessed the woman's slow surrender of her identity. Or maybe it's more than that. Maybe—just maybe—she *wants* to look into the Hypnotic Eye. Maybe underneath it all she wants to lose control over her actions—to lose her identity and become his helpless puppet.

I can remember no other film that makes loss of identity so sexy.—*AJL*

Identity (2003) [**split personality**] (Columbia). *D:* James Mangold. *S:* Michael Cooney. Cast: John Cusack (Ed); Ray Liotta (Rhodes); Amanda Peet (Paris); John Hawkes (Larry); Alfred Molina (Dr. Malick); Clea DuVall (Ginny); John C. McGinley (George York); William Lee Scott (Lou); Jake Busey (Robert Maine); Pruitt Taylor Vince (Malcolm Rivers); Rebecca De Mornay (Caroline Suzanne).

"As I was going up the stair, / I met a man who wasn't there. / He wasn't there again today; / I wish, I wish he'd go away."

This stark description of loss of identity was penned in 1899 by poet Hughes Mearns, and is the centerpiece of the film *Identity*. In the film, though, the poem was "made up" in childhood by Malcolm Rivers—a dissociative mass murderer whose prostitute mother so neglected and abandoned him that he "made up" 10 alternate personalities in order to cope with life. One of these personalities committed six murders on Malcolm's birthday four years ago.

The movie begins as misfiled evidence demonstrating Malcolm's insanity surfaces and compels a late-night hearing, putting the killer in transit on the eve of his execution. Meanwhile 10 strangers, compelled by car accidents and flooding, converge on a motel in the middle of the Nevada desert. In one car, an officer transports a felon convicted of multiple homicides. But the convict escapes; people start dying violently; and we are led to ask if the escaped convict is Malcolm, and if he has begun a new killing spree.

Not quite. For starters, the shackled convict is the third person to die. The cartoonish mayhem fits in the dreamworld inhabited by supernatural slashers and over-the-top theme killers, not in the realistic setting established in the film's introduction. And, in a page taken straight out of theme-killer movies, the characters discover that they possess odd thematic connections. They all are named after places (Rhodes, York, Dakota, Paris), and they all were born on May 10—Malcolm's birthday. In fact, as we learn late in the film, these characters are Malcolm's divergent personalities, individual pieces of his fractured identity, brought together in a psychiatrically induced fever-dream. Malcolm himself remains safely in custody.

The motel scenario is the psychiatrist's attempt to introduce Malcolm's personalities to each other, in hopes of killing off the peripheral personalities, leaving one emergent personality, and eliminating the personality who committed the murders in 1998. The strategy apparently works, with the judge granting Malcolm clemency. But there is one

problem. While the psychiatrist's motel scenario apparently kills off the characters sequentially in the reverse order from which they emerged (as indicated by the room keys the killer leaves on the bodies), one personality is actually left unaccounted for—the most important one.

So who are these personalities? Well, as we would expect, they consist largely of the sorts of people Malcolm would have come across, or fantasized about, as a boy growing up in cheap motels. And they all live in a world where reality is capricious, harsh, and frequently turned upside down. In Malcolm's dissociative world, people are never what they seem. He keeps meeting—or being—the "man who wasn't there."

His "motel proprietor" (personality #4) is actually a drifter who found the real proprietor face down in his food. His "cop" (#3) is one of two convicts who killed the driver of their transport. His "limo driver" (#2) is a cop on medical leave after a jumper jumped. His newlyweds (#9 & #5) married because the girl lied about being pregnant. His prostitute (#1) is seeking a second chance by purchasing orchard land in Florida. And even his middle-aged couple with a young boy (#7, #6) has been married only a year. The woman's former husband, like Malcolm's mother's johns, simply left.

At the motel, we are led to believe that the prostitute—Malcolm's idealized version of his mother—is the only survivor. But in reality, she is not the first personality who emerged from Malcolm, and she is not the only personality remaining. There is one personality who faked his death at the motel, committed or engineered all the other killings, and who is quite clearly the original personality—possibly even prior to Malcolm Rivers' fully dissociative state: the externally placid and quiet young boy, filled with rage and malice. This "boy" committed the murders in 1998, and dreamed of murder and mayhem in the long hours Malcolm spent abandoned and neglected during childhood. This is a boy of such terrifying hate that Malcolm sought refuge from him by living life in the other 10 personalities...until the boy's personality emerged with bloody slaughter on May 10, 1998.

Yes, the psychiatrist's treatment has worked in that it has gotten down to the core personalities of Malcolm's identity—the boy and the prostitute. But the killer remains. The boy finds his idealized prostitute, on her land, digging in the rich Florida soil. But in his world of malice and rage, "Whores don't get a second chance"—and apparently, in his real-world parallel, neither do psychiatrists. In the end, only the malevolent child—empowered by murder—remains. And even he is not truly "there."—*CCS*

I Married a Monster from Outer Space (1958) [**alien possession; doppelganger**] (Paramount). *D:* Gene Fowler, Jr. *S:* Louis Vittes. *Cast:* Gloria Talbot (Marge Bradley Farrell); Tom Tryon (Bill Farrell); Alan Dexter (Sam Benson); Robert Ivers (Harry Phillips); Chuck Wassill (Ted); Valerie Allen (hooker); Peter Baldwin (Officer Frank Swanson); Ty Hardin [as Ty Hungerford] (Mac Brody).

An intelligent, polished gem among so much rough-cut sci-fi dross of the 1950s, the sorely underrated *I Married a Monster from Outer Space* offers a tight, multi-layered script; involving direction; believable performances (particularly from Gloria Talbot as the beleaguered bride); uniquely impressive monsters; and one of the most terrifying loss-of-identity scenarios presented onscreen.

The story is every bride's nightmare—discovering that the man she just married is not really the man he pretended to be. Real-life horror arises when a wife finds that her husband has changed and is no longer the man she fell in love with, that she's now sleeping with a stranger. *I Married a Monster* takes this matrimonial anxiety far beyond real life and makes the husband not only an emotional stranger but an alien invader from another planet, who has stolen a man's identity (and place in the marriage bed) in an attempt to replenish his dying race!

Director Gene Fowler, Jr. makes the most of his low ($125,000) budget, frequently shooting on location (as well as on credible studio sets), and fully exploiting the truly unique and horrifying alien creatures. Former Universal effects ace John P. Fulton (*The Invisible Man* [1933 (*q.v.*)]) provides some impressive special photographic effects, particularly in his inventive use of a dense black cloud created by the aliens that billows out to envelop a person and then retreats, leaving only empty space where the victim

Marge Farrell's (Gloria Talbot) husband Bill (Tom Tryon) really was out of this world in *I Married a Monster From Outer Space*.

once stood. This serves as a powerful visualization of loss of identity, as the sinister cloud wipes away its victim's presence, leaving a completely alien being in its stead to do what it will while the original identity is literally hung up in a spaceship closet (the aliens keep their impersonated victims "on ice" by attaching them to machines that hold them dangling out of the way).

Fowler avoids the static, stagnant look of many of his contemporaries' efforts by utilizing mobile camerawork and frequent changes in set-ups. He fills his film with frightening touches, such as when the alien, now posing as Talbot's husband, gazes out at the stormy sky on their wedding night. A flash of lightning suddenly reveals his true countenance, and we catch a shuddery glimpse of the hideous otherworldly face under its human guise.

It's a shame editor-turned-director Fowler helmed as few films as he did (only seven in the late 1950s, including one other superior genre effort, 1957's *I Was a Teenage Werewolf* [q.v.], for which he proved himself adept at wringing every bit of nuance and mood from the few dollars available), before returning to the cutting room for such pictures as *It's a Mad Mad Mad Mad World* (1963), *Hang 'Em High* (1968), and *Caveman* (1981).

I Married's low budget shows through at times (particularly via some not-fooling-anyone day-for-night photography), but the occasional minor setback doesn't seriously detract from the fascinating story and exciting visuals. Given its superior acting, effects, photography, and direction—not to mention its terrifying "identity theft" scenario—*I Married a Monster from Outer Space* is a match made in 1950s sci-fi heaven.—BMS

Impostor (2002) **[doppelganger]** (Dimension Films, Marty Katz Productions, Mojo Films, P.K. Pictures). *D:* Gary Fleder. *S:* Norman S. Hall and Ray Trampe, Based on the Story "Imposter" by Philip K. Dick. *Cast:* Gary Sinese (Spencer Olham); Madeline Stowe (Maya); Vincent D'Onofrio (Hathaway); Tony Shalhoub (Nelson Gittes); Mekhi Phifer (Cale); Lindsay Crouse (the Chancellor).

A world constantly at war with an incomprehensible enemy. Democratic principles relinquished in the expedient name of security. A leader mouthing patriotic platitudes on television. Similar slogans festooned across the cityscape. Citizens monitored and scanned by an aggressive counter-terrorism force. Others subsisting in squalor, due to war-effort cuts in social services.

Sounds like Orwell's *1984*—or George W. Bush's America—but it's a cinematic dystopia sprung from the fertile mind of Philip K. Dick, a veritable font of some of the most intriguing science fiction concepts ever imagined. Dick's prose style was flatter than the Earth before Columbus, but that aspect of his writing has been rounded by the various scenarists who've fashioned screenplays out of Dick's work—*Blade Runner* (1982 [q.v.]), *Total Recall* (1990 [q.v.]), *Minority Report* (2002 [q.v.]), *A Scanner Darkly* (2006). Like those pictures, *Impostor* deals with issues of identity but, unlike them, doesn't enjoy the same high profile or regard. (Leonard Maltin reports *Impostor* was shelved for a year before being dumped into release.) Perhaps *Impostor*'s obscurity stems from the fact that it uses its running time to postulate a loss of identity only to end up *confirming* identity.

You are Spencer Olham, weapons expert in Earth's never-ending war against the Centauri. But you're beginning to have doubts about the venture. Still, life is good. You and your lovely wife, Maya (a compassionate doctor in a city hospital that cares for wounded war vets) have just returned from a weekend getaway and are looking forward to tonight's soirée with the Chancellor (known as "Big Sister" to some). Suddenly, you're seized by the ESA (Earth Security Authority) and harshly interrogated by agent Hathaway, who assures you that you are not *you* but a Centauri spy who killed the real Olham and is now cleverly disguised as you, right down to your DNA and most private memories. You're part of a plot to blow up the Chancellor with a sort-of time bomb rigged in your alien simulacrum heart.

How can you possibly convince this bastard that you are *you*—especially when he claims that x-rays (conveniently) can't detect the bomb, which only forms before triggering, that—as with the old "proof" by drowning that a woman *wasn't* a witch—the only way to reveal the truth is to drill into your chest cavity and extract the armed heart?

If you're Spencer Olham, you take advantage of an escape opportunity and struggle back to your wife's hospital for a full-body CAT scan. If it matches Olham's most recent scan, then you're still the same, right?

So Spencer Olham begins his desperate odyssey, and along the way, shows himself to be a good man but no superhero when it comes to street fighting and survival against the Gestapo trailing him—yet the movie leaves his identity in doubt, since that crucial CAT scan (which seems to be signaling something funny right around his aorta) is interrupted by his pursuers. The film's climax throws a curve—a double curve, a triple curve: Olham meets his wife at their hideaway spot; the ESA arrives; and Maya—who's only shown herself to be a doctor more concerned for her patients than the war—turns out to be an impostor. (We see her real body—throat slit—and then the ESA shoots her in the back.). And *then* it turns out that the real Spencer also had *his* throat slit and our Spencer is just what Hathaway said he was. Spencer's heart breaks (from the loss of his wife, from the realization?) and explodes, taking Hathaway, various ESA agents, and a

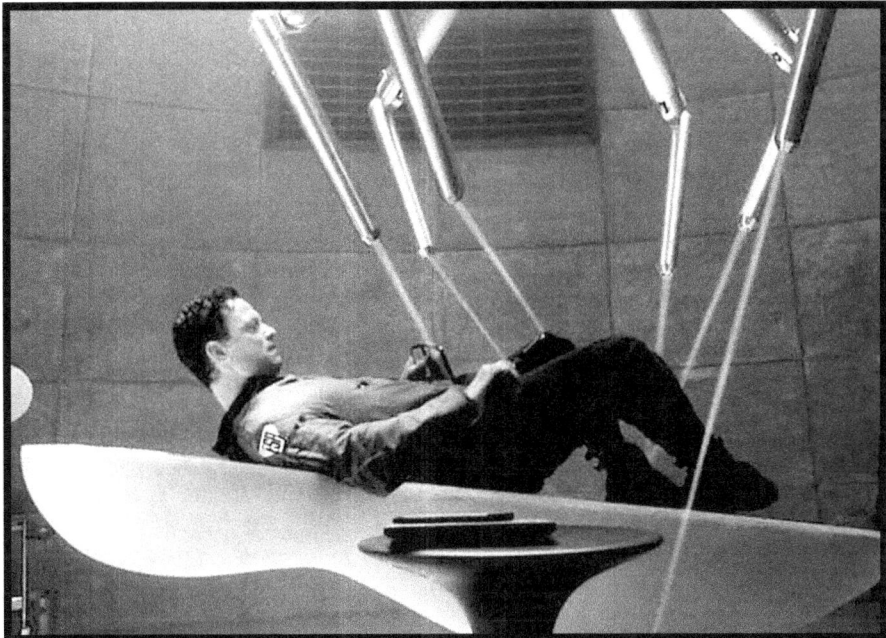

Spencer Olham (Gary Sinese) find himself suspected of being an imposter and must escape and prove he is human in *Impostor*.

large chunk of land with him. But, hey, the Chancellor's safe, and Cale, the proletarian who accompanied Olham on his journey to the hospital, has gotten the drugs he needs to cure his sick wife and many of the lower-class denizens of the inner-city underworld.

Impostor is a non-loss-of-identity loss-of-identity movie. From the beginning, Olham and his wife are already not themselves—but they don't know that. They make love and act for all the world like a human couple. And, if the pair retains all the thoughts and memories and feelings and moral sense of Spencer and Maya *before* they were replaced, what's the difference?

In an attempt to be oh-so-clever, the film is ultimately silly. (It is just following the parameters of the short story here, in which Olham, alone, is indeed the alien-weapon-in-human-clothing—but we can get away with that sort of twist ending in a short-story or *Twilight Zone* episode, whereas we can't in a novel or a feature-length movie.) A better scenario would be for Olham to have been somehow implanted with this device without his knowledge and then have to get it removed before (a) it exploded and/or (b) the ESA got him. But then we wouldn't be talking about the movie as LOI (and didn't they already do something like that in *The Chairman* [1969], whose Chinese Communists put a bomb in Gregory Peck's brain?).

Impostor is a disturbing film, especially in light of events that have occurred since it was made (Abu Ghraib, the sanctioning of torture, and the suspension of *habeus corpus* in the name of the war on terror), because it says that the repressive government is right—right to be repressive, right to charge and hold (and kill) a man on the most preposterous of grounds because—see?—they *may* turn out to be true. (By accident, it *could* suggest that wars are futile and pointless; when we're fighting our foes, we're actually fighting ourselves. The "fake" Maya and Spencer enjoy lovemaking and aid their fellows, just like human beings. In the immortal words of Walt Kelly's Pogo, "We have met the enemy, and he is us." But this interpretation gives *Impostor* too much credit.)—*AFA*

Incredible Hulk, The (1977) [**dual personality; metamorphosis**] (Universal). *D:* Kenneth Johnson. *S:* Kenneth Johnson; "The Incredible Hulk is a character from the Marvel Comics Group." *Cast:* Bill Bixby (David Banner); Susan Sullivan (Elaina Marks); Jack Colvin (Jack McGee); Lou Ferrigno (The Hulk); Susan Batson (Mrs. Maier); Mario Gello (Mr. Bram); Eric Server (Policeman); Charles Siebert (Ben).

Marvel Comics' Incredible Hulk was inspired by the Frankenstein Monster and Dr. Jekyll and Mr. Hyde. After being caught in a gamma-bomb explosion, frail scientist Bruce Banner finds himself transforming into a powerful green giant (the Hulk) whenever he becomes upset or angry. Banner has no memory of what the Hulk does, while the Hulk denies that Banner is a part of him—in fact he wants to destroy Banner. The situation is a true loss of identity. After many incarnations of the Hulk (including a sly gray one, a Hulk with Banner's brain, etc), writer Peter David revealed that Banner suffered from multiple personalities and the various Hulks were facets of his own fractured self.

The made-for-television, two-hour pilot film *The Incredible Hulk* was released as a feature in Europe (where it out-grossed *Apocalypse Now* [1979]). In the telepic, Dr. David Banner receives an overdose of gamma radiation and now, whenever he gets angry, transforms into a snarling creature dubbed the Hulk by newspaperman Jack

McGee. But here and in the series that followed, producers stressed that the Hulk was a part of Banner. The opening quote "Within each of us there dwells a mighty raging fury" establishes the idea. Later, when Banner confides to his colleague, Dr. Elaina Marks, that he is afraid the Hulk will kill someone, she assures him that the creature won't kill because David Banner does not kill. The Hulk represents the childlike primitive inside us all. A creature of instinct, he is nevertheless partly human. The loss-of-identity theme is still there, though. The Hulk cannot communicate. Banner has no control over what the Hulk does, and Banner has no memory of the monster's actions. This loss of identity—this physical rebellion of the body symbolized by ripping clothes and white eyes—drives Banner crazy.

Lou Ferrigno as the Hulk on the television show *The Incredible Hulk*, which featured Bill Bixby as David Banner.

The magic of the film and the series was in the casting of Bill Bixby as Banner. A reliable television actor, Bixby plays Banner as a man suffering from a disease that he is desperate to cure. Banner is the nice guy who lives next door and wouldn't harm a fly yet finds himself losing control again and again and releasing the beast within. As a result, the audience feels sympathy for Banner because of his loss of identity (though guiltily we tune in week after week to see him get beat up). The film tugs at the viewer's heartstrings during its last scene. Before dying, Elaina confesses her love for Banner to the Hulk, but Banner never knows it because he does not remember events that occur while he is the Hulk. Later, by her grave, he says that he loved Elaina and thinks she loved him, even though she never said it. Sigh—*The Incredible Hulk* always was a sad show.

Banner truly loses his identity by the end of the telepic. Believed to have been killed by the Hulk during a laboratory fire, Banner must now travel the country under various pseudonyms (like Dr. Richard Kimble in *The Fugitive*), never revealing his true identity or occupation. (See *Bride of the Incredible Hulk, The* [1978], and compare *Hulk* [2003].)—*JSM*

Carey (Grant Williams) copes with his metamorphosis in *The Incredible Shrinking Man*.

Incredible Shrinking Man, The (1957) [**metamorphosis**] (Universal). *D:* Jack Arnold. *S:* Richard Matheson (and Richard Alan Simmons, uncredited), From Matheson's Novel *The Shrinking Man*. *Cast:* Grant Williams (Scott Carey); Randy Stuart (Louise Carey); April Kent (Clarice); Paul Langton (Charles Carey); William Schallert (Dr. Arthur Bramson); Billy Curtis (Midget).

One of the best-known—and just plain best—science fiction films of the 1950s, *The Incredible Shrinking Man* ranks as perhaps the finest work for both its director, Jack Arnold (*Creature from the Black Lagoon* [1953], *It Came from Outer Space* [1953 (*q.v.*)]) and its screenwriter, the prolific Richard Matheson (adapting his own novel). It's certainly the unrivaled pinnacle of star Grant Williams' career. The film chronicles the adventures of Scott Carey, who, after exposure to a mysterious radioactive cloud, begins to shrink, his size diminishing throughout the film. First, Carey becomes emotionally estranged from his wife and has an affair with a circus midget. Then he grows smaller still, and faces deadly perils posed by his pet cat and, later, by an ordinary spider (which now dwarfs him). The film touches on the loss-of-identity theme obliquely, by dramatizing the extent to which our physical form defines our inner selves, as so often happens in werewolf, cat-people, or Jekyll-and-Hyde films, wherein loss of self accompanies bodily transformation.

Although Carey remains in complete command of his mental faculties throughout, he grows bitter and despondent, referring to himself as "the shrinking freak" and questioning his own humanity. In the film's famous final scene, he finally comes to emotional terms with his condition. "To God, there is no zero. I still exist!" he exclaims, even as he shrinks to subatomic size.—*MDC*

Incubo sulla citta contaminate. See ***Nightmare City*** (1983).

Innocents, The (1961) [**possession**] Great Britain (20th Century Fox). *D:* Jack Clayton. *S:* William Archibald and Truman Capote, Based on the Story "The Turn of the Screw" by Henry James. *Cast:* Deborah Kerr (Miss Jessel); Michael Redgrave (the Uncle); Pamela Franklin (Flora); Martin Stephens (Miles).

For all the horrors, both implicit and explicit in *The Innocents*, it should,nonetheless be regarded as that most happy of occasions in the history of cinema—namely, when the stars line up in such a way that every element of a film perfectly complements the other. Jack Clayton, in his dual roles of director and producer, assembled a marvelous team and cast to interpret Henry James' classic tale, most notably the brilliant cinematographer Freddie Francis. The screenplay by Archibald and Capote is so very rich that one could expound on many aspects of it at lengths far exceeding the space and scope of this book.

The plot is very simple. A governess travels to a remote country estate to care for two young orphans—a brother and sister named Miles and Flora. During her stay, she comes to realize that not only is the house haunted but also that the children are becoming possessed by the spirits of their deceased former governess and her lover.

For both the source material and the film, one could make a case that the supernatural elements in each are in fact figments of a repressed spinster's mind. For our purposes we shall stick to the film—which seems to most clearly favor a supernatural explanation. What's more, neither approach changes the basic situation: Both of these children have had their identities robbed—or at the very least corrupted—by the actions of the deceased characters. That corruption was occurring long before the pair died.

Deborah Kerr, Pamela Franklin and Martin Stephens in *The Innocents*

As the film unfolds and we see the children behaving in increasingly inappropriate, shocking, and even profane fashion, the viewer can't help but think of the similar destinies of so many unfortunate youngsters, now that the issue of child abuse has become so visible and so discussed in our culture. *The Innocents* may remain tasteful—but it does not shrink from some very unpleasant situations. For example, young master Miles, a charming boy of perhaps nine, kisses his governess on the lips, in a very sensual fashion. It is a most disturbing moment—this little boy behaving like a suave seducer. His younger sister, Flora, when forced to confront the ghost of the governess, is reduced to a paroxysm of shrieking rage. While we do not hear it, we are told quite plainly that her fury has led to an outburst of obscenities no child of that time should have been capable of repeating.

While the film never ventures beyond the bounds of good taste, it still delivers a shock to the system. These two "innocents," Miles and Flora, are innocent no more. They are tools—perhaps not complicit, but tools nonetheless—and are being led down a path toward depravity at best, incest and madness at worst. As frightening as the scenes with the ghosts are—and they do indeed deliver some of the most chilling imagery imaginable—it is the invisible battle for the souls of the children that will haunt the viewer long after the film has ended. That and the recognition of battles of a similar nature going on around the world, with nary a ghost in sight.—*RJT*

Invaders from Mars (1953) [**hive mind; alien possession; mind control**] (United Artists) *D:* William Cameron Menzies. *S:* Richard Blake. *Cast:* Helena Carter (Dr. Blake); Arthur Franz (Dr. Kelston); Jimmy Hunt (David); Leif Erickson (George); Hillary Brooke (Mary); Morris Ankrum (Colonel Fielding).

William Cameron Menzies' production design and superb visual direction transform the low-budget *Invaders from Mars* into a perennial baby-boomer favorite, a movie that touches the little boy in all males. The curly-haired Jimmy Hunt is the perfect choice to play the iconic 1950s child, who has two loving parents raising him and comforting him when he wakes up abruptly in the middle of the night, a victim of childhood nightmares. However, young David's nightmares become reality—that is, until the very last minute of the movie. In this 78-minute production, David finds that his strong but nurturing father becomes an alien zombie who slaps the inquisitive child with little provocation; his mother becomes suspicious and slinky-eyed, and even the police chief is monotone and cold-hearted.

In other words, David's horror involves loss of identity. Not necessarily his own identity, but the identity of his idyllic world populated by people who love him. After Jimmy awakes to find a flying saucer embed itself under the sand pit in his back yard, he can only observe as trusted people lure other innocents to the pit and then watch as they are buried beneath the swirling sand. David sees that his father now has a bloody sensor in the back of his head. Even the little girl next door, carrying flowers no less, adopts an expressionless attitude, her eyes glazed over, as she sets her home on fire. People whom David knew intimately now speak without emotion and act out of character, always suspicious of David. The boy does not change; what changes is his entire universe, both his formerly safe environment and its inhabitants.

Director/production designer Menzies populates his bare-bone sets with obviously unrealistic flourishes. In the police station, telephones are either lacking wires or the wires seem to dangle and lead nowhere. The same with light fixtures that sit on a huge

empty desk. In Jimmy's distorted worldview even the reality of the setting is askew, reflecting the child's disconnection with his former perfect world. Such bare-bones sets continue with the design of service stations and chemistry labs, all featuring high ceilings and minimal window dressing.

David's only friends become scientist Dr. Kelston and Kelston's girlfriend, Dr. Pat Blake, the two people of science (David's love and religion) who are unwavering in their friendship and dedication to help him—though, when he meets Dr. Blake, David does ask first to look at her nape, to make sure he can trust her. In David's world, paranoia runs rampant.

By *Invader from Mars*' thrill-packed climax, David sees his parents transformed into alien espionage agents working against our government, and alien mutants attempt to drill into the back of Dr. Blake's head to make her one of them. David, underground in the alien hive, grimaces in terror as the grand intelligence of Mars, a grotesque head with tentacles, gives orders about the conquest of Earth while monstrous giant mutants carry it around in a glass globe. Such a nightmare come to life is the ultimate fear of loss of identity because, just as in a dream, reality is shattered, and one's entire sense of self is turned topsy-turvy.

Perhaps the film's defining sequence is when David goes to the police station and tells the chief of police that his father has changed, that "they" have taken over his brain. David is held in custody, in a jail cell, while the chief calls the boy's parents, against the boy's wishes. In the meantime, Dr. Blake comes to the station to find the distraught boy obviously shaken and very much afraid. When the dead-eyed parents arrive to take David home, Dr. Blake intervenes and acts as the child's advocate. To protect David, she lies that he might have polio and convinces the police chief (now taken over by aliens; he also has the metal probe in the back of his neck) that David needs to be isolated in the hospital. Imagine a child's horror of living in what is no longer a *Leave it to Beaver* world but one wherein he's afraid to go home with his formerly tender and loving parents. The fear in actor Jimmy Hunt's eyes says it all as his sense of self is drastically threatened, all as a result of that horrible dream where the flying saucer crashed into his backyard.

Loss of identity is not only horror for adults, but for children as well. *Invaders from Mars* combines creative set decoration (especially the haunting backyard sand dunes and the bungholes into which adults tumble to their doom), wonderful Cinecolor photography, and an involving nightmare of a plot that keeps the audience transfixed. But *Invaders from Mars* should be most noted for its subjective vision of loss of identity from a child's perspective.—*GJS*

Invaders from Mars (1986) [alien possession; mind control] (Cannon Group). *D:* Tobe Hooper. *S:* Dan O'Bannon and Don Jakoby, Based on the Screenplay by Richard Blake. *Cast:* Karen Black (Linda Magnusson); Hunter Carson (David Gardener); James Karen (Gen. Climet Wilson); Louise Fletcher (Mrs McKeltch); Timothy Bottoms (George Gardner); Laraine Newman (Ellen Gardner); Bud Cort (Mark Weinstein); Jimmy Hunt (Police Chief).

As the original 1950s B-movie already features in this book, there's little to add when discussing the remake, except to say that it's not particularly good. It follows the original in most of its major plot particulars: (1) Young David sees an alien craft land behind his house. (2) He's menaced by his parents and other adults (like the abhorrent schoolteacher, Mrs. McKeltch, a new character)—unwitting, unwilling co-conspirators of the space invaders, controlled through a peculiar mark they bear upon the back of their neck. (3) He finally finds a sympathetic, non-possessed adult, his teacher, Linda Magnusson. (She's not a doctor, like her counterpart in the original film, but she has no need of a "strong" man, as in the original—this being the 1980s, when a woman can take care of herself.) (4) They ultimately convince a military man to help them. (In the face of the Martian threat, General Wilson—who seems to be suffering from his own paralyzing loss of identity, born of living a life of inactive frustration throughout the

Cold War—rediscovers and unleashes his lust for battle, unhesitatingly taking the war to the invaders.)

Invaders from Mars deals with a communal loss and subsequent forced realignment of identity, as the town's inhabitants are brainwashed, transformed from mundane members of nondescript suburbia to servants of malevolent Martians. Sadly, by the time we get even a third of the way into this boring, cheesy, and poorly produced remake, we won't really give a damn.—*AJB*

Invasion of the Body Snatchers (1956) [**alien possession; doppelganger; eradication of self**] (Allied Artists). *D:* Don Siegel. *S:* Daniel Mainwaring, Based on the 1954 *Collier's* Serial *The Body Snatchers* by Jack Finney. *Cast:* Kevin McCarthy (Dr. Miles Bennell); Dana Wynter (Becky Driscoll); King Donovan (Jack Belicec); Carolyn Jones (Teddy Belicec); Larry Gates (Dr. Daniel Kaufman); Ralph Dumke (Nick Grivett).

Invasion of the Body Snatchers is the Queen Mother of loss-of-identity films.

One of the best-known science fiction movies of the 1950s, *Invasion* conveys a sense of paranoia that is gradually and skillfully revealed. The threat appears benign at first—an elusive malady plagues a small California town, causing people to think that their relatives have somehow changed. The disease begins to affect the patients of Dr. Miles Bennell, who initially writes it off as a mass delusion. When Miles discovers that alien seedpods are forming into duplicates of his old flame Becky Driscoll and friend Jack Belicec, he realizes that the problem is no mere hallucination. The full extent of the menace is then revealed—Miles and Becky are the last remaining survivors of a community whose residents are no longer human. Their only hope is to warn the rest of the world before it is too late.

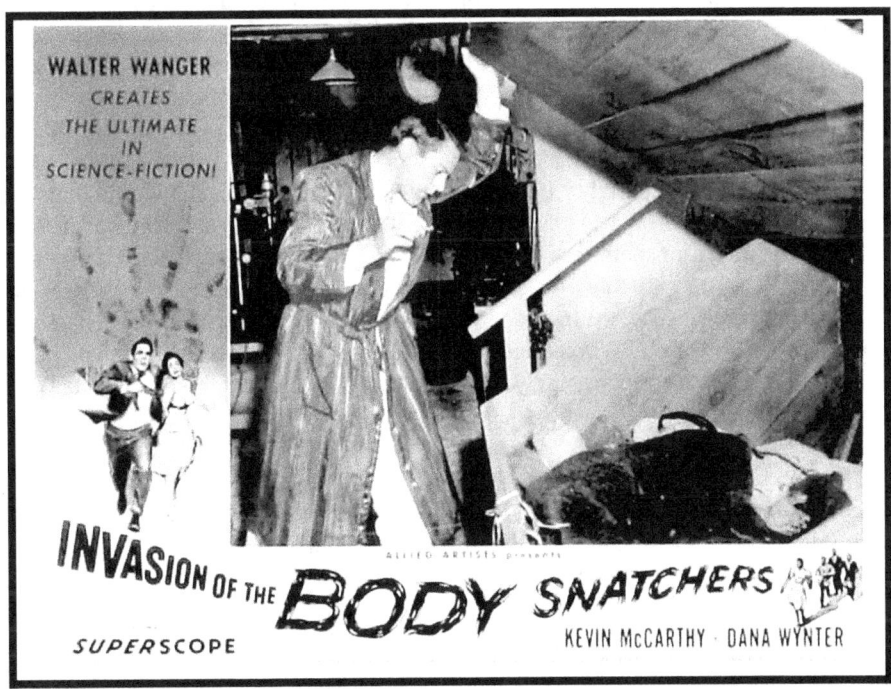

Miles (Kevin McCarthy) discovers a pod person in *Invasion of the Body Snatchers*.

Sleep becomes the film's metaphor for loss of identity. Like botanical Xerox machines, the fully formed seedpods take over their human hosts while they slumber. The sense of unease is thus heightened because it capitalizes on a fundamental human need, a fact made even clearer by the film's prospective working title, *Sleep No More*. The sleep allegory works on another level as well. "I've seen how people have allowed their humanity to drain away," Miles tells Becky at one point, a telling observation on the hardening of the heart that is common to the human experience. All of us are guilty, the film suggests, of letting compassion and human emotion die a slow, gradual death.

The identity issue is manifested in a loss of individuality. Although they retain the distinct appearance of the organisms that they clone, the alien replicons are utterly devoid of personality. They experience no wants or needs other than the drive to reproduce and dominate their new environment. The instinctive fear of the "other" is taken to extremes—the aliens are like us in every way except for the secret attributes that are known only to us and our loved ones. Human identity itself is called into doubt. When an organism looks like us, talks like us, and shares our thoughts and memories, we are forced to reassess the very definition of what is human and what is not.

The alien threat is explained in only the most vague detail, which heightens the film's menacing atmosphere. Miles is informed that the pods have the power to reproduce any life form, although apparently only human beings have been targeted. The changeover process itself is described as being quick and painless—once complete, the new "convert" is grateful that the process has taken place. This points out a bitter irony behind the alien methodology for conquest. In a world that has grown increasingly complicated, the promise of being reborn into an untroubled world has an appealing ring to it. Miles and Becky, both survivors of failed marriages, understand this appeal well. Only after reaffirming the value of love, grief, and beauty can they continue in their efforts to oppose the vision of a world in which everything sounds "so simple."

The success of *Invasion of the Body Snatchers* had an immediate impact upon the culture. [Its far-reaching effects spread at least as far as *The Dick Van Dyke Show*. In its second season, the popular television series offered a memorably hilarious and scary *Body Snatchers*' parody, "It May Look Like a Walnut."] Even today, the phrase "pod people" has a permanent place in the social lexicon. The mythos has proven to be highly adaptable; film commentators see in *Invasion* echoes of both the Soviet rhetoric of the 1950s and the anti-Communist hysteria of the same decade. Not surprisingly, the film still has resonance today. In an age where corporate and cultural forces conspire to control everything from fashion trends to political discourse, the value of independent thought has become an increasingly scarce commodity. Despite the film's tentatively optimistic finale, Miles Bennell's sobering warning, "You're next!" has proven to be uncannily accurate.—*SGT*

Invasion of the Body Snatchers (1978) [alien possession; eradication of self] Solofilm (United Artists). *D:* Philip Kaufman. *S:* W.D. Richter, Based on the Novel *The Body Snatchers* by Jack Finney. *Cast:* Donald Sutherland (Matthew Bennell); Brooke Adams (Elizabeth Driscoll); Leonard Nimoy (Dr. David Kibner); Veronica Cartwright (Nancy Bellicec); Jeff Goldblum (Jack Bellicec); Art Hindle (Geoffrey Howell); Kevin McCarthy (running man, uncredited); Don Siegel (cabbie, uncredited); Robert Duvall (man on swing, uncredited).

The original version of *Invasion of the Body Snatchers* left a lasting impact on America's collective cultural consciousness. Philip Kaufman's 1978 remake, which freely incorporated the societal changes that had taken place in the decades since, proved to be nearly as effective.

Set in contemporary San Francisco, the film depicts loss of identity as a social phenomenon as much as an otherworldly one. The society depicted in the film has begun to crumble under the weight of the ever-increasing complexity of modern life. Relationships are transitory, family units are fractured, and the inability to communicate has spread like the plague. Emotional intimacy is also in danger of becoming obsolete—even neighbors have become virtual strangers to each other. Against this chaotic backdrop, the robotic behavior of the duplicated humans easily passes unnoticed, leaving few obstacles in the way of a conquest from space.

Noteworthy too is the change in the depiction of authority figures. Government offers no hope of deliverance from the alien menace. Instead, the inevitable layers of bureaucracy found in City Hall impede any constructive action, as Department of Health official Matthew Bennell and lab worker Elizabeth Driscoll soon discover. Assorted police reports and phone calls to the mayor's office only get lost in a sea of paperwork and an onslaught of behind-the-scenes alien interference. By film's end, the helpful hand of official leadership is nowhere to be found. In a move that anticipates the political shifts of recent years, individual action is seen as the only hope against a world gone mad.

The alien invaders depicted in this film have no ulterior motive other than their own survival. Their promise of an "untroubled world" into which the subjugated humans will be reborn is less a rejection of love and emotion than a simple inability to comprehend these ideals. "Don't be trapped by old concepts," lectures pop psychologist-turned-pod-person Dr. David Kibner, as though the death of passion represents a step up the evolutionary ladder. This becomes the film's true loss-of-identity nightmare—human life has no more intrinsic value than the mindless seedpods that drift aimlessly through space.

The mythos of *Invasion of the Body Snatchers* has proven to be one of the most durable in all of genre cinema, adaptable to both the Cold War 1950s and the Counterculture 1970s. Both film versions demonstrate that loss of identity is a concept that speaks to every generation.—*SGT*

Invisible Ghost, The (1941) [**mind control**] Banner Productions Inc. (Monogram). *D:* Joseph H. Lewis. *S:* Al Martin and Helen Martin. *Cast:* Bela Lugosi (Charles Kessler); Polly Ann Young (Virginia Kessler); John McGuire (Ralph Dickson/Paul Dickson); Clarence Muse (Evans); Terry Walker (Cecile Mannix); Betty Compson (Mrs. Kessler).

The Invisible Ghost is one of those weird little Poverty Row thrillers that crept out of Sam Katzman's Banner Pictures back in the 1940s. It takes place in the home of Charles Kessler and his grown-up daughter, Virginia. Charles Kessler is haunted by the memory of his late, beloved wife. The memory is so strong that, on their wedding anniversary, he pretends to have dinner with her, making conversation with a woman who is not even in the room. Unbeknownst to all, however, Mrs. Kessler is *not* dead. Long ago she had tried to run away from her husband, but an automobile crash left her lover dead and Mrs. Kessler traumatized and brain damaged. She was found by the family gardener, who keeps the broken woman hidden away in a secret cellar, in hopes of restoring her to Kessler when her mind recovers. Periodically, however, Mrs. Kessler

Mrs. and Mr. Kessler (Betty Compson and Bela Lugosi) have a doomed relationship in *The Invisible Ghost.*

escapes from her cellar and confronts Kessler from outside the house. The sight of her causes Kessler to go into a kind of trance which is only relieved after Kessler commits murder. Upon waking, Kessler remembers nothing and goes about his life in perfect innocence. Until the next murder.

Okay, say it: In terms of plausibility, the plot of *The Invisible Ghost* is a total mess. And yet, and yet…the performances of Bela Lugosi and Betty Compson as Mr. and Mrs. Kessler are so good that they almost seem to fill in the background and evoke a strangely powerful story of identity and loss.

At every mention of his wife, Bela Lugosi evokes from Kessler a profound love and affection. Betty Compson conveys Mrs. Kessler's longing for her husband and a wish to be reunited with him. (So *why* did Mrs. Kessler leave her husband in the first place?) There is another bond between them that goes beyond love. Kessler seems to sense his wife's approach before she comes into view, and the film shows her communicating with him across distances where her voice cannot reach. Perhaps they share a love so great that their spirits seem to blend together. The idea is uneasily familiar to me.

Back in college I had my first romantic relationship (yeah, yeah, I was a late bloomer; give me a break). It was incredibly intense, from the first unexpected, passionate embrace that absolutely sealed our troth. Suddenly I found myself no longer just *myself*; I was now a *boyfriend*. I was a *couple*. What was I supposed to do? A boyfriend has obligations, and I was so clueless I had no idea what they were. When I didn't meet them, she was sometimes so hurt she cried. And, when she cried, it hurt me.

It got so *strong* I didn't know where I left off and where the relationship began. Where was this going? What was I turning into? After a while, I felt I was absolutely being eaten alive.

So how did I handle it? I panicked. And without warning, at the end of an ordinary date, blurted out that I wanted to break it all off. That was probably the first time in my life I ever really hurt somebody.

Did Mrs. Kessler feel the same panic I did? Was her attempted escape a last-ditch effort to assert her own identity? If so, then hers is a truly macabre story. She barely even got away from the house before sheer dumb luck killed her lover and left her incapable of any kind of independent existence. From her basement, she is inexorably drawn back to the house she so desperately wanted to escape.

When Kessler sees his wife, Lugosi's face becomes contorted with pain and anger. It is a rage so deep that Mrs. Kessler rightly fears "You'd kill me. You'd kill anybody." Kessler cannot raise a hand against his beloved, but, in the pain of her betrayal, Kessler symbolically murders her by strangling whomever he encounters. In one instance when there is no victim at hand, he mutilates his wife's portrait. Having sated his anger, Kessler must forget everything that has happened in order to continue living as the gentle man he knows himself to be. Only at the end of the film is Kessler is forced to acknowledge the murderer within himself, and for this sequence Lugosi delivers an absolutely Oscar-level piece of acting on the Poverty Row sound stages of a Sam Katzman production.

As we can see, there are a lot of identity issues at play in the mish-mosh that is *The Invisible Ghost*. (Lugosi and Compson deserve a lot of the credit for making it work, as does director Joseph H. Lewis for some authentically bizarre directorial touches.) For example, John McGuire's character is executed for murder half-way through the film, but McGuire returns almost immediately, playing a twin brother. Now *that* is weird.—*AJL*

Invisible Man, The (1933) [**madness**] (Universal). *D:* James Whale. *S:* R.C. Sheriff (and, uncredited, Philip Wylie and Preston Sturges), From the Novel *The Invisible Man* by H.G. Wells. *Cast:* Claude Rains (Jack Griffin); Gloria Stuart (Flora Cranley); William Harrigan (Kemp); Henry Travers (Dr. Cranley); E.E. Clive (police constable Jaffers); Una O'Conner (Jenny Hall, innkeeper's wife); Dwight Frye (reporter); John Carradine (phone informant).

How much of our identity resides in our physical appearance? If we lacked a physical appearance, would we *have* an identity? *The Invisible Man* suggests that we would not—or at least that we wouldn't be *all there*.

In James Whale's film, Dr. Cranley explains that the drug which makes a man invisible also affects his sanity. Certainly Jack Griffin seems to be going slowly (or already is)

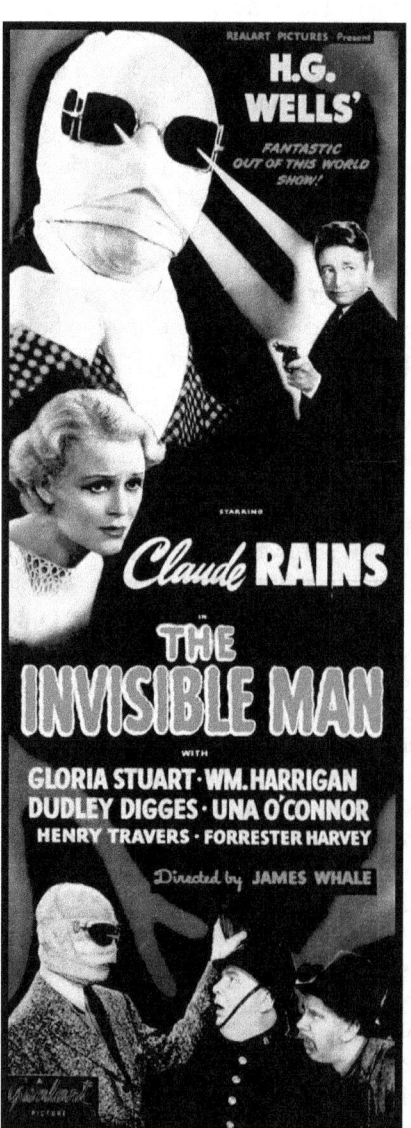

out of his mind from the moment he appears at the Lion's Head Tavern, heavily cloaked and bandaged. But one can almost conclude that the simple fact of invisibility—the absence of one's identifying features—is enough in itself to cause madness by denying the invisible one contact with or proof of his former identity or of *any* identity.

The tavern's denizens speculate that the strange guest in their midst is perhaps some horribly scarred veteran of the Great War. (See contributor Arthur J. Lundquist's "Battle-Scarred Horrors," *Midnight Marquee* 65/66 [2002], which deals with war-inflicted disfigurement and how it figured into the modern horror film.) Disfigurement affects one's sense of self (e.g., Karloff's Bateman in *The Raven* [1935 (*q.v.*)], who wonders aloud if a man who is ugly does ugly things). Imagine the increased risk of becoming unhinged if the "disfigurement" reduces a man to—*nothing*. (Significantly, the other great work of literature labeled *The Invisible Man* is Ralph Ellison's novel about a person whose identity is so submerged as to render him nonexistent.)

Invisibility is a funny malady. Half the time, filmmakers can't help playing it for laughs. (Witness the scene where the invisible man scampers along as nothing but a pair of pants, singing "Here we go gathering nuts in May.") The rest of the time, filmmakers try to instill in us a fear of what it's like to confront an invisible foe. (And Claude Rains' line readings when he speaks about how he'll start his reign of terror—"We'll begin with a few murders: murders of great men, murders of little men, just to show we make no distinction"—certainly achieves that chilling effect.)

Because fear of the unseen is one of the most frightening things known to humankind, why are invisible men just as likely to make filmgoers giggle as they are to make them jump? A possible explanation, at least for this film, is that Whale wants to keep us off guard about Griffin's true nature. I know I just said he was creepy from the first scene, but in the beginning, a viewer doesn't know necessarily *what* Griffin is—hero, menace, or clown. His gruff, secretive manner suggests one thing. The comic hijinks that ensue once he unwraps suggest another. We're constantly kept off balance by him and his behavior. Compare the opening of *Goodfellas* (1990), which introduces Joe Pesci's Tommy DeVito. I knew Pesci, previously, as a comedic actor. (I'm thinking of his "Okay, okay, okay" Leo Getz in 1989's *Lethal Weapon 2*, made just the year before.) So, when Ray Liotta's Henry Hill is smiling at him and DeVito asks, in his distinctive wheezy voice, "You think I'm funny?"...I didn't really understand the underlying menace that was there—which I *think* was director Scorsese's intention. When DeVito erupts into violence, we're doubly shocked. There's some of this, I think, in Claude Rains' invisible man. Sometimes he's funny; sometimes he's threatening.

Speaking of funny, "gaffe squads" for years have been laughing about the marks that the invisible man leaves in the snow at the film's climax: They're *shoe* prints, not footprints. But, in a way, this is fitting, as it suggests that Griffin's identity has been almost totally obliterated (to the point where he has no *sole*—or at least only an artificial one).

Ironically, as with filmic werewolves and Mr. Hydes, it's only after he's lost his identity for good, in death, that he regains it and his human form returns.—*AFA*

It Came from Outer Space (1953) [**alien possession; doppelganger; hive mind**] (Universal-International). *D:* Jack Arnold. *S:* Harry Essex; Story by Ray Bradbury. *Cast:* Richard Carlson (John Putnam); Barbara Rush (Ellen Fields); Charles Drake (Sheriff Matt Warren); Joe Sawyer (Frank); Russell Johnson (George).

Imagine an invasion from space that is confined to an isolated area, temporary, and expedient. Such is the premise of *It Came from Outer Space*, where a blazing flying saucer crashes into the Western desert. The one-eyed alien octopus needs human help to repair its spaceship to return to outer space. Thus, members of the local desert town are slowly being duplicated and replaced by aliens, while the original humans are held hostage back in the cave where the ship crashed.

Those sequences where the human victims are replaced with aliens are intense and visually interesting. In one spooky sequence, Frank and George are driving along a lonely desert road when a semi-cloud housing the one-orbed alien inside comes glaring subjectively right toward the audience (remember this film was originally released in 3-D). Then a transparent glistening eye fills the screen as we, the audience, become the alien and approach the terrified George, who recoils in horror. The eye alien slowly approaches George, who continues to back away as smoky clouds envelop him, and the human duplication commences. Soon the groggy George awakens to find an alien doppelganger speaking to him in a dull monotone, punctuated by archetypal science fiction music. Such sequences are visually arresting and imply the evil of outer-space invasion (which is later revealed to be totally pragmatic, as the humans are ultimately released once the space vessel is repaired).

Director Jack Arnold makes the Arizona desert a secondary character, mirroring the paranoiac horror of alien invasion. Sparkling, reflective metallic dust permeates the areas of the desert visited by aliens. Just as the small desert town has invaded the desert, astronomer John Putnam is a scientist/stranger who invaded the desert town (and is made to feel the outsider by the locals). Arnold, working with cinematographer Clifford Stine, uses every subtle opportunity to make the desert appear sinister and threatening, just like those quickly glimpsed creepy aliens who appear suddenly on the road. In one sequence, a Joshua tree's shadow makes heroine Ellen Fields scream because the tree's flash-lit presence seems otherworldly and threatening. In other sequences the subjective camera represents the presence of the all-knowing alien watching John and Ellen as they explore the desert for missing comrades—comrades that eventually return, but in slightly altered, alien forms.

The horror of loss of identity in *It Came from Outer Space* involves a subtly growing hive mentality where friends and loved ones act strangely once possessed by the alien life form. These doppelgangers keep unusually quiet, have shifty eyes, and behave in an off-kilter manner. (There's the odd touch of two men walking together, holding hands.) The alien humans carry strange electronic equipment to trucks for transport, speak very privately to one another, and emerge from dark passageways with eyes that glow in the dark. One alien even looks directly into the bright sun and comments how beautiful it looks. In most small towns, everyone knows everyone else intimately, but, once the alien transformation has occurred, even casual acquaintances notice the subtle differences in their neighbors.

Mystery and paranoia intensify as the human inhabitants of the small desert town are taken over, an act parallel to the mysteries and paranoia of the desert. The theme

The horror of loss of identity in *It Came from Outer Space* involves the glowing hive.

of the movie is that both mysteries are ultimately revealed to be harmless and non-threatening. The otherworldly desert with its tumbling weeds and strange landscape is no more harmful than the aliens who crash-landed here on Earth. By the film's end, the entire citizenry of the town has become an angry mob ready to destroy the compromised spacecraft and, along with it, the actual human hostages. Only brave scientist John Putnam has the courage to venture inside the spacecraft, confront and communicate with the alien hive leader, and work out a deal that includes the safe return of all human hostages and satisfies both parties.

Finally, all is right. The fireball space ship, repaired, returns to the skies. The hostages are freed. And John Putnam looks skyward with inquisitive eyes, wondering about what lies beyond.—*GJS*

[Editor's note: What lay ahead, 17 years in the future, was a television movie, *Night Slaves* (1970), a sort of extended *Twilight Zone* episode, directed by Ted Post and starring James Franciscus as the only person in a small Western town unaffected by the strange force that turns everyone else into zombified slaves at night (hence the title). They shamble off to the edge of town for some reason and wake up the next morning, with no recollection of what they did the night before. Turns out, in an obvious riff on *It Came from Outer Space*, that aliens whose ship is in need of repair are "borrowing" human bodies so that they can fix their rocket and move on. Forty-three years later, the Wheat brothers, Ken and Jim (responsible wholly or in part for acceptable-to-mediocre scripts such as *A Nightmare on Elm Street 4: Dream Masters* [1988], *The Fly II* [1989], *The Stepford Husbands* [1996], and *Pitch Black* [2000], among others), concocted a belated television-movie sequel, *It Came from Outer Space II* (1996), directed by Roger Duchowny and starring Brian Kerwin and Elizabeth Peña (as "Jack" Putnam and Ellen Fields). It came and went quicker than the aliens in the original.]

It's Alive! (1969) [**brainwashing; eradication of self; madness**] Azalea Pictures (American International Television). *D:* Larry Buchanan. *S:* Larry Buchanan. *Cast:* Tommy Kirk (Wayne Thomas); Shirley Bonne (Leilla Sterns); Bill Thurman (Greely); Annabelle Weenick (Bella); Corveth Outserman (Norman Sterns).

I don't blame anyone if he/she doesn't want to watch *It's Alive!* again.

It is, after all, one of those ultra-cheap movies made in Texas by Larry Buchanan back in the 1960s, that were never intended to be seen in theaters. No, their sole reason for being was to fill out an hour and a half of local television time as part of American International Pictures' television syndication package.

In *It's Alive!* Norman, Leilla, and Wayne, three innocents, fall into the clutches of Greely, a backwoods madman who traps people in the caves under his estate and feeds them to a giant prehistoric lizard that lives there. So isolated is the Greely estate that, to the outside world, his victims vanish without a trace.

The storyline has a certain potential, tapping into that fear of getting lost far from home and never being heard from again. That's a real and terrible loss of identity for anyone; the world forgets you, and there's nothing you can do about it. But the leaden pacing and general cheesiness of virtually every aspect of the production would cause pretty much any ordinary person to find something better to do.

However, its LOI heart is hidden away somewhere in *It's Alive!*'s 80-minute running time: a truly haunting story of identity stolen.

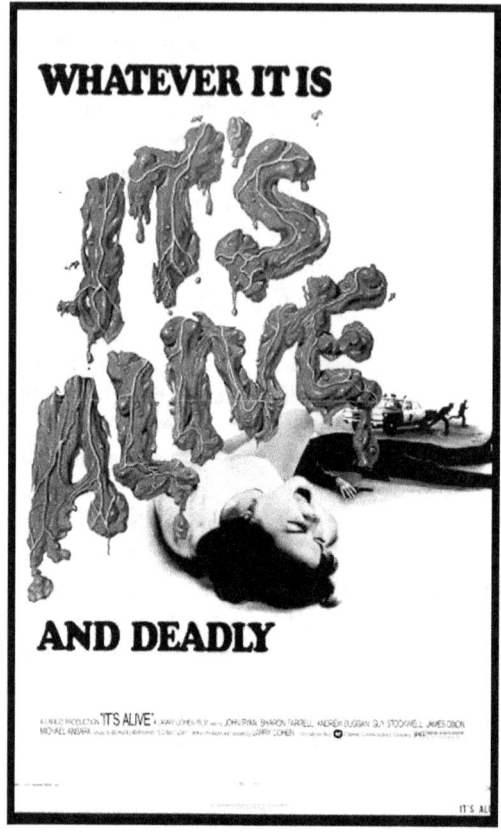

For there is one other character in the movie. Her name is Bella, a broken woman who tremblingly carries out Greely's wishes and lives in constant terror of incurring his displeasure. Many people who watch the film assume that she is Greely's wife, as if that affords her a degree of identity—or comfort.

She tells us her story, and in flashbacks we see an unmarried, 30-something schoolteacher, driving alone on vacation, looking for an affordable place to spend the night. As did so many others, her trail ends at Greely's. But Greely is not content, as he was with those others, to merely make her disappear.

He wants her to live. And, as the world outside forgets that she had ever been, Greely resolves through a combination of physical and emotional torture to break Bella down to a shell that has no existence beyond fulfilling his whims and wishes.

Yes, like the rest of the film, this flashback is overlong and paced like molasses. Yes, there is no synch-sound, only music and dubbed voices among interminable wordless stretches. In spite of all this, the story is truly frightening. And no technical flaw in the movie prevents this sequence from getting under our skin and haunting our private nightmares.

Because what we see has already happened. Greely's plan has worked. Evil has triumphed. No matter how long the flashback goes on, we know where it will lead. We've already seen the end of the story, and it is standing in front of us, in the person of the trembling, terrified Bella.—*AJL*

It's a Wonderful Life (1946) **[altered reality; eradication of self]** Liberty Films (RKO). *D:* Frank Capra. *S:* Frances Goodrich, Albert Hackett, Frank Capra, Jo Swerling (additional scenes), and Michael Wilson (uncredited), Based on the Story "The Greatest Gift" by Philip Van Doren Stern. *Cast:* James Stewart (George Bailey); Donna Reed (Mary); Lionel Barrymore (Mr. Potter); Thomas Mitchell (Uncle Billy); Henry Travers (Clarence Oddbody); Beaulah Bondi (Mrs. Bailey); Gloria Grahame (Violet); Ward Bond (Bert); Frank Faylen (Ernie); H.B. Warner (Mr. Gower); Samuel S. Hinds (Mr. Bailey).

The ultimate nightmare of identity loss—to see our life wiped out, erased; to never have been—is illustrated in this now-classic story, probably Frank Capra's darkest fable. He had been tending toward these bleaker and bleaker views of humanity and the human condition ever since he began his loosely related series of films about eponymous heroes who confront ever-greater evils, from small-town small-mindedness, to government corruption, to fascism. Each time, Capra's protagonist became mired deeply in a slough of despond, an almost intractable situation from which the director and his screenwriters were at pains to extricate him. Indeed, while Mr. Deeds' little-old-lady accusers reveal themselves for the pixilated folks they are (*Mr. Deeds Goes to Town* [1936]), the combined might of an institution offended and a vast political machine conspire to neutralize and render suspect Jefferson Smith's quixotic efforts, and only the last-minute reformation of Smith's mentor, the once-noble Senator whose slumbering conscience is jolted awake by Smith's filibuster for a lost cause (the "only one worth fighting for"), saves the exhausted, unable-to-admit-defeat-even-as-he-faints Smith from the ignominy and shame that would otherwise be his fate (*Mr. Smith Goes to Washington* [1939]). Two years later, in *Meet John Doe* (1941), another Capra protagonist unwittingly aids the forces of evil and only gets in deeper when he tries to repudiate them. Capra admitted that he had no idea how to get the character out of his predicament and experimented with several endings before deciding on the not-entirely-satisfying conclusion the picture now sports.

By the time of *It's a Wonderful Life* (*not* called *Mr. Bailey Never Leaves Town*), Capra apparently realized that nothing short of divine intervention could save the hero when he faced his dark night of the soul—more profoundly dark, perhaps, than anything all three of his predecessors, put together, confronted; hence, the bumbling, well-meaning Clarence the angel, who shows George the folly of suicide and the worth of his life by illustrating what would have happened if George had never been born. (To be fair, Capra does show "the people" coming through for his protagonist, gathering the money he needs to pay back the missing Mr. Potter–stolen funds. But George's faith in himself, apparently, requires a miracle.)

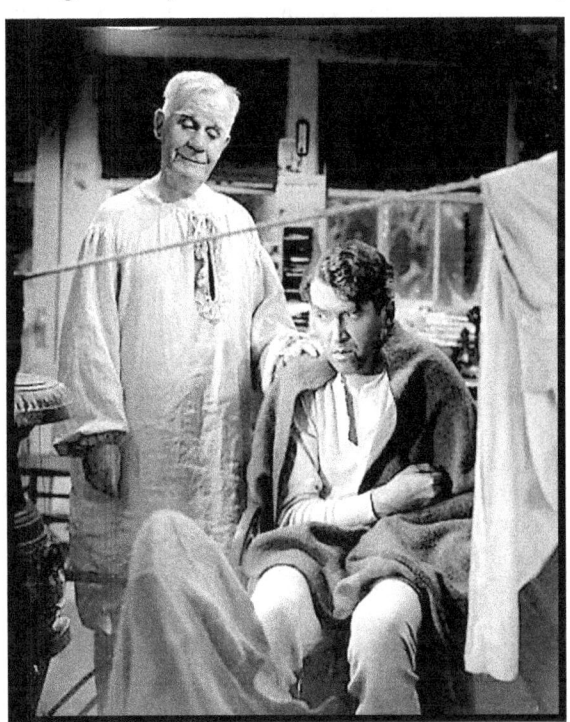

Clarence (Henry Travers) grants George Bailey's (Jimmy Stewart) wish that George had never been born in *It's a Wonderful Life*.

George proves remarkably slow on the uptake here, constantly inventing rationalizations to explain the townsfolk's strange behavior toward a person who never existed for them. This can be a little frustrating to the viewer, who's 'way ahead of George—who, in fact, may have spent the picture's careful build-up waiting for these fantasy scenes. Of course, the horror of *It's a Wonderful Life* is that George retains the memories from his nullified life, so it's perhaps understandable that he—as we probably would, in the same situation—cling to that now negated reality. (His behavior strongly suggests that George might not have been able to go through with the suicide to begin with.)

And Capra knows how to evoke the horror of the situation. Is there any more terrible scene than the one in which George confronts his would-have-been mother, now an old harridan, made scarier by the *mise-en-scène*, Beaulah Bondi's performance, and our knowledge of what she was in comparison to this frightening creature?

Not all of George's never-been encounters work so well. The best Capra and his screenwriters can come up with for wife Mary is the stereotype of the frigid spinster librarian. Would she have so shriveled up without a George Bailey in her life? Or would she have become rich Mrs. Sam Wainwright instead? ("Hee-haw!") The filmmakers do try to account for this anomaly. At one point, they have George wonder aloud to his wife why she ever married him, and she says—foreshadowing!—that she didn't want to end up an old maid. When he protests that she could have had anybody, Sam Wainwright, for instance, she deflects his remark by telling him that she "wanted our baby to look like you." And then we're off into the joyous news of pregnancy ("George Bailey lassos stork"), and the idea of Mary's desirability in a World-Without-George is dropped.

Reimagining a George-less Mary as a sexless prig is just about *It's a Wonderful Life*'s only flaw—save for another big flaw, which I guess either didn't cross the filmmakers' minds or which they felt they couldn't rectify without negating their own story, and that's this: If "each man's life touches so many others," the appropriate solution to George's dilemma would be for Clarence to make it so that *Mr. Potter* had never been. Then George—and everyone else in Bedford Falls—would have had a truly wonderful life. But, as satisfying as such a plot device might be, it would have denied us the nightmare descent into George Bailey's abyss of anonymity and the vicarious thrill we share with him when he gets his life back.

Of course, the irony of *It's a Wonderful Life*, as critic Robin Watson has pointed out in conversations with this author, is that George's identity has been shaped by Bedford Falls and the people around him from the very beginning. He never forges the identity for himself that he envisions—world traveler, architect, etc. But the life that he creates in reaction to and reluctant compliance with his environment turns out to be very wonderful indeed, enriching his neighbors and ultimately George himself, which is why he struggles so desperately to regain it after losing it.—*AFA*

I Walked With a Zombie (1943) [**voodoo**] (RKO). *D:* Jacques Tourneur. *S:* Curt Siodmak and Ardel Wray, Based on the Article "I Walked with a Zombie" by Inez Wallace and the novel *Jane Eyre* by Charlotte Bronte. *Cast:* Frances Dee (Betsy Connell); Tom Conway (Paul Holland); James Ellison (Wesley Rand); Christine Gordon (Jessica Holland); Edith Barrett (Mrs. Rand); James Bell (Dr. Maxwell); Theresa Harris (Alma); Sir Lancelot (calypso singer); Darby Jones (Carrefour).

The horror films produced by the Val Lewton unit at RKO gain much credibility by incorporating references to cultural mythology, both real and fictional. In *I Walked With a Zombie*, the second of Lewton's celebrated horror programmers, voodoo and the related loss of identity affect an entire family.

On the Caribbean isle of St. Sebastian, nurse Betsy Connell arrives to care for Jessica Holland, the apparent victim of a tropical fever. Devoid of willpower and unable to

Betsy Connell (Frances Dee) is confronted by the zombie-like Jessica Holland (Christine Gordon) in *I Walked with a Zombie*.

speak, Jessica is condemned to spend her remaining days as a mindless automaton. As the film progresses, the backstory of her condition is gradually revealed—the comely blonde was involved in a love triangle with her husband, Paul Holland, and his half brother, Wesley Rand. Driven half mad by the family crisis, Mrs. Rand, mother of the feuding brothers, prayed to the native gods, asking them to intervene. That very night, Jessica was stricken with her rare malady. Was it voodoo or mere coincidence? The film leaves the interpretation up to the viewer, although the suggestion is made that Jessica's lack of moral scruples rendered her subsequent loss of identity a moot point.

The aftermath of the incident has left its mark on both men. Holland has grown cold and cynical—there is no beauty on this island, he tells Connell, only "death and decay." Rand, although cordial and charming in social settings, routinely turns to alcohol for solace. Despite the fact that the pair have different last names, accents, and temperaments, they remain locked in an ongoing struggle of guilt and responsibility regarding the circumstances of Jessica's condition. Bound together by their mutual interest in the family sugar mill, they become targets for each other's unresolved anger.

Of the main characters, only Connell emerges unscathed from her time on the island. She comes to St. Sebastian in search of work, although she also seems to be searching for herself. She discovers much along the way, starting as a woman who is afraid of the dark and evolving into someone who is willing to risk a nighttime journey to the voodoo home fort to cure Jessica. Although her efforts are for naught, Connell's spirit remains formidable, and her identity is made stronger by the experience.

Various film writers have lauded *I Walked With a Zombie* for its moody atmosphere and strong characterizations. Now acknowledged to be a rough adaptation of Charlotte Bronte's *Jane Eyre*, the plot was officially credited to an article penned by Inez Wallace for *American Weekly Magazine*. Despite this potential identity crisis, the film remains one of the more distinctive zombie tales ever filmed.—*SGT*

I Was a Teenage Werewolf (1957) [**metamorphosis; scientific manipulation**] (American International Pictures). *D:* Gene Fowler, Jr. *S:* Herman Cohen and Aben Kandel (as Ralph Thornton). *Cast:* Michael Landon (Tony Rivers); Whit Bissell (Dr. Brandon); Yvonne Lime (Arlene); Tony Marshall (Jimmy).

It's a stereotypical 1950s high school, and one slicked-back rebel without a clue hovers near the entrance to the gym, the school bell directly overhead. Suddenly it rings, causing problem-teen Tony Rivers (a youthful Michael Landon) to curl his hands over his ears. Within seconds a deadly transformation occurs, the human morphing into a drooling, squinty-eyed werewolf. Tony has been eyeballing a sexy teen in skin-tight leotards, hanging upside down from the parallel bars, and, from her subjective point of view, she sees the predatory beast approach her. She screams at the top of her lungs and tries to run away but is captured, mauled, and slaughtered by the disturbed teen.

In Gene Fowler, Jr.'s iconic 1950s horror film, lycanthropy (that hairiest of all the losses of identity that can befall a human) overtakes complex, troubled youth Tony, a boy having issues with both his single-parent father (who can't control him) and his anger (which he can't control). A psychiatrist uses regression therapy to unleash the primeval ancestral beast within the anger-driven modern teen (indeed, within us all). Devious Dr. Brandon initially appears to be the concerned and caring father figure, but

Tony Rivers (Michael Landon) cannot understand what is happening to him as he transforms in *I Was a Teenage Werewolf*.

he soon uses hypnosis and Pavlovian suggestion (that bell) to exploit young Tony's aggression and rage in order to facilitate his attempt to revert the modern beast into a primitive one.

Tony Rivers becomes one evolutionary step closer to his inner beast when he's unable to socialize in the traditional manner. He has few friends; he's an outcast at school; his peers view him as a violent bully; he's unable to bond with his father or adults in general—thus casting him as a lone wolf in more ways than one. Once the adolescent becomes intimate with his inner, primordial self, his loss of identity transcends mere human-to-animal transformation; it is more like a sloughing off of modern man's anxiety and inability to express the rage we harbor inside. The release of the inner beast, the emergence of the savage, reveals the human being for the repressed animal he is.

The image of Tony Rivers wearing his high-school athletic jacket—wolf's fur covering his entire body, claws for fingernails, fanged bucked teeth with white saliva foaming from his mouth—becomes a visual metaphor for all the rage the boy feels inside, and the metamorphosis leaves him free to express all his pent-up anger without fear or guilt of societal morality or personal conscience. After a night of fury (where, as we see, his sexual lust can be expressed violently with the young gymnast), Tony becomes almost normal the next day, having released all his antisocial frustrations in the form of his werewolf murders. Such momentary loss of identity manifests itself as animalistic instincts held dormant for thousands of years. However, Gene Fowler, Jr., seems to be saying that mankind's actual identity involves coming to terms with the beast within. Tony Rivers is perhaps less able to disguise his inner beast when compared to his peers and the adults in his community, yet such internal savagery cannot be denied or ignored. It is truly part of our nature.

American International's 1957 production of *I Was a Teenage Werewolf* was intended for the teenage drive-in-theater circuit (where 20 million adolescent males hoped to turn into "wolves" themselves), yet its overriding message of one male's inability to become tamed and socialized by society's standards is a warning which teaches each of us that we must pay the penalty for failure to sublimate those bestial passions lurking deep inside which are still part of our character and heritage. Tony Rivers is not so much a throwback as he is the pet that society has been unable to potty train. His inner beast is not so much a flaw or a sin as much as it is an emblem of society's failure to tame that inner beast. For 21st-century viewers, the movie, with its high school and rock-'n'-roll setting, conveys this new-age beast in nostalgic settings.—*GJS*

Jacket, The (2005) [**altered reality; loss of affect; scientific manipulation**] Mandalay Pictures (Warner Bros.). *D*: John Maybury. *S*: Missy Tadjedin; Story by Tom Bleecker and Marc Rocco. *Cast:* Adrien Brody (Jack Starks); Keira Knightley (Jackie Price); Kris Kristofferson (Dr. Thomas Becker); Jennifer Jason Leigh (Dr. Lorenson).

Before you read this, please skip ahead to my take on *Jacob's Ladder* (1990). All done? Very well. As *The Jacket* begins with central character Jack Starks taking a bullet to the head during the first Gulf War, my immediate reaction was "Don't do the *Jacob's Ladder* thing again. Don't take us through an entire movie just so you can *surprise* us by revealing that he was killed in the first scene!" Thankfully, *The Jacket* offers nothing so simple. Jack's trauma is followed by more cruel twists—he's framed for a murder he didn't commit and winds up in an institution for the criminally

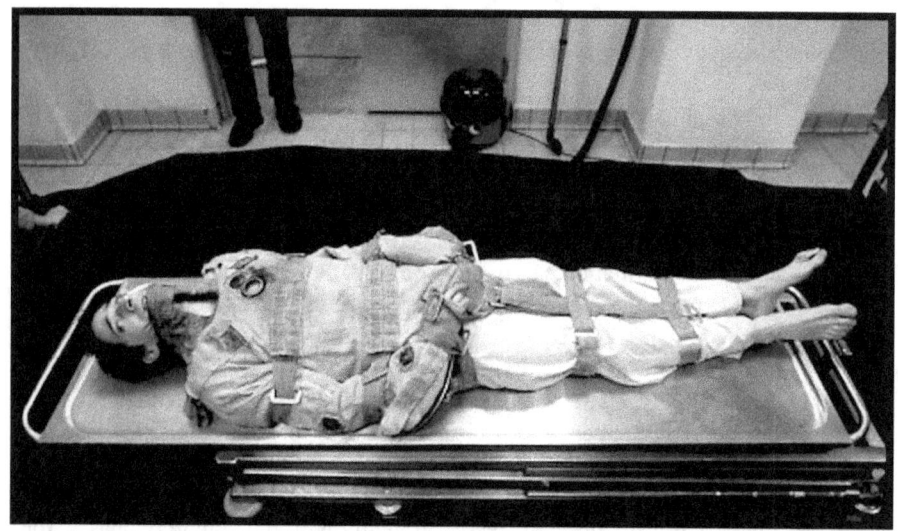

Throughout *The Jacket*, viewers are forced to wonder if Jack Starks (Adrian Brody) is alive or dead.

insane. And the therapy provided by one Dr. Becker involves forcing Jack into the title straitjacket and sealing him inside a morgue compartment for hours on end!

Via means known only to the filmmakers, this experience repeatedly sends Jack on a trip into the future—and not just in his own head, it would seem. Among other things, Jack is given the opportunity to right some wrongs in the life of his nominal counterpart Jackie (the older version of a little girl Jack met during his last day of freedom). But as Jackie reveals, the problem is that he couldn't possibly be Jack Starks—she happens to know that Jack Starks has been dead for years. Meanwhile, back in the "real" world, Jack is offered assistance by the sympathetic Dr. Lorenson (Jennifer Jason Leigh, following 2004's *The Machinist* [*q.v.*] with her second loss-of-identity film in a row).

Did Jack die back in the war? Did he die on the morgue slab? Is he actually having an effect in the future (thus breaking the "loss of affect" movie pattern)—and if so, is he even Jack anymore? *The Jacket* opts for ambiguity over easy answers in a move that undoubtedly hurt its box-office potential. Nevertheless, this is a rewarding and underrated entry in a cycle of films which had become far too predictable, finally proving that a return trip to Owl Creek Bridge doesn't always have to be part of the picture. (For a description of "An Occurrence at Owl Creek Bridge," see my entry on *Carnival of Souls* [1960].)— SMD

Jacob's Ladder (1990) [**altered reality; loss of affect**] (Carolco). *D*: Adrian Lyne. *S*: Bruce Joel Rubin. *Cast:* Tim Robbins (Jacob Singer); Elizabeth Peña (Jezebel); Danny Aiello (Louis); Matt Craven (Michael); Pruitt Taylor Vince (Paul); Jason Alexander (Geary); Ving Rhames (George).

As the film opens, Jacob Singer is wounded in action during a hellish Vietnam War incident. Flash forward to Jacob years later as he attempts to live a normal life as a New York City postman, only to fall prey to "loss of affect." Demons snarl at him from subway tunnels, fevers and seizures wrack his body as he seeks comfort from his

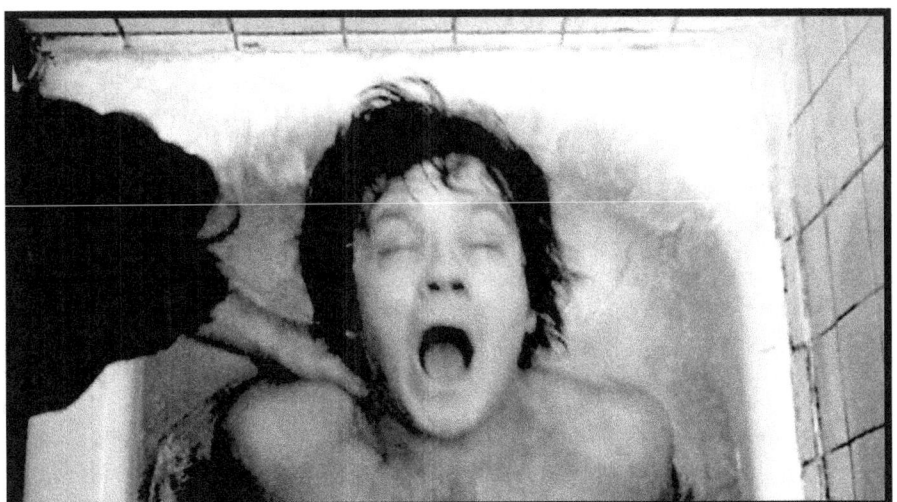

Vietnam veteran Jacob Singer (Tim Robbins) is on a terrifying trip into Hell in *Jacob's Ladder*.

friends (including significant other, Jezebel), and his stay at the local veteran's hospital becomes a trip into Hell. Is this post-war trauma? Is it the result of a covert drug experiment? Or is Jacob Singer on his way back to Owl Creek Bridge? (Yes, it's one of those stories again, just like "An Occurrence at Owl Creek Bridge" [see my entry on *Carnival of Souls* (1960)]: Jacob suffers the usual loss of affect that overtakes a protagonist who gradually comes to realize that he's been dead all along.)

Bruce Joel Rubin's script was once considered one of the 10 hottest unfilmed properties in Hollywood, and the combination of the writer of *Ghost* (1990) and the director of *Fatal Attraction* (1987) finally earned the project a green light. *Jacob's Ladder* features some undeniably nightmarish sequences (particularly in the hospital, where Jacob's doctors plainly inform him that he is not the living person he believes himself to be), and Danny Aiello offers immensely relieving support as Louis, the "good" doctor (possibly an angelic counterpart to "The Man" of *Carnival of Souls*) who tries to steer Jacob in the right direction. A subplot involving Jacob's reconciliation with his young son (an uncredited, pre-*Home Alone* [1990] Macaulay Culkin) is handled with notable sensitivity, as well. But the "surprise" finale still came as a letdown to many—especially to experienced "horror" fans drawn by the extreme material: They had predicted the ending from the very first scene of the film and wanted to be proven wrong.

Fifteen years later, *The Jacket* (2005 [*q.v.*]) would get off to a remarkably similar start, only to turn the "loss of affect" formula on its head.—*SMD*

Jekyll and Hyde...Together Again (1982) [**dual personality; metamorphosis**] (Titan/Paramount). *D:* Jerry Belson. *S:* Monica Johnson, Harvey Miller, Jerry Belson, and Michael Leeson, Based on the Novel *The Strange Case of Dr. Jekyll and Mr. Hyde* by Robert Louis Stevenson. *Cast:* Mark Blankfield (Jekyll and Hyde); Bess Armstrong (Mary Carew); Krista Errickson (Ivy); Tim Thomerson (Dr. Knute Lanyon); Michael McGuire (Dr. Carew); Neil Hunt (Queen); Cassandra Peterson (Busty Nurse); George Wendt (Injured Man); George Chakiris (Himself).

This Jekyll-and-Hyde spoof stars Mark Blankfield as Dr. Daniel Jekyll, a surgeon trying to create a substance to help patients avoid the operating table. He invents a white powder that brings out the user's animal instincts. Accidentally snorting the powder, Daniel transforms into Hyde, a sexually insatiable, drugged-out wild man. Though turning into Hyde causes him all kinds of problems, Daniel soon finds himself addicted to the powder.

Most of the movie's jokes are dated (and others are just overly tasteless), but the pic still has its funny moments. Hyde licking up the remnants of a line of powder is a visual crack-up, and many of the lines are still hilarious. (A woman screams "Rape!" and Hyde replies, "Later, if there's time.") Perhaps the funniest moment is when the dead body of Robert Louis Stevenson is shown rolling over in his grave.

It does not take a genius to figure out the symbolism in this film. The white powder is cocaine, and Jekyll becomes a coke addict. At one point, Daniel even uses a rolled-up dollar bill to snort his powder! (Jekyll's rationalization here is priceless as he reminds his "forgetful" self whose picture is on the bill, then starts rolling it up.) Jekyll's Hyde is a hepped-up, horny stoner with wild hair and one long fingernail (once a sign of a coke user). His transformation even has gold jewelry growing out of his skin! It all actually works despite the silliness and, in its way, cautions the public about drug abuse (without detracting from the overall comedic effect).

In the film, Jekyll loses his identity (just as previous screen Jekylls did) when he finds himself addicted to the powder. He even neglects his sweet fiancée and as Hyde starts seeing a hooker. And, like his screen predecessors, who were unable to control their transformations, Daniel is so addicted that he cannot control himself. However, this being a comedy, Jekyll's loss of identity does not lead to him hurting innocents, but it definitely affects his well-being and social position. The film is surprisingly faithful to primary elements of the original story, while also portraying a coke-head perfectly (though using comedy to do so). Scenes such as the aforementioned dollar-bill rolling, Hyde licking the table, Hyde sporting an erection he cannot get rid of, and others are all associated with the use and abuse of cocaine.

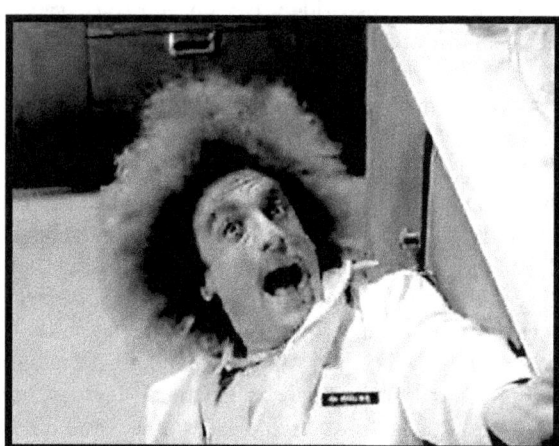

Jekyll (Mark Blankfield) turns into Hyde in *Jekyll and Hyde...Together Again*.

Cocaine was a popular and trendy drug at the time the film was produced, and applying it to the Jekyll-and-Hyde story is actually quite ingenious. Prolonged cocaine abuse does cause changes of identity. While on coke, people seem energized, overly sexual, with lowered inhibitions, doing things they wouldn't usually do in a more sober state. Craving the drug more and more, constantly seeking out more coke, addicts become paranoid, displaying new personality traits (irritability and nervousness) during the comedown periods. It is a Jekyll-Hyde situation that exists in reality and often leads to loss of identity. That just might make this the scariest version of the Jekyll-and-Hyde story to appear on screen!—*JSM*

Jiang shi fan sheng. See ***New Mr. Vampire, The*** (1987).

John Carpenter's The Thing. See ***Thing, The*** (1982).

Kabinett des Dr. Caligari, Das. See ***Cabinet of Dr. Caligari, The*** (1919).

Killer Bees (1974) [**possession**] Robert Stigwood Organization (ABC-TV). *D:* Curtis Harrington. *S:* John William Corrington and Joyce Hooper Corrington. *Cast:* Edward Albert (Edward van Bohlen); Kate Jackson (Victoria Wells); Gloria Swanson (Maria van Bohlen).

For many of us Baby Boomers, the idea that we were unique was one of our most prized possessions. And though it may seem strange today in an era when everybody rhapsodizes over "The Greatest Generation," one of our biggest fears was that we might wake up one day and find that we had turned into our WWII-era parents. I remember my buddy Rich complaining about the shock of discovering himself grunting Dad noises in the bathroom. Now, I had a pretty good relationship with my pappy, but I did not want to *be* him, and there is a very good chance that I would be a teacher today had it not been for my determination to go my own way at all costs.

The 1974 television movie *Killer Bees* works a genuinely creepy variation on the theme. The illustrious Gloria Swanson, in one of the grand lady's final film roles, stars as Maria van Bohlen, elderly matriarch of a California winegrowing family. Years before the film begins, she had abandoned a celebrated career of her own to take control of the van Bohlen family and of the hives of killer bees that buzz among its vineyards, with whom she seems to share a supernatural bond. Genre stylist Curtis Harrington's film positively exults in shots of Ms. Swanson covered from head to toe in masses of swarming bees. Grandson Edward van Bohlen (Edward Albert), has managed to pull himself free of the suffocating van Bohlen family with the help of his liberated girlfriend, Victoria Wells (Kate Jackson).

Killer Bees is 74 minutes long, and it is a measure of the effectiveness of the film that I have no recollection of what filled most of those 74 minutes. But for over 30 years I have been haunted by its climax, and if you haven't seen the film, I advise you to read no further. Victoria informs Ms. van Bohlen that she and Edward intend to raise a family far from the van Bohlen estate. The shocked matriarch suffers a heart attack and dies. During the funeral, while Victoria is packing to leave, the bees swarm about her, and, after they force her into a weird hive-like attic, she faints. When the young lady revives, she immediately assumes the

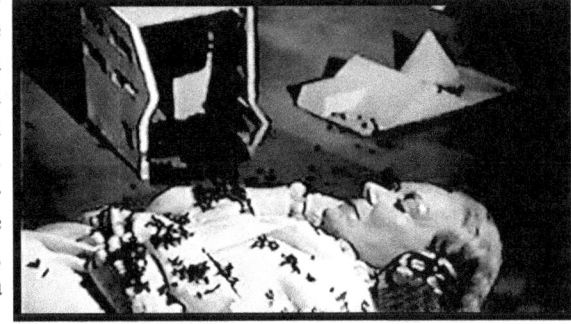

Maria van Bohlen (Gloria Swanson) dies of a heart attack surrounded by her bee friends in *Killer Bees*.

mannerisms of the elder van Bohlen, and, without a word, the rest of Edward's family begins treating her as their new matriarch. The film never states it in so many words, but it is obvious that Victoria is not Victoria anymore; her young body has become a new vessel for Maria van Bohlen. The film ends right there, on that familiar 1970s note of evil triumphant.

I tell you, that ending absolutely creeped me out. Not only has poor Edward lost the free spirit who gave him the courage to break away from his family, he now faces the prospect of living the rest of his life married to his own mother. A nightmare to make the blood of any true Boomer run cold.—*AJL*

King of the Zombies (1941) [**voodoo; hypnotism; scientific manipulation**] (Monogram). *D:* Jean Yarbrough. *S:* Edmund Kelso. *Cast:* Dick Purcell (James "Mac" McCarthy); Joan Woodbury (Barbara Winslow); Mantan Moreland (Jefferson Jackson); Henry Victor (Dr. Miklos Sangre); John Archer (Bill Summers); Patricia Stacey (Madame Alyce Sangre); Guy Usher (Admiral Wainwright); Marguerite Whitten (Samantha); Leigh Whipper (Momba); Madame Sul-Te-Wan (Tahama); Lawrence Criner (Dr. Couillie); Jimmy Davis (Lazarus).

"Can I help it 'cause I'm loquacious?"—New zombie Mantan Moreland being told that zombies can't talk.

A typical programmer from Poverty Row, *King of the Zombies* is memorable today for one reason and one reason only—the comic relief provided by the great Mantan Moreland. In fact, Moreland's one-liners and funny antics are so prevalent in the film that I would classify the picture as a horror-comedy in any study of genre spoofing. Rarely was the gifted comedian given such a chance to shine, and he makes the most of every minute he is onscreen. For viewers, it's a great opportunity to fully experience Moreland's screen *identity*. Especially since he is one of the characters who loses his identity as the plot progresses.

In the film, pilot James "Mac" McCarthy, investigator Bill Summers, and servant Jeff are flying south to Panama to search for the missing Admiral Wainwright, who has vital secrets relating to the war effort. They crash land on the island of sinister Dr. Sangre, who charmingly welcomes his guests but is secretly holding Wainwright hostage. Sangre has turned many of the island's natives—and even his own wife—into zombies who serve his evil will. He has also been trying to transform Wainwright into a zombie in order to learn his military secrets. Sangre is working for the Nazis! When Jeff comes too close to stumbling on to the plot, Sangre hypnotizes him into thinking he is a zombie, and he joins the undead at work. But beautiful maid Samantha restores him to normal by slipping some salt in his meal. Mac is accidentally killed, and he also becomes one of the walking dead. But during the picture's climax, Mac leads the zombies as they turn on Sangre and kill him.

The loss of identity in the film comes from both the zombies and Sangre's victims, who are hypnotized into thinking they are zombies. These unfortunates come under the control of Sangre and are forced to labor for him or carry out his orders. They're creepy enough, but they remain in the background for most of the picture, so there is little to dwell on regarding their loss of identity. Wainwright and Mac seem to retain something of their will and identities—Sangre is unable to obtain the admiral's secrets, and Mac is able to turn the tables on his so-called master. Perhaps the message here is to be true

Zombies and Nazis are evil compatriots in *King of the Zombies* as Dr. Sangre (Henry Victor) makes himself some new zombies, trying to force military secrets from Mac McCarthy (Dick Purcell).

to yourself and be of strong mind and spirit—then no voodoo master can fully control you. Or maybe the film was trying to warn us that the Nazis, if victorious, would turn us all into mindless drones with no identities of our own.

But the most memorable zombie transformation occurs to the most memorable character. Jeff figures out right away that something unnatural is going on, and his suspicions cause Sangre to get him out of the way. He hypnotizes Jeff and forces him to join the other zombies at work. ("Move over, boys; I'm one of the gang now.") Jeff quickly takes over as leader (in a way, it is he who is the titular "King of the Zombies"). This loss of identity is played strictly for laughs. In the film's stand-out sequence, Jeff leads the zombies to the dinner table for their regular meal. Even as a zombie, Moreland is hilarious, and the way his identity slowly emerges when the truth begins to dawn on him is priceless. True to form, once he is fully aware that he is human and not the undead, he rushes out of the kitchen as fast as his legs will carry him. Seldom has the loss of identity in a fantasy film been funnier than it is here.

In 1943, Monogram released *Revenge of the Zombies* (*q.v.*), which recycled this film's plot. It even featured Mantan Moreland back again as Jeff (but working for a new boss). Tom Weaver states in the book *Poverty Row Horrors* that the studio planned a third zombie film to feature Moreland, but it never came about. Too bad; more of Moreland is always welcome.—*JSM*

Land of the Dead (2005) **[zombification]** Romero-Grunwald Productions (Universal Pictures). *D:* George A. Romero. *S:* George A. Romero. *Cast:* Simon Baker (Riley);

John Leguizamo (Cholo); Asia Argento (Slack); Robert Joy (Charlie); Dennis Hopper (Kaufman); Eugene Clark (Big Daddy).

With *Land of the Dead*, George A. Romero's ground-breaking flesh-eater concept (first put forth in 1968's crude but stylish *Night of the Living Dead* [*q.v.*]) comes full-circle. As in *Night*, *Dawn of the Dead* (1978 [*q.v.*]), and *Day of the Dead* (1985 [*q.v.*]), the recently deceased, reanimated by some unknown phenomenon, hunger for human flesh and attack the living; those who die from being bitten return to seek living victims. The situation takes on apocalyptic proportions as the zombie population increases exponentially and the remaining human survivors must fight the flesh-eaters—and each other—for survival. One of Romero's themes throughout the series is that man's inability to communicate and adapt properly to crises ultimately causes his downfall. Another theme is that we can't rely on the familiar anymore; we never know *who* might become undead. A friend, acquaintance, or some normally benign individual could lose his/her identity, just like that, which is what makes Romero's work so scary. At any time, any place, we can be attacked. Loved ones, security figures, and trusted individuals—Goofy at Disneyland or even the new Pope—could haul off and take a bite out of you.

While the remaining humans hole up in strategic, walled-in locations, like Pittsburgh's exclusive Fiddler's Green complex, the living dead have inherited the Earth, performing the barely remembered mechanics of daily lives lost, of identities now altered. Reanimated band members attempt to play in an outdoor gazebo; a service-station bell sets a ghoul attendant in gas-pumping motion. [*He* must have become a zombie a *long* time ago.] Into the small, overrun borough of Uniontown roars a fortified, military-like vehicle, operated by a paramilitary scavenging crew, led by cocky Cholo (who wants "something more"—i.e., admittance to Fiddler's Green) and cautious Riley

With *Land of the Dead*, George Romero's flesh-eater concept comes full circle.

(who wants "something beyond"—i.e., life beyond the city). They ransack the shops and massacre many of the dead.

Disturbed by this slaughter, one-time gas-station attendant now flesh-eater Big Daddy tries to save his fellow ghouls. Exhibiting memory and even emotion, Big Daddy sees the glowing city on the horizon and sets his sights on it. Somehow banding together hordes of the dead, he has them approach the city en masse.

A class structure, left over from the "less brutal" days of humanity and capitalism, exists inside the protected city's confines. A select elitist few, the rich and oblivious, live in Fiddler's Green, an opulent skyscraper filled with restaurants, shops, and other consumerist distraction. Lording over this haven (and the surrounding community of the poor and depraved outside) is Kaufman, an opportunist not unlike the survivalists of *Dawn of the Dead* who took over the Monroeville mall, except that Kaufman's community exists to serve the needs of the rich (and is protected by the paramilitary minions and their massive tank, Dead Reckoning). Kaufman has not simply made a grab for the gold; he's adapted to the apocalypse and learned to profit from it (in a world where money ultimately means nothing). On the other hand, while the world has turned upside down, life for the street-level people continues pretty much as before: The tough survive; the weak are exploited; drug use and "perversion" run rampant. People are played for sport, having to fend off tethered flesh-eaters in dirty cage-matches. It's a no-frills depiction of man's weakness, ugliness, inhumanity, and tyranny from pre-apocalyptic times. The same games, but with the underlying tyranny undisguised.

As with all Romero Dead films, the major loss-of-identity themes are reflected in what the living must resort to (usually fear, flight, or hiding) in order to survive, and with the living dead themselves (although it could be argued that the dead's evolution and learning ameliorate, to some extent, their identity loss). We are the living dead; we're already all dead in a sense: in our behavior and preoccupations, in what drives us mad or delirious, in how we rationalize our relationships and lack of humanity. As in Romero's other work (*Night*'s upstairs/basement territoriality, *Dawn*'s "it's all mine" philosophy, *Day*'s military-vs.-science squabbling), class divisions, greed and passion, and the inability to communicate, evolve, and adapt to given circumstances cause man's recurring downfall. Throughout the tetralogy, man's inhumanity repeats and repeats in a downward spiral until the final battle here, where the last humans lose the spoils of a war they've already lost. (We may have further to fall, since a fifth *Dead* installment could be in the works; *Land* hints at similar outposts remaining in the U.S.) The dead represent the bare-bones hunger and madness that our systems and societies reduce us to, civilization and sophistication merely an illusion. The dead are indeed us, and, as we are in this world, we indeed deserve to be them: bad jokes of our former, desperate selves. Though, in death, we all "win."—*ABJ*

Last Man on Earth, The (1964) [**zombification**] Produzioni La Regina (Associated Producers Inc.). *D:* Ubaldo B. Ragona, Sidney Salkow (dubbing supervision). *S:* Richard Matheson (as Logan Swanson) and William Leicester (uncredited), From Matheson's Novel *I Am Legend*. *Cast:* Vincent Price (Robert Morgan); Franca Bettoia (Ruth Collins); Emma Danieli (Virginia Morgan); Giacomo Rossi-Stuart (Ben Cortman).

Screenwriter Richard Matheson has nothing good to say about *The Last Man on Earth* (based on his own classic horror novel *I Am Legend*), which he felt lost its iden-

Robert Morgan (Vincent Price) is attacked by a vampirish zombie in *The Last Man on Earth*.

tity two or three times on the way from page to screen. "The [story's] initial sale was to Hammer Films," Matheson related (at the 1993 *Famous Monsters* Convention in Arlington, Virginia). "I went over there [to England]; I was living there for about two-and-a-half months working on the script for *I Am Legend*. They told me later on that the censor would not pass it…it was too horrific. So they sold it back to the United States, to producer Robert Lippert." [*Loss # 1.*] Matheson maintains that Lippert promised him acclaimed filmmaker Fritz Lang (*M* [1931], *Scarlet Street* [1945]) as director but delivered only Italian neophyte Ubaldo B. Ragona and television-journeyman Sidney Salkow (*77 Sunset Strip, The Addams Family*). [*Loss # 2.*] Not only that, "they had some guy named William Leicester do a revision on [the script]. I hated it." [*Loss # 3.*] As a result, Matheson hid his identity, employing the pen name "Logan Swanson" (derived from his mother-in-law's and mother's maiden names) for his screen credit. Of the finished film, Matheson concluded, "I thought it was pretty bad." He was wrong.

Set in the "near future" of 1968, the story centers on Los Angeles–based scientist Robert Morgan, seemingly the only person in L.A. left alive (thanks to some kind of natural immunity) after a mysterious plague annihilates the population, transforming its victims into vampire-like zombies. Morgan spends his days hunting down the sleeping creatures and driving wooden stakes through their hearts and his nights holed up in his barricaded home trying not to go crazy as the monsters (once his friends and neighbors, now something entirely other) attempt to get at the "last man on Earth."

In a world where everyone else has lost his/her identity, how does one man hold on to his? As Morgan, Vincent Price is onscreen nearly every second, painting an effective and poignant portrait of a man stripped of everything he holds dear (indeed, stripped of everything that defines his very identity—including every other human being), going through the motions of living while sinking deeper into loneliness and despair. Price excels at revealing his character's near-breaking-point anguish, such as when he watches home movies of his family shot at a circus and begins to laugh, his giddy laughter gradually degenerating into agonizing sobs.

The horror quotient rises steadily, with a disturbing montage of Morgan searching out and staking the sleeping zombies, then the nighttime assault on his home by the walking dead (who beat feebly on the house and tonelessly cry, in the dead voices of those who have no identity—or perhaps whose only identity is in seeking to destroy the sole person *with* an identity, "Morgan, come out, come out..."), while Morgan drinks wine and listens to jazz records in a vain attempt to both recapture some sense of normalcy and drown out the horror of what those he knew have now become and what he's become in relation to them.

Admittedly, the film falters during its later stages (after Morgan learns he is not alone), resulting in a tepid action "chase" sequence, and an ill-conceived and rushed wrap-up. But the frightening images of the near-mindless walking dead (the LOI cinematic ancestors of Romero's zombies in *Night of the Living Dead* (1968 [*q.v.*]) and all the zombies who came after), combined with Price's convincing portrayal of loneliness and despair, as a man clinging to identity, make *The Last Man on Earth* both involving and horrific.

"I think it was better than [the second adaptation of *I Am Legend*,] *The Omega Man* (1971 [*q.v.*]), which Charlton Heston did later," opined Price to interviewer Lawrence French. "It had a kind of amateur quality about it."

This unpolished aspect actually serves the story well, lending a gritty edge and air of immediacy to the proceedings that the bigger-budgeted, glossier *Omega Man* lacks. And the despondent, sport-jacket-wearing Price makes a far more believable "everyman"—a man whose identity and loss of same we can relate to—than the two-fisted, bare-chested Heston.—*BMS*

Leopard Man, The (1943) **[split personality; madness]** (RKO). *D:* Jacques Tourneur. *S:* Ardel Wray, with additional dialogue by Edward Dein, Based upon the Novel *Black Alibi* by Cornell Woolrich. *Cast:* Dennis O'Keefe (Jerry Manning); Margo (Clo-Clo); Jean Brooks (Kiki Walker); Dr. Galbraith (James Bell); Margaret Landry (Teresa Delgado); Abner Biberman (Charlie How-Come); Isabel Jewell (Maria, the Fortune Teller).

When it comes to the great horror films of Jacques Tourneur (*Cat People* [1942 (*q.v.*)] and *I Walked With a Zombie* [1943 (*q.v.*)]), Val Lewton's other Tourneur production, *The Leopard Man*, is forgotten. But *The Leopard Man* is an essential loss-of-identity entry. This classic episodic chiller, focusing upon the external perceptions people create to hide their inner identities, features multiple losses of identity.

Leopard Man's first example of LOI begins with Charlie How-Come, the self-proclaimed Leopard Man, who travels around the southwest, performing with his cat. Slick PR agent Jerry rents the cat to promote nightclub performer Kiki Walker. The rival talent, castanet-snapping Latin dancer Clo-Clo, attracts all the attention, and Jerry figures Kiki will steal Clo-Clo's thunder if she enters the hotel nightclub with a leopard in tow. However, the determined Latina aggressively approaches the cat and rattles her castanets, and the leopard breaks loose of its leash and runs into the streets. Soon, young girls die, mangled and torn to shreds by the escaped cat…or is it the cat?

Jerry believes the first victim *was* murdered by the cat (as depicted in the classic sequence where a young girl encounters the leopard beneath a train tunnel and runs for her life—only to be locked out of her home by her own mother!). But Jerry believes a human fiend is responsible for the subsequent mutilations. Still, the poor leopard gets total blame, maintaining the identity of mauler and killer. Charlie How-Come claims, "My cat did not kill that girl in the cemetery…cats don't go looking for trouble. That cat ain't mean. For six years I fed him out of my own hand." However, Charlie himself is prone to alcoholic blackouts and fears his own dark nature; he has the sheriff arrest him and hold him in custody.

Next, we have the relationship between Jerry and Kiki, two hardened city types who look upon their brief stay in this dusty New Mexican town as a minor inconvenience. Outside the funeral parlor, after the first murder, Kiki sneaks the family some money, but when Jerry condescendingly asks Kiki whether he should donate something to the family, she states tersely, "Don't be soft!" Kiki's career and Jerry's profits are what matter the most to the two of them, but slowly, both become caught up emotionally in the plight of the formerly carefree little town.

> *Kiki*: Maybe I am tired of pretending that nothing bothers me and that all I care about is myself. Myself and my two-by-four career.
> *Jerry*: What else do you care about?
> *Kiki*: You… us! We got too busy trying to be tough guys. (*They kiss*.) Confession…I'm a complete softie.
> *Jerry*: There's two of us.

Two hard-boiled, tough-skinned urbanites, slumming and passing time in a sleepy, slow-paced desert town, finally admit that they are not as tough-skinned as they pretend to be…a loss of one identity and acceptance of another.

Clo-Clo and the town museum curator, Dr. Galbraith, both of whom are not what they seem, represent another kind of loss of identity. The film introduces Clo-Clo in her dressing room, clicking her castanets and annoying new arrival Kiki, causing Kiki to slam her dressing-room door shut in anger. After Clo-Clo frightens the leopard in the nightclub, the feisty performer breezes past Jerry and asks, "Who needs a publicity man when one has talent?" Walking down the street, Clo-Clo is brazen, acting as though she owns the world. However, the performer's hard shell melts when she shares a drink with a well-dressed older man. Clo-Clo admits she is a gold-digger, but then she reveals the details of her harsh life. Clo-Clo says she loves the boy who works at the grocery store, and she is worried about money—paying bills, making rent—and caring for her little girl as a single parent. She is a survivor and works hard for her money. Her harshness and arrogance are merely a cover for her life as a hard-working parent, who only desires to make enough money to provide for herself and her child. Another identity transformed!

When Clo-Clo consciously tries to alter her own identity, her own destiny, she doesn't fare so well. Her fortune-teller friend always draws the ace of spades when predicting her future…reluctantly telling her that something black threatens! That's why, that night, out on the street, Clo-Clo turns down the offer of a lift from a man driving a black car. Clo-Clo goes home and promises to buy her daughter the best dress in the world, tomorrow. But she discovers her money is missing and goes back outside to find it—a fatal mistake. Alone in the dark, she hears lumbering, tentative footsteps as a figure approaches in the night. She screams, becoming the latest victim of the Leopard Man.

In the same vein—this one more horrific—Dr. Galbraith seems mild-mannered, well educated, and always willing to show off his museum. In his talks with Jerry throughout the movie, we soon sense a sinister underbelly to this benign character. When Jerry refers to men with kinks in their brains, Galbraith mentions men who kill for pleasure. Jerry, who believes that the leopard is innocent, asks whether a psychopath might be the murderer. Galbraith answers, "He'd be a hard man to find, particularly if he's a clever man. He'd go about his ordinary business calmly, except when the fit to kill was upon him." Jerry responds, "You thought about all this before! You know it wasn't the leopard, don't you?" Of course Galbraith knows the truth, because he *is* the Leopard Man, a human fiend who uses the actual claws and hair from Charlie How-Come's traveling leopard, an animal he shot, to commit murder. Shades of *Psycho* (1960 [*q.v.*])! Like Norman Bates one generation later, Galbraith is the passive, withdrawing entity who assumes another persona (in this case the leopard) in order to kill. (Bates is obsessed with birds—and his mother; Galbraith with leopards.) One passive, harmless persona melts away to reveal the beast within.

Almost everyone in *The Leopard Man* fronts an identity that is gradually lost or transformed, as the truth emerges, sometimes for the better, sometimes for the worse.—*GJS*

Machinist, The (2004) [**altered reality; loss of affect; split personality**] Filmax International (Paramount Classics). *D*: Brad Anderson. *S:* Scott Kosar. *Cast:* Christian Bale (Trevor Reznik); Jennifer Jason Leigh (Stevie); John Sharian (Ivan); Michael Ironside (Miller).

It's easy to believe gaunt, emaciated machine-shop employee Trevor Reznik when he claims that he hasn't slept in over a year—something is quite literally eating away at him, but he's at a complete loss when it comes to identifying it. That is, until Ivan shows up at the shop. Huge-bodied, bald, and sporting a mangled left hand, Ivan is Trevor's physical opposite—and this opposite certainly seems to be a fatal "attraction" where Trevor is concerned. When Trevor's carelessness causes one of his crewmates (Michael Ironside) to lose an arm on the job, he blames the accident on Ivan's distracting presence. The trouble is that nobody else has ever seen or even heard of Ivan.

Ivan is the latest in the string of cinematic strangers that signal a huge change in either the life or the identity of a film's protagonist. And, from Ivan's first appearance, *The Machinist* begins to play like a "loss of affect" film à la *Carnival of Souls* (1960 [*q.v.*]), wherein the protagonist gradually comes to realize that he has lost his identity, that he can no longer have any effect on the events around him. As hers did for Mary Henry in *Carnival of Souls*, Trevor's life takes a turn for the surreal—the film's most nightmarish sequence even takes place on a carnival ride. (Trevor attempts to ease his mind by escorting a waitress he's befriended—and her young son—to an amusement park, but his efforts nearly send him and the boy straight to hell.) So is Trevor dead? Or is Ivan going to bring him back to face a reality he created for himself? (Perhaps the answer given to the question raised by the nameless title protagonist of the television series *The Prisoner* is relevant here: "Who is Number One?" "*You are*, Number Six!")

Trevor Reznik's (Christian Bale) life takes a turn for the surreal in *The Machinist*.

The details need not be spelled out here—but *The Machinist* reaches its turning point as Trevor looks into the mirror and states not "I know what you did," but "I know who you are." And, from there, for all of its horrific content, the film proceeds to what is perhaps the most relieving conclusion in the entire loss-of-identity/loss-of-affect cycle.

Jennifer Jason Leigh has a superb supporting role as Stevie, a sympathetic prostitute who believes that she and Trevor might actually have a chance to achieve genuine happiness together. She would go on from there to provide hope for another LOI victim in *The Jacket* [*q.v.*], released early the following year.—*SMD*

Mad Ghoul, The (1943) [**scientific manipulation**] (Universal). *D:* James P. Hogan. *S:* Paul Gangelin and Brenda Weisberg, Story by Hanns Kräly. *Cast:* George Zucco (Dr. Alfred Morris); David Bruce (Ted Allison); Evelyn Ankers (Isabel Lewis); Turhan Bey (Eric Iverson); Robert Armstrong ("Scoop" McClure); Milburn Stone (Sgt. Macklin); Rose Hobart (Della Elliot).

He did it all for the nookie.

Dr. Alfred Morris, that is, played to perfection by George Zucco in Universal's *The Mad Ghoul*. Unlike the run-of-the-mill madmen Zucco played in his PRC horror shows, Morris isn't after power or fame or revenge. He commits his crimes in the name of love, or at least of desire, which brings an atypical measure of pathos to the character. In turn, Zucco's superb lead performance brings distinction and class to this otherwise routine mad-science yarn.

Throughout his career, Zucco's icy, understated style set him apart from the overheated overacting of most other screen villains. His placid façade only made Zucco's villains seem more confident, more powerful, more dangerous. Meanwhile, his roving, blazing, pinball eyes convinced audiences that something unspeakably wicked lurked behind that polished, calm exterior. That's certainly the case with Morris, who remains aloof, imperious, and cold as a stone—a conniving, egomaniacal sociopath. But he's also something else—an incurable romantic.

Dr. Morris (George Zucco) turns his assistant Ted (David Bruce) into a living zombie in *The Mad Ghoul*.

Morris discovers an ancient potion that enables him to place subjects in a state of "living death." He can return his subjects to normal with a special concoction of herbs and other elements. Unfortunately, one of those elements must be extracted from the heart of a living or recently deceased victim. At first he experiments only with monkeys, but even this upsets his squeamish assistant, Ted, who complains that there must be "something evil in all this." [The spoilsport colorless character is played by the equally monochromatic David Bruce, in a Universal role that has Lon Chaney, Jr. written all over it: a sap who gets transformed by a crazy professor (think *Man Made Monster* [1940 (*q.v.*)], suffers torment, and loses his life, and the girl—Evelyn Ankers, here (as is often the case with Chaney).]

Morris dismisses Ted's moral concerns out of hand. He devotes considerably greater attention to Ted's fiancée, Isabel. She joins Morris and Ted for a drink but seems distracted. Morris guesses (correctly) that she is no longer in love with Ted [which already says something about Ted's identity, or lack thereof], and assumes (incorrectly) that she has fallen in love with him. The scientist decides to kill two birds with one stone by tricking Ted into becoming the subject of a human experiment with the "living-death" gas. He turns his assistant into a zombie, robs a grave, and collects the heart from a desecrated corpse. Using the stolen heart, he brews up the zombie antidote and restores Ted to his former self—but not before leaving his assistant a post-hypnotic message: "You will forget Isabel." He also removes from Ted all memory of the grave-robbery.

Shortly afterward, however, the monkey that Morris and Ted had previously revived returns to its zombie state. Morris realizes the same thing will happen to Ted—that he's doomed to re-lose whatever little personality he has and that Morris will be forced to continue robbing graves or even killing to keep his assistant from remaining a zombie forever. (If it weren't that Ted's condition would draw suspicion upon Morris, would he bother?) Then Morris learns that Isabel is in love—not with him but with her accompanist, Eric. For a moment, Morris sits in stunned silence. "We see what we want to see most of the time," Morris says, finally, Zucco's voice full of quiet heartache. "Even I, a scientist, have such moments of weakness." Morris, however, isn't about to give up on Isabel. He tries ordering the zombie-ized Ted to murder Eric and then commit suicide—setting up the film's frantic climax.

With its outlandish storyline and gory plot elements—not only zombie-ism and murder, but also robbing graves and cutting victims' hearts out—*The Mad Ghoul* ranks among the most, well, *ghoulish* of Universal's 1940s chillers. Thanks to Zucco's winning lead performance, it's also among Universal's most underrated.—*MDC*

Mad Love (1935) [**madness**] (Metro Goldwyn Mayer). *D:* Karl Freund. *S:* Guy Endore, From Florence Crewe-Jones' Adaptation of the Novel *Les Mains d'Orlac* by Maurice Renard. *Cast:* Peter Lorre (Dr. Gogol); Francis Drake (Yvonne Orlac); Colin Clive (Stephen Orlac); Ted Healy (Reagan); Sarah Haden (Marie); Edward Brophy (Rollo); Henry Kolker (Prefect of Police Rosset); Keye Luke (Dr. Wong); May Beatty (Françoise).

Many films treat loss-of-identity topics as exclusively a psychological phenomenon. *Mad Love*, one of MGM's last attempts to jump on the horror bandwagon of the 1930s, uses the transplantation of body parts to tap into an entire range of identity-based fears.

Stephen Orlac is a successful concert pianist until his hands are mangled in a train accident. In place of the damaged digits are grafted the hands of an executed murderer,

Dr. Gogol's (Peter Lorre) love for the wife of a concert pianist brings his twisted fantasies to a horrifying conclusion in *Mad Love*.

Rollo, a circus knife thrower. The presence of replacement body parts begins to take its toll on Orlac's psyche. Initially, Stephen is humbled by the loss of his musical prowess, which he can relive only through phonographic recordings. But in its place he discovers he has inherited a new and more disturbing talent—the ability to hurl knives with deadly accuracy. When his stepfather is found dead with a knife in the back, Orlac begins to doubt his own sanity. The premise of hands having a will of their own implies a loss of control that is fundamental to all loss-of-identity fears.

The crime's real culprit turns out to be Dr. Gogol, who performed Orlac's life-saving operation. Gogol secretly covets Orlac's wife, Yvonne, whom he first saw performing at a Grand Guignol theater. Before long, his obsession with her quickly spirals into full-fledged madness. After Yvonne spurns his advances, Gogol decides to take advantage of Orlac's fragile mental condition and concocts a plan to frame him for murder. Along the way, Gogol also plays a few identity games of his own. At one point, he poses as a reanimated Rollo, his hands encased in glowing metallic splints and his head supported by a ghastly neck brace. Gogol also confesses a strong identification with Pygmalion, the mythological sculptor who formed the figure of Galatea out of marble and saw it come to life in his arms. When Gogol gazes upon a wax statue of Yvonne, whose hair he strokes lovingly, he imagines himself as an incarnation of Pygmalion, a role that will consume him as he becomes further detached from reality.

As an actress, Yvonne Orlac is likewise skilled at the art of identity shifting. She is the headliner at the Théâtre des Horreurs, where her nightly torture scenes are a hit with the thrill-seeking audience. Quite unwittingly, Yvonne's thespic exploits feed the twisted fantasies of Gogol, who shows up dutifully night after night to watch the lurid play. Yvonne's playacting world and Gogol's disturbed fantasies collide head-on in the film's finale when she is forced to stand in for her own wax likeness, using her skills as an actress to engage in her own (faux) loss of identity. When a scratch on the cheek gives her away and she apparently comes to life, Gogol shouts in rapture, "I am Pygmalion!" Yvonne had known that Gogol was unstable, but she doesn't realize how out of touch he is with reality until her "awakening" triggers this emotional outburst. Then she realizes, nearly too late, the vulnerable situation in which she has placed herself. Though she'd been able to stave off Gogol's advances by "losing" her identity and masquerading as a wax figure, she accidentally plays into and feeds Gogol's mad certainty that he has created her new identity.

A failure at the box office, *Mad Love* is one of the more grotesque of the Golden Age horrors. Missing body parts, forbidden obsessions, and loss-of-identity themes are freely combined to make Peter Lorre's American film debut an auspicious one. Adding to the frisson is Lorre's memorable pronouncement that "each man kills the thing he loves." Organ/body transplants are still a common device in genre films today, but seldom is the potential for identity issues handled in such a skillfully horrific fashion.—*SGT*

Manchurian Candidate, The (1962) [**brainwashing; mind control**] (United Artists). *D:* John Frankenheimer. *S:* George Axelrod, John Frankenheimer (uncredited), From the Novel *The Manchurian Candidate* by Richard Condon. *Cast:* Frank Sinatra (Bennett Marco); Janet Leigh (Eugenie Rose Chaney); Laurence Harvey (Raymond Shaw); Angela Lansbury (Mrs. Iselin); James Gregory (Sen. John Iselin); Leslie Parrish (Jocelyn Jordan); John McGiver (Sen. Thomas Jordan); Khigh Dheigh (Dr. Yen Lo); Henry Silva (Chunjin).

A masterpiece of political thrills, John Frankenheimer's *The Manchurian Candidate* remains one of the most brilliant films of the 1960s. A stylish combination of paranoia and satire, the picture boasts a first-rate cast, effective direction, and a tight script by George Axelrod that closely follows Richard Condon's 1959 source novel. Frank Sinatra stars as Ben Marco, leader of a group of Korean War veterans who warmly support their dour comrade, Raymond Shaw, who has been nominated for the Congressional Medal of Honor. Yet Shaw's wartime heroism is a sham; he and his party were captured and brainwashed by Communist agents, and now the Reds are using Shaw as a pawn in a bizarre scheme to capture the White House and destroy America from within.

The theme of loss of identity is most profoundly demonstrated in Laurence Harvey's masterful performance as tortured Raymond Shaw, the unlikable scion of a hellish mother (Angela Lansbury, deservedly Oscar-nominated for her performance) and her drunken McCarthyish husband, Senator John Iselin. Certainly Shaw has been brainwashed, but a careful viewing of the film reveals the protagonist as a victim of a lifelong identity crisis. Shaw hates his ravenously ambitious mother and stepfather, who have tried to force him into being a model son for most of his life; the Medal of Honor business is primarily a gambit to improve Iselin's political standing. His family conflicts have made Shaw grow into the unfriendly jerk he appears to be, but his love for the daughter of his stepfather's rival reveals how kind and sensitive he truly is when in the proper company. Among the highlights of Harvey's performance is a scene in which the unfortunate Shaw, his programming accidentally activated, is inadvertently told to go jump in the lake—which he promptly does, silently and robotically, on the coldest day of the year. There is genuine anguish in Harvey's voice when he says to Sinatra's Major Ben Marco, "They can make me do anything, Ben, can't they? Anything."

Bennett Marco (Frank Sinatra, left) and his fellow prisoners are brainwashed by Communists in *The Manchurian Candidate*.

Shaw is not the only victim of brainwashing; so are his remaining compatriots, including Ben Marco, whose vivid nightmares of being conditioned by a Communist scientist indicate that the perfect brainwashing technique isn't quite infallible. Marco's attempts to master his own mind are dramatic and unnerving. Even the demonic Mrs. Iselin and her dullard husband aren't quite what they appear to be; circumstances as much as conspiracy have compelled them to project identities that do not truly reveal their natures, and in projecting these identities, the Iselins have in a sense become the people they seem to be.

The film's only serious misstep is the overnight romance that develops between Marco and Rosie, a girl he meets by happenstance on a train. The love story seems awfully rushed and out of place—but it is more or less a faithful translation from Condon's novel. Nevertheless, the coy dialogue between Marco and Rosie, particularly during their first meeting, feels like it has wandered in from another movie altogether. [*Cf.* another movie altogether: *The Manchurian Candidate* (2004).]—*JML*

Manchurian Candidate, The (2004) [**brainwashing; mind control**] (Paramount). *D:* Jonathan Demme. *S:* Daniel Pyne and Dean Georgaris, Based on the Screenplay by George Axelrod and the Novel *The Manchurian Candidate* by Richard Condon. *Cast:* Denzel Washington (Ben Marco); Meryl Streep (Eleanor Shaw); Leiv Schrieber (Raymond Shaw); Kimberly Elise (Rosie); Jon Voight (Sen. Thomas Jordan); Vera Farmiga (Jocelyn Jordan).

One improvement in Jonathan Demme's intermittently intriguing but ultimately inferior remake of the 1962 Frankenheimer classic (*q.v.*) is the romance between hero Ben Marco and Rosie. In the newer version, Rosie turns out to be part of the conspiracy, as her new beau Marco discovers when he tries to determine the truth behind Raymond Shaw. This time around, Raymond's mother, Eleanor, is the ambitious Senator—no need for her to have a husband to fill that role—and the Manchurian of the title refers to Manchurian Global Corporation, the multinational bent on world domination.

Ben Marco (Denzel Washington) is held prisoner and brainwashed in the remake of *The Manchurian Candidate*.

Streep is particularly effective as the duplicitous Senator, but otherwise the remake loses much of its punch by substituting corporate conspiracy for political shenanigans. The fall of Communism in Europe certainly indicates a new bad guy is appropriate for the 21st century, but the fact that Red China is still this nation's single greatest economic and military threat suggests that director Jonathan Demme and company have underestimated the danger of contemporary Communism. Or maybe they have simply been brainwashed. (Conspiracy theorists, start your blogging!)—*JML*

Man Made Monster (1940) [**zombification**] (Universal). *D:* George Waggner. *S:* George Waggner (as Joseph West), From the Story "The Electric Man," by Harry Essex, Len Golos, and Sid Schwartz. *Cast:* Lionel Atwill (Dr. Rigas); Lon Chaney, Jr. ("Dynamo" Dan McCormick); Anne Nagel (June Lawrence); Sanuel S. Hinds (Dr. Lawrence).

A year prior to *The Wolf Man* (1941 [*q.v.*]), director George Waggner and star Lon Chaney, Jr., collaborated on the underrated *Man Made Monster*. Although not in the same league as *The Wolf Man*, *Man Made Monster* remains an effective chiller and offers an interesting twist on the familiar loss-of-identity theme.

Chaney plays "Dynamo" Dan McCormick, a circus performer who's developed a resistance to electrical shocks in the course of doing his sideshow act. Kindly scientist Dr. Lawrence recruits McCormick to assist in his research into "electro-biology." But Lawrence's assistant, Dr. Rigas, sees Dan as the perfect guinea pig to test his own radical theories and begins conducting secret experiments that slowly transform the gregarious young man into a mindless, glowing, electrically charged automaton. At Rigas' command, McCormick murders Lawrence. He's captured, tried, and sentenced to die—but the electric chair only strengthens McCormick's powers, and he goes on the rampage.

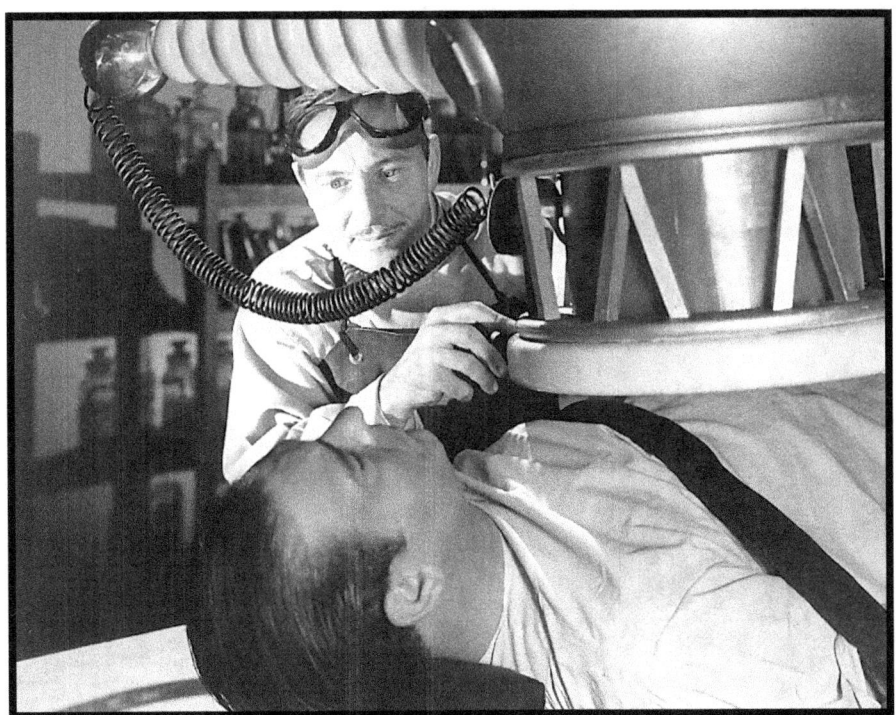

Dr. Rigas (Lionel Atwill) conducts secret experiments on Dynamo Dan McCormick (Lon Chaney, Jr.) in *Man Made Monster*.

Chaney is in fine form here, but Lionel Atwill as Rigas steals the show with a wildly over-the-top portrayal that earned him the nickname of "Hollywood's maddest doctor." Waggner's direction is swift and sure, and John P. Fulton's visual effects are first-rate. In his circus act, McCormick is billed as "The Electrical Man," which also served as the working title of the film. (Behind-the-scenes LOI: At one time, this project was going to be a Karloff-Lugosi vehicle, with Karloff in the Chaney part and Lugosi in the Atwill role—until its identity was altered.)—*MDC*

Man with Two Faces, The (1934) **[hypnotism]** First National Pictures, Inc. (Warner Bros.). *D:* Archie Mayo. *S:* Tom Reed and Niven Busch, Based on the Play *The Dark Tower* by Alexander Woollcott and George S. Kaufman. *Cast:* Edward G. Robinson (Damon Welles/Jules Chautard); Mary Astor (Jessica Wells); Ricardo Cortez (Producer Ben Weston); Mae Clarke (Daphne Flowers); Louis Calhern (Stanley Vance); Arthur Byron (Dr. Kendall); John Eldredge (Horace "Barry" Jones); David Landau (Sergeant William Curtis); Emily Fitzroy (Hattie, Martha's Housekeeper); Henry O'Neill (Inspector Crane).

On November 25, 1933, *The Dark Tower*, styled by its authors as "a melodrama," opened on Broadway at the Morosco Theatre and ran for 57 performances. Nine months later (August 4, 1934), *The Man with Two Faces*, Warner Bros.' retitled film version, premiered.

Despite its pedigree (written by the odd couple of Alexander Woollcott and George S. Kaufman, both members of the Algonquin Round Table but quite different person-

alities), *The Dark Tower* remains obscure in both of its dramatic incarnations, which is a shame because it features one of the slimiest villains to ever slink across stage or screen (a defining role for Louis Calhern in the film)—an example *not* of the satanic hypnotic powers of a Dracula, Svengali, or Rasputin, but the nonchalant command over women exerted by an immoral gigolo.

Stanley Vance possesses the uncanny power (never rationally explained) of complete dominance over certain women. One of these is Jessica Wells, celebrated Broadway-actress sister of celebrated Broadway actor Damon Wells. Whenever Vance is around, Jessica falls into a trance-like state, obedient to Vance's every whim. (To his regret, the irony is that, although Vance has complete control over the poor woman, it's at the cost of her vitality and drive, the things that make her a successful actress—and his meal ticket.)

The story cleverly withholds Vance's appearance, leading up to it by showing Jessica's concerned friends and family relieved that she's rid of her slave master and is her old self again (she and her brother have just triumphantly opened a new play). But Vance waltzes back into her life so the audience can see the effect—her complete and immediate deterioration and degradation.

Nothing remains, of course, but for Vance to be eliminated, and his greed sets him up, since he leaps at the chance to sell Jessica's half-share in the (now jeopardized) play. The out-of-town backer who apparently wants to buy into the play murders Vance instead and then seemingly disappears from the ship on which he booked passage—a suicide? Sharp-eyed film buffs will immediately see through the disguise of the nonexistent Jules Chautard (Max Sarnoff in the play); it's Damon incognito, he's subsumed his own identity (no great feat for an actor) in order to give his sister hers back.

The film, following the recently strongly enforced Production Code, cannot allow someone who took the law into his own hands, even for a noble cause, to go free. So the movie cop catches on to Damon's deception, and the actor turns himself in, whereas, in the play, he gets off scot free; the policeman is stymied; and everyone lives happily ever after. —*AFA*

Matrix, The (1999) [altered reality; scientific manipulation; search for self] (Warner Bros.). *D:* Andy and Larry Wachowski. *S:* Andy and Larry Wachowski. *Cast:* Keanu

Reeves (Neo); Laurence Fishburne (Morpheus); Carrie-Anne Moss (Trinity); Hugo Weaving (Agent Smith); Gloria Foster (the Oracle); Joe Pantoliano (Cypher).

When considering loss of identity in genre cinema, there's arguably no more dynamic and thought-provoking moment in movie history that more vividly encapsulates said concept than the sequence midway through this film, when Neo finally wakes up and sees the "real" world for the first time.

Emerging from a comatose state of existence, within which he has thus far spent his entire natural life, Neo begins a path toward a new identity.

Known within the simulated world as Thomas Anderson, he has lived a relatively mundane existence, programming software codes by day and engaging in illegal hacking activities by night, while all the time harboring the feeling that something is inexplicably wrong with his life and the world around him. Communicating under the alias Neo, he is soon contacted by Morpheus, a man revered by some and vilified by law-enforcement agencies across the globe, and who teases Neo with hints of an unspeakable truth about his life.

Neo progresses from temptation about the prospect of such a revelation to fraternization with the wanted man and his associates (including Neo's soon-to-be-love-interest Trinity), until Morpheus finally leads him to a simple choice, which, he is informed, will irrevocably alter his life.

Shortly after deciding to discover the truth, Neo learns that his entire life has been led within a computer simulation.

Let's just stop a moment to consider the enormity of this scenario within the context of loss of identity. Imagine if the world containing everything and everyone we ever knew that defined our life, whether conscious or otherwise, did not actually exist except as part of a virtual world designed to hold us in bondage. All the external forces that mold us into individuals—society, class, relationships, dreams, and so on—would remain powerfully resonant parts of our consciousness but would no longer exist tangibly in our true reality.

People who escape the matrix must come to terms with this fact—that their entire being and self-perceived identity has been formulated from variables within a software program designed to hold us captive.

However, perhaps the most salient question here, as Morpheus occasionally states, is, "What is 'real'?" Would a person have the same identity if he developed within a subconscious world identical to the so-called real one? Or, if someone spent several years of his life doing nothing but playing out life on a computer simulation, would he then take on the identity of the role he performed within that virtual world? And more importantly, if the simulated world is as tangible, sustainable, and *real* as the matrix, is there any difference between it and the actual "real" world?

Obviously, in this film the answer would be *yes*, as Neo quickly learns that reality is living the life of prey on a dark, turgid, and dangerous planet.

Blue pill, anyone?

Neo's personal situation is perhaps initially a little more challenging than that of others who, like him, opt for the red pill, for when he "awakes," Morpheus informs him that he is "the One," the prophesied legendary being who will stand against the domination of the machines over humanity and bring an end to the war that has resulted in most people living lives of virtual desperation.

Neo (Keanu Reeves) awakes to discover the true nature of mankind's existence in *The Matrix*.

So, rather than facing an internal struggle to determine exactly who he is, Neo must engage in a different, more dramatic struggle to accept whether he is actually the embodiment of humanity's renaissance. As far as his comrades on Morpheus' hovercraft are concerned, Neo doesn't have to establish (or re-establish, depending on our own perception of the matrix in comparison to reality) his identity as the One (although that identity evidently proves to be a bone of contention for some, such as the backstabbing Cypher). But Neo himself must confront this dualism of identity within his new surroundings: He grapples with both Morpheus' fundamental conviction that he is the One and his own doubts about the truth. But after a discussion with the Oracle, a woman who seems to know everything that happens within the matrix, and some ferocious combat with his soon-to-be mortal enemy, Agent Smith, it all becomes clear to him; Neo finally accepts his super-powered identity and takes to the skies, preparing to change the destiny of mankind.—*AJB*

Matrix Reloaded, The (2003) [**altered reality; scientific manipulation**] (Warner Bros.). *D:* Andy and Larry Wachowski. *S:* Andy and Larry Wachowski. *Cast:* Keanu Reeves (Neo); Laurence Fishburne (Morpheus); Carrie-Anne Moss (Trinity); Hugo Weaving (Agent Smith); Gloria Foster (the Oracle); Lambert Wilson (Merovingian); Helmut Bakaitis (the Architect).

Throughout *The Matrix* (1999 [*q.v.*]), its protagonist and hero Neo seems to be unsure of his identity, both within himself and in the wider world, especially upon his "awakening" when he sees the world as it truly is. Obviously by the end of the film he believes he understands the path that has been laid out before him as "the One"— namely, to guide humanity to survival and peace with the machines.

As *Reloaded* gets underway, we soon realize that his status as the savior has been well and truly accepted, not just by Neo but by the majority of inhabitants of the last human city, Zion. Of course, this reverent acceptance from many within Zion causes many of the survivors to discard their ability to help themselves, preferring instead to relinquish their identities and hurl themselves at the feet of the One to beg for deliverance.

Morpheus, in the role of apostle, is responsible for spreading the gospel of the One to the populace, proclaiming to all at every opportunity that Neo is the savior, and professing unshakeable faith in the new icon of hope. Indeed, Morpheus' character alters significantly from the first film; he has changed from a believer to an outright fundamentalist, which seems to color his thinking in every matter, whether he is addressing the council of Zion, the general commanding the city's defense, or the large crowd that gathers for a Dionysian shindig in the depths of the city.

Likewise Trinity, who slips almost comfortably from the role of hardened guerrilla warrior to the messiah's love interest. It's difficult to tell at times whether she truly loves Neo or is actually just another believer caught up in the possibility that he can save her from extinction—this ambiguity possibly stemming from her own doubts about their future together.

For Neo's part, the mantle of the One seems to rest a little uncomfortably upon his shoulders, but he gets on with it, occasionally spending time to indulge the masses who worship him, either through genuine pity for their circumstances or perhaps in an attempt to maintain solidarity in the face of a pending all-out assault by the machines.

However, things take a turn when he is confronted by another revelation about his existence and his powers to combat the machine menace. Both the all-knowing Oracle and the Merovingian, a gangster and powermonger code built into the matrix, initially hint at this revelation, which is finally unveiled during Neo's eventual confrontation with the Architect, the program responsible for contriving the matrix itself. The Architect informs Neo that he is the latest in a line of saviors, all of whom stood before the Architect and were forced to make a choice to save a remnant of or condemn all of humanity. (So far, the preceding five opted for the former course.)

Neo (Keanu Reeves) seeks insight from the Oracle (Gloria Foster) in *The Matrix Reloaded.*

Neo (Keanu Reeves) must face a titanic battle of good against evil to save humanity from slavery in *The Matrix Revolutions*.

Thus Neo discovers that he is far from the unique and infallible savior that Morpheus and other believers think he is. Even so (or perhaps because of this fact), he decides that he cannot select a mere handful of people to escape the coming Zion apocalypse and instead chooses to fight. [In this decision, at least, he is unique among Ones.]

Meanwhile, Agent Smith is also undergoing a transition, returning from his apparent demise at Neo's hands to attain the ability to take over everyone within the matrix, literally removing their identity and appearance and changing them into clones of himself. The process allows Smith the opportunity to take command of the network and bring about its demise; the people who fall to him are, quite literally, removed from conscious existence within the program.

With this film, the Matrix license itself seems to undergo a loss of identity of sorts throughout this poorly contrived and badly told story. Although *Reloaded*'s special effects and fight sequences are enjoyable, it expands upon the simple yet thought-provoking themes of the first film in a manner akin to the most laughable of pseudo-philosophical concepts; the dialogue suffers shockingly as some ludicrous lines spew from the mouths of the characters. Indeed, it's almost as if the filmmakers have been bullied into producing a money-spinning sequel, without any prior thought or plans about how they would actually make it work.

I'm too weak to suppress my own identity and not state how bad this movie actually is...—*AJB*

Matrix Revolutions, The (2003) [**altered reality; scientific manipulation**] (Warner Bros.). *D:* Andy and Larry Wachowski. *S:* Andy and Larry Wachowski. *Cast:* Keanu Reeves (Neo); Laurence Fishburne (Morpheus); Carrie-Anne Moss (Trinity); Hugo Weaving (Agent Smith).

"Everything that has a beginning has an end."

Thankfully, after the unappetizing *Matrix Reloaded* (2003 [*q.v.*]), the end to the Matrix trilogy is a palatable affair, culminating in a titanic battle between Neo and Agent Smith.

At the last, we are presented with the polar opposites of good and evil, as Neo, humanity's savior, confronts Smith, the archetypal megalomaniac seeking domination over both humans and machines alike.

Ultimately good triumphs over evil, and Neo releases humanity from slavery.

Both his and Trinity's sacrifices allow the remnants of the human race to be released from their shackles, making the transition from enslaved and hunted creatures to free beings. [Machines bear Neo off; is he unplugged for good, free at last?—or, as at least one critic wondered, will his coding be reinserted into the matrix, his identity lost to or absorbed in the matrix Oversoul?]

All that remains is for Morpheus to lead his congregation in worship of his dead god, and for the free to learn how to live without fear.—*AJB*

Memento (2000) [**amnesia**] I Remember Productions LLC (Newmarket Films). *D:* Christopher Nolan. *S:* Christopher Nolan, more or less Based on Jonathan Nolan's Story "Memento Mori" (written concurrently). *Cast:* Guy Pearce (Leonard); Carrie-Anne Moss (Natalie); Joe Pantoliano (Teddy Gammell); Mark Boone Junior (Burt); Russ Fega (Waiter); Jorja Fox (Leonard's Wife); Stephen Tobolowsky (Sammy).

You have a brain injury that prevents you from making new memories. You can't remember where you're staying, people you know, things you've done, conversations you've had—anything, really—since the injury. Except that you sort of *can* remember some things—like that you really *really* want to kill John G., the guy who raped and murdered your wife, and injured you. And except that maybe your wife didn't die in the assault, if this cop Teddy is to be believed. What if *you* killed her accidentally, and have killed multiple John G.s to avenge her death? And, worse, what if you have constructed an elaborate set of lies to prevent you from ever learning the truth about yourself?

That, in a nutshell, is the nightmare scenario facing Leonard Shelby in the multifaceted loss-of-identity thriller *Memento*. Is Teddy ("Don't believe his lies") telling the truth? And if so, can we trust anything, really, that we learn from Leonard, a man with no reliable memory? Is Leonard essentially still a former insurance investigator now on a mission to "make things right"? Was he ever an investigator? Is he now some "sad pathetic freak" living off the grid, killing at the whim or purpose of whoever sets up the next "John G." to be the fall guy? Is his entire quest really just about assuaging his own conscience for giving his wife too much insulin? Who knows? But we're getting ahead of ourselves.

Memento has a notoriously complex structure, with the plot itself moving backwards and overlapping in order to simulate

Leonard's own confusion, while a secondary plot (the story of Sammy Jankis—Leonard's attempt to explain his "condition") moves forward through a series of phone calls.

In the backwards-motion plot: After Leonard (at film's end) kills a John (actually, Jimmy) G., Teddy tells him "the truth"—a truth which shows Teddy (the cop on his wife's case) playing Leonard as mercilessly as Bytes and the Night Porter play John Merrick in *The Elephant Man* (1980). Leonard keeps this memory active long enough to set up Teddy ("John Edward Gammell") to be the next John G. And, in the movie's opening chapters, we watch Leonard execute this new John G.

Between killing Jimmy and Teddy, Leonard wanders into an involvement with Jimmy's girlfriend, Natalie, who plays on his weakness as mercilessly as Teddy does, but who uses feminine vulnerability to cover up her intentions. Still, we are left in the end with questions: When Natalie gives Leonard the DMV info to help him identity his new John G., is she aware that this John G. is the "Teddy" who had her boyfriend killed? Is she setting Leonard up to take a fall for killing a cop? Is she making Leonard her thrall, as he apparently was Teddy's? Or has her attitude changed? Is she now helping Leonard in his quest? How much of a femme fatale is she, anyway? Once Teddy is gone, we must wonder if Leonard will continue—John G. after John G.—at Natalie's whim (as he seemingly did at Teddy's), or if he has been freed from endless "revenge" by the snapshot of this new dead John G. Since the movie ends with a snapshot, not a tattoo, we are left not knowing. But that is the one constant in this film: not knowing.

This not knowing is taken to elaborate lengths in the Sammy Jankis plot. Sammy, Leonard states, had a head injury and short-term memory loss, but when testing could not condition habits into a different part of his brain, his problem was ruled mental, not physical. He should have been able to make new memories. When Leonard (the claims investigator) rejected Sammy's claim, Sammy's wife began testing her husband to see if he could be jolted out of his short-term memory loss. Eventually, she had him inject her multiple times with insulin, resulting in her coma and death. According to Teddy's "truth," though, Sammy had no wife. Leonard's wife was the diabetic, and Leonard injected her.

Teddy's "truth" forces us to question just how much of Sammy's story is really a projection of Leonard's own experience. Was Leonard subjected to Pavlovian conditioning tests? Was his insurance claim thrown out? Was his wife skeptical about his condition? If his condition is truly physical, then how did he retain these memories from after his injury, distorted, and transformed as they are? And how is it that sometimes even in his old memories, his wife's face is exchanged for a new face—Natalie's? Is Leonard's condition, as he concluded Sammy's was, "mental" rather than physical?

We don't know. But when we watch Natalie play his weakness (taunting Leonard into smashing her face, then telling him a few minutes later that Dodd—a man she fears will kill her—did it), we do know that no amount of conditioning can make Leonard's life workable. Conditioning didn't work for Sammy...and it doesn't work for Leonard either, no matter how often he proclaims it does.

Leonard's life, as Teddy tells him for his own purposes, is a lie. He has no idea, really, who he is or what he has become. He can't accurately trust a man's life to a few slips of paper when he doesn't know exactly where he got his "facts." He can't even guess correctly where he got (Jimmy's) Jaguar or suit.

Memory may, as Leonard claims, be unreliable. But facts without the glue of memory are even more so. And so we reach Leonard's core problem—his *noir* problem:

By playing a game of death, totally divorced from context, he has made himself a thing to be played. Any unscrupulous person can manipulate Leonard's "facts" to make drug money for himself or settle old scores. And Leonard—or whatever's left of whoever he was—will never know.—*CCS*

Mephisto Waltz, The (1971) [**possession; body switching**] Quinn Martin Productions (20th Century Fox). *D:* Paul Wendkos. *S:* Ben Maddow, Based on the Novel *The Mephisto Waltz* by Fred Mustard Stewart. *Cast:* Alan Alda (Myles Clarkson); Jacqueline Bisset (Paula Clarkson); Barbara Parkins (Roxanne Delancey); Bradford Dillman (Bill Delancey); Curt Jurgens (Duncan Ely); William Windom (Dr. West); Pamelyn Ferdin (Abby Clarkson).

In the wake of *Rosemary's Baby*, horror films found a receptive audience by catering to the mainstream audience of the late 1960s. *The Mephisto Waltz* follows this trend, incorporating loss-of-identity elements into a seemingly normal domestic situation.

Struggling journalist Myles Clarkson strikes up a friendship with concert pianist Duncan Ely after he is granted an interview with the musical luminary. Ely and daughter Roxanne Delancey sense a nascent talent in Myles and encourage him to pursue his musical ambitions, despite the protests of his wife, Paula, that "they're too damn friendly." When Ely succumbs to leukemia, his will stipulates that Myles is to receive his cherished Steinway along with $100,000 to further his musical career. Myles begins practicing rigorously and, with emotional support from the duplicitous Roxanne, prepares to make his concert debut.

But other changes are soon evident in Myles. He quickly tires of his conventional lifestyle and develops a taste for fine dining and expensive liquor. Myles also prefers to spend all his waking hours at Roxanne's stately home, continually refining his musical prowess. Paula's fears are aroused when she experiences a frightful dream, during which

Myles Clarkson (Alan Alda) will soon be a lot closer to Duncan Ely (Curt Jurgens) then he could ever imagine in *The Mephisto Waltz*.

Ely menaces her young daughter, Abby, while claiming "it's part of the bargain." After Abby is stricken with a fatal disease, Paula discovers that Ely's wife also died under mysterious circumstances—and uncovers rumors of his involvement with a satanic cult. To her horror, Paula begins to suspect that Ely has taken possession of Myles' body, extending his own life and affording him the opportunity to continue his incestuous relationship with Roxanne. When Myles performs his first concert in front of a rapturous audience, Paula becomes convinced that the devil's bargain has been cinched.

Knowledge of Ely's demonic game plan proves dangerous to Paula, who soon finds her own life in jeopardy. In a classic case of "if you can't beat 'em, join 'em," Paula turns the tables on her pursuers and makes her own deal with "the master." The spells are recited, the ceremony is performed, and the film concludes with Paula, after apparently committing suicide, trading places with Roxanne. Her quest to be reunited with "Myles" is successful, although the long-term stability of the relationship remains open to question [especially since Myles is really Ely, the man Paula hated and feared, so why she would give up her Jacqueline Bisset body for a Barbara Parkins model, just to be reunited with the husband who isn't her husband is a good question that the story's creators never bothered to answer].

Like many "respectable" horror movies, *The Mephisto Waltz* downplays any supernatural elements, preferring instead to suggest that the horrors may only be a figment of Paula's overwrought imagination. As such, it appears sober and staid at a time when genre films had begun to turn increasingly exploitive. The denouement begs credibility too, although it is suggested that Paula enjoys a heightened sense of carnality that motivates her eventual acceptance of the dark side. In the final analysis, the film implies that none of the principals are capable of retaining their innocence. This, along with the film's presentation of soul transference, is the film's most noteworthy contribution to the loss-of-identity cinema.—*SGT*

Minority Report (2002) [**scientific manipulation; eradication of self**] (20th Century Fox). *D:* Stephen Spielberg. *S:* Scott Frank and Jon Cohen, Based on the Story "Minority Report" by Philip K. Dick. *Cast:* Tom Cruise (John Anderton); Colin Farrell (Danny Witwer); Max Von Sydow (Lamar Burgess); Kathryn Morris (Lara); Samantha Morton (Agatha); Peter Stomare (Dr. Solomon Eddie); Jessica Harper (Anne Lively); Tim Blake Nelson (Gideon).

To say that *Minority Report* concerns a loss of *eye*-dentity is not to be clever but merely to take a description from the movie itself, in which Precrime cop John Anderton finds himself accused of a yet-to-be-committed homicide and must get his eyeballs switched in order to elude the authorities; in the world of 2054, retina scans are used as biological IDs. But, before he gets his new orbs, Anderton has already lost his identity as Precrime's chief investigator—reduced to a common would-be criminal and forced to flee the very authorities who once answered to him. (A visual image of Anderton's total loss occurs after he's caught: Immobilized and nearly naked, incarcerated in an individual holding tube, he's shelved away with his fellow future criminals, their cells forming a sort of hydraulic living crypt.)

Minority Report begins with a typically tautly edited Spielberg suspense sequence, introducing the audience to the Precrime Division, the Precogs who see future murder, and the method Precrime cops use to thwart a killing about to happen. The sequence ends with the arrest of the suspect just seconds before he's about to commit his preordained murder. His protest that he hasn't done anything falls on deaf ears as he's carted away (but it introduces another wrinkle for the audience—about the infallibility and ethics of Precrime). Obviously, if the murders that the Precogs see can be prevented, then the future they predict is *not* preordained or fixed. (Philip K. Dick spells out this aspect in his short story: "If only one time-path existed, precognitive information would be of no importance, since no possibility would exist, in possessing this information, of altering the future." Knowing the "future" means that one can alter it. In the movie, the Precog Agatha stresses to Anderton that he has a *choice*.)

In Dick's story, characters raise the possibility that Precrime detection/detention may

John Anderton (Tom Cruise) will soon find that everything he believed in was wrong when he is accused of a murder before it happens in *Minority Report*.

net innocent men, but that idea is eventually discarded (the system *is* infallible), and the heroes must protect the agency from bad guys working to undermine it, to prove fallibility in order to discredit and disband Precrime. In the movie, the bad guy is Lamar Burgess, the "father" of Precrime, who's trying to preserve and promote the practice *at all costs*. The film's approach is just the opposite of its source's—which, ultimately, makes it superior to the story and a more successful film than, say, *Impostor* (2002 [*q.v.*]), another Dick adaptation, which is truer to Dick's text and thus ends up embracing some very questionable moral positions. (Summarizing Dick's "Imposter": "Even though you feel human, you're an alien because we say so—and we're right." Summarizing Dick's "Minority Report": "Even though you'd never kill anyone, especially a man you don't know, you will because we say so—and we're right.")

The other loss of identity in *Minority Report* is the humanity of the precognitives. Dick callously treats them as mere devices (in the story they're gifted with second sight but otherwise mentally and physically disabled); characters refer to them as monkeys and put audible quotation marks around their names—"Mike," "Donna," "Jerry"—as if the idea of calling them anything is absurd. The film's Precogs possess actual names (Agatha, Arthur, and Dashiell—no quotation marks but named by the screenwriters after Christie, Doyle, and Hammett, three practitioners of detection) and suffer from no visible defects. However, they are stripped of their individuality and personality and kept doped up in an induced trance/lethargy (in part, it's claimed, to protect them from being overwhelmed by their visions). Their only activity is to dream what's to be and announce an upcoming murder (via the wooden balls on which their brainwaves inscribe victim's and killer's names), and provide images for the cops to record and study.

The prime mover behind both the Precogs' loss of identity and John Anderton's is Lamar Burgess. Because the Precogs (and especially Agatha, the most talented seer) were integral to Precrime's success, Burgess resorted to homicide when Agatha's formerly drug-addicted, now-clean mother, Anne Lively, demanded her daughter back. To ensure that Agatha remained under Precrime control, he used the "echo" effect of the Precogs' vision (re-seeing a murder already visualized)—hiring a patsy of a hitman, who was apprehended, and then cleverly copy-catting the man's actions to commit Lively's murder. To ensure that the program can expand and "go national," he is willing to sacrifice his protégé Anderton by framing him for a future murder. (The twists that the scripters wring from the plot match the spirit of Dick's puzzles and solutions in the short story.) But even Burgess, after his machinations have been exposed, rediscovers himself and his scruples—and proves his Precrime practices wrong—when, instead of killing Anderton as predicted in the Precogs' vision, he turns the gun on himself.

The end of *Minority Report* is a triumph for identity regained, free choice asserted. (*Cf.* the issues explored in that other LOI picture, *A Clockwork Orange* [1971 (*q.v.*)]) The three Precogs have been given their lives back, given a chance at life, living on their own, removed from the inundation of human thought in the city. Anderton has been reunited with his estranged wife, and they're expecting their second child. (This element is perhaps Spielberg's only misstep—he sometimes has a tendency to go sentimentally overboard, as in the coda that concludes *Saving Private Ryan* [1997]. An important plot point involved the kidnapping and probable murder of Anderton's young son several years before, which led to his dedication to Precrime, the disintegration of his marriage, and the "hook" that allowed Burgess to set up Anderton's future murder. Bringing the couple back together would have been enough. Showing Lara pregnant is perhaps a bit much. But maybe that's me—maybe the filmmakers felt they needed to show Anderton with his entire identity regained: policeman, husband, father.)—*AFA*

Misterious de ultratumba. See **Black Pit of Dr. M, The** (1959).

Mr. Vampire (*Geung si sin sang*) [zombification; mind control] (1985) Hong Kong (Bo Ho Film Company Ltd./Golden Harvest Company Ltd.). *D:* Ricky Lau. *S:* Ricky Lau, Chuek-Hon Szeto, and Barry Wong; Story by Ying Wong. *Cast:* Ching-Ying Lam (Master Gau); Siu-hou Chin (Chou); Ricky Hui (Man Choi); Moon Lee [as Choi-fung Li] (Ting-Ting); Billy Lau (Wai); Pauline Wong (Jade).

The Chinese undead, whom we meet in this Hong Kong horror classic, serve as prime examples for loss of identity in cinema.

Unlike her Western counterpart, a Chinese female ghost is a fearsome creature, more like a succubus than an incorporeal spirit. She is sexually insatiable, but in her insatiability, she controls the mind and slowly drains the life of the men she seduces. A Chinese vampire is even more fearsome. True, he hops. But his hopping batters

Mr. Vampire (Yuen Wah) pretty insulted that he was buried vertically, takes it out on his family and anyone else in the vicinity in *Mr. Vampire*.

down well-bolted gates. His long fingernails rip through walls. He does not talk. He cannot hear. He cannot see. Breath and smell are the only things he shares with the living...whom he can find only by smelling their breath. And *when* he finds them, he tears at their flesh with all the ferocity of a werewolf or flesh-eating zombie.

A Chinese vampire is as feral and single-minded as one would expect a predator ruled entirely by instinct to be. He has no personality. He has completely lost his identity. All that remains is an insatiable desire to rip into the living. A female ghost, on the other hand, robs her sexual target of his identity.

In *Mr. Vampire*, Master Gau, a Taoist priest, and his two hapless assistants are hired by a rich man to dig up the man's father and rebury him in order to bring good fortune. They soon discover that the dead man was buried vertically...an insult to the dead, which probably accounts for why his corpse has not decayed in 20 years. The priest orders his assistants, Chou and Man Choi, to place incense on the graves to appease the spirits of the dead, but in doing so, the handsome assistant, Chou, excites the interest of a young woman's spirit.

In the world of Chinese horror, none of this is good news. The female ghost soon succeeds in seducing the handsome Chou. The undecayed father, of course, turns into a vampire and escapes his restraints almost effortlessly. This newly unbound "Mr. Vampire" soon shreds his millionaire son's throat, turning him into a (ferocious, but quickly subdued) vampire. And the next night an increasingly powerful Mr. Vampire bites the un-handsome assistant, Man Choi, who begins transforming into a vampire himself. Chaos and comic hijinks ensue.

In her seduction, the ghost, of course, controls Chou's mind, placing him in an illusory world where her decaying face is still beautiful, where her rotting abode is still palatial, where even Master Gau's efforts to free his assistant appear to Chou as a loutish rival's attempt to rape his ghostly love.

In the end, though, Master Gau does free Chou, and the priest and his assistants succeed in subduing Mr. Vampire. But given that these are the *Chinese* undead, they are subduable only by distinctly Chinese means...martial arts, applied potions, yellow paper quoting Taoist scripture, and lots and lots of sticky rice. When all else fails, there's always fire.

Mr. Vampire is a seminal film in the Hong Kong horror canon. It turned actor Ching-Ling Lam (Master Gau) into the quintessential Taoist vampire-hunter, and spawned sequels and imitations galore—giving us reels and reels of the hopping dead.—*CCS*

Monster and the Girl, The (1941) [**brain switching**] (Paramount). *D:* Stuart Heisler. *S:* Stuart Anthony. *Cast:* Ellen Drew (Susan Webster); Robert Paige (Larry Reed); Paul Lukas (W.S. Bruhl); Joseph Calleia ("Deacon"); Onslow Stevens (J. Stanley McMasters); George Zucco (Dr. Perry); Rod Cameron (Sam Daniels); Phillip Terry (Scot Webster); Marc Lawrence (Sleeper); Gerald Mohr (Munn); Charles Gemora (Gorilla, uncredited).

The Monster and the Girl is a fun little picture that fuses film-noir elements with classic horror-genre motifs. In a shocking plot development for the time, beautiful but naïve Susan Webster is tricked into a marriage with Larry Reed. After their wedding night, Larry reveals himself to be part of a criminal gang that forces Susan into prostitution. Susan's brother, Scot, attempts to help her, but the mobsters frame him for murder. Unfairly sentenced to die (his lawyer is also part of the gang), Scot is approached by Dr. Perry on the eve of his execution. Scot agrees to donate his body to science. Perry's experiment is transplanting a human brain into a gorilla. The gorilla—with Scot's brain—escapes and goes on a killing spree, murdering the gang members one by one. Eventually, the police shoot and kill the beast, but not before Susan is freed of the mobsters' control and returned to a respectable life.

Arguably, there is no loss of identity in this film. The picture makes it quite clear that the gorilla has retained Scot's memories and intelligence after the operation. There is no other explanation for its behavior as it kills each of the gangsters (acts that the audience cannot help but root for). So any loss of identity here is actually very minor. In fact, it is only Scot's exterior or physical identity that is lost. He is, obviously, no longer human—he is a gorilla. And were he not killed by the police, he would continue to be a gorilla. But Scot does not let this setback keep him from achieving his revenge-driven goals. Instead, he actually uses his newfound strength and agility to do what needs to be done. Even Scot's dog sees through the physical exterior and recognizes his master's true self. In a touching subplot, the dog follows on the gorilla's heels and is last seen by the side of the dead gorilla, mourning the death of his master.

If anyone loses identity in this film, it is not the monster but the girl. Susan starts off as a likable young woman hoping to find success in the big city. Caught up in circumstances beyond her control, she is forced into a life of prostitution. This is not a life she would have chosen for herself, nor is it a position in which she wants to remain. But the gangsters give her no choice—they force her to become someone else. They force a loss of identity on her. This is the film's tragedy, reflecting the real-life downfalls of girls who lose themselves in big cities to lives of prostitution and drug abuse. If only there actually was a guardian gorilla out there protecting fallen women.

The Monster and the Girl is not wholly original. The plot is reminiscent of *The Walking Dead* (1935 [*q.v.*]) while the idea of transplanting a man's brain into a gorilla's head is also hinted at in *The Strange Case of Dr. Rx* (1942). And those are just two examples of movies that this one apes (pun intended). Yet the film stands on its own two feet as a tight little thriller that should satisfy fans of both horror and gangster pictures.—*JSM*

Monster on the Campus (1958) **[metamorphosis]** (Universal International). *D*: Jack Arnold. *S*: David Duncan. *Cast*: Arthur Franz (Professor Donald Blake); Joanna Moore (Madeline Howard); Judson Pratt (Lt. Mike Stevens); Troy Donahue (Jimmy Flanders).

Horror films of the 1950s delved into a specific subgenre many times, that of modern man reverting to his primordial self. *The Neanderthal Man* (1953) was one of the first, and *The Vampire* (1957 [*q.v.*]) became the cinema's finest variation on that theme. (We can see echoes in 1980's *Altered States* [*q.v.*].) Less than a year after *The Vampire*, Universal attacked the subject with *Monster on the Campus*, another scientific-regression trip back to the Stone Age. Unfortunately this Jack Arnold–directed programmer is generally loathed as the nadir of his career and considered to be one of the 1950s' worst B horror features. While the film is about on the same level as 1960's *The Leech Woman* (which is slightly more original), *Monster on the Campus* is not without its merits. Perhaps its chief strength is Arthur Franz's star performance as Professor Blake; he delivers an intense, fun-filled turn as the pipe-smoking college professor who gets caught up in his work.

Like Universal's earlier LOI-themed *Tarantula* (1955 [*q.v.*]), *Monster on the Campus* first depicts animals undergoing a loss of identity. Here Samson, man's best friend, playfully laps up the bloody water flowing from the crate carrying the thawing prehistoric fish that Blake exported from Madagascar (the fish itself is not prehistoric,

Professor Donald Blake (Arthur Franz) injures himself in the lab and transforms into a murderous fiend in *Monster on the Campus.*

but the species has not evolved for millions of years...and this specific one has been preserved with gamma-ray radiation). Within minutes, the poor hound sprouts elongated canine teeth and attacks his human friends, including student Jimmy. By that evening, Blake cuts his own hand on the fish, drawing blood, and accidentally soaks his ailing hand in the fishy waters that turned the dog momentarily insane. Becoming very ill, Blake asks a female colleague to drive him home, but once there he transforms into an unseen monster who frightens the young woman to death and leaves her hanging by her hair in the garden.

Of course the next day the dog is perfectly normal, as is Blake, but the scientist pursues his regression theories to their final ends. Soon a dragonfly feeds off the ugly, monstrous fish and transforms into a gigantic prehistoric version of itself, only to be speared by the brave Blake. Unfortunately, when he extracts the spear, blood from the blade drips into Blake's pipe. (What are the odds of *that* happening?) Naturally, the well-intentioned professor is quite unaware of this contamination. So, as the doctor opens one of his texts to read about the prehistoric dragonfly, his vision becomes cloudy and he hallucinates. During this trippy interlude, the enlarged dragonfly shrinks back into its smaller, modern version. And Blake succumbs one more time to the regression process and, as the unseen monster, once again kills an innocent victim.

By this time, the college superiors begin to suspect that Professor Blake is ill and needs a vacation, so his boss offers Blake use of his isolated mountain cabin. Blake plans to continue his work there, now suspecting that he himself might be the murderous prehistoric fiend. Tying strings to multiple cameras aimed from every angle to capture the transformation—if that is what indeed is occurring— Blake injects himself with his formula. Afterward, having learned the truth that he has regressed to aggressive ancient-human status, Blake is prepared to sacrifice his life for the advancement of science, arranging his own death while being observed by his scientific superiors. (Unfortunately, Universal, so famous for its monstrous makeup conceptions, here substitutes a floppy rubber mask and beefed-up chest-and-shoulder body suit to very ridiculous effect. No wonder only grunts and a hairy hand and arm are depicted in the earlier transformations.)

What makes *Monster on the Campus* so interesting and suspenseful is the fact that, until the final reel, Blake is never sure he is the fiend—and he is not convinced he is until he views the results of the photos taken at the mountain cabin at the very end. He begins to piece the mystery together, realizing that whenever he awakens in the park or on the lawn, a victim of foul play always turns up not far away. (Once, Jimmy—always trying to protect his beloved professor—even slips the professor his pipe after Jimmy recovers it at a murder scene.) Blake suspects the truth after his entire laboratory is destroyed—furniture thrown around, priceless equipment ruined—but remains true to the scientific method: He demands bona fide proof. And when he gets his proof, he then sets himself up to be shot to death by the called-for police (in fact instructing them to shoot to kill!). So, in this low-rent scientific rethinking of the Jekyll-Hyde theme, once he confirms that he indeed is the fiend, our Professor Blake understands he must pay the ultimate price for his loss of human identity. And *Monster on the Campus* deserves some credit for that.—*GJS*

Mummy, The (1932) [**reincarnation; hypnotism**] Universal. *D:* Karl Freund. *S:* John L. Balderston, story by Nina Wilcox Putnam and Richard Schayer. *Cast:* Boris Karloff (Imhotep/Ardath Bey); Zita Johann (Helen); David Manners (Frank); Edward Van Sloan (Dr. Muller); Bramwell Fletcher (Ralph).

The iconic Universal horror classic *The Mummy* surprisingly becomes a thought-provoking example of the horror of loss of identity. At heart a reincarnation romance with a monster, *The Mummy* deals with the horrors of loss of self through the revelation, to Helen Grosvenor, that she is the reincarnated Egyptian lover of Imhotep, now revived and living as Ardath Bey. While Ardath Bey's memories are always of his former life as an Egyptian high priest, Helen Grosvenor considers herself modern in every way. The thought that she might be linked to a woman who lived 3,500 years ago is simply absurd.

But Ardath Bey has the mystified woman gaze into the fascinating Pool of Time to see her past lives. Many reincarnation sequences were deleted from the final theatrical print, but the one remaining makes clear that she loved passionately the decaying corpse before her. No longer is such a romance appealing, not after thousands of years. Besides, Helen is currently falling in love with hero Frank Whemple, and her heart now belongs to him.

As *The Mummy* unwinds, Ardath Bey is able to grow stronger and assert more and more control over the human pawns that he seeks to dominate, including Helen. Bey is able to control her telepathically (her eyes glaze over; she enters a trance-like state) and bid her to do his will. At the film's climax, Helen, still in a trance, scantily dressed in ancient Egyptian clothing, willfully lies supine on the sacrificial altar, not yet conscious

Ardath Bey (Boris Karloff) seeks to regain his lost love in Helen Grosvenor (Zita Johann), the reincarnation of the Egyptian princess, in *The Mummy*.

of what Ardath Bey has in store for her. Raising a huge sacrificial knife, Bey wishes to end Helen's life so that, using the powers of the god Amon Ra, he can see his Princess reborn in Helen's body, both of them to be immortal and able to smooch throughout all time.

Such loss of identity involves the fading memory of Helen Grosvenor and the awakening consciousness of her Egyptian former self. In *The Mummy*, loss of identity is actually the substituting of one collective human memory for another, since the theory of reincarnation implies that all of us have lived multiple lives but only remember our current one. Under Karl Freund's visually arresting and somber direction, Zita Johann's performance becomes intense as the cosmopolitan everywoman slowly comes to see herself as a different entity entirely, her face and eyes bulging in fear and anticipation. Helen never embraces her former life, but she seems totally overwhelmed to actually discover she lived many lives throughout history; and to a superficial gal, this news is *more* than overwhelming.

Boris Karloff's deliberate, slo-mo performance, his obsession to regain the love of his distant life, contrasts nicely to Zita Johann's fear, confusion, and vulnerability. Remember, Ardath Bey does not win his lover's heart back again with smooth words or presents; Bey uses the power of the gods and Egyptian magic to win domination of her soul. In other words, Bey does not fight fair, and the only concern he seems to express is his ultimate power of will. He'll never be the romantic lover; he remains the power-obsessed male determined to control his Princess in any way possible, but always against her will (the will that wants to remain Helen).

Zita Johann submits one of the most disturbing and convincing portrayals of loss of identity in the horror film, and her arsenal of emotions, as she ventures from being David Manners' purring love interest to the dazed and confused pawn of Boris Karloff, makes this performance richer as time goes on.—*GJS*

New Mr. Vampire, The (***Jiang shi fan sheng***) (1987) [**zombification; soul transference**] Hong Kong (Focus Films Co., Ltd.). *D:* Billy Chan and Leung Chung. *S:* Liang Hua. *Cast:* Chung Fat (Master Chin); Chin Siu-ho (Wang Choi); Lui Fong (Tai-fa); Pauline Wong (His-wan); Ku Feng (Criminal Boss).

The New Mr. Vampire (unrelated to the old one) presents us once again with a fierce, feral, utterly instinct-driven Chinese vampire—a vampire with no personality, no human identity. But the vampire is actually the least of this movie's loss-of-identity depictions.

In *The New Mr. Vampire*, there is no all-powerful Taoist priest who can control the living dead. Instead, there are two warring Taoist priest brothers...one of whom undermines the efforts of the other. When a local crime lord chooses Master Chin over his brother, Priest Wu, to bury a Mafia Boss in the boss' home town, the vengeful Wu stows away in Chin's wagon and attempts to awaken the dead man and discredit his brother. Unfortunately for Chin, Wu's efforts take place during the yin hour of the yin day of the yin month...during a full moon. Naturally, when moonshine falls on the corpse, it awakens and becomes a vampire.

Chin easily subdues it, but soon after, a young graverobber who had sneaked into a young woman's grave now has the woman chasing him, through Master Chin's camp. As it happens, lightning struck while he was stealing her jewels—letting in the full moon, awakening the dead woman, fusing their souls together, and thus causing her to mimic every action he makes. He runs; she runs. He falls; she falls. Of course, all this is set-up for what will happen when the company arrives in Boss Vampire's hometown.

In a hotel in town, we soon find that the young woman was the concubine of a lord, despondent over her loss. When he discovers that she has been revived (after a fashion), the film becomes an unstoppable steamroller of slapstick action, involving the lord's attempts to restore his love to at least a semblance of her former self.

Not surprisingly, Wu shows up and *again* revives the vampire, this time feeding it snake blood and teaching it the smell of his brother's hair cream. When the vampire action gets going, the vampire is primed to attack Master Chin. In a curious subversion of Chinese-vampire conventions, this vampire has apparently escaped the onset of rigor mortis. In other words, he does not hop. Instead, the Mafia Boss Vampire is limber enough to run through the halls of the hotel, chasing his intended prey. The film subverts another convention in showing that the brothers' Taoist spells ultimately cannot control the super-vampire that Wu has created. Perhaps, if they'd brought enough sticky rice to burn his feet, they could have gotten the better of him. But alas, they never so much as mention the awesome power of sticky rice. Instead the army is forced to take action...and, in the ultimate slap at vampire-hunting convention, blast the vampire to bits.

Though the vampire plotline is clearly the main draw for this film, the concubine plot presents the most striking image of loss of identity. The original *Mr. Vampire* (1985 [*q.v.*]) played briefly with the notion of controlling another's actions, but *The New Mr. Vampire* presents an extended version of this concept as the young woman's corpse moves through scene after scene, with no thought or will of her own. The lord may be so lovesick that he is willing to have the young man dance on the side so that he can "dance" with his woman, but in reality there is nothing of her that remains. He dances only with a corpse. A mobile, mindless corpse.—*CCS*

Nightmare Castle (*Amanti d'oltretomba, Gli*; *Faceless Monster, The*; *Night of the Doomed*) (1966) [**possession**] Italy: Emerci-SRL (Allied Artists). *D:* Mario Caiano (as Alan Grunewald). *S:* Fabio de Agostino, Mario Caiano. *Cast:* Barbara Steele (Muriel/Jenny); Paul Miller/Muller (Stephen); Helga Liné (Solange); Lawrence Clift (Dr. Joyce); John McDouglas/Giuseppe Addobbati (Jonathan); Rik Battaglia (David).

Between 1960 and 1966 the iconic 1960s horror-movie "scream queen" Barbara Steele starred in 10 terror titles, most of them of European origin. After *Black Sunday* (1960) and perhaps *The Pit and the Pendulum* (1961 [*q.v.*]), the Gothic Italian period horror film *Nightmare Castle* may very well be the best, as well as the entry that best serves Steele the *actress*, allowing her far greater range than most—not to mention allowing her to participate in a solid loss-of-identity scenario.

Steele plays Muriel, the sexy but shrewish wife of sadistic scientist Stephen, who likes to experiment with electricity. When Stephen finds his wife in the arms of her lover, he tortures them both to death (dripping burning acid on Muriel, and using a red-hot poker on her paramour). Learning that Muriel left all her wealth to her stepsister, Jenny (Steele again), Stephen woos and wins the naïve, high-strung girl, plotting to drive his new bride mad. Amazingly, these two "stepsisters" appear to be identical in every way except hair color, which allows for "twinning" and gives Jenny a headstart in the loss-of-identity department! Soon Jenny is wearing Muriel's clothes, playing Muriel's

music, drinking Muriel's brandy, and behaving as if possessed by the dead woman's ghost. Is it delirium, or have the dead returned to seek retribution?

As the heartless Muriel, Steele is at her coldest *and* most alluring. With Muriel's death and Jenny's arrival, the actress transforms herself into a nervous and ultimately terrified victim—before turning terrifying herself at the end as she gleefully loses herself to Muriel and exacts Muriel's gruesome revenge. And the climactic appearance of the ghost remains one of the eeriest sequences in 1960s horror cinema. As Muriel slowly approaches the disbelieving Stephen, her raven tresses hang down, obscuring her beautiful face. Stephen abruptly pulls back the hair to reveal a horribly ruined countenance—the gruesome shock augmented by Muriel's demonic laughter. (And this over three decades before Japanese entries like *Ringu* (1998) made such an image a horror movie staple).

With its loss-of-identity mix of gruesome shocks and shuddery Gothic atmosphere (augmented by the opulent—and authentic—castle setting, mobile camerawork, intriguing angles, and evocative lighting), *Nightmare Castle* truly lives up to its name, standing as one of the best Italian horrors of the decade.—*BMS*

Nightmare City (***Incubo sulla citta contaminate***) (1980) [**zombification**] Italy: Dialchi Film/Lotus Films/Televicine S.A. de C.V. (21st Century Distribution). *D:* Umberto Lenzi. *S:* Antonio Cesare Corti, Luis Maria Delgado, and Piero Regnoli. *Cast:* Hugo Stiglitz (Dean Miller); Laura Trotter (Dr. Anna Miller); Maria Rosaria Omaggio (Sheila Holmes); Francisco Rabal (Major Warren Holmes).

Somewhere in Europe, in the *Nightmare City* of the title, an event involving a toxic spill and the resultant psychosis in the indigenous population results in a nasty, ugly, and damn fine zombie film. Cinematically the zombie has always been a threatening, amoral, and perhaps even tragic beast. However, here the creatures are utterly malevolent. Arguably, within the context of this film, the concept of identity loss, or loss of humanity seems like a reasonable trade for the incredible strength and durability that the monsters attain. Zombie fans will instantly notice something different here; the dead move swiftly, have superhuman strength, and even use an arsenal of weapons, from axes and knives to submachine guns, pushing the genre, and indeed the concept of loss of identity via zombification, into dark new terrain.

Witness to the first massacre is news reporter Dean Miller, who, after passively watching the slaughter, flees to his television studio to make an emergency report that is promptly censored by the inflexible Major Holmes. Obviously this media suppression doesn't stop the killings; instead the hapless citizens go about their business without any warning as the film moves from one bloodbath to the next. The blood-sucking zombies storm television studios, army barracks, hospitals, and other venues, butchering everyone in their path as they go. Meanwhile, having abandoned his studio, Miller swiftly loses his identity as well, undergoing a startling transition from genial, mild-mannered reporter into dynamic, fearless guerrilla, shooting, bludgeoning, and punching his way through the zombie ranks across a panic-stricken city whilst desperately trying to locate his wife, Anna.

It's just as well that he responds with such vigor, as here, the undead do not dodder or fall over; these zombies are all action in the ruthless pursuit of their objectives. In this respect, director Umberto Lenzi is quite ambiguous.since, apart from creating a new order of ghouls upon the Earth, he leaves it to the viewer to ponder what the redefined identity of the creatures actually is. Are they executing the master plan of a deviant super villain or simply doing what comes naturally for a flesh eater, albeit with consummate style and a tactical approach previously unseen in the genre (such as when they cut the power to the city)? In this respect, the loss of identity of the zombified is difficult to quantify, as the hordes seem to be acting upon more than simple instinct, but the source of their motivations is left unresolved by the end of the film.

Conversely, although the idea of super-strong, armed zombies is perhaps anathema to some purists, in the hands of a gore master such as Lenzi it makes for highly entertaining and indeed, compulsive viewing, as the undead trade fire with hapless soldiers and hack up semi-naked dancing girls with hatchets. Thankfully, the loathsome creatures can still be put down with a bullet to the brain, but the fact that these ghouls can and will fire back means that only those with the steadiest of hands, plus a serious cache of ordnance, have a chance of survival.

And then, at the very end, Lenzi pulls an incredible stunt, as Miller wakes up next to his wife and discovers that it has all been a dream! However, his elation is short lived, since his first assignment of the day leads him right back to the start of the invasion, and the nightmare begins for real…—*AJB*

Night of Dark Shadows (1971) [**possession; reincarnation**] MGM. *D:* Dan Curtis. *S:* Sam Hall; Story by Sam Hall and Dan Curtis. *Cast:* David Selby (Quentin Collins/Charles Collins); Kate Jackson (Tracy Collins); Grayson Hall (Carlotta Drake); Lara Parker (Angelique Collins); John Karlen (Alex Jenkins); Nancy Barrett (Claire Jenkins); James Storm (Gerard Stiles); Diana Millay (Laura Collins); Christopher Pennock (Gabriel Collins).

Night of Dark Shadows lost its identity on the cutting-room floor. As written and filmed, Dan Curtis' follow-up to *House of Dark Shadows* (1970 [*q.v.*]) would have been superior to that film and could have been a minor masterpiece of early-1970s horror cinema because of its numerous timely qualities (*déjà vu*, reincarnation, witchcraft, ghosts, and a downbeat ending). Instead, Curtis was forced, under a tight deadline, to cut his 129-minute film to 97 minutes. The studio subsequently cut it even further, to 93.5 minutes, at the behest of the MPAA. What's left is a confusing, often unsatisfying narrative which nevertheless delivers a strong theme of loss of identity even though—or perhaps *because*—the film lost its *own* soul as it was hastily shortened.

Under the best circumstances, *Night of Dark Shadows* faced an uphill battle. It was released four months after ABC-TV's *Dark Shadows* was cancelled, and it was missing Jonathan Frid as the vampire Barnabas Collins, who had spectacularly decimated the cast of *House of Dark Shadows*. After that film's relentless bloodbath, *Night of Dark Shadows* was a more cerebral exercise in ghostly possession. Patterned in part after *Rebecca* (1940) and the television serial's own 1970 Parallel Time storyline, *Night of*

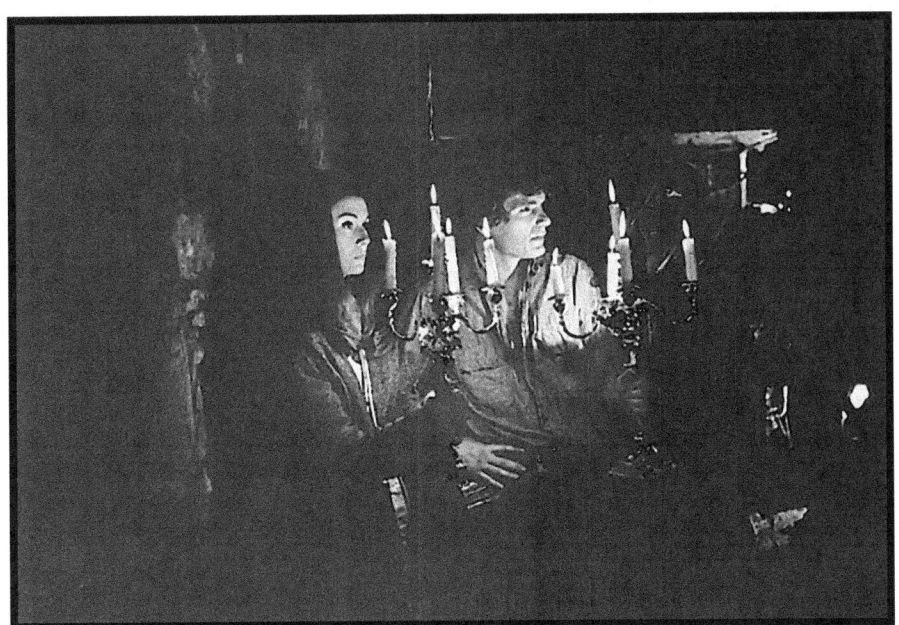

Quentin (David Selby) and Tracy Collins (Kate Jackson) move into a sinister Collinwood in *Night of Dark Shadows*.

Dark Shadows is even more similar to Roger Corman's *The Haunted Palace* (1964 [*q.v.*]), with David Selby, Kate Jackson, and Grayson Hall essentially playing the Vincent Price, Debra Paget, and Lon Chaney, Jr. roles of possessed husband, victimized wife, and sinister housekeeper.

Artist Quentin Collins and his wife, Tracy, move in to Quentin's inheritance, the Collinwood estate, sternly run by Carlotta Drake and handyman Gerard Stiles. Soon, Quentin begins having dreams and visions of the life of his look-alike ancestor, Charles Collins, also a painter, who lived at Collinwood in 1810. Quentin is especially drawn to Collinwood's mysterious tower room, where Charles had an affair with his brother Gabriel's wife, Angelique, before her public hanging for witchcraft. Angelique's spirit still haunts Collinwood, and—as Quentin begins to come unmoored from his own identity—Carlotta tells him that he is the reincarnation of Charles Collins and the vessel through which Angelique and Charles' love will live again. (Carlotta declares that she herself is the reincarnation of a young girl who lived at Collinwood in 1810 and who witnessed Angelique's hanging.)

Quentin falls under the spell of the house and its beautiful ghost, losing his identity to that of Charles and at one point even attempting to rape and later drown Tracy. However, with her help and the help of their novelist friends Claire and Alex Jenkins, he fights to resist his possession.

Despite its similarities to *The Haunted Palace* and other sources, *Night of Dark Shadows* contains more original and unusual subject matter for a *Dark Shadows* movie than *House of Dark Shadows,* which was a mere retelling (with extra blood and gore) of the television serial's 1967 storyline. However, when Dan Curtis delivered his 129-minute opus to MGM, CEO James Aubrey demanded drastic cuts—and gave Curtis as little as 11 hours to deliver them! (Aubrey, the "Smiling Cobra" who at different times tyrannized MGM and CBS, was the basis for the ruthless television executive Robin Stone in Jacqueline Susann's novel *The Love Machine*.) In his film career, Aubrey was known for tampering with movies by Blake Edwards, Ken Russell, and Sam Peckinpah, as well as Dan Curtis. Therefore, on a moment's notice, Curtis and an MGM staff editor were forced to eviscerate *Night of Dark Shadows* to please Aubrey.

As a result, several of Quentin's dream sequences are consolidated, causing his pajamas to change from yellow to blue in the course of one night's sleep. The Jenkinses are edited out of some scenes, and much of Angelique's part is cut. As the film now stands, the audience does not know how Gerard and Carlotta are related (he is her nephew), why Tracy goes to the poolhouse (she had a dream about it), why Quentin/Charles tries to drown her there (Charles drowned his wife, Laura, in 1810), why Quentin/Charles limps (off-camera, he fell off his horse), or why Laura laughs during Angelique's funeral (Angelique's body is not really in the coffin). Reverend Strack's line about Angelique's "threats" no longer makes sense because Curtis had to delete the scene in which she cursed her executioners (and thus had to jettison the film's original title, *Curse of Dark Shadows*). And viewers now see Carlotta *rehang* Angelique's portrait when they never saw it removed to begin with! Most heartbreakingly, what would have been the film's most important and powerful scene—a séance conducted by Quentin, Tracy, Alex, and Claire, which reveals that Angelique was *not* a witch—does not appear in the movie and shortchanges the effect of the ending. Nevertheless, the final moments—when the audience learns the fates of the characters and the crushing force of identity loss—still have the power to stun.

For the 1989 Dark Shadows Festival, I wrote *The Night Before*, a play which reinstated many of the missing scenes and afforded *Dark Shadows* fans a seriocomic feel for what the complete *Night of Dark Shadows* might have been like. In 1997, film historian Darren Gross definitively reconstructed the film in the pages of *Video Watchdog* magazine (number 40). In 1999, Gross did the impossible by finding the long-lost, one-and-only 129-minute color separations (footage) in a film-storage vault in a Kansas City salt mine. Now, Gross and Dark Shadows Festival chairman Jim Pierson are spearheading an effort to reconstruct the film for a possible 2008 or 2009 DVD release. Because only 100 minutes of soundtrack survive, the film's living stars—Kate Jackson, David Selby, Nancy Barrett, John Karlen, Diana Millay, James Storm, and Lara Parker—have re-recorded some or all of their missing dialogue. Three dozen years after a sadly truncated *Night of Dark Shadows* fell far short of its potential, the complete film may yet be appraised and appreciated by critic and fan alike. Its identity as a loss-of-identity film will finally be re-established.

In 1976, *Night of Dark Shadows* seemed to live again as Kate Jackson once more played the victimized wife of a man under a ghostly thrall in the television movie, *Death at Love House* (*q.v.*), and Dan Curtis himself appropriated the downbeat ending of *Night of Dark Shadows* for his 1976 film *Burnt Offerings* (*q.v.*).—JDT

Night of the Comet (1984) [**zombification**] (Atlantic Releasing Corp.). *D:* Thom Eberhardt. *S:* Thom Eberhart. *Cast:* Robert Beltran (Hector Gomez); Catherine Mary Stewart (Regina Belmont); Zoe Kelli Simon [known as Kelli Maroney] (Samantha Belmont); Sharon Farrell (Doris Belmont); Mary Woronov (Audry White).

If the majority of humanity were to die tomorrow, leaving only one or two survivors, how would the remnants of humanity respond? Post-apocalyptic movies from

A Boy and His Dog (1975) to *Mad Max 2* (1981) or even *Waterworld* (1995) indicate that the aftermath will impose a huge change on the behavior and conduct of survivors, pushing them away from their previous identities into a new and usually more barbaric lifestyle. However, in stark contrast to this are the characters of *Night of the Comet*, which begins with a mass assembly of humanity (most of whom are decked out in the most garish of 1980s party clothes) to witness the passing of a comet that will be visible as it travels through Earth's atmosphere. Very few fail to attend the street parties and gatherings across the globe, and thus—when the comet starts emitting a deadly radiation—billions die, and the remnants are mutated into psychotic, putrefying zombies, proving that congregational celebrations can be very bad for the health.

However, walking tall across this barren, post-apocalyptic cityscape are two "Valley Girls"—sisters Regina and Samantha, who gradually come to terms with the loss of everyone and everything they know while fighting alongside Hector (a pre-*Star Trek: Voyager* Robert Beltran) against the undead, visiting deserted malls to look for new clothes, and avoiding several sinister scientists who want to consume their blood. The girls take several steps away from their former lives with survivalist activities such as machine-gun practice, but manage to balance these changes by maintaining certain "normal" activities such as shopping and flirting with any unmutated guys they can find.

Night of the Comet draws obvious influence from a range of sci-fi survival-horror films such as the movie version of John Wyndham's *Day of the Triffids* (1962), *The Omega Man* (1971 [*q.v.*]), and, of course, George A. Romero's *Night of the Living Dead* (1968 [*q.v.*]), thrusting its characters from mundane suburbia into a (relatively) hostile

Samatha Belmont (Kelli Maroney) finds herself in the undead arms of the law in *Night of the Comet*.

environment within which they must fight not only for survival but also to rediscover themselves in a new world virtually bereft of life. Samantha in particular struggles to accept the reality of her situation, before eventually finding her feet when she assumes the broadcast mantle at a deserted radio station. The zombies for their part are disappointingly few, but on appearing badmouth the girls in several confrontations and retain the motor capacity to use firearms and bludgeoning tools. So, although driven to random and unprovoked homicide, the undead retain certain traits of their former humanity, although not enough to render them exempt from the girls' bullets. By contrast Hector seems jovially merciful with the creatures; in one scene he runs away from a teenage zombie, shouting "Lucky for you I've always liked kids!" *Night of the Comet* is hardly a classic but certainly one for 1980s film buffs interested in considering a light-hearted teen movie about the end of the civilized world and those who inherit the aftermath.—*AJB*

Night of the Doomed. See **Nightmare Castle** (1966).

Night of the Living Dead (1968) [**zombification**] Image Ten/Laurel Group (Continental Distributing, Inc.). *D:* George A. Romero. *S:* George A. Romero and John A. Russo. *Cast:* Duane Jones (Ben); Judith O'Dea (Barbra); Karl Hardman (Harry Cooper); Marilyn Eastman (Helen Cooper).

When one considers the concept of loss of identity in contemporary zombie movies, the pivotal, defining point is George A. Romero's masterpiece, *Night of the Living Dead*. Shot in black and white on a budget of $114,000, featuring a little-known cast, minimal special effects, and a score comprising library music, *Night of the Living Dead* truly rewrote the rules for the genre, and in doing so altered the interpretation of loss of identity for both the zombified humans and those who fought them to survive. First, to consider loss of identity from the undead perspective, earlier zombie features such as *White Zombie* (1932 [*q.v.*]) through to Hammer's *Plague of the Zombies* (1966) usually depicted zombies as tragic human victims reduced to mindless subservience as a result of voodoo incantations and the like, and usually acting at the behest of an evil, yet very human, master. Additionally, these hapless creatures were not completely beyond redemption, as both myth and movies dictated that the zombie could be released from the spell they were under with a variety of means, from the death of their master to eating salt, which allegedly reinvigorated the parts of the brain rendered inactive by the process of zombification. Therefore there was a certain lack of permanence to these beasts, who might recover at least in part from their condition. However, with *Night...*, Romero redefined the concept completely and unleashed the living dead as slaves only to their most basic instinct, which in this case is the need to feast on human tissue. And for those unlucky enough to suffer the fate of zombification in Romero's movie, the loss of identity is permanent; the individual's death triggers the horrific transition, and then the only possibility of salvation is at a spiritual level, provided by a bullet (or blunt implement) to the brain.

Based on a premise drawn more from science fiction than voodoo folklore, *Night...* begins with radio reports of an unmanned space probe returning from a mission to Venus and exploding in the Earth's outer atmosphere, releasing a deadly form of radiation that reactivates the corpses of those who have recently died. The first people in the film to encounter the undead are Johnny and his sister, Barbra, who are visiting a relative's grave

Night of the Living Dead **became the ultimate zombie movie and made George Romero the king of the zombes.**

when attacked by one of the creatures. After watching her brother lose a grim struggle with a tenacious flesh eater, Barbra essentially surrenders her identity. Overcome, she flees to a nearby farmhouse and is joined there by Ben, a man who, as a result of his drive and determination to survive, has narrowly escaped from a city overrun by the undead. As Barbra sinks into a catatonia from which she never recovers, he becomes her protector.

As the film progresses, Romero clarifies his revised scientific blueprint for the creatures via a series of news broadcasts that inform both the viewer and the disbelieving characters that "the recently deceased are returning to life and attacking the living." All the while, the number of zombies gathering at the house increases steadily and, although the undead are individually weak and easily dealt with, the seven humans are too busy waging their own insular power struggles to deal with the growing threat, which is a theme the director expands upon in the sequels, *Dawn of the Dead* (1978 [*q.v.*]), *Day of the Dead* (1985 [*q.v.*]), and *Land of the Dead* (2005 [*q.v.*]). In the farmhouse, conflict rages primarily between Ben and a stubborn, argumentative, and thoroughly unpleasant individual, Harry Cooper, who along with his wife Helen and their injured daughter, has adopted the cellar as his personal haven and refuses to assist the others in fortifying the windows and doors on the ground floor.

Indeed, the humans in the film (apart from the comatose Barbra, who never recovers from the loss of her brother) spend more time asserting their individuality than in taking group action, to the ultimate detriment of their survival. Both here and within the wider context of Romero's tetralogy, this flaw eventually proves to be the defining, decisive failure of humanity. Conversely, the zombies, whether formerly children or adults, black or white, male or female, or anything else, unify as one force in their pursuit of food, a mechanical single-mindedness in the face of which a divided humanity has no response. This then is perhaps the ultimate irony of Romero's seminal zombie movies, in that as the undead forfeit their human identities to become automatons unknowingly colluding within an undefined yet substantial union, the humans struggling to maintain and assert their own identities and ideals to outlast their insatiable predators isolate themselves and are consumed.—*AJB*

Night of the Zombies. See ***Virus*** (1980).

1984 (1984) [**regimentation; eradication of self**] Great Britain: Umbrella-Rosenbloom Film Productions/Virgin (Atlantic Releasing Corp.). *D:* Michael Radford. *S:* Michael Radford, From the Novel *1984* by George Orwell. *Cast:* John Hurt (Winston Smith); Richard Burton (O'Brien); Suzanna Hamilton (Julia); Cyril Cusack (Charrington).

[*1984* is a milestone in loss-of-identity literature—a devastating portrait of 1948 U.S.S.R. in thinly veiled science fiction disguise that only a disillusioned Socialist like George Orwell could imagine. The various film versions—the 1954 teleplay starring Peter Cushing and André Morell; the 1956 Michael Anderson feature starring Edmund O'Brien and Michael Redgrave; and this one—all follow the novel fairly closely. Thus, we're allowing this possibly last version to stand for them all (since time and events—e.g., the dissolution of the Soviet Union—have perhaps overtaken *1984*).]

1984 is loss of identity in three acts. Act 1 introduces a protagonist with no identity save for the regimented one doled out to him by the omnipresent, nearly omniscient State, symbolized by its leader, Big Brother, whose image is everywhere and whose Party controls the population with an iron fist, wielded by the deadly Thought Police, reinforced by the unceasing propaganda that perpetual war engenders (see the Cold War, the war on drugs, the war on terror, etc.), and monitored by the elaborate "telescreen" surveillance system (not to mention a network of informants and snitches) that notes the minutest deviation from the Party line. Act 2 features our protagonist revolting, in his small way, trying to assert his identity amidst the mass conformity and in spite of the odds against him. Act 3 shows the protagonist suffering the full weight of the State for his "sins"—losing his little identity for good, having it shredded, and leaving him with less (if possible) than he had at the beginning.

Winston Smith, a small cog in the massive bureaucratic wheel, works in the Ministry of Truth's records department, which continuously alters written records of history to provide The Party with infallibility (i.e., they're constantly recreating the society's collective identity). He indulges in occasional small yet unforgivable betrayals of Big Brother, such as writing in secret. However, he is eventually stung into actively seeking to change the course of society when he comes across irrefutable proof that The Party is lying to both him and everyone else. (From this point on, he seals his own fate, as recognition, and pursuit, of the truth—i.e., assertion of individual identity—is an act of thoughtcrime, and no thoughtcrime goes unpunished.)

Following this revelation, Winston's outlook on life changes radically, to the point where this timid, downtrodden man defies Big Brother by falling in love, the ultimate defiance toward a state that demands its citizens' undivided and unequivocal adoration.

Despite the ironclad certainty of discovery by the Thought Police and resultant incarceration, torture, and death, Winston and his lover, Julia, indulge in a series of clandestine meetings in an attempt to experience life without fear or suspicion. He rents from Charrington, owner of a dusty curiosity shop, an upstairs room that has no telescreen. Winston and Julia also connect with O'Brien, a member of the Inner Party, who informs them of an underground movement against Big Brother and inducts them into the cause with a book which reinterprets the world from a perspective different from Party propaganda.

Julia and Winston temporarily create a bubble around themselves in Charrington's spare room, impervious to the outside world—until the tramping of steel-capped boots echoes up the stairs and the full force of the police state shatters their shared illusion of happiness and sanctuary.

Actual identities are revealed: Charrington is a member of the Thought Police. He hands Winston over to O'Brien, who also drops the mask of co-conspirator and embarks upon a savage disassembly of Winston's self identity through a series of beatings, interrogations, forced medication, and torture. Winston clings desperately to some strand of himself, attempting to hold fast to his love for Julia and his belief that he is right and sane.

He can't do it. Perhaps the greatest facet of the movie, and central to Orwell's supreme masterpiece, is the concept of doublethink, a framework within which a falsehood is always one step ahead of the truth in the mind of the individual exercising said discipline. Previously, Winston had rejected the concept as madness, but O'Brien forces him to consider the premise of doublethink as crucial to survival for a disciplined, stable mind. And possibly the most frightening thing about O'Brien's logic is its raw sincerity: The Party crafts your identity for you—or else you'll have *no* identity. Agreeing that two plus two equals five, three, or nothing, according to The Party, is obviously insane, but who would reject such reasoning if his life depended on it?

Indeed, doublethink, more than anything else, sums up the complete submission of identity to Big Brother and, although it takes a momentous, shattering event for Winston to grasp its intricacies, at the end he too accepts it, along with love for Big Brother. He becomes a shell of a man, his identity irreovocably erased.—*AJB*

[Editor's note: *1984* and Big Brother live on—in *Brazil* (1985 [*q.v.*—working title: *1984 1/2*]), *The Handmaid's Tale* (1990 [*q.v.*]), and *V for Vendetta* (2006), to name three examples, and even in a rumored (as of this writing) new version (2009?)—not to mention in the George W. Bush administration.]

Nutty Professor, The (1963) [**dual personality; metamorphosis**] (Paramount). *D:* Jerry Lewis. *S:* Jerry Lewis and Bill Richmond. *Cast:* Jerry Lewis (Professor Julius Kelp/Buddy Love/Baby Kelp); Stella Stevens (Stella Purdy); Del Moore (Dr. Hamius R. Warfield); Kathleen Freeman (Millie Lemmon); Howard Morris (Elmer Kelp); Elvia Allman (Mother Kelp); Milton Frome (Dr. M. Sheppard Leevee); Buddy Lester (Purple Pit Bartender); Marvin Kaplan (Man at Nightclub); Les Brown and His Band of Renown (Themselves).

Almost everybody considers *The Nutty Professor* Jerry Lewis' best film, and I agree. It's the one picture he helmed where everything comes together beautifully, most of the gags work, the pathos is not overloaded, and the comic scenes are cut at the right moment rather than drawn out past the point of being funny. It's also Lewis' most complex picture with a powerful message and a true sense of black comedy. Of all his films, this one will go down in the books as Jerry's greatest work—in fact, it already has.

The movie tells the story of pathetic Professor Julius Kelp, a buck-toothed, nasal-voiced, out-of-shape nerd intimidated by everyone around him from the college dean to his own students. Kelp is in love with one of those students, the beautiful Miss Purdy, but he feels she could never fall for someone like him. Thankfully, Kelp does have some good qualities—he is a brilliant chemist—and after some disastrous trips to the gym, Kelp creates a potion which will bring out his better self. But the serum unleashes Buddy Love, an egotistical lout who entertains the local students and romances Miss Purdy. Eventually, Love is asked to entertain at the school dance, but during his big number, he is unable to control his transformation back into Kelp.

There is no denying the theme of loss of identity in this film. Just like Dr. Jekyll (Stevenson's Jekyll/Hyde novella is the inspiration for the picture), Dr. Kelp scientifically transforms himself, leading to a loss of identity as his new persona gradually takes control of his life. The question here is *who* is Kelp's Hyde—"Who is Buddy Love?"

Many over the years have assumed that Buddy Love is a parody of Lewis' former comedy-team partner, Dean Martin. Though there are minor similarities, Lewis denies any connection (see the bonus features on the recent DVD release). Stella Stevens herself told me that Jerry did not have Dean in mind when he created Love. I am more inclined to agree with Danny Peary, who, in the book *Cult Movies*, argues that Love is a reflection of Lewis himself—the smug, self-serving Lewis seen during the Labor Day telethons and in interviews—"that conceited fellow with the slick-backed hair who is either… teasing his guests or insulting them." (p. 232-233). Love very well may be someone lurking within Lewis—his own wife would not permit their children to see the film and witness their father's darker side.

The picture does have a positive message regarding identity: Embrace who you are inside. Prof. Kelp gives a long speech to the student body at the conclusion of the film, saying essentially that you cannot expect others to like you for who you are if you do not like yourself. *The Nutty Professor* stresses the importance of being true to yourself and retaining your individuality. Conforming to the ideal or trying to be like everyone else can only lead to a loss of identity, and that is when someone like Buddy Love can emerge. This theme is more important today than ever before. In an age where billboards dictate what is beautiful, where children still mock those who are different, where racial intolerance is still a national problem, "to thine own self be true" is a motto that should not and cannot be ignored. Thankfully, animated films have today become the mouthpieces for the idea, and pictures such as *Antz* (1998) and *A Bug's Life* (1998) continue to remind new generations (and some old ones) of that important lesson.

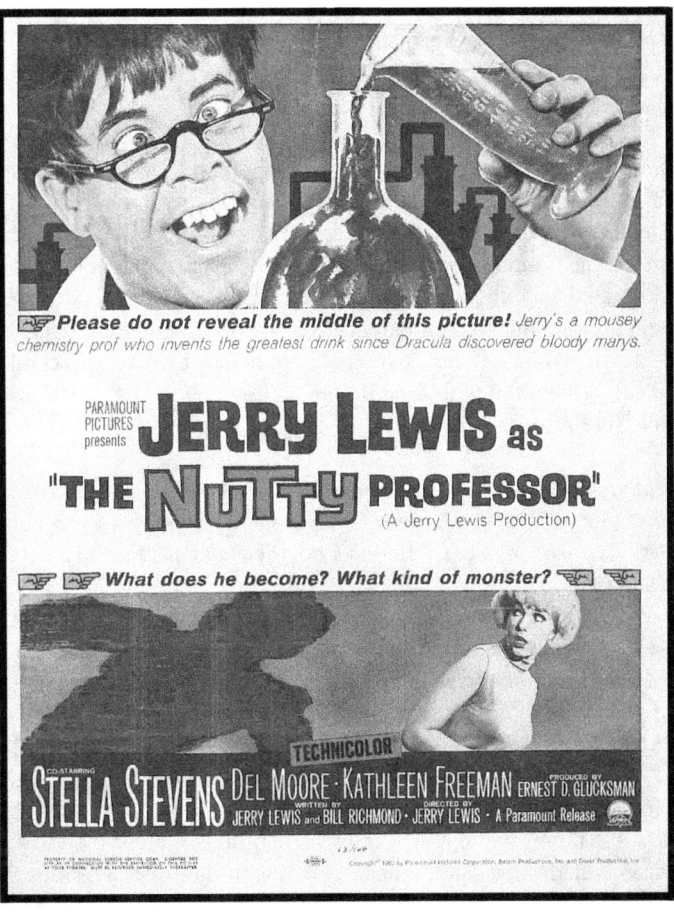

Some could argue that Lewis' film seems to reverse its stance near the end. Miss Purdy is running off with Kelp to get married. She has decided she loves Kelp for who he is. Yet she is seen taking some of Kelp's formula—presumably for the wedding night. I don't see this truly affecting the theme—it's just a very funny closing gag. Buddy Love may thrill the college students (and even some of the faculty), but the objective viewer sees that Love is a repulsive, arrogant jerk. Lewis makes this clear in the wonderful sequence where Buddy walks to the local tavern after the first transformation. We see the shot through Buddy's point of view and witness people on the street running away in hysterical terror as they encounter Love. When we finally see what Love actually looks like, he is just a handsome lounge lizard. But Lewis has made his point—we should not admire Buddy Love. In fact, Miss Purdy is just as equally repulsed by Buddy as she is attracted to him. Deep down, she knows it's what's on the inside that matters, and Buddy has nothing good inside.

The Nutty Professor was later remade as an Eddie Murphy vehicle in 1996. In this new version, Prof. "Klump" is a gigantic fat man who makes a potion that will transform him into a virile thin man. But once again, an obnoxious Buddy Love emerges. The theme is thankfully the same, updated for modern audiences yet packing the same importance. Interestingly, these films make the same comment about what forms an individual's identity: In both the Lewis and Murphy versions, the main characters are who they are due to their parents. Kelp had an ineffectual father dominated by a shrew of a wife, while Klump's parents (giant beings themselves) coddled their son and continually filled him with food. In the battle of nature vs. nurture, the *Nutty*s continually vote for nurture.—*JSM*

Oldboy (2004) **[eradication of self; search for self]** South Korea: Egg Films/Show East (Tartan USA). *D:* Park Chan-wook *S:* Hwang Jo-yun, Lim Chun-hyeong, and Park Chan-wook. *Cast:* Min-sik Choi (Dae-su Oh); Ji-tae Yu (Lee Woo-jin); Hye-jeong Kang (Mi-do).

Oldboy is situational horror—the horror of finding one's self in a situation from which there is seemingly no way out; the horror of the unseen—of being tormented for some unknown reason by some practically invisible foe; and ultimately, the horror of discovery—of the secret that led to incarceration and of the devious manipulation endured once "free."

Oldboy initially seems to be the story of Dae-su Oh, an uncouth and belligerent family man who is abducted and imprisoned in solitary confinement in a small windowless room, without any knowledge of his crime or the identity of his jailer. While incarcerated, he is conditioned to fall unconscious upon hearing the sound of a particular melody, which, throughout the duration of his custody, is piped into his room on a regular basis to herald the administration of a potent sleeping gas. Hence, under these conditions, his social identity as husband and father and reasonably productive member of society is totally removed, and throughout his detention he teeters on the edge of sanity, desperate to know why he has been imprisoned and by whom. We quickly learn he is not the most popular of individuals, highlighted by the list of enemies he checks off while contemplating who his jailer might be. Then, sometime into his stretch, he is informed that his wife has been murdered and that he is a prime suspect. Spurred on by this knowledge, his desperation to know the fate of his young daughter, and an overwhelming desire for revenge upon his keeper, he contrives an escape plan.

As the years roll slowly by, Dae-su teaches himself to fight by boxing the walls of his cell until his fists and feet have been bruised and bloodied so much that they are as hard as tempered steel, changing his body from a bloated and unfit vessel to a formidable vehicle of vengeance. Simultaneously, he uses the chopsticks given to him at mealtimes to scrape away at the mortar of one wall, hoping he can eventually loosen enough bricks to escape. Throughout this time he broods and fantasizes about the brutal reprisal he will eventually take on the mystery jailer responsible for his wasted years. As he enters his 15th year of captivity, he finally manages to remove enough bricks in the wall to escape.

Swiftly abandoning any cursory attempts to make sense of the new world, Dae-su initiates his efforts for retribution. However, while wandering the city streets in a daze, he is handed a cell phone, which immediately begins to ring. The caller reveals that he is the jailer and advises Dae-su that he has not finished exacting his own revenge for a past transgression. Given only five days to discover the answers over which he has obsessed for so long, "Oldboy" embarks upon a violent and uncompromising journey toward the truth, at times oddly reminiscent of Michael Caine's relentless pursuit of answers in *Get Carter* (1971). Indeed, Dae-su's transformation from loud-mouthed drunkard at the film's beginning to the steel-fisted, unstoppable brawler that he becomes during his passage from one hell to another highlights the loss of identity blighting his character throughout.

Dae-su Oh (Min-sik Choi) is unknowingly seduced by his biological daughter Mi-do (Hye-jeong Kang) in *Oldboy*.

On his journey he falls in love with Mi-do, a young waitress who serves him at a sushi bar and takes care of him after her phone curiously plays a ring tone of the same melody that renders Dae-su unconscious. Eventually his enemy is revealed to be Lee Woo-jin, a long-forgotten classmate of Dae-su's, initially appearing as a genial, cultured playboy until his own shocking motives of vengeance are revealed. In the conclusion he invites Dae-su to his penthouse and reveals that his sister had committed suicide after a drunken Dae-su shamed them when he discovered and revealed details of their incestuous relationship to their classmates. He then invites Dae-su to leaf through a dossier of photographs featuring Dae-su's daughter in various stages of growth during the time of his imprisonment, with the final photograph revealing her to be Mi-do, who has also been conditioned by Lee Woo-jin to seduce her own father. (Neither father nor daughter can call their identities their own.) Ultimately Dae-su flees both physically and psychologically from this terrible truth and opts to undergo surgical treatment to permanently remove his tortuous memories, voluntarily relinquishing his identity, leaving him smiling vacantly as the tragic playboy's revenge attains closure (thus ending where 2004's *Eternal Sunshine of the Spotless Mind* [*q.v.*] begins).—*AJB*

Omega Man, The (1971) [zombification; eradication of self] Walter Seltzer Productions (Warner Bros.). *D:* Boris Segal. *S:* John William Corrington and Joyce Hooper Corrington, Based on the Novel *I Am Legend* by Richard Matheson. *Cast:* Charlton Heston (Colonel Robert Neville); Anthony Zerbe (Matthias); Rosalind Cash (Lisa); Paul Koslo (Dutch); Lincoln Kilpatrick (Zachary).

This second version of Richard Matheson's *I Am Legend* (after *The Last Man on Earth* [1964 (*q.v.*)]) is a minor sci-fi classic with a cult following—a heady 1960s-era Christian allegory with a campy deification of star Charlton "Moses" Heston, post-*The Ten Commandments* (1956), as a man who must cling to his identity in a world where the normal anchors that reinforce it have come unmoored. That identity undergoes a radical change in the course of the story. (The Robert Neville of the excellent source novel becomes a necessary monster to be publicly executed, feeding "a new vampiric world order"; he realizes that his attempts to destroy the vampires have earned him a new, perhaps unwanted, identity as a boogeyman among the new vampire-like race that has sprung up and that his passing bestows upon him another: legend. *The Omega Man*'s Neville becomes a Christ-like creator-destroyer: He is compared to God several times—Dutch calls Neville an "exterminating angel" and later refers to him indirectly as Christ; a little girl asks Neville if he's God; in the end, he is literally crucified.)

For two years following a China-Russia war, Neville—the lone survivor of world-destroying germ warfare, a Biowar scientist vaccinated and immune to plague—fends off the nightly attacks of the Family, an organization of plague mutants who have long since lost their identity. This organization bears the "scars of Punishment" (the plague and death that modern man brought down upon himself): painful light-blindness, grotesque lesions, and albinism.

By day, Neville—this "last man on Earth"—hunts these "barbarians" (his term), desperate to kill them as they sleep. At night, inside his barricaded townhouse, Neville fortifies himself with drink and tries to retain his sanity while, outside, charismatic madman Matthias and his followers call out to him as they've done every night for years, commanding him to submit to judgment by fire. Neville snaps and throws his drink, "Why the hell can't you leave me alone?" But in reality, Neville's only identity now is that conferred upon him by the Family. A creature of the wheel, a scientist whose science has decimated mankind and the Earth. He's *the* representative of the dying order that the Family's pledged to eradicate.

For, in spite of science destroying "normal" man by the billions, Matthias and the Family (insane mutants all) have survived—granted, as a twisted, dying society, but as a relatively organized one. They've gotten people together, building and working for a purpose. They may follow a mad showman with his own perverted agenda, but in a way these mutants *embrace* their new identities and tasks. Neville's bulldozing, ego-stroking thieveries and murder sprees (reflecting his territorial fears and ego-paranoia) perpetuate the true culture of fear, loss of humanity, and death. How can one *not* root for the mutants?—*ABJ*

Peeping Tom (1960) [**madness; mind control**] Great Britain: Anglo-Amalgamated Productions/Michael Powell (Theatre) (Astor Pictures Corporation). *D:* Michael Powell. *S:* Leo Marks. *Cast:* Carl Boehm (Mark Lewis); Anna Massey (Helen Stephens); Maxine Audley (Mrs. Stephens); Moira Shearer (Vivian); Esmond Knight (Arthur Baden); Shirley Anne Field (Diane Ashley); Jack Watson (Chief Insp. Gregg).

The cinema of Great Britain produced some of the most thought-provoking films of the late 1950s and early 1960s. Although seldom screened today, certainly in comparison to its 1960 American counterpart, *Psycho* (*q.v.*), *Peeping Tom* became the British equivalent of Hitchcock's movie—i.e., a film so notorious that it left critics sharply divided even while it left audiences startled out of their wits.

Peeping Tom relates the tale of Mark Lewis, a cameraman and amateur filmmaker, whose hobby provides an outlet for his voyeuristic tendencies. Lewis' development was warped by the experiments of his father, an eminent psychologist, who was fascinated with the nature of the fear response. From an early age, the young boy was subjected to a series of nocturnal shocks and surprises, all dutifully monitored and recorded by his father's ever-present recording devices. Now, thanks to his unorthodox upbringing, Lewis is unable to relate to the world in anything resembling a normal fashion, his condition a realistic and highly disturbing example of loss of identity.

Lewis' phobia manifests itself in a variety of ways—eavesdropping on neighbors through a window, gazing at a lovers' tryst in the park, and, most significantly, stalking unsuspecting women and recording their murders on film. The film's opening sequence details Lewis' chillingly casual manner as the crime is committed. A prostitute is spotted on a street corner. (As Lewis watches through the camera viewfinder, the image suggests the crosshairs of a rifle.) She quotes the going rate, and he follows her up the stairs and into her bedroom. As she disrobes, Lewis reveals a knife blade hidden in the leg of his camera tripod. He then incorporates a bizarre touch—the use of a mirror that allows the viewer to watch her own fearful reaction as the attack concludes. The viewer thus becomes an observer, and unwilling participant, in her own death.

Painfully shy in social settings, Lewis is aware of his aberration but is unable to resist its lure. His budding relationship with Helen Stephens, a fellow boarder in his rooming house, provides hope for a more normal way of life. "Not you," he screams as Helen points the camera to herself, "It will never see you." Ironically, Helen's blind mother, immune to the seductive power of the moving image, sees Lewis most clearly and senses his problems most acutely. After showing Helen the films of his childhood,

Mark Lewis (Carl Boehm) uses a camera to satisfy his voyeuristic tendencies in *Peeping Tom*.

which disturb her greatly, he contemplates a change and eventually discusses his problems with a psychiatrist. But Lewis' murders of a movie stand-in and a model at a pornographic photo shooting demonstrate that he is unable to escape the stamp of his early psychological imprinting.

Peeping Tom anticipates the heightened use of sexuality in the cinema, a phenomenon that would become a virtual obsession in subsequent decades. Models, attired in provocative, semi-nude outfits, give the camera a healthy slice of cheesecake. Another sequence, played for comedic effect, features an elderly man who asks about "special" photographs at the camera shop where Lewis freelances ("How much would the whole lot be?" asks the old codger). The film is also notable for the way it explores the relationship between fantasy and reality, and the manner in which photographed images can blur that distinction. This observation, one understood by all movie fans, makes *Peeping Tom* one of the more daring entries in the loss-of-identity cinema.—*SGT*

Performance (1970) [altered reality; metamorphosis] Great Britain: Goodtimes Enterprises (Warner Bros.). *D:* Donald Cammell and Nicholas Roeg. *S:* Donald Cammell. *Cast:* James Fox (Chas); Mick Jagger (Turner); Anita Pallenberg (Pherber); Michele Breton (Lucy); Johnny Shannon (Harry Flowers); Anthony Valentine (Joey Maddocks); Stanley Meadows (Rosie).

Performance is an unusual, intense, and unsettling experience that merges two separate worlds—linked by the madness of performance—which intertwine as players from each world meet. At first hyperkinetic, with wild time and space displacements, the film changes pace along with its protagonist, a brutal casual agent of fear who, for self-preservation, slips into a thick, hedonistic environment of decadence and slow death.

Macho East London underworld enforcer Chas runs afoul of his employer and must run for his life, going underground by altering his appearance and stealing into a subleased room. There he meets ex-rock-star Turner, who has gone into retirement to find himself (and trip out with two trippy chicks, Pherber and Lucy). As barriers begin to break down, and appearances and realities change, Chas loses his sadistic kineticism and is seduced into numbed hedonism. Turner is momentarily re-energized, and they both play out their final performances.

When we first see him, sadist Chas represents the ultimate male fantasy: macho, self-occupied, forceful, and dynamic. A misogynist, he treats a female sex partner almost as badly as he treats his clients. He gleefully creates terror and wreaks havoc, quite effectively performing ill-will as an art. As an egocentric, self-professed artist, he freely challenges the will of his boss, Harry Flowers. Chas believes he can get away with murder simply because his ego says he can. Chas kills small-time bookmaker Joey Maddox to prove a point, literally declaring himself to be the bullet that kills Joey (a homosexual subtext runs beneath the gang's activities and interactions). He has a mind like a steel trap and is a tight and fastidious character, clean-cut and fit. Chas is an egomaniac beyond his boundaries, whose ego is gradually stripped away to reveal hidden personality facets. His ordered structure fragments and dissolves, and he becomes susceptible and seduced by sex, drugs, and rock 'n' roll: Chas unwittingly eats psilocybin mushrooms, dresses up like a hippie, and, succumbing to the mushrooms, has sex with Lucy, then is seduced by Turner in kind. (Turner performs a musical number—"Memo from T"—to Chas, and Chas hallucinates homoerotic visions involving not just Turner but Harry and the gang.) Turner comes alive during his performance, at one point screaming like an animal. But naturally, after the 'shrooms begin to wear off, Chas falls back on brutality and in effect kills himself by killing Turner, by killing that element within himself represented by Turner. Then Chas walks off to his own physical death, essentially committing suicide. (As Chas goes passively to his death at the hands of his former gang, the figure seen as the car passes now resembles Turner.) The killer, once artist, now burned out, is on his way to death.

Faded rock star Turner has retreated into drugs and sex, a slow-death escape covering a lost or dormant muse. Turner has already lost much of his identity as a fiery rock star, almost a sort of castration (though in theory everything still works). He remains an egomaniac, but fallen and absorbed. As an artist, he understands the only performance is one that achieves madness, and in Chas he sees danger and power, a way to absorb that energy and play to it. Though there's still fire there, Turner's age shows, and in the end an almost willingness to give in to death or execution takes over. The artist, once killer, now burned out, is on his way to death.—*ABJ*

Pillow of Death (1945) [**madness**] (Universal). *D:* Wallace Fox. *S:* George Bricker; Story by Dwight V. Babcock. *Cast:* Lon Chaney, Jr. (Wayne Fletcher); Brenda Joyce (Donna Kincaid); J. Edward Bromberg (Julian Julian); Rosalind Ivan (Amelia Kincaid); Clara Blandick (Belle Kincaid); George Cleveland (Sam Kincaid).

This last-gasp effort in Universal's "Inner Sanctum" mystery-thriller series would scarcely rate a mention here if it weren't for the pattern set by the films that preceded it, namely *Calling Dr. Death* (1943), *Weird Woman* (1944), *Dead Man's Eyes* (1944), and *The Frozen Ghost* (1945). Some were more "supernatural" than others, but they essentially told the same story: Our protagonist (always played by Lon Chaney, Jr.) found himself accused of murder thanks to damning circumstantial evidence—only to prove himself innocent in the last reel. (Okay, so the fifth entry, *Strange Confession* [1945], didn't really fit the pattern, but that film's status as an unauthorized remake of *The Man Who Reclaimed His Head* [1934] kept it out of circulation for decades, and most people still haven't seen it.)

So, as *Pillow of Death* proceeds, any new viewer familiar with the series will take for granted that Chaney's character, Wayne Fletcher, a lawyer, is completely innocent of the smothering of which he is accused—never mind that the murder of his wife would seem to clear the way for him to further pursue a relationship with his secretary, with whom he is having an affair. And, near the end of the film, when he starts describing the murder in detail—confessing as if he were a man possessed? What of it? It's a trick—he's about to expose the true guilty party, right? And when he takes a suicidal leap out of a window to wrap things up? Hmmm… might we have been mistaken?

Fletcher (Lon Chaney, Jr.) points the finger of guilt at Julian Julian (J. Edward Bromberg) in *Pillow of Death.*

Pillow of Death is a minor effort at best, but it's a nice joke on the unsuspecting viewer as well, as Fletcher's madness (he truly *did* believe himself to be innocent in the early going), nudging it into the loss-of-identity category in the meantime.—*SMD*

Pinocchio (1940) [**metamorphosis**] Walt Disney Pictures (RKO). *D:* Hamilton Luske and Ben Sharpsteen. *S:* Aurelius Battaglia, William Cottrell, Otto Englander, Erdman Penner, Joseph Sabo, Ted Sears, and Webb Smith, Based on the Novel *The Adventures of Pinocchio* by Carlo Collodi. *Voice cast* (all uncredited on screen)*:* Dickie Jones (Alexander/Pinocchio); Cliff Edwards (Jiminy Cricket); Christian Rub (Geppetto); Evelyn Venable (The Blue Fairy); Frankie Darro (Lampwick); Mel Blanc (Cleo/Figaro/Gideon/Additional Voices).

When critics discuss the horror films of the 1930s and 1940s, they usually don't mention Walt Disney, even though those same critics have often pointed to sequences in Disney pictures that scared the bejeezus out of the children (and, probably, the adults) who saw them. From the Mickey Mouse short "The Mad Doctor" (1933), to the terrifying (if illogical) transformation of the Wicked Queen in 1938's *Snow White* (illogical because why would anyone so concerned about her beauty purposely transform herself into an old hag rather than donning a disguise, as in the source tale?), to the nightmarish "Elephants on Parade" dream sequence in *Dumbo* (1940), to the living nightmare of the uncontrolled, uncontrollable mindless water-carrying brooms in the "Sorcerer's Apprentice" segment of *Fantasia* (1940), through to the harrowing Headless Horseman's pursuit of hapless schoolteacher Crane that caps the first half of *The Adventures of Ichabod and Mr. Toad* (1949), Disney's animators provided viewers with some of the most heart-stopping sights and sounds of the period.

But the most frightening by far—not only for the gripping climax involving the terrifying Monstro the whale—has to be what many consider Disney's animation masterpiece, *Pinocchio*, in large part because of its graphic depiction of loss of identity.

Pinocchio is all about identity, concentrating as it does on an animated wooden mannikin who wants to be a "real boy," and who tries on different identities (school boy, puppet without strings), none of which he can be, none of which fit him. Eventually, Pinocchio ends up on Treasure Island, where, in the film's most disturbing scene, he almost loses what little identity he has, nearly succumbing to the temptations that transform his pool-playing, beer-drinking, cigar-smoking comrades into jackasses. (The moment when Lampwick starts to transform, braying instead of laughing, is chilling.) Pinocchio himself (saved by the timely intervention of his conscience in the person of Jiminy Cricket) ends up half-metamorphosed, sporting ears and a tail, accoutrements he keeps until after the climactic struggle with the whale, when he asserts his humanity by saving his father and is rewarded with flesh to match.

The generations of children who saw *Pinocchio* upon its initial release (and subsequent rereleases)—the kids who weren't allowed yet to see "monster movies"—first ran up smack-dab against the horror of loss of identity in this cartoon guise, the boys-into-donkey transformations probably preparing them for the wolf men and cat people to come.—*AFA*

Pit and the Pendulum, The (1961) [**madness**] (Alta Vista/American International Pictures). *D:* Roger Corman. *S:* Richard Matheson. *Cast:* Vincent Price (Nicholas/Sebastian Medina); John Kerr (Francis Bernard); Luana Anders (Catherine Medina); Barbara Steele (Elizabeth Medina); Anthony Carbone (Dr. Charles Leon).

The cycle of Edgar Allan Poe films produced by American International Pictures in the 1960s routinely incorporated loss-of-identity themes into their Gothic-tinged plot lines. In *Pit and the Pendulum*, insanity is the catalyst that triggers such a change, leading to one of the more flamboyant performances of Vincent Price's career.

In Spain, 1547, nobleman Nicholas Medina mourns the loss of his wife, Elizabeth. The brother of the dead woman, Francis Bernard, calls to pay his last respects but finds the initial explanation of his sister's death less than convincing. Medina's erratic behavior also gives him pause, despite the reassurances of Nicholas' sister, Catherine, who explains that her brother's neurosis is rooted in a ghastly childhood trauma. Eventually, Nicholas confesses his suspicion that the malignant atmosphere of the family castle, once presided over by his father, infamous torturer Sebastian Medina, led to Elizabeth's death. Another shock waits in the family crypt when they discover that Elizabeth was apparently interred alive.

The death turns out to be a ruse perpetrated by Elizabeth and her lover, family physician Dr. Leon, to drive poor Nicholas out of his mind. But the strategy works all too well, and Nicholas responds by adopting the murderous persona of his father. Elizabeth and Dr. Leon fall victim to Nicholas' vengeful tirade, and Bernard is mistakenly imprisoned in the "ultimate device of torture"—the pit and the pendulum. Only a last-minute rescue prevents a further calamity, allowing the film to end on one of the supreme shock sequences of the 1960s.

Nicholas Medina's loss of identity occurs in multiple stages. As a boy, he witnessed the execution of his mother and uncle at the hands of his father when their illicit love affair was exposed. Nicholas now carries with him both a bizarre fascination with his father's world of torture and a shared sense of guilt over the family's sins. "Am I not the spawn of my depraved blood?" Nicholas laments as he recounts his horrific background to Bernard. Nicholas' take on reality is thus skewed, rendering him vulnerable to the deception of his wife and her secret lover. "Elizabeth was too sensitive, too aware," he mistakenly declares; "the atmosphere of the castle destroyed her." For Nicholas Medina, it is safer to dwell on his tragic family history than to acknowledge the treachery of the female heart.

Nicholas Medina (Vincent Price) descends into madness in *The Pit and the Pendulum.*

The shock of his wife's "resurrection" nearly frightens Nicholas to death—and indeed his old self is now vanquished from his consciousness. Instead, the identity of his late father comes to the fore, triggered by circumstances that are eerily similar to his tortured memories. The denouement too recreates past history, although this time "Sebastian" shares in the fate of his victims. In his adopted guise, Nicholas' viewpoint becomes even more distorted—out of touch with reality, he is unable to distinguish between the guilty and the innocent. Torturing others, as he has been tortured, Nicholas finds only damnation in his compulsion to relive the past.

Vincent Price takes full advantage of his colorful role as Nicholas/Sebastian and delivers a performance that pulls out all the stops. From his first appearance onscreen, he appears fearful and high-strung; once madness sets in, he chews the scenery with wild theatrical abandon. Critics remain split over his work in this film, although his final-reel soliloquy ("You are about to enter hell...") is a superb and memorable moment. As such, *Pit and the Pendulum* demonstrates the opportunity that the loss-of-identity cinema provided for actors, a fact often taken for granted.—*SGT*

Planet of the Apes (1968) [**altered reality; eradication of self**] (20th Century Fox/AP-JAC Productions). *D:* Franklin J. Schaffner. *S:* Michael Wilson; Rod Serling, Based on the Novel *La Planète des singes* by Pierre Boulle. *Cast:* Charlton Heston (Taylor); Roddy McDowell (Cornelius); Kim Hunter (Zira); Maurice Evans (Dr. Zaius); Linda Harrison (Nova); James Whitmore (President of the Assembly); James Daly (Dr. Honorius).

Anyone of a liberal bent who was conscious back in the 1960s and 1970s can remember the feeling of being ashamed of America. Hey, back in my college days, I was angry with America; I was bored with America, I wanted out. (Give me a break, it was the 1970s!) So I got out, and spent three years studying acting in England. It was a pretty big jump, and, in those uneasy days of the Cold War, I didn't really know if I'd ever see home again.

A funny thing happened over there. The harder I worked to achieve a Standard English Pronunciation, the more American my voice became. The phrase "y'all" started creeping into my daily speech. By the end of three years, it was painfully obvious that I was not going to make my living performing Noel Coward. By then I had found the America in myself, and was ready to go home again.

At least I had an America to return to. The 1968 film *Planet of the Apes* introduces us to Taylor, an embittered astronaut on a spaceship bound for the stars. Due to the effects

Taylor (Charlton Heston) faces a grim new reality in *Planet of the Apes.*

of traveling near the speed of light, hundreds of years have passed since lift-off. Any home he has ever known has turned to dust.

This is no big loss to Taylor. He treats his abandoned world and every vestige of it with unveiled contempt. "I can't help thinking," he says, "somewhere in the universe there has to be something better than man."

However, Taylor lives in the *Twilight Zone* universe of co-writer Rod Serling: There is a god, and he has a sense of humor. In short order Taylor is marooned on a planet ruled by intelligent, civilized apes, where the only human beings are mute savages. He soon finds himself caged with the other humans in a hospital devoted to animal research.

Alone, stripped of his uniform, of his rank, and, thanks to a throat injury, unable to speak, Taylor is to the apes a stereotypical human: filthy, dangerous—an animal fit only for medical experimentation. No matter what he does, his every action is interpreted in that light.

Thus, *Planet of the Apes* presents an intriguing variation on the fear of loss of identity, one that in 1968 appealed to audiences on a variety of levels across a spectrum of post-Eisenhower, post-Watts, pre-Women's Liberation, pre-Stonewall America. How do you maintain your identity when the society that gave that identity meaning has ceased to exist, in a culture that insists you are less than human?

Taylor's fight to find and assert that identity is the primary conflict for much of *Planet of the Apes*. To preserve their status quo, the apes are prepared to resort to the ultimate solution, lobotomy, and impose by force their image of human beings on Taylor. But when Taylor finally succeeds, forcefully asserting himself as an intelligent, civilized human in the faces of a crowd of gawking apes, 1968 audiences cheered.—*AJL*

Possession of Joel Delaney, The (1972). [**possession**] ITC Productions (Paramount Pictures). *D:* Waris Hussein. *S:* Irene Kamp and Matt Robinson, From the Novel *Possession of Joel Delaney* by Ramona Stewart. *Cast:* Shirley Maclaine (Norah Benson); Perry King (Joel Delaney); David Elliott (Peter Benson); Miriam Colon (Veronica); Lisa Kohane (Carrie Benson); Barbara Trentham (Sherry Talbo); Lovelady Powel (Dr. Erika Lorenz); Edmundo Rivera Alvarez (Don Pedro).

Prior to 1973's fiery tale of demonic possession, *The Exorcist* (*q.v.*), an obscure but more realistic and unapologetic horror-thriller hit the screens without much attention, save for a little controversial full-frontal child nudity and humiliation. *Joel Delaney* is a socio-polemic with some potent observations about white-Hispanic class conflicts, an unabashed horror picture, and a brutal loss-of-identity exploration in which a woman begins to realize her brother has fallen under a Santeria possession—a spell to which she herself also succumbs!

Somewhat snooty Manhattan socialite Norah Benson is reunited with her younger brother, Joel Delaney. She's very protective of him, even around his old girlfriend, Sherry, and people at a party think Norah and Joel are lovers. Through his friendship with Tonio Perez, a powerful and evil practitioner of Santeria, the weaker-willed Joel loses himself when Tonio's stronger will possesses him from beyond the grave. Via Joel (and Joel's own resentment and rejection of upper-class society), Tonio's contempt and hatred for what Norah represents is reanimated; Tonio can kill again. Regular Joel struggles throughout to maintain his sanity, waking from psychotic "Tonio" episodes as if from a deep sleep. By the end, he becomes completely possessed and wreaks horrible vengeance via torture and humiliation (making Norah's son completely strip and dance, forcing Norah's daughter's face into a bowl of dog food)—besides continuing Tonio's practice of decapitation.

Norah herself gradually loses her grip on her identity as Joel's apparent madness grows. As she becomes immersed in the underground of Spanish Harlem and participates in a Santeria ritual, in an effort to help her brother and save him from his increasingly erratic behavior, she begins to lose her stuffy socialite posturing. Her ignorance and fear overshadow/overwhelm her wealth, comfort, and decadence. She becomes desperate and flees with her children. And, further losing herself (or perhaps seduced by the Tonio side of her brother), she almost reciprocates when the possessed Joel violently kisses her during their climactic, brutal struggle. But when he slashes her daughter's throat (the child survives), Norah snaps back momentarily long enough to remember her children. Then, as Joel (shot by police) dies in her arms, her grief makes her vulnerable, Tonio's spirit enters her body (power of faith or spirituality overcoming hollowness from upper-class trappings), and (in a typical 1970s "evil-lives-on" ending) she picks up Joel's blade, wielding it against a policeman. We can only imagine what happens after the film's final freeze-frame on her sneer.—*ABJ*

Psycho (1960) [**split personality; madness**] Shamley Productions (Paramount Pictures). *D:* Alfred Hitchcock. *S:* Joseph Stephano, Based on the Novel *Psycho* by Robert Bloch. *Cast:* Anthony Perkins (Norman Bates); Janet Leigh (Marion Crane); Vera Miles (Lila Crane); John Gavin (Sam Loomis); Martin Balsam (Arbogast); Simon Oakland (psychiatrist).

Hitchcock's low-budget experiment in efficiency, shot in black and white by his *Alfred Hitchcock Presents* television crew, is a genuine horror classic with the Master's usual touches of wit and black humor, trademark duplicities, and psychological ills and twists—and was the scariest, most controversial film of its time. Lurid and sensational, it's a screaming example of identity loss and transmutation, moving from one impulsive act of desperation to defining madness—the unraveling of the psyche of a murderous monster.

Attempting to escape to a better life, Phoenix real-estate secretary Marion Crane impulsively steals $40,000 entrusted to her for bank deposit, taking off by car toward boyfriend Sam Loomis, a divorcé stuck with debts from his dead father's hardware business. During a slashing rainstorm (prefiguring the slashing indoor shower to come), Marion loses her way and ends up in the middle of nowhere—namely, the seemingly deserted Bates Motel. Boyish caretaker Norman Bates is upbeat and accommodating (though troubled and troubling, but Marion attributes his disquiet and outburst to the argument she overheard him having with his mother). Marion's conversation with Norman convinces her to do the right thing; she decides to go back to Phoenix, return the money, and face the consequences of her actions. In her room, she takes a symbolically cleansing, refreshing shower—and Hitchcock breaks the rules, throwing the audience's "viewer identity" into question by letting the person whom everybody expected to be the main character get murdered in the bathroom. Forty minutes into its running time, *Psycho* changes identities to become the story of poor Norman, covering up his mother's crimes—until the film's final, sensational surprise revelation (which everybody knows by now) that Norman *is* "Mother."

Duplicities of character and characters permeate the sensational aspects of the film, giving them depth. Through Marion's actions of desperation—her flight and guilt and fear of being caught—we come to understand split personality or fragmentation of self and its concomitant fabrications and illusions (and also a sense of extreme passion and need). Marion, a trusted employee of long standing (though prone to naughtiness in the name of love, as illustrated by her lunchtime rendezvous with Sam), suddenly commits a criminal act. She's "not herself" (just as Norman explains his mother is not when he apologizes for Mother's rant later on). Marion becomes paranoid, trying to ditch the cop (her conscience?) who's dogging her, imagining voices and making up conversations. She becomes lost in the wet night and ends up at the door of a real monster, Norman, a devil hiding behind innocence and charm. Seeing in Norman a similar trapped soul, she only catches a glimpse of his madness when he raves. Her failure to realize the degree of his insanity proves fatal.

Psycho **Belgium poster**

As for "Dr. Norman and Mrs. Bates," the young man has neatly consigned all that is atrocious about himself to his "Mother" guise (fitting, since Mrs. Bates—significantly first-named Norma—apparently was the one who "made him what he was") so that he can retain his aura of nice-guy normalcy.

A graphic example of the power of personality occurs at the movie's climax, when Sam Loomis overpowers "Mother" in the cellar. Sam's relatively easy vanquishment of someone whom we've come to regard as a formidable foe might seem like typical Hitchcock climax-rushing (the Master is often in a hurry to wrap things up), but here it visually illustrates a truth about identity in *Psycho*: As soon as "Mother's" wig falls off during the tussle with Sam—as soon as Norman loses his identity (clothes *do* make the man, or woman, in this case)—Norman becomes powerless, reduced once again to his helpless, hapless self. And, in the end, after Norman has been found out, "unmasked"—*e-feminated*, as it were—he can do a complete 180, "becoming" Mother for good and blaming all the criminal actions on her wayward son (who did, after all, commit them). Norman must be put away, like he should've been years ago. He was always *bad*! Mother thinks if she sits nice and quiet, knowing they're watching her, they'll see and know how harmless she is. She wouldn't even harm a fly.—*ABJ*

Quatermass and the Pit. See **Five Million Years to Earth** (1967).

Quatermass II. See **Enemy from Space** (1957).

Quatermass Xperiment, The. See **Creeping Unknown, The** (1956).

Raven, The (1935) [**disfigurement/medical intervention; madness**] (Universal). *D:* Lew Landers (as Louis Friedlander). *S:* David Boehm, Suggested by the Poem "The Raven" and the Story "The Pit and the Pendulum" by Edgar Allan Poe. *Cast:* Bela Lugosi (Dr. Richard Vollin); Boris Karloff (Edmond Bateman); Lester Matthews (Dr. Jerry Halden); Irene Ware (Jean Thatcher); Samuel S. Hinds (Judge Thatcher); Spencer Charters (Colonel Bertram Grant); Inez Courtney (Mary Burns)

The Raven, the second of Universal's Karloff-Lugosi pairings, is best remembered as the sole entry in which Bela Lugosi enjoyed the dominant role. The film has the added benefit of dealing with two loss-of-identity topics—disfigurement and madness.

The plot explores the relationship between appearance and self-identity. Criminal Edmond Bateman recruits the help of surgeon Dr. Richard Vollin to transform his facial features in an effort to hide from the law. Bateman's actions have a secondary implied motivation as well—ever since childhood, his appearance has been a source of personal rejection. "Makes me feel mean," he confesses to Vollin. "Maybe if a man looks ugly, he does ugly things." Vollin immediately notes the significance of Bateman's statement. Our appearance influences how others treat us, as well as how we see ourselves.

Unfortunately for Bateman, Vollin has his own agenda. He surgically paralyzes one side of Bateman's face to blackmail him into assisting in a bizarre revenge scheme. Vollin's actions put Bateman's philosophic observation to the test—transformed into something monstrously ugly, he will now be asked to perform horrible deeds. Bateman's identity change is so complete that his very presence in the room will later unnerve a group of strangers.

From the moment the film introduces him, Vollin's own identity is warped by a touch of madness. He lives, almost literally, in the shadow of Edgar Allan Poe, as suggested

Vollin (Bela Lugosi) agrees to help Bateman (Boris Karloff) change his appearance but disfigures Bateman so he will help him with his evil plans in *The Raven*.

by the image of the raven that appears in his opening scene. Called in on a medical emergency, Vollin saves the life of lovely Jean Thatcher; she soon becomes the object of his desire, as well as the source of his torment. When Judge Thatcher implores the surgeon to forget his daughter, Vollin is outraged, declaring later, "When a man of genius is denied his great love, he goes mad!," an axiom he proceeds to prove by kidnapping Jean and her family and subjecting them to Poe's devices of torture. "My brain—your hand," he tells Bateman, implying a bizarre forged identity that is greater than the sum of the parts.

The obsession with torture reveals additional aspects of Vollin's character. He describes his construction of the death devices with grand relish, telling one character, "It's *more* than a hobby." Later, Vollin joyfully demonstrates the workings of his full-sized pendulum, enthusiastically lying on the table while he allows the manacles to be fastened in place. As the plan for vengeance commences, Vollin's mania intensifies, as does his empathy with his imaginary mentor. "Poe only conceived it; I have done it!" he boasts to Bateman when his goal is finally in sight. Vollin eventually reaches identity fulfillment when his talents for physical torture match Poe's gift for the horrors of the mind. "*Poe—you are avenged!*" he pronounces to the world, confirming that his identification with the dark side is now complete.

In the film's final act, Bateman overcomes his facial deformity and discovers in himself the human compassion for which he had earlier yearned. The catalyst for this awakening is a beauty-and-beast relationship between Jean Thatcher and Bateman, implying that love can also help shape our identity. Vollin, conversely, becomes a victim of his personal obsessions. His inner torment is made manifest in the physical torture to which he is subjected in the closing reel. Thus, one man overcomes his identity issue, while another suffers because he immerses himself in the "wrong" identity.

Questions of identity aside, *The Raven* ranks as one of the lesser entries of Universal's Golden Age due to its overripe melodramatics and thrill-a-minute exploits. In a curious twist of cinematic irony, the film's opening and closing credits incorrectly credit Spencer Charters with the role of Geoffrey Burns and Ian Wolfe with the part of Col. Bertram. Even the film's secondary players, it would seem, experienced some identity issues.—*SGT*

Return of the Jedi. See *Star Wars: Episode VI – Return of the Jedi* (1983).

Return of the Living Dead (1985) [**zombification**] (Hemdale/Orion). *D:* Dan O'Bannon. *S:* Dan O'Bannon, Story by Rudy Ricci and Russell Steiner. *Cast:* James Karen (Frank); Don Calfa (Ernie Kaltenbrunner); Thom Matthews (Freddie); Beverly Randolph (Tina); Clu Gulager (Burt Wilson); Jewel Shepard (Casey); Linnea Quigley (Trash).

Based loosely upon the events of *Night of the Living Dead* (1968 [*q.v.*]), the superb *Return of the Living Dead* provides a tongue-in-cheek look at the painful process of zombification. It begins with two workers in a storage facility being exposed to a noxious gas that transforms them into the undead and is then released into the atmosphere to reactivate corpses buried in a nearby graveyard. Frank and Freddie, the unfortunate warehouse caretakers who accidentally break open a canister containing the monster-making gas, then spend the rest of the film writhing and shrieking in agony whilst trapped in the local mortuary. Ernie, the swastika-armband-wearing coroner, monitors their gradual deterioration, while his mortuary is under siege from the ghoulish army that has risen from the grave searching for brains to eat.

Finally, despite retaining the ability to speak and interact, both discard any pretense of humanity and seek the nearest source of food available, culminating with Freddie hunting his girlfriend, Tina, through the mortuary. The surviving humans holed up in the town manage to secure their refuges and settle in to await assistance from the military. However, the National Guard decides to quell the zombie outbreak by obliterating the town with tactical nuclear weapons (which not only spells doom for the survivors but spreads the airborne zombie plague to the world).

Obviously *Return...* features the usual loss of identity associated with zombification, but its fly-on-the-wall voyeurism of the painfully slow transition from human to zombie of the two wretched individuals (a theme examined in a more serious and poignant manner in 1993's *Return of the Living Dead 3* [*q.v.*]) makes this piece a valid entry here.

We'll not discuss *Return of the Living Dead Part II* (1988), since it's essentially a redo of this picture. In it, James Karen and Thom Matthews as Ed and Joey assume roles quite similar to their Frank and Freddie here. (The best line in that movie is when one tells the other that he has a sense of *déjà vu*, as if this has all happened before!)—*AJB*

Return of the Living Dead 3 (1993) [**zombification**] Vidmark (Trimark). *D:* Brian Yuzna. *S:* John Penney. *Cast:* Kent McCord (Col. John Reynolds); Melinda [Mindy] Clarke (Julie Walker); J. Trevor Edmond (Curt Reynolds).

An up-close and personal look at a very protracted and occasionally poignant process of zombification amid the conflicts and challenges of coming of age, Brian Yuzna's unique take on undead mythology focuses upon teenage couple Curt and Julie, who suffer tragedy when Julie is killed in a motorbike accident. However, Curt discovers his dad, Col. Reynolds, is in charge of a military research project aiming to create and control undead soldiers, and consequently the plucky teen tearaway [British slang: wild, reckless person] illicitly utilizes this process to reanimate his dead girlfriend. *Return...* is a very different film from its similarly named predecessors, the special distinction being that the transformation of Julie from teenage bad girl into zombie is not as immediate as perhaps it should be. She doesn't instantly become a mindless flesh eater upon revival, as is usual in most zombie films; Julie's resurrection initially allows her to retain her memory and behavioral traits, and even as her humanity ebbs slowly away, she desperately fights her cravings before eventually being overwhelmed with bloodlust.

Julie Walker (**Mindy Clarke**) tries to prove dead girls have more fun in *Return of the Living Dead 3*.

The film's consideration of its protagonist's preservation of memory, morals, and identity poses some interesting issues for the zombie enthusiast. Although there are other zombie movies within which certain characters peer slightly less than mindlessly through the shroud of living death and assert indications of previous memories and experiences (the loveable "Bub" from Romero's 1985 *Day of the Dead* [*q.v.*] springs instantly to mind), not many actually chart a prolonged course illustrating the struggle against loss of identity as a result of zombification. Indeed, most zombie films feature the living fighting against the undead for survival; *Return...* actually takes this a step further and looks at the doomed struggle to survive when the person in question is already dead.

Julie's experience of zombification is in stark contrast to the rest of the undead in the movie who, within seconds of lying down as quivering, partially eaten shreds of tissue, rise up again as mindless meat-eating automatons with no qualms whatsoever about devouring the nearest source of warm flesh. Obviously such antics prompt the question of why she does not similarly lose her identity with the same swiftness and finality, and here *Return...* hints controversially that the process might be controllable, or at least limited, if the individual is subjected to certain emotional variables.

From death to undeath and beyond, Julie evolves both physically and mentally toward her inescapable destiny and even briefly seems to realize emancipation when completing her transition to the nightmare vision she becomes, as she routs and devours her enemies. Ultimately her humanity reasserts itself at the very end thanks to Curt's efforts to save her from imprisonment and subsequent experimentation at the military lab, and director Brian Yuzna and scenarist John Penney hint intriguingly that perhaps love can conquer the trials and terrors of zombification. Let's hope not!—*AJB*

Revenge of Frankenstein, The (1958) [**brain switching**] Great Britain (Hammer Films). *D:* Terence Fisher. *S:* Jimmy Sangster. *Cast:* Peter Cushing (Dr. Victor Stein/Frankenstein); Francis Matthews (Dr. Hans Kleve); Eunice Grayson (Margaret); Michael Gwynn (Karl); John Welsh (Bergman); Lionel Jeffries (Fritz); Oscar Quitak (Karl); Richard Wordsworth (Slensky); Michael Ripper (Kurt).

One of the hallmarks of Hammer Films' long-running Frankenstein series was the chronic inability of cinema's most infamous mad doctor to achieve his life goal. Whether through personal oversight, the meddling of others, or just plain bad luck, his tireless attempts to transfer life to a new body prove to be frustrating and fruitless. In *The Revenge of Frankenstein*, Hammer's second entry in the series, the simple act of brain switching generates deadly and unforeseen consequences.

The film's identity victim is Karl, a paralysis sufferer who longs to escape his crippled shell of a body. After making a deal with the condemned Dr. Frankenstein to save him from the guillotine, he volunteers to become a subject for the doctor's unconventional experiments. The arrangement is equitable—Karl gets a new body and Frankenstein dodges his appointment with death.

Frankenstein's best-laid plans soon go awry, of course. One of the doctor's earlier subjects, a chimpanzee, is revealed to have traits of cannibalism. Frankenstein is certain that this will not occur again as long as Karl's brain is given time to properly heal. But after Karl sustains a serious beating, his body regresses—the paralysis returns, and his tastebuds develop a protein craving that would make Jeffrey Dahmer proud. Karl's

Dr. Hans Kleve (Francis Matthews) and Frankenstein (Peter Cushing) transplant a brain from a dying man into a new body in *The Revenge of Frankenstein*.

crisis quickly becomes acute. He cannot escape his old identity, is unable to adapt to his new one, and slowly finds himself transforming into something monstrous.

Dr. Frankenstein engages in some identity deception as well. His last-minute escape is achieved by trading places with a priest, a substitution that sends the pious man to a burial in unhallowed ground. Later Frankenstein assumes the persona of Dr. Stein before taking up residence in the village of Carlsbruck. There he develops a successful new practice and, after gleefully thumbing his nose at the local medical council, continues in his efforts to create life in his own image by pilfering body parts from the patients in his charity ward.

In the final reel, Frankenstein's past comes back to haunt him. When his identity is revealed to all, his patients rise up in revolt, nearly beating him to death in the process. Frankenstein's assistant, Dr. Hans Kleve, helps his mentor carry out the ultimate escape plan by removing the brain from its dying body and transplanting it into a new human shell. Frankenstein then achieves the ultimate loss of identity by shedding his old mortal coil and starting life anew as Dr. Franck.

The Revenge of Frankenstein is one of Hammer's most entertaining chillers. Benefiting from a fine performance by Peter Cushing and sure-handed direction by Terence Fisher, the film's handling of the loss-of-identity issue only adds another layer of interest to its smart and compelling narrative.—*SGT*

Revenge of the Stepford Wives (1980) [**mind control**] Edgar J. Scherick Associates (NBC). *D:* Robert Fuest. *S:* David Wiltse, Based on the Novel *The Stepford Wives* by Ira Levin. *Cast:* Sharon Gless (Kaye Foster); Julie Kavner (Megan Brady); Audra Lindley

(Barbara Parkinson); Don Johnson (Officer Andy Brady); Mason Adams (Wally); Arthur Hill (Dale "Diz" Corbett).

See commentary under *Stepford Wives, The* (1975).

Revenge of the Zombies (1943) [**voodoo; scientific manipulation**] (Monogram). *D:* Steve Sekely. *S:* Edmond Kelso and Van Norcross. *Cast:* John Carradine (Dr. Max Heinrich Von Altermann); Gale Storm (Jennifer Rand); Robert Lowery (Larry Adams); Bob Steele (Agent); Mantan Moreland (Jeff); Veda Ann Borg (Lila Von Altermann); Barry McCollum (Dr. Harvey Keating); Mauritz Hugo (Scott Warrington); Madame Sul-Te-Wan (Mammy Beulah).

Revenge of the Zombies is practically a remake of *King of the Zombies* (1941 [*q.v.*]), even down to the casting of Mantan Moreland and Madame Sul-Te-Wan in similar roles. Because of this, critics often put down the film. I'm not so picky—I don't mind the repetition, and I can get past the similarities to enjoy the movie on its own merits. Besides, the movie features John Carradine as a mad doctor and contains comic relief by the always reliable Moreland. I will admit that his jokes do not seem as funny this time around—for example, the old chestnut "I gotta go home; there's something I forgot—to stay there" is used for the umpteenth time. Still, the film is great fun for a Saturday afternoon of old-horror-movie viewing.

In the picture, Dr. Von Altermann is a mad scientist devoted to creating zombies for his home country (the word "Nazi" is never used, but it's fairly clear who the doctor's employers are). He has even transformed his own wife, Lila, into the walking dead! Lila's brother is alerted to her demise and hires a private investigator to help clear up the matter (for no apparent reason, the two exchange identities—some minor "loss of identity" that plays no part in the overall theme). Larry the detective also brings his driver, Jeff, who is among the first to encounter the zombies that lurk nearby. Lots of comings and goings ensue before Lila leads the zombies against the doctor for the titular revenge.

Loss of identity comes into play with the zombies that the doctor has created—men who have lost their own will and are under the control of Von Altermann. But the film adds little to the overall idea. However, real-life women who feel they lost their identities when they got married can relate to the doctor's wife, whom he has also turned into a zombie. A visual representation of a woman's subjugation to a man, Mrs. Von Altermann is under the total control and power of her mad husband. She has lost her own identity. As a result, one cannot help but root for her when she fights back against his hypnotic control and causes her husband's inevitable downfall. Unfortunately, Lila's predicament may not be all that unusual, especially to battered women or those who find themselves trapped in any kind of abusive marriage.

The other zombies are not very impressive. In *King of the Zombies*, at least some of the undead were somewhat disturbing and menacing, but here the zombies are dull and uninteresting. Some are too fat, some are too thin, and none of them stand out as particularly frightening or memorable menaces. One of them even plays straight man to Mantan Moreland! Most of the walking dead in this film are little more than background figures, and as a result, they add nothing to any overall theme of identity loss.

But as with *King*, the theme of loss of identity is linked with control by a foreign power. Both films warn against the Nazis by showing how normal men and women would become "zombies" under their control. A wartime loss to such a power would result in surrendering our very souls and identities to these horrible people.

Nazis and zombies would combine on celluloid at least one more time, in the film *Shock Waves* (1975), but since that's about mindless Nazi stormtroopers becoming mindless zombie-Nazi stormtroopers, there's not much identity to lose.—*JSM*

Rollerball (1975) [**regimentation; eradication of self**] Algonquin Productions (United Artists). *D:* Norman Jewison. *S:* William Harrison, Based on his Story "Roller Ball Murder." *Cast:* James Caan (Jonathan E); John Houseman (Mr. Bartholomew); John Beck (Moonpie); Maud Adams (Ella); Ralph Richardson (librarian).

Somewhat of a sci-fi cult classic due to its creation of the title sport, *Rollerball* is another heady, big sci-fi picture from the 1970s falling into the future-shock category where individuality has been absorbed and processed into bought-off dehumanization. In the not too distant future, 2018 to be exact, multinational corporations such as Energy, Luxury, Food, and Transport, control the world. War, violence, poverty, and crime have been eliminated via the creation of a numbed, presumably docile working populace, who eat mood-altering pills like candy. Information and all forms of stimuli are controlled and regulated by the quasi-Communist structure, with corporate wars and the public need for violence by proxy fed by the brutal, gladiatorial sport of rollerball (a skating and motorbike contest played on a tremendous, banked-hardwood circle; it's a combination of roller derby, football, and rugby, and employs various self-defense tactics as players attempt to field a heavy, cannon-fired steel shotput and slam it into a magnetized goal). It's a game designed to show the futility of individual effort, not a game where there are superstars or players who grow old in the game. Even with rules and penalties, there are always injuries and sometimes even deaths.

Jonathan E, a battle-scarred Rollerball veteran of 10 years, is captain of Houston's Energy-sponsored team. (His identity is inextricably linked to the team he represents; his company *gives* him his identity, for his last name is synonymous with Energy's corporate symbol—*E.*) He plays with ferocity while covering a deep wound in his soul: When Jonathan was a young rookie fresh from university training, a corporate executive wanted his wife, Ella, and used her. Powerless, Jonathan took his pain and became the best at his game, leading the Houston team into several world championships over the years. Now, older but no less mean, Jonathan (who has become a cultural folk-hero figure, much to the dislike of the corporate executives) seeks to discover the truth

Jonathan E (James Caan) tries to fight the corporations, who have turned society into mindless workers, in *Rollerball*.

about corporate decision-making and control of society and to heal the wounds of his past. Because he is both a hero to billions and a threat to the societal structure created by the corporate world, corporate heads determine to force retirement on Jonathan to eliminate him from the game. When he refuses to go quietly (in part in support of his team, especially when teammate Moonpie is made a vegetable during a horrifying match against Tokyo), the game rules are gradually eliminated until all skate in a no-penalties, no-time-limit contest to the death.

In a world where corporations make all decisions and control all lives, the loss of individual choice (much as in 1971's *A Clockwork Orange* [*q.v.*]) here signifies man's *mass* loss of identity. Under the corporate class system, man has become a simple, mindless tool, a working beast whose denied bloodlust must inevitably be appeased. Jonathan, who is aware of his power to obtain "concessions" in his quest for knowledge (but isn't yet aware of his true stature), comes to realize how utterly powerless (though dangerous) he is. He's the tough jock who's had it all for so long, then one day can't understand why he suddenly must retire. Not told why he's wanted out, he becomes, of course, defiant, leading to a power struggle of sorts between Jonathan, seeker of knowledge and truth (whose search leads him to kooky computer librarian Ralph Richardson, and ultimately nowhere), and Bartholomew, representative of the power structure that denies individual freedom/Truth (but is too afraid of Jonathan to simply kill him outright). Through his defiance, and his survival of the contest where he ultimately refuses to make the final kill but wins the game anyway, Jonathan transcends his trappings (a world of numbed, mindless obedience to conformity) and becomes a true warrior legend broken free, asserting an identity forged from pain.—*ABJ*

Rosemary's Baby (1968) [**madness; erasure of self**] William Castle Productions (Paramount Pictures). *D:* Roman Polanski. *S:* Roman Polanski, Based on the Novel *Rosemary's Baby* by Ira Levin. *Cast:* Mia Farrow (Rosemary Woodhouse); John Cassevettes (Guy Woodhouse); Ruth Gordon (Minnie Castavet); Sidney Blackmer (Roman Castavet); Maurice Evans (Edward "Hutch" Hutchins); Ralph Bellamy (Dr. Abraham Sapirstein); Patsy Kelly (Laura Louise); Elisha Cook, Jr. (Mr. Nicklas); Charles Grodin (Dr. Hill); Victoria Vetri (as Angela Dorian) (Terry Gionoffrio).

One of the all-time horror classics, *Rosemary's Baby* is a superb treatment of deception and paranoia, of mounting terror culminating in shock, acceptance, and insanity. A young pregnant woman suspects her actor husband has sold his soul—and their unborn baby—to a coven of witches in return for fame. Years ago, another film critic named Andrew (Sarris—not me) suggested that *Rosemary's Baby* was the perfect metaphor for a woman's fears during pregnancy, and he's probably right. The film is at once a psychological, supernatural horror film, and a black-comedy take on birth and the birth of modern evil.

Fragile, child-woman Rosemary Woodhouse (raised Catholic but now uncertain about her faith, trying to mold an identity for herself as a housewife) and her frustrated actor/husband Guy (who lies about what he's acted in, trying on whatever identity will further his prospects) move into NYC's Bramford apartment building (played by the real-life Dakota, a building which lost its own identity in 1980 when resident John Lennon was assassinated outside of it). Immediately they are taken under the overbearing wing of their elderly neighbors, Roman and Minnie Castavet, who take a proprietary interest in Guy's career and Rosemary's plan for a family.

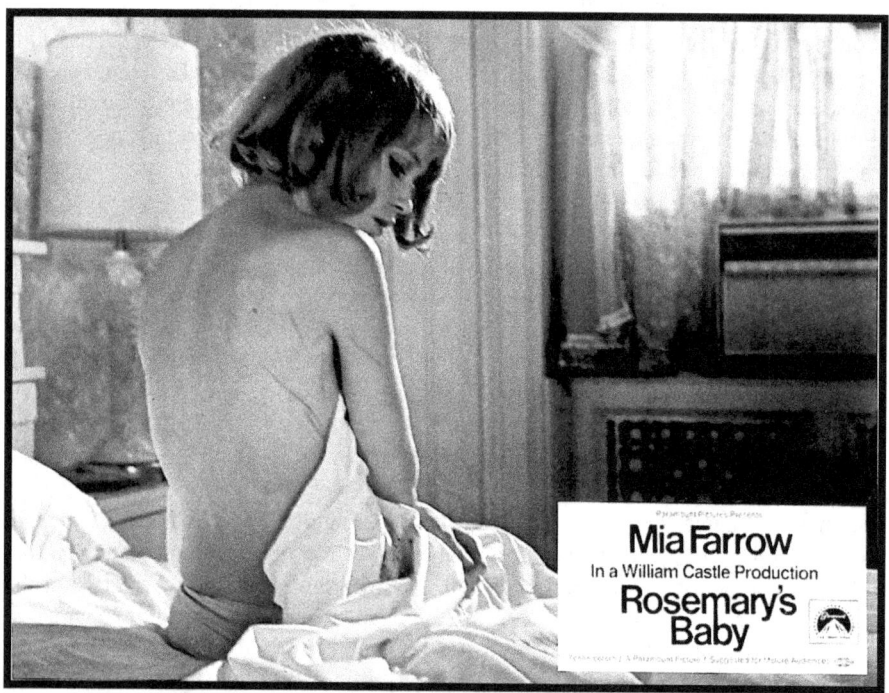

Rosemary Woodhouse (Mia Farrow) finds her life out of control as she slowly learns she is carrying the son of Satan in *Rosemary's Baby.*

In short order, Guy gets his break and Rosemary gets pregnant, but neither event occurs in the way she expects. A competing actor suddenly, mysteriously goes blind, so Rosemary's happiness for Guy is tempered by the regret and—yes—guilt she feels for the original actor's fate. And Rosemary conceives during a drug-induced nightmare, wherein she experiences feelings of shame (and more guilt), subdued by naked onlookers and essentially raped by something *beastly*.

From then on, as Guy's career soars, Rosemary's life sinks out of control. She can't call her soul her own anymore. Guy, the Castevets, and world-renowned obstetrician Abe Sapirstein see to it that she conforms to the confining regimen they set for her. While everything's coming up roses for successful Guy, Rosemary suffers through a less-than-successful pregnancy—no rosy maternal glow for her: She loses weight, becoming chalky, ghostly. Her one attempt at asserting her increasingly subsumed identity is the very short Vidal Sassoon haircut she gets (which only makes her look more like a concentration-camp inmate and accentuates her internal pain).

Just when Rosemary fears she can't take it anymore, the pain stops; the baby moves and is alive. But the disappearance of physical discomfort merely allows Rosemary to dwell on mental anguish. She learns that Roman is really Steven Marcato, son of satanist/warlock Adrian Marcato. She reads that witches perform ritual magic and cast spells, using the force of their combined will to influence others. And that they use baby's blood in their rituals! She becomes convinced that the Castevets, witches, want her unborn baby for some sort of ritual sacrifice and begins to suspect that Guy and Dr. Sapirstein are involved in a conspiracy to harm her unborn baby. But she can't escape their clutches, goes into labor, and is delivered of her child—who vanishes. Dead, she's told.

By this point unwilling to believe anyone, Rosemary eschews the sedative they've been feeding her and, bolstered by a large kitchen knife, seeks the source of the muffled cries she's been hearing. Sure enough, she finally discovers not only her baby but the Truth (of which the audience has been aware ever since the ad campaign): She has given birth to Satan's son. But the Satanists are proving to be lousy surrogate parents. Rosemary, as if in a trance, is drawn to her child, and it warms to her. Giving herself over completely, she accepts the infant as her own, rocking it slowly to sleep.

Rosemary's Baby is a loss-of-identity movie from the get-go. Rosemary begins the film as a lapsed Catholic already, who casually initiates sex and jokes about marijuana and eating children. She still retains feelings of shame and guilt and defers, with 1950s female subservience, to her frustrated egomaniac actor-husband Guy, but there is a sense of spiritual blurriness about her (possibly in part because she's caught between the changing youth culture of the late 1960s and the residual desire to conform). Rosemary herself represents a sort of disassociated innocence—something in transition, slightly independent but trusting, easily manipulated.

With Guy's allegiance to the coven and consequent deception of her, Rosemary allows herself to be robbed of her free will by trusting Guy and the Castevets. Soon they manipulate her food and vitamin intake, her stimuli, her movements. Due to emotional trauma and Guy's sudden personality changes (and "handling" of her), Rosemary's uneasiness becomes suspicion, reinforced by strange physical change and constant pain. As the pain increases, fear creates paranoia, leading to the idea of conspiracy and jeopardy for her unborn child. Even after the pain stops, she acts desperately, running out on her doctor's appointment, frantically calling her previous doctor, Dr. Hill, for help.

Her unraveling and investigation, her need to know, lead to her astonishing discovery (she's the mother of Baby Satan!), and her acceptance of her destiny (her undying maternal instinct) is her madness. Loss of identity—monstrous transformation! Her own identity completely lost, she accepts her destiny and the identity that has been created for her as the mother of Satan's son.

As a final note here, Mia Farrow suffered her own loss of identity during production: Frank Sinatra had her served with divorce papers on the set (and then Ruth Gordon got the Academy Award).—*ABJ*

San daikaijû: Chikyu saidai no kessen. See **Ghidrah, the Three-Headed Monster** (1964).

Scanners (1980) [**scientific manipulation**] Canada: Canadian Film Development Corporation (CFDC)/Filmplan (AVCO Embassy Pictures). *D:* David Cronenberg. *S:* David Cronenberg. *Cast:* Jennifer O'Neill (Kim Obrist); Stephen Lack (Cameron Vale); Patrick McGoohan (Dr. Paul Ruth); Lawrence Dane (Braedon Keller); Michael Ironside (Darryl Revok); Louis Del Grande (First Scanner).

Scanners was the film that pushed David Cronenberg to the forefront of the American popular consciousness. This may have happened initially due to rather explicit special effects, but ultimately because we were witnessing a gifted filmmaker hitting his stride, one who had something to say about our relationships with science and technology and the ultimate merging of the two quite literally with the human body. Our generation's Mary Shelley—a storyteller whose deep-seated studies masqueraded as exploitive genre films. *Scanners*' title refers to people who are born with a unique ability—they can "scan" other humans—and through scanning they can physically control their victims' very metabolic/neurological makeup—causing heartbeats to rise, muscles to ache, skin to tear. At one point, through scanning, a man's head is literally caused to explode.

For me *Scanners* has achieved an unexpected resonance, not unlike the way Stephen King's novel *The Stand* took on a whole new meaning in post-AIDS society. My son is autistic, and all evidence points to the presence of mercury in the ridiculous battery of vaccinations he was subjected to. As a result of this poisoning, my son lost his ability to speak, to attend to others, to socially interact. He in essence lost his identity, and by the age of two would no longer even allow me to hug him. After several years of biomedical interventions, he is slowly recovering. But will he ever become the person he was supposed to be? This is one of the identity-centered questions that *Scanners* presents.

The lead character, Cameron, after a lifetime of psychotic-induced homelessness and sensory-integration dysfunction, is suddenly (through medication) functioning normally. Whereas before his scanning was ever-present, unfocused, and resulted in a bombardment of the neuroreceptors, post-medicated he is in complete control of his faculties. The film takes some license—there's no real mention of how Cameron would even be able to read, given the intense nature of his original condition. But generally the conceit is effective. We feel for this man-child as he struggles to understand the whole of his existence at once—the revelation of heretofore unknown family members, the possibility of romantic love, the desire to find his place in the world, and of course, his coming to terms with the immense power he now wields.

Like my son, Cameron was the innocent victim of supposedly good-intentioned science run amok. (An interesting side note and then I'm off the soap box—but the rate of autism in countries implementing the WHO vaccine schedule dwarfs those countries that do not participate. And before the letters flood in, let me assure you—I am all for vaccinating to prevent dreaded diseases and epidemics. I merely question the necessity of including highly toxic metals in the vaccines.) The film postulates that, years before, a food supplement given to infants resulted in the scanners' development. And, as in the case of the real-world autism epidemic, none of those responsible in the film own up to their guilt. Meanwhile, Cameron's identity shifts throughout the film—from homeless person, to high-functioning responsible member of society, to rogue investigator/activist, to son, to brother, to avenger, to healer. But, in the end, who is Cameron really? It doesn't matter that he can function normally—for one may never know what impact the original drug had on his brain and organs—nor can we be certain what long-term complications the mitigating drug will have on those same areas. In addition, the effect of living his childhood in a perpetually disoriented state also contributes to his "self" being more than a little ill-defined. And thanks to these variables, as in the case with my son, will we ever know what identity it was that Cameron lost?—*RJT*

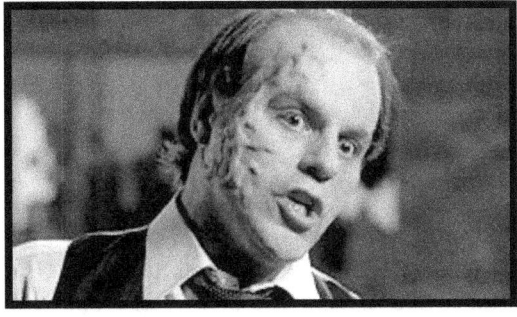

Cameron Vale (Stephen Lack, above) and Darryl Revok (Michael Ironside, below) were unknowingly part of an experiment that turned them into *Scanners*.

Scared Stiff (1953) [**voodoo**] (Paramount). *D:* George Marshall. *S:* Herbert Baker and Walter de Leon, additional dialogue by Ed Simmons and Norman Lear, Based on the Play *The Ghost Breaker* by Paul Dickey and Charles W. Goddard. *Cast:* Dean Martin (Larry Todd); Jerry Lewis (Myron M. Mertz); Lizabeth Scott (Mary Carroll); Carmen Miranda (Carmelita Castina); George Dolenz (Mr. Cortega); Dorothy Malone (Rosie); William Ching (Tony Warren); Paul Marion (The Carriso Twins); Jack Lambert (The Zombie).

The Ghost Breakers (1940 [*q.v.*]) was remade in 1953 as *Scared Stiff* and starred the comedy team of Dean Martin and Jerry Lewis. Also directed by George Marshall, the new film made few changes to the story except for adding musical numbers and a role for Carmen Miranda. A zombie did appear again, though it was not as frightening as the one in the Bob Hope film, thanks to toned-down makeup. Again, nothing new was added to the theme of loss of identity; the zombie plays a relatively minor role.

Dean Martin, Lizabeth Scott and Jerry Lewis in *Scared Stiff*, a remake of *Ghost Breakers*.

[Some find evidence of this toning down in the punchline that follows the description of a zombie. "A zombie has no will of its own. You see them sometimes, walking around blindly with dead eyes, following orders and not knowing what they do, not caring." Instead of the original's political line "You mean like Democrats," the remake substitutes sexual politics: "You mean like husbands."] There *is* a funny moment when Larry and Myron lock the zombie in a closet. Standing guard, Myron asks "Are you in there, zomb?" The monster replies by beating against the door, frightening Myron.

Forming a connection to the previous picture, Bob Hope (with Road movie pal Bing Crosby) makes a cameo during the film's fadeout gag.—*JSM*

Seconds (1966) [**disfigurment; eradication of self**] Gibraltar Production/Joel Productions/John Frankenheimer Productions Inc. (Paramount Pictures). *D:* John Frankenheimer. *S:* Lewis John Carlino, Based on the Novel *Seconds* by David Ely. *Cast:* Rock Hudson (Tony Wilson); John Randolph (Arthur Hamilton); Salome Gems (Nora Marcus); Will Geer (Old Man); Jeff Corey (Mr. Ruby); Richard Anderson (Dr. Innes).

You know, the Age of Aquarius could not have been easy on my old man. Think of it—turning 40 when young people are running around barefoot with flowers in their hair and mini-skirts barely covering their legs, co-habiting without marriage, attending happenings and love-ins, all the while saying the institutions and culture are morally bankrupt. The fact that he pretty much agreed with them probably didn't help. We gotta wonder if he ever looked at his secure existence with wife and kids, thought back to himself as a young man returned from WWII attending college on the GI bill, and wondered, "How the hell did I get here?"

John Frankenheimer's 1966 weirdie *Seconds* was made for men of my Dad's generation. In this, it hardly stood alone. Hell, Rod Serling made almost a second career weaving fantasy scenarios about men wondering where their lives had gone. There are enough movies out there like *The Man Who Haunted Himself* (1970), *Charly* (1968), *Watermelon Man* (1970), and even *The Incredible Shrinking Man* (1957 [*q.v.*]) to justify a special category of LOI films, "the Depression/WWII-generation male-mid-life-crisis movie."

The opening 20 minutes or so of *Seconds* paint the life of quiet desperation of successful middle-aged businessman Arthur Hamilton: the job that bores him, the wife he barely listens to. Minor background details, like a tennis trophy with "Fidelis eternis" scratched in its base, nudge us toward the theme of idealistic youth lost.

Mr. Hamilton, however, has a chance to escape. He receives an offer from a mysterious organization. For $30,000 he will be given a new life. Plastic surgery will change his face, his signature, his voice. A new identity, a new name, a new career complete with all documentation will be established for him. A surgically altered corpse will legally end Mr. Hamilton's old life. His estate will be managed to leave his survivors in comfort and to underwrite his fresh existence far from home.

Mr. Hamilton is not a hard-sell. In fact, he is aching to light out for the frontier as soon as the movie opens.

Words fail to do justice to the nightmare quality of *Seconds*. Frankenheimer, screenwright Lewis John Carlino and cinematographer James Wong Howe have obviously watched too many episodes of *The Twilight Zone* (especially the classic "Eye of the Beholder") as they create the gray wasteland of Mr. Hamilton's home life, and the organization's nightmare maze of corridors and empty rooms. Actually, after a while we kind of wish they'd lay off a little with the distorting lenses and disorienting compositions.

At last the bandages are removed and the newly born Tony Wilson, now played by Rock Hudson, steps into the world to begin his new life. "You are alone in the world, absolved of all responsibility, except to your own interests. Isn't that marvelous?" And then, giving away the game *Seconds* has been symbolically playing, "You've got what almost every middle-aged man in America would like to have. Freedom. Real freedom."

What will he do? Where will he go? Straight to the nearest singles bar to grab the first college co-ed inside the door? Will his new face make him a new man? The artist he always dreamed of being? Or will old patterns reassert themselves, ultimately leaving him in a caricature of his old life?

Alas, viewers will look to *Seconds* in vain for answers to these questions. With freedom, Frankenheimer and Carlino seem to lose their way. Mr. Wilson/Hamilton is so nondescript, there is nothing he seems particularly driven to do, whatever face he wears. So *Seconds* flounders around for an hour or so before giving up and proceeding to one of the most ghoulish finales in the history of moving pictures. (Stick around for it!)

Ultimately, the moral of *Seconds* seems to be "Be happy with who you are. It can only get worse." And to tell the truth, from above the frayed social safety net at this end of the 21st century, Mr. Hamilton's settled and arid existence doesn't look all that bad.

"Fidelis eternis"—*AJL*

Secret Window (2004) [**madness; split personality**] (Tristar). *D*: David Koepp. *S*: David Koepp, From the Novella *Secret Window, Secret Garden* by Stephen King. *Cast:* Johnny Depp (Mort Rainey); John Turturro (John Shooter); Maria Bello (Amy Rainey); Timothy Hutton (Ted Milner); Charles S. Dutton (Ken Karsh); Len Cariou (Sheriff Dave Newsome).

Professional author Mort Rainey receives a surprise visit from one John Shooter, a disgruntled writer who claims to be the victim of an act of plagiarism on Rainey's part. Rainey protests his innocence and attempts to dismiss Shooter as a crank, but the intruder won't be put off so easily. Positive proof of Rainey's original authorship seems to be the only thing that will stop the escalating tide of intimidation and violence that follows.

Those familiar with Stephen King's novel *The Dark Half* (or George A. Romero's 1993 film adaptation) will recall that it involved a novelist's alter ego (inspired by King's second authorial identity as "Richard Bachman") brought to homicidal life via supernatural means. Therefore, few readers were truly surprised when John Shooter turned out to be an extension of Mort Rainey himself in King's novella *Secret Window, Secret Garden*—but Shooter is no supernatural entity.

When a mysterious stranger shows up to bedevil the protagonist in a movie—and does so completely unacknowledged by anybody else—then that either means that the central character is actually dead without knowing it (see the "loss of affect" films starting with 1961's *Carnival of Souls* [*q.v.*]); or that he's going to be forced to acknowledge a side of his identity that he's desperately tried to suppress (the case both here and in *The Machinist* [*q.v.*], released later the same year). *Secret Window* is perhaps the most subtle example of its type—it avoids the surrealism embraced by most of its companions (such as the aforementioned *Machinist* and the non-horror-themed *Fight*

Mort Rainey (Johnny Depp) is haunted by a mysterious stranger (John Turturro) in *Secret Window*.

Club [1999 (*q.v.*)]) and allows the story to be conveyed almost exclusively through the interaction of Depp and Turturro. Though not an outstanding shocker, *Secret Window* was more likely to surprise people than King's source story, earning it footnote status in loss-of-identity cinema.—SMD

Serpent and the Rainbow, The (1988) [**voodoo; possession; zombification**] (Universal). *D:* Wes Craven; *S:* Richard Maxwell, A.R. Simoun, "Inspired by the book *The Serpent and the Rainbow* by Wade Davis." *Cast:* Bill Pullman (Dennis Alan); Cathy Tyson (Marielle Duchamp); Zakes Mokae (Dargent Petraud); Paul Winfield (Lucien Celine); Brent Jennings (Mozart); Conrad Roberts (Christophe); Michael Gough (Schoonbacher).

The investigations of Harvard ethnobotonist Wade Davis, chronicled in his books *The Serpent and the Rainbow* and *Passage of Darkness* (detailing Davis' search for a Haitian "zombie poison"), offer convincing evidence that zombies do indeed exist—though not as the walking corpses of Hollywood fantasy. Through an engulfing tide of cultural tradition and psychological belief, and aided by the physiological properties of neurotoxins and psychotropic drugs obtained from local flora and fauna, victims' wills and individual identities can be stripped from them. These unfortunate creatures are not decomposing cadavers, however, but living persons whose memory and personality have been sublimated and even partially erased.

"[A zombie is created] by means of a slow-acting poison that is applied directly to the intended victim," writes Davis in *The Serpent and the Rainbow*. "That poison contains tetrodotoxin, which acts to lower dramatically the metabolic rate of the victim almost to the point of clinical death. Pronounced dead by attending physicians, and considered materially dead by family members and even by the bokor [voodoo sorcerer] himself, the victim is in fact buried alive.…In those cases in which the victim receives the correct dose of the poison, [he or she] wakes up in the coffin, and is taken from the grave by the bokor. The victim, affected by the drug, traumatized by the…total experience, is bound and led before a cross to be baptized with a new name. After the baptism, or sometimes the next day, he or she is made to eat a paste containing a strong dose of a potent psychoactive drug, the zombi's cucumber, which brings on a state of disorientation and amnesia."

The Serpent and the Rainbow is one of the few horror films to highlight the *real* horror of "zombies": loss of identity. For Haitians, the fear is not of being harmed by a zombie but of *becoming* one.

The story follows anthropologist Dennis Alan, who journeys to Haiti to investigate rumors of a "zombie drug." There Alan befriends psychiatrist Marielle Duchamp and a friendly voodoo priest but soon runs afoul of the intensely

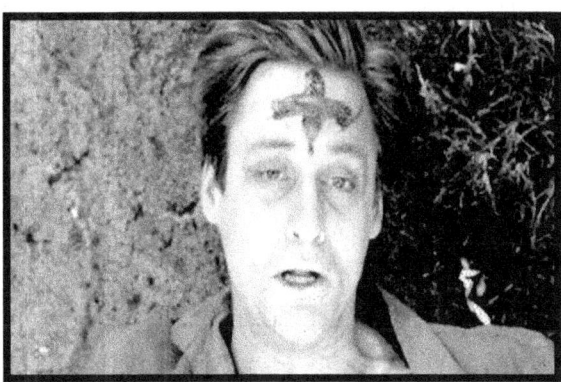

Dennis Alan (Bill Pullman) pays the price for delving into secrets of voodoo in *The Serpent and the Rainbow*.

Captain Petraud (Zakes Mokae), a voodoo sorcerer, begins to manipulate Alan in *The Serpent and the Rainbow.*

malevolent Captain Petraud, the corrupt head of the dreaded secret police—and a voodoo sorcerer—who warns the anthropologist off his quest, eventually resorting to intimidation and torture. Soon Petraud begins to manipulate Alan's subconscious and invade his dreams. With Haiti erupting in revolution (as the dictatorial Duvalier family takes flight), Alan must battle the evil sorcerer for his very soul—to preserve his identity.

Apart from zombie-making, possession rears its ugly loss of identity head after Alan flees back to the States and begins analyzing the zombie powder. At a small dinner party given by a pharmaceutical executive in honor of the anthropologist's success, the hostess becomes possessed and lunges at Alan with a knife. "You've been warned," she hisses in Petraud's voice. "You're going to die!"

The Serpent and the Rainbow comes the closest of all its cinematic brethren to an accurate depiction of the zombie phenomenon. Not surprisingly, however, the movie both romanticizes and simplifies the motivation behind zombification. The "recovered" zombie whom Alan contacts in the film, Christophe Durand, is the big-screen counterpart of the real-life Clairvus Narcisse, whose extraordinary case had drawn Wade Davis to Haiti in the first place. In reality, however, Clairvus was not "a grade-school teacher [who] wasn't afraid to speak out for the people, for freedom" (as his character is described in the film), but a greedy, ambitious pariah at odds with his family (even coming to blows with siblings) and his community.

But because *The Serpent and the Rainbow* deals with the horror of loss of identity, it's better that the film provides Durand with a decent identity to lose. The movie's dramatic simplification adds to the theatrical value of the story (and creates a fascinating antagonist in the form of the ruthless identity-depriving bokor Petraud), marking *The Serpent and the Rainbow* as a thoughtful, frightening, and entertaining loss-of-identity movie.—*BMS*

Shaun of the Dead (2004) [zombification] Great Britain (Rogue Pictures). *D:* Edgar Wright. *S:* Simon Pegg and Edgar Wright. *Cast:* Simon Pegg (Shaun); Kate Ashfield (Liz); Nick Frost (Ed); Lucy Davis (Dianne); Dylan Moran (David); Penelope Wilton (Barbara); Bill Nighy (Philip); Jessica Stevenson (Yvonne).

As of this writing, horror-comedy fans have not had much to celebrate. Notoriously difficult to pull off, horror spoofs of late have been limited to multiple entries in the *Scary Movie* series. However, two recent films have been causes for celebration—*Bubba Ho-Tep* (2002) and the subject of this entry, *Shaun of the Dead*.

Shaun may well go down in film history as the definitive spoof of the George A. Romero living-dead pictures. It follows the adventures of 30-something Brit slacker Shaun, who awakens the morning after having been dumped by his girlfriend to find himself in the middle of the Apocalypse. The dead have risen, and they are eating the living! With his best friend, Ed, Shaun crosses the city and avoids the undead (and the word "zombie") to rescue his mother and his girl and make it to his favorite pub for a few pints. Filled with sly British wit and punctuated with numerous references to *Night of the Living Dead* (1968 [*q.v.*]), *Dawn of the Dead* (1978 [*q.v.*]), *Evil Dead* (1983), *28 Days Later* (2002 [*q.v.*]), and their ilk, *Shaun of the Dead* is an incredibly entertaining rollercoaster ride that manages to be uproariously funny, surprisingly scary, and of course, ghoulishly gory.

As in the living-dead films, the loss of identity here comes from the zombification of the recently deceased and any of the general populace unfortunate to get bitten by the dead. Unlike most fantastic films dealing with the subject—including traditional zombie films such as *White Zombie* (1932 [*q.v.*]) or *King of the Zombies* (1941 [*q.v.*])—the loss of identity here is not reflected by the individual but by the society around him. Living-dead films tend to focus on the plight of a handful of individuals who remain human while everyone around them loses their identities (like *Invasion of the Body Snatchers* [1956 (*q.v.*)]).

The horror of this particular loss of identity comes from the terror of such a situation. Everyone around the central characters has become a mindless zombie driven solely by the need to consume human flesh. Hence, the main characters are in constant danger. In addition, the loss of identity is so complete that there is absolutely no reasoning or communicating with these creatures as they use their ever-growing number to overwhelm the survivors. In all the subgenres of the horror film, it is difficult to find more frightening—or more depressing—films than the living-dead pics.

Still, *Shaun* is a comedy as well as a horror picture, and it plays jokingly with the theme of loss of identity. The characters never seem all that concerned about what is going on around them. The Apocalypse is more of an inconvenience than a severe life change. For example, stoner Ed uses the occasion to drive his roommate's car, and later he pauses in the midst of a zombie attack to field a cell phone call. And the mindless zombies themselves become targets for Shaun and Ed to pitch records at, drive over, take photos of, etc. Yet *Shaun of the Dead* is also surprisingly touching as it plays with its theme. Just before he dies, Shaun's hated stepfather waxes poetic and changes Shaun's feelings toward him. Even more painful, Shaun is forced to kill his own mother when she transforms into a zombie, losing her own identity—and finally bringing home to the characters the gravity of their situation.

Shaun even finds his own identity as the horrific events unfurl. Considered a loser and a failure by those around him, Shaun rises to the occasion by becoming a leader

***Shaun of the Dead*, a surprising little gem from Britain, breathes fresh life into the zombie film.**

and taking his friends to safety. He also wins back his girlfriend. By the end, Shaun has regained his self-confidence and revels in the now-accepted happiness of his humdrum life.

Shaun of the Dead subtly subverts the theme of loss of identity by showing that many of the zombies retain elements of their original personality. For example, Shaun tries to explain to his mother that there is nothing left of her husband Philip in his current state of zombiedom. Yet, right after he says that, undead Philip (locked inside his car) reaches to the dashboard to switch off the blaring rock music that he found so annoying during his life. There's also Ed who, after rising from the dead, spends his days locked in the shed playing video games and vegging out—just as he did when he was alive. In the chaos of *Shaun of the Dead*, loss of identity may just be an exaggeration, while being undead (or loving someone who is undead) simply means adjusting one's lifestyle.

The film also warns us that we may already be dead and therefore may have already lost our identities (reminiscent in many ways of Romero's *Dawn of the Dead*). Opening scenes show lethargic laborers slaving away at their meaningless jobs, riding the bus in an almost comatose state, waiting in long lines, staring ahead, and going about the daily grind of their lives with no enthusiasm or semblance of emotion. Even after becoming zombies, the undead of the film stay in the same location doing virtually the same things they did when alive, be it approaching Shaun for money, playing ball in the street, cuddling outside the pub, etc. It is why Shaun and Ed barely notice that the dead have risen—society has already transformed most of us into mindless drones. Sadly, it's true—we are brought up to conform; we lose our creativity and childlike innocence in order to fit into our society. The film seems to be warning us to retain our individualism and believe in who we are—all the better to survive and combat the living dead when they surround us. This is *Shaun of the Dead* at its most serious, but that level of seriousness in no way detracts from the overall fun to be had with this unique motion picture. It's still one hell of a ride.—*JSM*

She Creature, The (1956) [**hypnotism; reincarnation**] (American International Pictures). *D:* Edward L. Cahn. *S:* Lou Rusoff. *Cast:* Chester Morris (Dr. Carlo Lombardi); Marla English (Andrea Talbott); Tom Conway (Timothy Chappel); Lance Fuller (Dr. Ted Erickson); El Brendel (Olaf, the butler).

In this devilishly outré 1956 B production from A.I.P., Edward L. Cahn creates one of his most offbeat horror entries that showcases everyone's favorite Paul Blaisdell monster. The film opens as manipulative hypnotist Dr. Lombardi emerges from a beach house where the young occupants have been savagely murdered (the male victim falls stiffly directly toward the camera). Lombardi is not the murderer, but he is responsible nonetheless. A former carnival groupie, Andrea Talbott, young and terribly sexy, who always wears a sheer white nightgown, has become the tool of the lustful doctor. Lombardi, whose work in Age Regression was ridiculed by his colleagues, has been able to hypnotize Talbott and revert her soul into its earliest incarnation millions of years ago. In those slimy primordial times Talbott was the She Creature, a sea creature half human and half amphibian with claws and crusty hard-shelled skin, whose urges—then, as now—were simply to kill, kill, kill! Once Talbott is defenseless and in a trance state, Lombardi forces her to become her own ancestral killing machine. Often he leaves Talbott in a semi-comatose state during the day, lying supine on a couch, staring at the ceiling, while her spirit is transformed into the at-first translucent fiend who gradually takes on flesh-and-blood features.

Interestingly, in this wonderful example of cinematic loss of identity, the Talbott character is viewed throughout the movie as lacking individual identity. All the viewer knows about the brunette knockout is that she was a carnival groupie who fell under Lombardi's spell. While she's in a trance, the doctor tries to seduce his defenseless victim with a passionate kiss, but even he realizes that he can make her do anything except love him. [*Cf. The Man with Two Faces* (1934 [*q.v.*]), and *Svengali* (1931 [*q.v.*]).] She is a blank tablet for most of the movie, in a trance-like state and reliving the reincarnated former lives of women and creatures she used to be. Foremost is the reincarnated Elizabeth Wetherby, a feisty woman who lived during the 1600s. When she is not reliving the life of Wetherby, she is the reincarnated monster from the past, the She Creature. Only the battle of wills between conniving Lombardi and actual doctor Ted Erickson (Lance Fuller) gives Talbott the chance to live a normal life. Lombardi, with an ego that knows no limits, tries to use Erickson in his experiments to lend validity to his work, and Erickson is slowly convinced that Lombardi's work is not hokum. In the process, Erickson falls in love with the mysterious assistant and fights to free her soul from Lombardi's grip (despite the fact that Talbott fails to display any type of personality as her present-day incarnation and instead only seems to come to life when she has been reincarnated into one of her past lives).

In the film's clumsy climax, Lombardi pretends to free Talbott's soul from her mind trance when he is in fact forcing her spirit to enter the guise of the fiendish She Creature one last time. After the monster appears from the surf and attacks a policeman, the monster runs amok and, like Universal's Kharis the Mummy, slowly stalks victims who stand within arm's reach firing a worthless pistol at the creature. It does not take much

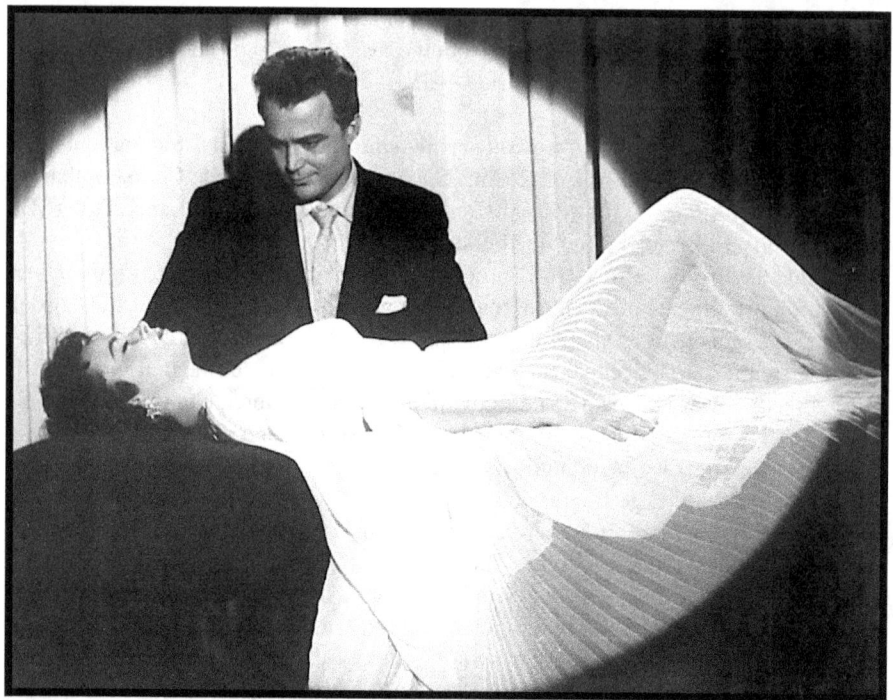

Lombardi (Chester Morris) uses his powers for evil as he turns Andrea Talbott (Marla English) into *The She Creature*.

for the monster to raise its arm and clobber the puny human to the ground. Lombardi, who orders the She Creature to kill his rival Erickson, of course sees the She Creature turn against him and batter him to the ground. Before dying, Lombardi frees Talbott from her spell, allowing her to live a normal life with Erickson, as the She Creature vanishes into mist and vapors for the final time, returning to the sea. [Whether or not Talbott has gained an identity (as Mrs. Ted Erikson?) remains to be seen.]—*GJS*

Shrine of Lorna Love, The. See **Death at Love House** (1976).

Silver Bullet (1985) [**metamorphosis**] (Paramount). *D:* Daniel Attias. *S:* Stephen King, From his Book *Cycle of the Werewolf*. *Cast:* Gary Busey (Uncle Red); Corey Haim (Marty); Megan Follows (Jane); Terry O'Quinn (Sheriff Joe Haller); Everett McGill (Reverend Lowe); Bill Smitrovich (Andy); Robin Groves (Nan); Lawrence Tierney (Owen); Kent Broadhurst (Herb).

At the heart of every werewolf movie lies a warning and admonition: Lose your identity, and become a (literal) monster. *Silver Bullet* is one of the better renditions of this monstrous metaphor, showing that even a respected "man of God" will become a beast when he succumbs, even temporarily, to a loss of self.

The ever-popular Stephen King here adapts his old-fashioned werewolf "novelette," *Cycle of the Werewolf*, for the—*ahem!*—silver screen. Set in Tarkers Mills (Small Town, USA), *Silver Bullet* is every kid's escapist fantasy of meeting and ultimately defeating a real, live monster, and first-time director Daniel Attias manages to retain much of the small-town charm as well as the midnight horror of King's novelette.

Silver Bullet is more a character-driven film than a lunar-driven one, making it an unusually mature monster movie, and hammering home the more intimate loss-of-identity horror found in the werewolf trope. The three main protagonists (a wheelchair-bound boy, a sister resentful of the attention awarded her handicapped brother, and their disreputable but good-hearted alcoholic uncle) all have their own internal demons to fight right alongside the furry external one. "What we tried to deal with, kind of subtextually throughout the film," explained director Daniel Attias to *Fangoria*'s David Everitt, "is the notion that crippledness is more a function of one's own image of oneself than anything else. That fact that the boy is physically crippled does not *make* him crippled. The movie becomes his progress toward accepting himself and gaining acceptance from his family." This *finding* of identity by the young protagonist effectively serves as reflective counterpoint to the antagonist's monstrous *loss* of identity.

Attias (who cut his industry teeth working as assistant director for such cinematic giants as Steven Spielberg and Francis Ford Coppola) and cinematographer Armand Nannuzzi create several standout set pieces involving striking camerawork and edge-of-the-seat suspense. Utilizing POV shots (as the hitherto unseen monster begins to climb to an upper window where an unsuspecting victim awaits), menacing noises (which one victim-to-be investigates among the shadowy forms in a darkened greenhouse), and quick, frenetic cuts (flashing claws, demonic eyes, snarling fangs) when the monster finally attacks, Attias carefully constructs his scenes for maximum build-up that ultimately explodes in a terrifying frenzy. Sadly, Attias, who showed such promise in his debut film, soon forsook his feature-film identity for the more secure, anonymous

In *Silver Bullet* a small town church harbors some dark and frightening secrets.

clime of episodic television, working steadily on such hit series as *Beauty and the Beast, Northern Exposure, Beverly Hills 90210, Lois and Clark,* and *Ally McBeal.*

Some "television" atmosphere seeps into this production: Attias occasionally goes a bit overboard on the "family feature" quality, at times trying to inject a little too much *Afterschool Special* into what is in truth a gruesome R-rated horror film (especially one whose very first scene concludes with a decapitated head flying through the air!). But in the end, it's still an enjoyable monster movie with appealing characters (no easy task considering two of them are pre-teens) and a satisfying ending. *Silver Bullet* has not received the recognition it deserves, especially since, to my mind, there's always room for an uplifting creature feature.—*BMS*

Sien nui yau wan. See **Chinese Ghost Story, A** (1987).

Son of Dracula (1943) [**hypnotism; eradication of self**] Universal. *D:* Robert Siodmak. *S:* Eric Taylor; Story by Curt Siodmak. *Cast:* Lon Chaney, Jr. (Count Alucard); Louise Albritton (Kay Caldwell); Robert Paige (Frank Stanley); J. Edward Bromberg (Professor Lazlo); Frank Craven (Dr. Brewster); Evelyn Ankers (Claire Caldwell).

Son of Dracula, released the year before *Double Indemnity* and *Murder, My Sweet* (both 1944)—and directed by Robert Siodmak (Curt's brother), who went on to make *The Killers* (1946), *Criss Cross* (1949), and other films in the same vein—is just as much a *film noir* as its famous hard-boiled contemporaries and Siodmak's later, acknowledged *noirs.* This "Vampire Always Rings Twice" features a typical *noir* triangle: a love-sick sap of a hero (who'll do anything—even murder—for the twist who's got him twisted around her finger—though here he manages to resist temptation in the end), a *femme fatale* who initially appears to be a naïve innocent but turns out to be calling all the shots (think *The Maltese Falcon*'s Brigid O'Shaughnessy), and the dumb cluck patsy of a husband who thinks he's in charge even as the woman has him exactly where she wants him.

In this respect, *Son of Dracula* turns the typical vampire loss-of-identity scenario on its head. Instead of telling the tale of a young virgin who loses her free will to the hypnotic power of a vampire, transforming into a blank, staring zombie (as in *Dracula* [1931 (*q.v.*)]), it depicts the machinations of a cunning schemer who uses the vampire to unleash her inner sinner. Louise Albritton offers a fine performance, altering both her look and her voice once she's vampirized, providing the audience with a chilling picture of a person deprived of humanity, and then slowly revealing to her clueless boyfriend (and to us viewers) that she'd planned this transformation all along (suggesting that she didn't so much lose her human identity as *shed* it, like a snake its skin, to reveal her true self beneath). As such, *Son of Dracula* is perhaps an *anti*-loss-of-identity film—at least in comparison to its vampire kin. Of course, the titular character suffers his own loss of identity—loss of face, loss of respect, loss of affectiveness—in light of the fact that he's played so spectacularly for a sucker by a "mere" woman. From the beginning, he's had to hide his identity behind the lame anagram "Alucard" (suggesting just how backward this vampire is), and he's reduced to nothing more than a catalyst, seduced by the woman he thinks he's seducing, who uses him as a means to an end (eternal life) and then regards him as an inconvenience to be disposed of. (*Cf. film noir* golddiggers who marry rich husbands for their money and then need to get rid of the husband.)

Who is under whose spell in *Son of Dracula*—**Kay Caldwell (Louise Albritton)** or **Count Alucard (Lon Chaney, Jr.)**?

Among horror-film fans, debates will continue unabated about whether this vampire is Dracula himself or his offspring. (Professor Lazlo, the Van Helsing character in the film, suggests he could be either.) Obviously, Universal's publicity powers-that-were meant the *Son* of the title to refer to star Lon Chaney, Jr. (son of Mr. Monster—Lon Chaney, Sr., who, before his early death, was reportedly considered for the role that made Bela Lugosi famous)—and also to stir memories of its recent (1939) *Son of Frankenstein* success. In the 1940s, Chaney, Jr. played all the famous monsters (save the Invisible Man); his Frankenstein monster was definitely the same as Karloff's creature, though his Kharis the mummy was not Karloff's Im-Ho-Tep but just a poor unfortunate who shared a similar backstory. So is his Dracula *the* Dracula? Who knows? This uncertainty underscores the identity confusion the hapless vampire endured from the get-go.—*AFA*

Soul Survivors (2001) **[altered reality; loss of affect]** (Artisan). *D*: Stephen Carpenter. *S*: Stephen Carpenter. *Cast:* Melissa Sagemiller (Cassie); Wes Bentley (Matt); Casey Affleck (Sean); Eliza Dushku (Annabel); Angela Featherstone (Raven); Luke Wilson (Jude).

While scarcely deserving of an entry to itself in this project, the existence of *Soul Survivors* provides an opportunity to sum up a few other offshoots and side effects of the "loss of affect" film cycle. The film is not to be confused with Thom Eberhardt's *Sole Survivor* (1983)—a low-key *Carnival of Souls* retread in which a young woman (Anita Skinner) suffers guilt over her title status as the only passenger who didn't die

Cassie's friend Annabel (Eliza Dushku) starts acting strange after a car accident in *Soul Survivors*.

in a plane crash. Of course, by the end of the film, she realizes she has nothing to feel guilty about.

Wes Craven "presented" a nominal remake of *Carnival of Souls* (directed by Adam Grossman and Ian Kessner) in 1998. Accident victim Alex Grant (Bobbie Phillips) was made to face sinister clown Louis (Larry Miller) in a story far removed from the original, save for the premise/punchline. Sure enough, at least one reviewer accused it of ripping off *Jacob's Ladder* (1990 [*q.v.*]).

Bruce Willis discovered that he had actually died in the first scene of *The Sixth Sense* in 1999—but he was so focused on his "patient" Haley Joel Osment ("I see dead people") throughout that his own identity was never a concern to him. And the protagonists of the *Final Destination* films (2000, 2003, 2006) really *did* avoid the catastrophes that opened the respective stories: The fact that Death felt cheated and came back to finish the job had nothing to do with "loss of affect."

And somewhere in between, *Soul Survivors* gave us Cassie, a high-school grad who survives a grisly auto accident—or does she? Her friends start acting weird; sinister "Goth" types come after her; a kindly priest tries to help her, etc. But, in an apparent effort to avoid a downer ending and thus please the target youth audience, the film doesn't make Cassie go through with the expected trip to Owl Creek Bridge—she wakes up in bed surrounded by her concerned loved ones after her terrible dream. I don't normally talk in movie theaters, but I couldn't resist firing off "And, oh, Auntie Em, there's no place like home!" at the end of *Soul Survivors*. The three other people in the theater laughed.—*SMD*

So, You've Downloaded a Demon [possession] (2007) Accidental Films/Compass Films. *D:* Todd Livingston. *S:* Todd Livingston and Nicholas Capatanakis. *Cast:* Casidee Riley (Miranda); Sommer Fain (Cat); Zak Kreiter (Dave); Daniel Paul Schafer

(Brian); Todd Livingston (Dr. Malcolm); Xenia Seeberg (Noel); Nicholas Capetanakis (Doctor Wicker).

Okay, full disclosure time. Todd Livingston is my friend and sometime collaborator. And his debut feature film, *So, You've Downloaded a Demon* was not in general release at press time. [It did, however, receive a DVD release from Pop Cinema.] But there was an aspect of this film so relevant, given the parameters of this book, that I felt compelled to write about it. *So, You've...* is a horror/comedy about demonic possession. Dave, a candidate for student-body president of his college, accidentally becomes possessed by a demon via the internet. And, as Todd would say, "Hijinks ensue."

The film is very funny, and the director coaxes relaxed, believable performances from four unknown actors. Despite its extremely low budget and the accompanying hurdles all filmmakers encounter, *So, You've...* manages to move briskly and deliver plenty of laughs. Todd and co-writer Nicholas Capetanakis milk the jokes resulting from the possession for all they're worth. And what's interesting about Dave's possession by Anticus (a demon from Hell) and the subsequent "hijinx" is the very real way in which his friends roll with his goofy behavior.

Sure, Dave (like all cinematic possessed folk post-*The Exorcist* [1973 (*q.v.*)]) vomits on everyone he encounters while campaigning door to door—his campaign manager chalks it up to Dave's low tolerance for beer. Then there's the Goth chick Dave is sweet on. She's a witch-in-training herself, and not exactly closed off to Anticus' lewd suggestions. Even his deeply disturbing stump speech gets the student body pumped up.

All of this rings kind of true to me, I guess, which allows me to suspend disbelief and follow Livingston and company to the film's conclusion. And one of the things that I kept thinking about was this: I've had friends who've lost themselves. Maybe not to demons from Hell (or maybe it was, in the case of some guys in Hollywood) but to other "demons"—like drugs or alcoholism. And it's amazing how we go along with it, for whatever reasons: denial, indifference, embarrassment, cowardice. It usually takes a while—something big has to happen; they have to lose a job or a marriage or rob our piggy banks—before we accept the fact that the person we knew isn't there anymore. They have indeed lost their identity. At that point, we encounter the next stumbling block: What—if anything—are we going to do about it?

In *So, You've Downloaded a Demon*, Dave is fortunate. He's got some committed friends who ultimately aren't afraid to face the truth and then commit themselves at great personal risk to his salvation. We should all be so lucky.—*RJT*

Star Wars (***Star Wars: Episode IV – A New Hope***) (1977) [eradication of self; search for self] Lucas Film Ltd., (20th Century Fox). *D:* George Lucas. *S:* George Lucas. *Cast:* Mark Hamill (Luke Skywalker); Harrison Ford (Han Solo); Carrie Fisher (Princess Leia Organa); Peter Cushing (Grand Moff Tarkin); Alec Guinness (Ben Obi-Wan Kenobi); Anthony Daniels (C-3PO); Kenny Baker (R2-D2); Peter Mayhew (Chewbacca); David Prowse (Darth Vader); James Earl Jones (voice of Darth Vader).

See commentary under ***Star Wars: Episode VI – Return of the Jedi*** (***Return of the Jedi***) (1983).

Star Wars: Episode I – The Phantom Menace (1999) [eradication of self; search for self] Lucasfilm Ltd. (20th Century Fox). *D:* George Lucas. *S:* George Lucas. *Cast:* Liam Neeson (Qui-Gon Jinn); Ewan McGregor (Obi-Wan Kenobi); Natalie Portman (Queen Padmé Amidala); Jake Lloyd (Anakin Skywalker); Pernilla August (Shmi Skywalker); Frank Oz (voice of Yoda); Ian McDiarmid (Senator Palpatine); Oliver Ford Davies (Gov. Sio Bibble); Ray Park (Darth Maul); Hugh Quarshie (Capt. Panaka); Ahmed Best (voice of Jar Jar Binks); Anthony Daniels (C-3PO); Kenny Baker (R2-D2); Terence Stamp (Supreme Chancellor Valorum); Brian Blessed (voice of Boss Nass).

See commentary under ***Star Wars: Episode VI – Return of the Jedi*** (***Return of the Jedi***) (1983).

Star Wars: Episode II – Attack of the Clones (2002) [eradication of self; search for self] Lucasfilm Ltd. (20th Century Fox). *D:* George Lucas. *S:* George Lucas and Jonathan Hales; Story by George Lucas. *Cast:* Ewan McGregor (Obi-Wan Kenobi); Natalie Portman (Senator Padmé Amidala); Hayden Christensen (Anakin Skywalker); Christopher Lee (Count Dooku/Darth Tyranus); Samuel L. Jackson (Mace Windu); Frank Oz (voice of Yoda); Ian McDiarmid (Supreme Chancellor Palpatine); Pernilla August (Shmi Skywalker-Lars); Rose Byrne (Dormé); Temuera Morrison (Jango Fett); Daniel Logan (Boba Fett); Jimmy Smits (Senator Bail Organa).

See commentary under ***Star Wars: Episode VI – Return of the Jedi*** (***Return of the Jedi***) (1983).

Star Wars: Episode III – Revenge of the Sith (2005) [eradication of self; search for self] Lucasfilm Ltd. (20th Century Fox). *D:* George Lucas. *S:* George Lucas. *Cast:* Ewan McGregor (Obi-Wan Kenobi); Natalie Portman (Padmé); Hayden Christensen (Anakin Skywalker); Ian McDiarmid (Supreme Chancellor Palpatine); Samuel L. Jackson (Mace Windu); Jimmy Smits (Senator Bail Organa); Frank Oz (Voice of Yoda).

See commentary under ***Star Wars: Episode VI – Return of the Jedi*** (***Return of the Jedi***) (1983).

Star Wars: Episode IV – A New Hope. See ***Star Wars*** (1977).

Star Wars: Episode V – The Empire Strikes Back (***Empire Strikes Back, The***) (1980) [eradication of self; search for self] Lucasfilm Ltd. (20th Century Fox). *D:* Irving Kershner. *S:* Leigh Brackett and Lawrence Kasdan; Story by George Lucas. *Cast:* Mark Hamill (Luke Skywalker); Harrison Ford (Han Solo); Carrie Fisher (Princess Leia Organa); Billy Dee Williams (Lando Calrissian); Anthony Daniels (C-3PO); David Prowse (Darth Vader); Peter Mayhew (Chewbacca); Kenny Baker (R2-D2); Frank Oz

The sad journey of Anakin Skywalker/Darth Vader becomes the link between the six *Star Wars* films.

(Voice of Yoda); Alec Guinness (Ben Obi-Wan Kenobi); James Earl Jones (voice of Darth Vader, uncredited).

See commentary under *Star Wars: Episode VI – Return of the Jedi* (*Return of the Jedi*) (1983).

Star Wars: Episode VI – Return of the Jedi (***Return of the Jedi***) (1983) [**eradication of self; search for self**] Lucasfilm Ltd. (20th Century Fox). *D:* Richard Marquand. *S:* Lawrence Kasdan and George Lucas; Story by George Lucas. *Cast:* Mark Hamill (Luke Skywalker); Harrison Ford (Han Solo); Carrie Fisher (Princess Leia Organa); Billy Dee Williams (Lando Calrissian); Anthony Daniels (C-3PO); Peter Mayhew (Chewbacca); Sebastian Shaw (Anakin Skywalker); Ian McDiarmid (The Emperor); Frank Oz (voice of Yoda); James Earl Jones (voice of Darth Vader); David Prowse (Darth Vader); Alec Guinness (Ben Obi-Wan Kenobi); Kenny Baker (R2-D2/Paploo).

Six years after Darth Vader first strode onto the screen, audiences finally learned the name he bore before turning to evil: Anakin Skywalker. Before that moment, we knew the mask, the suit, a few stories from George Lucas about Vader's being burned to a crisp in a volcano, and Vader's revelation to Luke at the end of Episode 5 that he was the boy's father. But aside from that single revelation, Anakin Skywalker had been erased, stripped of his identity, his story transformed into a tale of two different people, one of whom had become the bogeyman (Vader) who "killed" Luke's father and obsessively hunted down rebels. Then the boogeyman merged into the father, but sought to turn his own son over to the evil Emperor.

The son, though, sees what nobody else can—that there is still good in Vader. Despite Vader's denial that Anakin still resides in his mechanized shell, Luke believes that Anakin Skywalker is "the name of [Vader's] true self, which [he has] only forgotten." Luke's eyes of love see a hope that his father, marred as he is by lava and hate, can be turned back from evil to this true self. And so the *Star Wars* saga becomes a story not

Anakin Skywalker (Hayden Christensen) gives himself to the dark side of the force to try to save his beloved wife in Episode 3.

only of identity lost, but also one of identity regained. The Anakin trilogy (completed 28 years after audiences first met Obi-Wan, Luke, and the droids on Tatooine) presents the story arc leading up to Anakin's loss, whereas the original trilogy depicts the long process of Anakin's restoration—while at the same time showing the son make wiser choices than his father.

When we first meet Anakin—a boy born into slavery but immensely powerful in the Force—he is an idealistic nine year old. Raised with no sense of greed and a burning desire to free slaves, Anakin himself is liberated from slavery by Qui-Gonn Jinn of the Jedi, who recognizes the boy's immense power and believes he may be the Chosen One of Jedi Prophesy, destined to destroy the Sith and bring balance to the Force. But Anakin's liberation comes not without cost. He leaves behind his mother in slavery. He receives training from a barely minted Jedi (Obi-Wan) who can be only a brother, not a father, to him. And worst of all, Chancellor Palpatine (the unknown Dark Lord of the Sith) takes an interest in Anakin and becomes the father figure the boy never had. By the time Anakin becomes a bratty teenager, impatient and extremely powerful in the Force, Palpatine has begun a campaign to convince the youth that he will someday be the greatest of all Jedi, that he will be invincible.

And so, little by little, Anakin moves away from his natural and Jedi ideals and assumes more and more of the power-oriented ideology embraced by the Sith. By the time Anakin's mother dies, he blames himself for not being "strong enough" to save her…and vows someday to learn how to stop people from dying—an unnatural power, which he later learns is pursued only by those devoted to the Dark Side. In Episode 3, when Anakin is confronted with the possibility of losing Padme, his wife, in childbirth (a possibility Palpatine terms a certainty), the young man crosses fully over to the Dark Side, submits himself to the Dark Lord's teachings, and accepts the Sith identity Darth Vader.

Anakin's willful loss of his true identity, though, has implications not only for himself but for the galaxy. When Anakin becomes Darth Vader, Palpatine is finally able to unveil all his plans: The Republic loses its democratic identity and becomes an Empire; the Jedi are destroyed, and the survivors go into exile (Obi-Wan becoming the hermit "Ben" in the wastes of Tatooine). But the devastation extends into Anakin's family as well: Padme loses the will to live, and her twin children (Luke and Leia) are separated at birth and do not know their true identities until they are adults. Luke never even hears of the Force until he meets up with Obi-Wan. And on Dagobah with Yoda, he is skeptical of Force powers that any Jedi Temple youngling would have seen with his own eyes by the age of five.

The good news is that Luke gets the chance to choose differently than his father, *in* his father's presence. When Yoda and Obi-Wan look at Luke, they see only Anakin's bad choices, not Padme's idealism and inner strength. They believe that the boy he will fall to the Dark Side (as his father did) if he goes out to rescue his friends without completing his training, But Luke in many ways is Padme's son. He is not interested in hoarding Force powers to save people from dying; he wants only to use what powers he has to defend his friends. On the platform above the cloud city, Vader offers his son the same temptation he offered Padme on Mustafar: to join with him and rule the galaxy together. But Luke, like his mother before him, recoils in horror, preferring to die rather than betray his ideals.

Likewise, in the presence of the Emperor, when Luke has beaten down his father and cut off Vader's mechanized right hand, he refuses to kill this Sith apprentice as Anakin killed the disarmed Dooku so many years before. By preferring to die rather than lose himself to the Dark Side, Luke not only re-awakens Anakin's memories of Padme and Dooku (why else would Lucas have written the parallels into Episode 3?), but shows his father that a different path is possible. It is *not* too late for him: Vader does not have to die the Emperor's Sith slave. By making a better choice himself, Luke offers Vader a second chance to make a better choice.

And so, as the Emperor slowly kills the one person who still loves and sees hope for him, Anakin Skywalker re-emerges to destroy the Dark Lord of the Sith... and restore balance to the Force.
—*CCS*

[*Editor's note:* When it comes to *stolen* identity, critics have listed George Lucas' many sources of inspiration for *Star Wars*, including—but not limited to—the Universal *Flash Gordon* serials and Akira Kurosawa's *The Hidden Fortress* (1958), but we've never seen mention in print of his *major* inspiration: Jack Kiry's early-1970s *New Gods* comic-book series. Kirby's hooded villain, Darkseid (who resembles his Dr. Doom for *The Fantastic Four*) is an obvious forerunner of Darth Vader. The heroes obtain strength and power from "the Source," and one hero is named, not Luke Skywalker but Mark Moonrider. Another, Scott Free (Mr. Miracle), turns out to be Darkseid's son. Coincidence? I think not.]

Stepford Wives, The (1975) [***not* mind control**] Fadsin Cinema Associates and Palomar Pictures (Columbia). *D:* Bryan Forbes. *S:* William Goldman, From the Novel *The Stepford Wives* by Ira Levin. *Cast:* Katharine Ross (Joanna Eberhart); Paula Prentiss (Bobbie Markowe); Peter Masterson (Walter Eberhart); Nanette Newman (Carol Van Sant); Tina Louise (Charmaine Wimperis).

The trouble with *The Stepford Wives* is that it *doesn't* make use of the theme of loss of identity—at least, not the way it should. When the secret of Stepford is revealed at the film's end, it is certainly shocking to learn that the town's husbands are having their spouses done in and replaced by android doubles—that's definitely not good news for the murdered wives, but it's simply not as horrifying a revelation as it would have been if the women had been *altered* and turned into obedient sex slaves. What's worse?—your hubby dumping you (homicidally, admittedly) for a bimbo who reminds him of you or your hubby transforming you, against your will, into a creature forced to carry out his every whim?

Wives is as marred as that other, non-LOI 1970s SF film—*Soylent Green* (1973)— was, by an insufficiently shocking ending. When you stop to think about it, the revelation that "soylent green is people" makes perfect sense in an overpopulated world where other foodstuffs are scarce. If the authorities were actively "cultivating" the food—by butchering people instead of giving old folks pleasant dying experiences (as Edward G. Robinson's character has—which is probably better for the meat, like humane slaughterhouse practices)—or if soylent green turned out to be something of absolutely no nutritional value, processed human waste, say ("Soylent green is shit!")—*that* would have been something.

The immediate sequel to *The Stepford Wives*, the television movie, *Revenge of the Stepford Wives*, was wise enough to rectify the original's error, having the in-thrall females not be robot duplicates but flesh-and-blood women deprived of their reason (until the spell is broken at the end, for the wives' revenge of the title). After giving

This lobby card for the original *The Stepford Wives* shows the android slaves in a grocery store.

birth to our daughter the day before, my wife was in the hospital, in the maternity ward, on Sunday, October 12, 1980, when NBC first broadcast the film. She noted that *every* television in the ward (hers included) was tuned to that movie: These new mothers who'd so recently lost control during the process of labor were looking to gain a little vicarious *Revenge* of their own.

The *Stepford Wives* remake (2004) similarly corrects the flaw in the original while introducing some inconsistencies of its own. Perhaps we shouldn't expect coherent logic from a comedy, but its contradictions do destroy credibility for an audience. At first screenwriter Paul Rudnick plays off viewers' knowledge of the original, by having the wives of Stepford perform or malfunction as only machines could (shorting out—with sparks flying; enlarging their breasts automatically; spitting out cash like an ATM), but he ultimately reveals that the mechanism that controls them is computer- and microchip-based mind control (except, of course, for the plan's "mastermind," who turns out to be a bona fide android à la Ash in *Alien* [1979]). No doubt Rudnick and director Frank Oz hated to forgo the women's robotic aspects, both for comic/visual reasons and audience misdirection, but it hurts the film and prevents the development of an (*ahem!*) organic story line.—*AFA*

Stepford Wives, The (2004) [**mind control**] Paramount/Scott Rudin Productions/De Line Pictures/Dreamworks SKG (Paramount). *D:* Frank Oz. *S:* Paul Rudnick, Based on the Novel *The Stepford Wives* by Ira Levin. *Cast:* Nicole Kidman (Joanna Eberhart); Matthew Broderick (Walter Kresby); Bette Midler (Bobbie Markowitz); Glenn Close (Claire Wellington); Christopher Walken (Mike Wellington); Roger Bart (Roger Bannister); David Marshall Grant (Jerry Harmon); Jon Lovitz (Dave Markowitz).

The remake of *The Stepford Wives* made barely a dent at the box office.

See commentary under ***Stepford Wives, The*** (1975).

Strange Possession of Mrs. Oliver, The (1977) [**amnesia**] Shpetner Company (NBC). *D:* Gordon Hessler. *S:* Richard Matheson. *Cast:* Karen Black (Miriam Oliver/Sandy Logan); George Hamilton (Greg Oliver); Robert F. Lyons (Mark); Lucille Benson (housekeeper); Jean Allison (Mrs. Dempsey); Gloria LeRoy (saleslady); Burke Byrnes (bartender).

Two years after her portrayal of a woman with a split personality in Dan Curtis' *Trilogy of Terror* (1975 [*q.v.*]), Karen Black once again plays a woman with severe identity problems. Miriam, an unfulfilled housewife, seems to be "possessed" when she suddenly begins dressing and acting like a persona whom she names "Sandy." Suddenly, people begin *recognizing* Miriam as "Sandy," and someone wants her dead. Richard Matheson's script leads the audience to believe that Miriam is losing her identity, but the twist is that she already lost it half a decade earlier—when the real Miriam died in a fire set to kill Sandy. "Miriam" is *really* Sandy, who years ago began dressing and acting

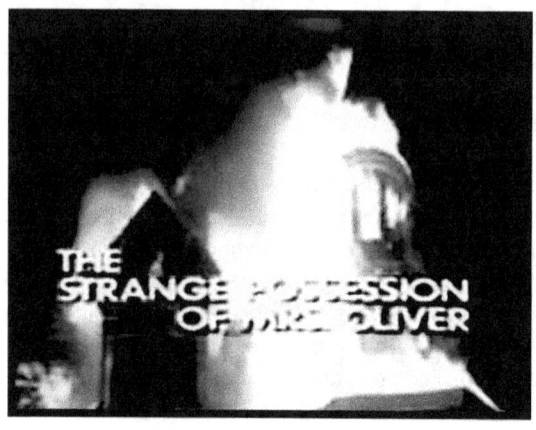

like her dead friend in an attempt to let her live again. Karen Black's performance, as well as Morton Stevens' background music and its interpolation of the golden oldie "Venus" (composed by Ed Marshall), gives this television movie its memorable identity.—*JDT*

Student of Prague, The (*Der Student von Prag*) (1926) [**doppelganger**] Germany (Sokal). *D:* Henryk Galeen. *S:* Henryk Galeen. Based on the Novel *Der Student von Prag* by Hanns Heinz Ewers, derived from the story "William Wilson" by Edgar Allan Poe. *Cast:* Conrad Veidt (Balduin); Werner Krauss (Scapinelli); Agnes Esterhazy (Countess Margaret); Elizza La Porta (Liduscha); Ferdinand von Alten (Baron Waldis Schwarzenberg); Fritz Albert (Count Schwarzenberg); Erich Kober (student); Max Maximillian (student).

The Student of Prague was filmed three times, but the 1926 version is the most deserving of critical attention. Set in 1820, the plot concerns Balduin, a poor student, whose fortunes improve after he unwillingly sells his soul to Scapinelli, an incognito Satan. The film's noteworthy contribution to loss-of-identity cinema is its prevalent use of the doppelganger (ghostly-double) theme.

Myths regarding alter egos are common fixtures of world folklore. Author Jean Paul Richter coined the term "doppelganger" in relation to paired siblings who shared a psychic bond. The concept found widespread influence in 19th-century literature and in the German Expressionist cinema, which often utilized characters of a dual nature or paired characters who were locked in a symbiotic relationship. Among the films that fit this model are *The Cabinet of Dr. Caligari* (1919 [*q.v.*]), *Der Januskopf* (1920), *The Hands of Orlac* (1924), and *Faust* (1926).

The use of the doppelganger theme reached its zenith in *The Student of Prague*. In the film's most striking sequence, a dejected Balduin is approached by Scapinelli and offered 600,000 gold pieces in exchange for the right to take any of the meager possessions in Balduin's room. Scapinelli beckons him to a full-length mirror—Balduin then watches in astonishment as his image takes corporeal form, departs from the looking glass, and walks away. Balduin's double, an expressionless automaton, haunts him throughout the remainder of the film, reminding him of his unholy bargain. When Balduin backs down from a swordfight with Baron Waldis, his romantic rival for the hand of Countess Margaret, his "other" carries out the deed in his place. The Baron is slain, leading to Balduin's expulsion from school and his ultimate rejection by Margaret's family.

Mirrors and mirrored images reinforce the film's primary theme. Seemingly innocuous scenes, such as Balduin practicing his fencing or Margaret primping at her vanity, foreshadow the significance of the reflected image. While attending a formal reception, Balduin hurriedly ushers Countess Schwarzenberg, Margaret's mother, to the dance floor to avoid the damning reflection of a nearby mirror. Late in the film, Balduin encounters Margaret a final time to plead for her love. When she begs for an explanation of the events that led to Baron Waldis' death, he leads her to a mirror and makes the truth known to her. The film's final sequence features a protracted encounter between Balduin and his wayward image. They finally confront each other in the room where the original Faustian bargain was struck. As Balduin fires a pistol, his image disappears and the mirror behind him shatters. Balduin rejoices when he sees his face reflected in the broken glass, only to expire moments later when he realizes he has been mortally wounded.

As presented in the film, the doppelganger provides a subconscious wish fulfillment for actions that we fear but secretly desire. It is also reflective of a loss of spiritual identity. Like misplaced thoughts, our "other self" takes on a life of its own, revealing inner conflicts that we long to keep hidden. In the case of Balduin, the issues of class separation and the moral bankruptcy of sudden riches become the source of unassailable guilt. By film's end, that guilt manifests itself in self-destruction, a common denouement of doppelganger stories.

The Student of Prague has few of the visual flourishes of the best Expressionist horror films. Its leisurely pacing and naturalistic setting prove to be notable liabilities. To its benefit, however, the film's use of the doppelganger theme left a small but significant mark on German cinema. Author Theodore Price also believes that the film was a key influence on Alfred Hitchcock, who later included doppelganger-like pairings in *Shadow of a Doubt* (1943), *Strangers on a Train* (1951), and *Frenzy* (1972).—SGT

Student von Prag, Der. See **Student of Prague, The** (1926).

Supernatural (1933) [**possession**] (Paramount). *D:* Victor Halperin. *S:* Harvey Thew and Brian Marlow, from a story by Garnett Weston. *Cast:* Carole Lombard (Roma Courtney); Randolph Scott (Grant Wilson); Vivienne Osborne (Ruth Rogen); Alan Dinehart (Paul Bavian); H.B. Warner (Dr. Carl Houston); William Farnum (Nick Hammond); Beryl Mercer (Madame Gourjan).

The Golden Age horror films of Paramount lack the Gothic styling and thematic consistency of Universal's classic horror tales, focusing instead on production gloss and marquee-name power. Carole Lombard provided the latter in 1933's *Supernatural*, a tale of murder, revenge, and ultimately, loss of identity in the form of possession from beyond the grave.

As the film opens, mass murderer Ruth Rogen (Vivienne Osborne) is sentenced to death for killing three lovers after a "riotous orgy." Dr. Carl Houston (H.B. Warner), anxious to test his theories concerning the pernicious influence of evil personalities, hopes to prevent a spate of copycat crimes by isolating the energy that emanates from Rogen's dead body. An entirely separate plot thread develops involving wealthy Roma Courtney (Carole Lombard), who is contacted by phony spiritualist Paul Bavian (Alan Dinehart) following the accidental death of her brother. The disjointed story eventually comes together when it is revealed that Bavian was Rogen's lover until the bogus medium betrayed her to the police. During a chance visit to Houston's laboratory, Roma is exposed to "microgenetic" rays from Rogen's body and becomes a host for the dead woman's personality, setting the stage for some well-deserved retribution.

Rogen's initial possession of Roma is deliberately underplayed. After interrupting Houston's Frankenstein-like experiment, Roma moans and clutches her throat, after which she appears to be normal. But during an elaborately staged séance, the image of Rogen materializes and settles in for good. Roma opens her eyes, grasps her hands, and flashes a wry smile in a manner reminiscent of the late murderess. Her laugh, too, takes on Rogen's jaded, dare-you-to-stop-me quality. Roma then makes romantic overtures to Bavian, inviting him first to Rogen's old boarding house and then to her own stately

Grant Wilson (Randolph Scott) must save Roma (Carole Lombard) from being possessed by a killer because of the experiments of Dr. Houston (H.B. Warner) in *Supernatural*.

yacht, waiting for the opportunity to enact a ghostly vengeance. Although Rogen is clearly in charge, the memories of Roma are still intact, implying some sort of dual residency in the woman's soul. Roma finally gets her chance after Bavian is plied with liquor; she wrestles him to the couch and begins to garrote him. "I am Ruth Rogen," she announces triumphantly, "I'm gonna to kill you before I leave this body that you like so much." Before sweet retribution is achieved, however, boyfriend Grant Wilson (Randolph Scott) intervenes, allowing karma to resolve itself in a more traditional manner.

The film incorporates a number of touches that pave the way for the metaphysical journey of Lombard's character. Roma's expression of grief for her late brother plays out in an extended sequence that is both somber and touching. Her later attempts to contact the dead sibling, although clearly misguided, are presented in a sympathetic light. Conversely, Bavian is depicted as an absolute slimeball—among his many crimes is the murder of an intrusive landlady, who enacts an ill-advised blackmail scheme. One can easily understand Rogen's motivation for seeking vengeance, even if she must return from the grave to achieve it. Although one of the minor thrillers of the 1930s, *Supernatural* demonstrates how quickly Hollywood gravitated towards loss-of-identity themes in an effort to extend the Golden Age horror bandwagon.—SGT

Svengali (1931) [**hypnotism**] (Warner Bros.). *D:* Archie Mayo. *S:* J. Grubb Alexander, From the Novel *Trilby* by George Du Maurier. *Cast:* John Barrymore (Svengali); Marion Marsh (Trilby); Donald Crisp (the Laird); Bramwell Fletcher (Billee).

Svengali wasn't the first movie, or even the first memorable movie, to explore hypnosis as a mechanism for the loss of identity. It's predated by, among others, Robert Weine's seminal *Cabinet of Dr. Caligari* (1919 [*q.v.*]). In fact, *Svengali* wasn't even the first screen version of this story! By 1927, there had been at least seven silent-movie adaptations of George Du Maurier's novel (the majority filmed under its original title, *Trilby*). Nevertheless, director Archie Mayo's 1931 *Svengali* remains a minor milestone as the first talkie on its theme, as the definitive cinematic version of Du Maurier's novel, and for star John Barrymore's bravura portrayal in the title role.

Barrymore, working under heavy and obvious makeup that makes him look like Rasputin, gives a rococo performance from the Snidely Whiplash school of moustache-twirling villainy. But he spikes this broad characterization with a dash of sardonic humor, which helps elevate *Svengali* from hoary melodrama to *enjoyable* hoary melodrama.

The eponymous villain is a conniving voice teacher with powerful hypnotic abilities who seduces his young female "students," then robs and abandons them. His latest target is Trilby, a naïve young girl with prodigious vocal talent. Svengali mesmerizes Trilby, fakes the young woman's death, and then launches a high-grossing theatrical career for the hypnotized singer (under an assumed name). He also marries her. These steps give him complete command of Trilby's life and career, as well as her mind. But he cannot control her heart. [*Cf.* the effect of such hypnosis in *Dracula* (1931 [*q.v.*]), *The Man with Two Faces* (1934 [*q.v.*]), and *The Hypnotic Eye* (1960 [*q.v.*]).]

Svengali can bend Trilby to his will, can make her have sex with him, and can even make her *say* that she loves him, but he can't make her *truly* love him. The mesmerist grows dissatisfied with the masturbatory nature of making love to a woman robbed of the power to resist him. "You are beautiful, my manufactured love, but it is only Svengali talking to himself again," he laments.

Svengali (John Barrymore) keeps the beautiful Trilby (Marion Marsh) under his spell in *Svengali*.

The screenplay never explains why such romantic ideas should trouble Svengali, who in the film's early scenes appeared concerned only with money. Yet this becomes the film's overriding concern, finally resolved in the picture's astounding conclusion: Svengali, dying, appeals to God for Trilby's love—and has his wish granted! In other words, the bad guy wins.

Despite (or maybe because of) its arch melodramatics and offbeat finale, *Svengali* was a sensation in its day. Its popularity was so great that the word "svengali" entered the American vernacular, as a generic term for anyone who exerts a malign influence over a naïve innocent.

From a 21st-century perspective, most of the film's lingering interest rests with Barrymore's barnstorming lead performance, and with a handful of beautifully executed sequences from Mayo, who uses Expressionist-influenced sets and eerie lighting to maximum impact. In one unforgettable scene (reminiscent of *Caligari*), the camera pans from Svengali's burning eyes, out a window and across a miniature city, into a distant bedroom window and over to Trilby, lying in her bed. Even miles (or at least blocks) away, Svengali's control over her is complete.

During those moments, *Svengali* proves mesmerizing indeed.—*MDC*

Tarantula (1955) **[disfigurement/medical intervention; metamorphosis]** (Universal International). *D*: Jack Arnold. *S*: Robert M. Fresco and Martin Berkeley; Story by Jack Arnold and Robert M. Fresco. *Cast*: John Agar (Dr. Matt Hastings); Mara Corday (Stephanie "Steve" Clayton); Leo G. Carroll (Professor Gerald Deemer); Nestor Paiva (Sheriff Jack Andrews).

Jack Arnold's *Tarantula* is iconic not only because of its amazing special effects but because of its subplot which addresses a world population increasing "at the rate of 25 million a year" and the need to feed that ever-expanding population. But why should one of the classic 1950s giant-monster-on-the-loose movies be included in a book on loss of identity?

The movie opens as a horribly disfigured man wearing pajamas, dress shoes, and socks wanders weakly through the southwestern desert, soon collapsing and dying. The official cause of the scientist's death (he is Eric Jacobs, a biologist working with Professor Gerald Deemer) is acromegaly, but the man appeared normal only days before, and the disease typically takes years to produce such disfigurement. In his laboratory, Professor Deemer, working on a synthetic non-organic nutriment to feed the world, gives said nutriment to gigantic white rats, guinea pigs, monkeys, and tarantulas via hypodermic needle. He says that Jacobs complained of muscular pain only four days ago before becoming hallucinatory and wandering off into the desert to die.

Paul, Deemer's second assistant—also a horrible victim of acromegaly—attacks him, ranting about how they are both going to die. Paul smashes the laboratory, setting it ablaze and freeing the already over-sized tarantula. The lab goes up in flames, and before collapsing, Paul injects the unconscious Deemer with a syringe. Deemer awakens in time to extinguish the fire, but all his experimental animals burn to death, and the conflagration destroys part of the lab. He then buries his former friend in the desert, obviating the need for a medical autopsy.

Deemer lurks unseen, in dark shadows, while graduate-student Stephanie (who goes by the name Steve—the usual masculine-feminine identity of so many 1950s lady

Dr. Matt Hastings (John Agar) and Steve Clayton (Mara Corday) try to help Professor Deemer (Leo G. Carroll) in *Tarantula*.

researchers) shows homegrown scientist Matt Hastings how the animals in Deemer's lab have amazingly doubled in size only a few hours after injection. After Hastings leaves, Deemer rushes in "My laboratory is not open to the public, Miss Clayton!" he yells, revealing a visage grown jowly—dark and elongated. "Professor, your face!" she cries, retreating upstairs. Deemer goes to the lab and observes his changing features in a mirror. He holds up the hypo that Paul jabbed him with and silently realizes he now has a lifespan of only a few days in which to validate his work.

Matt—called to Deemer's house later—finds the doctor slumped across his desk, semi-conscious, his face now grown monstrous and deformed. When Hastings, ever hopeful, tells Steve that they can do for the professor everything a hospital can do, Deemer reveals the truth: "There's nothing you can do, doctor, nothing anyone can do": Eric and Paul injected themselves with the nutriment four days before they died; the nutriment mutated inside both men, driving them insane and monstrous; Paul injected Deemer before he died. "You should have seen them [the animals] before the fire… eight times their normal size… living only on my nutriment… all lost… all burned."

Imagine the horror of devoting one's life to a grand scientific enterprise only to succumb to impatience, injecting oneself with the unproven formula. Not only does the deadly serum produce monstrous physical changes, making the men look more like monsters than their former selves, but the formula produces delusions and insanity before bringing about a violent end 96 hours later. Imagine such a loss of identity…both physical and mental, all within four days. And pity the eminent Professor Deemer, cruelly punished by his former colleague Paul, who injected the scientist knowing full well he was conferring a four-day death sentence upon the man. Deemer has only those few days in which to transform failure into success, before his eventual end.

And what about the tarantula growing monstrous and attacking the small desert town, ultimately destroyed by napalm explosives fired from jet planes? Well, even for the tarantula, a loss of identity has created fits of violence for the formerly benign creature. Having existed in a world where buildings are gigantic and human beings were the over-sized monsters, the pathetic tarantula finds itself in an altered reality, with an altered sense of identity, where now it has become the giant, monstrous creature and the puny humans its food. In Jack Arnold's world, loss of identity affects the entirety of nature itself, both animal and humans, each driven to violent actions by virtue of an unproven formula injected inside both that produces physical and neurological changes. Pity the three pathetic humans. Pity the poor tarantula as well.—*GJS*

Tenebrae (***Unsane***) (1982) [**madness**] Italy:Sigma Cinematografica Roma (Bedford Entertainment, Inc.). *D:* Dario Argento. *S:* Dario Argento. *Cast:* Anthony Franciosa (Peter Neal); Daria Nicolodi (Anne); John Saxon (Bullmer); Giuliano Gemma (Detective Germani).

Crime novelist Peter Neal (Anthony Franciosa) travels to Rome to promote his latest novel. From the moment he arrives, he finds himself drawn into a web of murder. A deranged killer is modeling his methods on those in Peter's book. And Peter is on his list of future victims.

Why do I keep choosing films whose twisted plots prevent me from fully explaining the impact identity loss has on the story? Probably for the same reason I continue to search for more tortured definitions of the same! With *Tenebrae* Argento returned to his work in the *giallo* genre. (*Giallo*—Italian for "yellow"—is a term used to describe certain Italian murder mysteries which have several defining characteristics, including murders seen subjectively through the eyes of the killer.) The film generates plenty of tension and numerous jolting scares. The plot is more coherent than much of the director's later work, even though the logic is a bit strained at points. As with much of Dario's canon, the film is well worth seeking out, provided audiences can look past the gory bits and the occasionally uncomfortable elements of misogyny. But I digress, as I search for a way to discuss loss of identity without loss of surprise for those of you who haven't yet seen the film!

Somewhat akin to *Psycho* (1960 [*q.v.*]), Argento does an interesting bait-and-switch with a lead character. However, instead of killing the ostensible heroine part-way into the film as Hitchcock did, *Tenebrae* eliminates the killer! And, through a clever bit of chicanery, the "Italian Hitchcock" is able to blur the audience's idea of just who the "new" killer is, although I suspect today's viewer is a little more savvy, living in the post-Shyamalan age, and will likely figure the mystery out. What remains interesting, however, in addition to Argento's visual virtuosity, is the identity switch that gives birth to the second killer. Someone "becomes" the apparently deceased killer by adopting, to a point, the killer's m.o. So, while the original killer had adopted his persona from Peter Neal's book, the "killer-of-the-killer" adopts the latter's identity, which in fact means he's merging with not one but *two* identities. And upon further investigation we discover that he/she had also been responsible for an unsolved murder decades earlier, the details of which lead this person to struggle with certain segments of society—and identity. Through a series of flashbacks from the perspective of one of the killers that involves implied oral rape, homosexual assault, and murder, we learn that one of the killers struggles mightily with all sorts of residual emotions, and apparently a confused sense of self. To top it all off, the person from the past who acts as both tormentor and victim in these flashbacks is an attractive young woman—who on closer inspection seems rather masculine—a part for which Argento did in fact cast a man! Identities are shed like snake skins in *Tenebrae*—but not so easily the effects of a first-time viewing of the film.—*RJT*

They Live (1988) [**altered reality**] (MCA/Universal Pictures). *D:* John Carpenter. *S:* Ray Nelson and John Carpenter (as Frank Armitage). *Cast:* Roddy Piper (Nada); Keith David (Frank); Meg Foster (Holly Thompson); George "Buck" Flowers (drifter); Peter Jason (Gilbert); Raymond St. Jacques (Street Preacher).

How much of one's identity is defined by one's environment? Is identity a purely internal phenomenon, or do external forces shape and mold one's personality? It's the old nature-vs.-nurture question, and the reasonable answer is that identity springs both from an individual's inherent traits

Eve Robins is the girl on the beach in *Tenebrae*.

and molding external factors. Radically alter or manipulate those external factors, and a person's identity comes into question; can it even be lost altogether. Such a terrifying prospect is taken to a global level in writer-director John Carpenter's *They Live*. (Though the film officially credits one "Frank Armitage" as scripter, star Roddy Piper revealed that it was Carpenter himself who penned the screenplay—despite Carpenter's [no doubt tongue in cheek] statements to *Cinefantastique* magazine that his supposed co-author "thinks along the same line as I do," and that "this guy is like my brother.")

"Imagine that the Reagan Revolution is run by aliens from outer space," suggested Carpenter in describing his new twist on the aliens-among-us theme pioneered by films like 1956's *Invasion of the Body Snatchers* and 1957's *Enemy from Space* (*qq.v.*; both favorites of Carpenter). "It's a kind of modern, 1980s *Invasion of the Body Snatchers*, but slightly different in that you don't lose your humanity when you get taken over—or at least, you don't become physically different—all you're doing is selling out your values. There's no change; you just get rich. Everybody wants to get rich, right?"

In the first half-hour of *They Live*, Carpenter treats us to a masterful bit of mood building as he introduces John Nada (Roddy Piper), an honest, hard-working regular Joe down on his luck who's come to the big city looking for work. Focusing on a modern-day shantytown location, Carpenter effectively establishes the down-and-out climate of Reaganomics woes that existed side-by-side with the bright shiny skyscrapers of prosperity just over the hill. After the movie engages in a bit of mystery building, Nada discovers that our whole economic and political system is being run by aliens

who keep the human populace unaware and complacent (save for a select few—the "power elite") through the use of a sophisticated system of subliminal control. The ugly aliens, skull-like in appearance, seem normal to humans due to the use of a perception-altering beam transmitted through television. Nada stumbles onto a small resistance movement and acquires specially made sunglasses that enable him to see the aliens and his environment for what they really are. The sight of a normal cityscape transformed into a sterile-looking forest of messages like "OBEY," "CONFORM," "MARRY AND REPOPULATE," and "WATCH TV" plastered everywhere is unnerving in its visual depiction of an entire culture stripped of its collective identity. Billboards, business signs, magazines, and product labels all consist of these subliminal messages designed to keep the human race apathetic and productive for the alien entrepreneurs running the show. Even the dollar bill carries a message in bold black letters: "THIS IS YOUR GOD." These scenes effectively touch on the social and political paranoia inherent in many Americans—the distrust of government and authority in general and the loathing of being duped or manipulated—while at the same time making a caustic statement about the power of greed. "Basically the aliens are Republicans," remarked Carpenter, revealing his particular view of politics in the 1980s.

Carpenter pushes some emotional buttons in the viewer by showing how everyman (in the persona of Nada) can stand up and buck the system. "It's really kind of an existential Western," described the director. "It's got a loner hero, a kind of everyman. He's really the only one who can do anything about [the invasion]. He doesn't sell out to the aliens as most people do. It's about control, loyalty, morality." Of course, such nonconformist defiance on Nada's part is not without cost, and Carpenter wisely avoids shooting the ending through rose-colored lenses. The denouement is not downbeat, however, but neither is it neatly wrapped up in a bright tidy package.

The middle portion of the film, in which Nada tries to convince first television station employee Holly and later fellow construction worker Frank of the nefarious conspiracy, drags somewhat. For instance, the sequence in which Nada has to fight his doubting co-worker in order to convince him to put on the revealing sunglasses goes on far too long (seven-and-a-half minutes, to be precise!). The seemingly endless bout of fisticuffs quickly becomes both ridiculous and tiresome, making one wish Nada would just hurry up and beat the guy senseless so he can place the glasses on his face. (According to Piper, Carpenter "wanted the longest fight scene in cinema history" and had his star watch John Wayne in *The Quiet Man* [1952] for inspiration.) The sequence is obviously a showcase for Piper's big-time-wrestling talents, since Piper was known as "Rowdy Roddy Piper" on the professional wrestling circuit when not acting in films. But its interminable repetition of senseless punches threatens to cause the movie to lose *its* identity. Fortunately, the final 30 minutes, when Nada and Frank start shooting aliens and searching for the secret signal transmitter, is great non-stop action.

Piper's background is uncomfortably close to his onscreen persona; he himself was homeless as a youth. "I've been on the streets since I was 13, have been a professional fighter since 15, have been electrocuted once, and stabbed three times. John [Carpenter] could see that I had experienced what the character of John Nada required, so he incorporated those things into the film. And, since the character was essentially me, who better to play him?"

As a political paranoia thriller and a shoot-'em-up sci-fi actioner, *They Live* satisfies on both counts.—*BMS*

Thing, The (***John Carpenter's The Thing***) (1982) [**alien possession; hive mind**] (Universal). *D:* John Carpenter. *S:* Bill Lancaster, From the Story "Who Goes There?" by John W. Campbell, Jr. *Cast:* Kurt Russell (MacReady); A. Wilfred Brimley (Dr. Blair); T.K. Carter (Nauls); David Clennon (Palmer); Keith David (Childs); Richard Dysart (Dr. Copper); Richard Masur (Clark).

Imagine an alien invasion of the most personal kind. Instead of death machines blazing laser beams down on populated cities and leveling buildings to their foundations, perhaps an even more insidious kind of invasion might take place. An invasion where our humanity—indeed, our entire human fiber—would be copied and replaced by alien predators. This is the premise of John Carpenter's 1982 remake of the 1952 *Thing from Another World* directed by Christian Nyby/Howard Hawks, based upon the classic science fiction story by John W. Campbell, Jr., "Who Goes There?"

In Antarctica, an American team finds a deserted Norwegian military camp and evidence that the humans there discovered a spacecraft buried deep within the snow and ice. A humanoid creature appears to have been freed, but there is no sign of life. Then a few remaining Norwegians show up, pursuing a dog via helicopter. The Americans quickly kill these armed men, rescue the dog, and place it in their kennel with their own dogs. Unfortunately, the dog is actually the alien terror, and from its canine hiding place, the alien life source is able to infiltrate the humans and slowly become them.

The rule of the universe is survival, and this shape-shifting alien entity has only that goal, to survive. By morphing into humans before the actual humans are even aware a change has been made, the aliens have a distinct advantage. Clark, who tends the kennels, is obviously one of the first men to be infiltrated because he is nearest to the alien dog. However, only he knows what he has become, because Clark the alien looks exactly like Clark the human. When the change occurs, the movie audience never gets inside the alien consciousness to know the aliens' level of intelligence or their ultimate goal (other than planet-wide conquest). The fear of not knowing if your best friend is still human is at the heart of the horror of *The Thing*. The fear that I am human one minute but may not be the next is perhaps the ultimate human fear. We see men performing their bland chores, listening to music, skating through the barracks, doing their jobs, but over all permeates a dread of the horror of losing, not one's life, but more appropriately, one's human soul. Similar to the fear of becoming a vampire, this alien terror is not one between life and death but between humanity (being a fully functioning person) and soullessness (becoming an empty shell and host for an alien parasite).

Slowly, the truth of this identity usurpation dawns on the humans. In one key sequence, Dr. Blair, who has remained isolated from the other men, goes ballistic—ranting, waving his gun, threatening to kill anyone who approaches his personal space. Blair understands exactly how the invasion is playing out. The sequence at first seems overdone, but Dr. Blair is literally fighting for his humanity and does not know who is human and who is alien.

One fear of loss of identify that *The Thing* magnifies is the fear of loss of our body and its familiar form and shape. This transformation from human to alien is more than mental; it is physical and horrible at the same time. And the fear only becomes intensified when the men at the military base realize this is exactly what is happening. Thus, audiences understand Blair's total freak-out. Blair is fighting to remain not only human but to retain every memory and feeling he ever experienced.

In the film's most riveting sequence, MacReady has concocted a blood test to prove just who is human and who is alien. Unfortunately, when the blood test is administered, one man at a time, all the men at the base are tied together. Thus, when the alien is ultimately revealed, the humans are still restrained and unable to move as the supposed human right beside them instantaneously morphs into an alien monster, the vulnerable, helpless humans screaming and yelling at the top of their lungs. This fascinating episode

The remoteness of Antarctica only adds to the terror as the men no longer know whom they can trust in *The Thing*.

illustrates the horror of loss of identity, where human beings see their comrades lose the last vestiges of their humanity and fear that the alien parasite might be growing inside them.

By the film's ending only two men survive. After MacReady has found the alien entity beneath Blair's hut and attempted to blow it up, MacReady and Nauls sit around and watch the camp go up in flames, each man deciding to stay for a little while longer to wait and see if both men are human or if one of them is now an alien. Each is willing to die in the Antarctic cold to save humanity and not allow the alien infestation to spread to mainland civilization. And on that note of altruistic, noble, desperate, futile assertion of human identity, the movie ends.

Very few films have captured so perfectly the inner fear of being taken over and transformed into something that is not us, so rapidly, so insidiously, that not even our closest friends will be able to discern that a change has come. That's the true horror of *The Thing*.—GJS

Total Recall (1990) [**scientific manipulation; search for self**] Carolco Pictures (TriStar Pictures). *D:* Paul Verhoeven. *S:* Ronald Shusett, Dan O'Bannon, and Gary Goldman, From a Screen Story by Ronald Shusett, Dan O'Bannon, and Jon Povill, Based on the Story "We Can Remember It for You Wholesale" by Philip K. Dick. *Cast:* Arnold Schwarzennegger (Douglas Quaid/Hauser); Sharon Stone (Lori); Michael Ironside (Richter); Rachel Ticotin (Melina); Ronny Cox (Vilos Cohaagen); Marshall Bell (George/Kuato); Mel Johnson, Jr. (Benny).

We gotta hand it to Philip K. Dick; he can ring in more variations on loss of identity than any three other writers. This ingeniousness is demonstrated full force in *Total Recall* (in which three writers—*Alien* co-scripters Ronald Shusett and Dan O'Bannon, along with Gary Goldman—elaborate upon Dick's original story).

Total Recall is an appropriate title for this loss-of-identity movie, which peels off layer after layer of its protagonist's conflicting memory/identity. Regular-guy Douglas

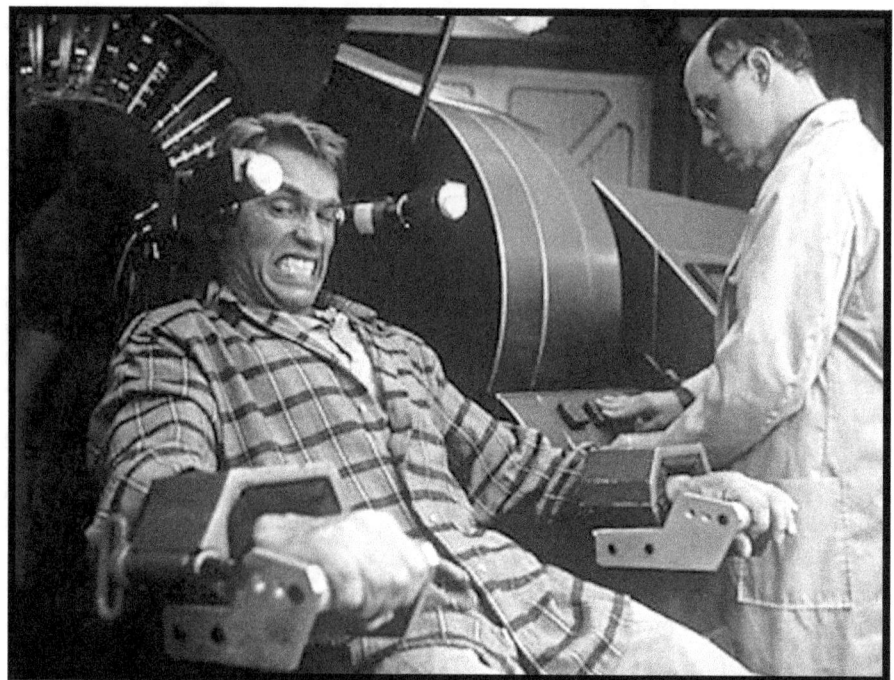

Blue-collar worker Douglas Quaid (Arnold Schwarzennegger) finds himself with memories and abilities he doesn't understand after a virtual vacation in *Total Recall*.

Quaid—a blue-collar worker, plagued by dreams of Mars—decides to take a virtual trip to the Red Planet (since his wife, Lori, is dead-set against an actual journey there). During the memory-implant session (for which Quaid has picked a secret-agent persona for himself), his erased memories are unleashed, and he realizes that he actually *was* a secret agent on Mars, originally sent to infiltrate the Martian rebels but eventually defecting to their side.

After an abortive attempt by the memory people to convince Quaid, who used to be Hauser, that he's merely having a psychotic episode, Quaid/Hauser escapes to Mars, joins up with the rebels, and tries to foment the revolution. Until, when he inadvertently leads the authorities to the rebel leader, it's disclosed that Quaid/Hauser (when he was Hauser) had *voluntarily* undergone memory erasure just so his memory could be restored later and he could, without guile, infiltrate the rebels and expose the leader. Of course, the irony of the story is that the authorities have done their job *too* well: Quaid/Hauser is *not* Hauser the counterspy but a man who has embraced his rebellious implanted identity and rejected his real one.

Throughout the film, various people turn out not to be whom they seem. Lori is not Quaid's wife but a government agent sent to keep an eye on him; other double agents include one of Quaid's co-workers and the supposedly helpful cabbie who drives him around Mars. And one of the rebels, George, has a *dual* identity: Kuato, the mysterious, elusive rebel leader, is a Siamese-twin-like appendage who emerges from George's chest. (These people, along with dozens of government agents, rebels, and innocent bystanders, are blown away by either Quaid/Hauser or the people chasing him;

for a science fiction film, *Total Recall* has all the rapid-fire shoot-'em-up of a typical Schwarzennegger action picture—which gives it some identity confusion of its own.)

All the gunplay and carnage covers up the basic, unnecessary contrivance of the government plot: Why didn't they just wait until Hauser gained the rebels' complete confidence and got in good with Kuato, as he apparently was on his way to doing, instead of concocting this elaborate memory-erasure ruse that would take just as long (if not longer) to pull off? If we can ignore that minor detail, it's fun to watch the contrivances unfold. The film as a whole suffers from the usual one-note performance of Arnold Schwarzenegger, although maybe, in this case, that's a good thing: The viewer always wonders "Who is he now?"—Quaid, Hauser, or Quaid/Hauser—because he's always the same. (He does have one great line—which sort of sums up his problem in the film: "If I'm not me, who the hell am I?")—*AFA*

Torture Ship (1939) [**brainwashing; scientific manipulation**] Producers Pictures Corporation (Producers Distributing Corporation). *D:* Victor Halperin. *S:* George Wallace Sayre, Suggested by the Story "A Thousand Deaths" by Jack London. *Cast:* Lyle Talbot (Lieutenant Bob Bennett); Irving Pichel (Dr. Herbert Stander); Jacqueline Wells (Joan Martel); Sheila Bromley (Mary Stavish); Anthony Averill (Dirk); Russell Hopton (Harry).

The beleaguered Dr. Herbert Stander is about to be indicted for his illegal experiments. Determined to continue his efforts to "cure criminality" with endocrine extracts, Stander helps a number of notorious killers escape and makes them an offer they can't refuse: "In return for helping me with my experiments, I'll give you safe passage to another country." Among the murderers are "Harry the Carver," "Machine Gun Slayer" Jesse, "Bluebeard Killer" Ezra Matthews, and "Poison Mary." Captained by his innocent nephew, Navy man Bob Bennett, the doctor's yacht hastily departs with its cargo of criminal guinea pigs. Stander then begins his experiments. After several failures (resulting in madness and death for his subjects), the determined medico even experiments on his own nephew, temporarily turning Bob into a homicidal imbecile! When the doctor threatens to use Bob's love interest, Joan, in the experiment, the recovered Bob leads the criminals in a mutiny against the doctor and his crew. Of course, the felons soon turn on Bob, but he once again gets the upper hand and subdues the killers. When "Poison Mary" (the latest experimental subject) suddenly turns over a new leaf, the dying doctor (shot by one of the criminals) sees his theory proven correct before he succumbs.

A few worthwhile ideas can be found on this *Torture Ship*. The concept of forcing criminals to participate in experiments to cure their "criminality," à la *A Clockwork Orange* (1971 [*q.v.*]), is rife with moral dilemmas (such as whether the act of altering someone's personality/identity against his/her will is justified by the result of making that individual a subjectively "better" person). Too bad such potential ethical conflicts remain largely unexplored. Even more intriguing is the hero-turned-monster scenario. By transforming Bob into a Monster (albeit temporarily) and having him menace the very person he has vowed to protect (Joan), a unique conflict arises that becomes both disturbing and perversely satisfying. Along the lines of Jekyll and Hyde, this transformation suggests that even the most noble and courageous individual has something dark and violent inside him or her. The notion of losing control over one's own behavior, over

one's nature, over one's *identity*—to have it changed against one's will—is a truly terrifying concept.

While the film's production values and photography are generally adequate for a low-budget "B," the picture needed more than a minimal technical competency to hold it together. Mundane direction from Victor Halperin (who offers none of the macabre flourish displayed in his 1932 *White Zombie* [*q.v.*]), bland acting from a subdued Irving Pichel as Stander (in a part that simply cried out for some Bela Lugosi–style bombast), a complete lack of atmosphere (Halperin does nothing with the inherent possibilities of shipboard menace; for all the use made of the setting, the picture might just as well have taken place on dry land), and a bad case of wasted opportunities ultimately sink this *Torture Ship* at the dock.—*BMS*

Trilogy of Terror (1975) [**split personality; possession**] Dan Curtis Productions/ABC Circle Films (ABC). *D:* Dan Curtis. *S:* Richard Matheson and William F. Nolan; Stories by Richard Matheson. *Cast:* Karen Black (Julie Eldridge/Millicent Larimore/Therese Larimore/Amelia); Robert Burton (Chad Foster); James Storm (Eddie Nells); Gregory Harrison (Arthur Moore); John Karlen (Thomas Anmar); George Gaynes (Dr. Chester Ramsey).

Like his *The Night Stalker* in 1972 and *Dracula* in 1974, Dan Curtis' television movie *Trilogy of Terror* made a ratings splash in 1975 and is fondly remembered by viewers to this day. Karen Black portrays four different women awash in identity problems. "Julie" is a seemingly mousy college English professor who exerts an unexplained, wicked influence over a series of her male students. At least one of them, Chad, thinks that he has the upper hand, but it is Julie who actually has caused *him* to lose his will. "Millicent and Therese" are vastly different "sisters" who are revealed to be *one* woman with "the most advanced case of dual personality" that her doctor has ever seen. (Two years later, Karen Black would play essentially the same role—a woman with two personalities—in the memorable 1977 television movie *The Strange Possession of Mrs. Oliver* [*q.v.*], another Richard Matheson story.)

The third segment of *Trilogy of Terror* is the one that everyone remembers so well. Based on Matheson's story "Prey," "Amelia" tells the tale of an unhappy, mother-dominated woman who seeks to find her own identity apart from her mother by moving away from home and dating a gentleman friend. When she buys a Zuni fetish doll for her friend for his birthday, the ferocious-looking doll comes to life and stalks Amelia through her apartment. The film's final, unforgettable image is the very picture of loss of identity: After Amelia succeeds in burning up the doll, the spirit of the Zuni warrior that inhabited it enters *her* body. (Compare Karen Black's character's fate in Curtis' 1976 theatrical feature, *Burnt Offerings* [*q.v.*].) Twenty-one years later, Dan Curtis revisited the Zuni doll in *Trilogy of Terror II* (1996 [*q.v.*]).—*JDT*

Trilogy of Terror II (1996) [**possession**] Power Pictures/USA Pictures/Wilshire Court Productions (USA Network, Inc./ Wilshire Court Productions). *D:* Dan Curtis. *S:* William F. Nolan, Richard Matheson, and Dan Curtis; Stories by Henry Kuttner and Richard Matheson. *Cast:* Lysette Anthony (Laura/Bobby's mother/Dr. Simpson); Geraint Wyn Davies (Ben); Matt Clark (Roger Ansford); Geoffrey Lewis (Arleigh Stubbs).

The horror anthology *Trilogy of Terror II* lives up to its name even more than the classic original. This television movie presents three truly scary stories, all starring Lysette Anthony, who played Angelique in Dan Curtis' 1991 reprise of *Dark Shadows*. "The Graveyard Rats," one of the most terrifying stories ever told on television, is a film which I pair with Henry Kuttner's short story and share with my Tennessee State University students every Halloween. Richard Matheson's "Bobby" is a faithful, frightening remake of the final segment of *Dead of Night*, Curtis' 1977 made-for-television horror trilogy.

"He Who Kills" is both a sequel to and a remake of Matheson's "Amelia"/"Prey" story about the Zuni fetish doll in Curtis' 1975 *Trilogy of Terror* (*q.v.*). This story begins soon after Amelia's story has ended. Amelia, possessed by the spirit of the Zuni warrior, has died after killing her mother, and the police take the charred Zuni doll to Dr. Simpson, a scientist who examines it at her office in a museum after hours. The Zuni doll comes back to life and stalks her, and what follows is a close remake of the original trilogy's frantic, bloody battle of wits between woman and doll. This time, Dr. Simpson manages to dump the Zuni in sulfuric acid, but it re-emerges and possesses her in time for the film's final, murderous image. A decade later, Matheson and Curtis' Zuni doll lives again in the form of a collectible action figure!—*JDT*

28 Days Later (2002) [**zombification**] British Film Council (as UK Film Council)/Canal+/DNA Films (Fox Searchlight Pictures). *D*: Danny Boyle. *S*: Alex Garland. *Cast:* Christopher Eccleston (Major Henry West); Brendan Gleeson (Frank); Cillian Murphy (Jim); Naomie Harris (Selena); Megan Burns (Hannah).

My first reaction to this movie was, "Hey, these guys wanted to make an indie but switched to horror to make a profit!" And I remain convinced of the accuracy of that first impression.

Admittedly, the film's horror premise *is* scary: All of England, and possibly the world, is either infected by the virus "rage" or terrorized by those infected; people have 30 seconds after transmission of the virus to be killed or become transformed into murder machines; the whole of London—and probably the world—is a ghost town, with no hope of recovery. And the uncoordinated but also terrifyingly, preternaturally *fast* movements of the infected hordes are enough to give anyone used to seeing slow-shambling zombies the creeps. But the film is called "28 days *later*," and while part of the reason for that title is because it's when Jim, Our Hero, wakes from his coma into this not-so-brave new world, it's also because the real horror is in the effects of the plague on the few people who've survived. Selena, the tough woman who helps rescue the confused Jim, is—or professes to be—utterly without feeling, able to kill her friend Mark in seconds and without compunction when he appears to be infected. This is all that's left, she tells the appalled Jim, no time for sentiment, nothing but survival.

She's soon forced to change her opinion, though, after she and Jim team up with the father-daughter team of Frank and Hannah and travel out of London in search of the source of a radio broadcast promising military safety and "the answer to infection." The film becomes a human drama exploring the characters' tentative, joyous return to humanity and fellow-feeling after their world has been destroyed.

Their new peace is short-lived, however, as they are met with an even greater terror that's quite likely in the aftermath of all disasters, supernatural or otherwise: military take-over—not of countries, for the small unit is only holding an old mansion, but of

Zombies are re-emerging as a horror-film favorite in films like *28 Days Later.*

the *minds* of troops—and of any of the innocents captured by them—as Selena and Jim and Hannah are. Rather than discovering a haven, the three find themselves the prisoners of troops who have been "promised women" by their chilling commander, with Jim expendable and Selena and young Hannah objects of possessive desire. The movie becomes a commentary on the grotesque effects of survivalist and colonial mindsets: Desperate to maintain the world as they know it, the soldiers want women—not just to engage in lawless, brutal sex with them, but because they have a terror of being the Last Men on Earth. In order to ensure the continuation of a species, they're willing to commit any and all acts of savagery and dehumanization. By the end of the film, the conflict is between the mob mentality of the military and the human, humane desires of the three heroes; the infected hordes are really only peripheral. In fact, Jim makes use of one of the infected, a former soldier the troops have been keeping chained up to "study," in order to create a diversion and help his friends escape. Even before the typical world-overrun-but-not-*entirely* happy ending, the real relief is seeing the three protagonists break free of the dystopia created by the troops. Zombie-like monsters we can deal with, but heaven preserve us from the minds of men.—*OVA*

Undead, The (1957) [**hypnotism; reincarnation**] (American International Pictures). *D:* Roger Corman. *S:* Charles Griffith, Mark Hanna. *Cast:* Pamela Duncan (Diana Love/Helene); Richard Garland (Pendragon); Allison Hayes (Livia); Val Dufour (Quintus Ratcliff); Mel Welles (Smolkin); Dorothy Neumann (Meg Maud).

Director-producer Roger Corman is best known for two types of movies—his schlocky-but-beloved sci-fiers of the 1950s (*Day the World Ended* [1956], *It Conquered the World* [1956], *Attack of the Crab Monsters* [1957 (*q.v.*)], etc.) and his stylish-and-even-more-beloved Poe series of the 1960s (*House of Usher* [1960], *Pit and the Pendulum* [1961 (*q.v.*)], *The Masque of the Red Death* [1964], etc.). Falling in between these two cinematic poles is *The Undead*, his one-of-a-kind stab at a medieval horror-fantasy. The film stands between the two subsets in terms of quality as well, for it's much cleverer than his sci-fi entries but not nearly as engrossing as his Poe films. It's not nearly as beloved as either. And there's the rub, for *The Undead* is an intriguing—even entertaining—experiment in loss of identity that, while not wholly successful, still delivers enough to make it a cinematic trip worth taking.

Inspired by the then-topical Bridey Murphy craze (resulting from a popular book titled *The Search for Bridey Murphy* by Morey Bernstein, in which Bernstein claims to have used hypnotism to regress a woman named Ruth Simmons back to a previous life as an Irish woman named Bridey Murphy), Corman intended to capitalize on the hot topics of reincarnation and hypnotism. "I told [Roger] that, by the time we got the thing out, [reincarnation] would be a dead issue," deadpanned scripter Charles Griffith to author Mark Thomas McGee. "Then the Paramount movie based on Bernstein's book bombed, so Roger changed the picture from *The Trance of Diana Love* to *The Undead*." Its original identity hidden, *The Undead* still emerged as a solid little LOI film.

The rediscovery-of-lost-identity plot involves a maverick psychiatrist who offers prostitute Diana Love $500 to participate in a dangerous experiment in hypnosis and past lives. Regressing the girl backward to medieval times, he finds that she was a young maiden named Helene, wrongly sentenced to die for witchcraft. When the girl's "modern mind" somehow informs her earlier self how to escape, this positive change

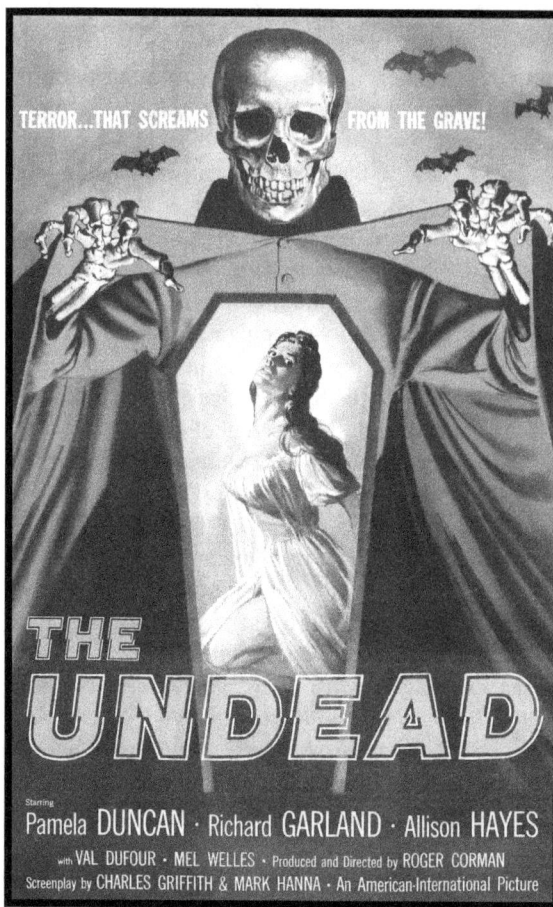

in the past paradoxically jeopardizes all her future lives, putting her in danger of losing those identities for good (a common-enough event in written science fiction, later played variation on in the *Back to the Future* trilogy [1985, 1989, 1990]). The psychiatrist then must thrust himself back into time with her (via some further hypnosis and an odd electrical machine) to try to rectify matters. Complicating things is an evil coven of witches, led by the voluptuous Livia, who not only sets her satanic sights on Helene's knightly beau but conjures up the Devil himself.

A bizarre film as is, *The Undead* could have been even more extraordinary. "Chuck Griffith wrote that script completely in rhyme, in *couplets*, the first time," explained actor Mel Welles (who played the crazy but sympathetic gravedigger) to interviewer Tom Weaver. "It was a wonderful script, and it probably would have been *the* cult film had it been shot that way. But either Roger or someone at American International Pictures didn't think that it was commercially viable to do it that way, and at the last minute a decision was made to rewrite the script without that."

Even minus its iambic-pentameter rhyme, the movie possesses an almost fairy-tale quality—but one with an even darker tone than that found in the Brothers Grimm, making it a sort of Hansel-and-Gretel-Go-to-Hell scenario. It is filled with strikingly bizarre characters: a gorgeous, alluring witch who periodically transforms into a lizard, cat, mouse, and bat (actually Paul Blaisdell's flying Venusian creature from *It Conquered the World*); a half-mad gravedigger with a penchant for singing morbidly twisted nursery rhymes ("Hey diddle diddle, the rat and the fiddle, the corpse jumped over the tomb/The murderer laughed to see such a sight, as he strangled a girl in the gloom"); an evil imp (played by dwarf actor Billy Barty) with pointy ears, pointy shoes, and ever-present pointy grin; a "good" witch with the worst false nose and chin this side of Oz; a psychiatrist who can't help loving every minute of the hell he's created for his patient; a "wanton woman of the streets" for a main character, whose past life saw her in the role of innocent maiden; and of course, Satan himself. Add to this cast of characters a cramped woodland setting through whose perennial fog the sun never penetrates ("We almost died of asphyxiation from all the creosote fog that was created in that place," recounted Welles), the stilted yet oddly appealing dialogue that somehow suits the medieval milieu, and we have a savory witch's brew for those whose taste runs to the offbeat.

When it comes to the actors, *The Undead* would have been better named *The Uneven*. Mel Welles (best know as the greedy flower-shop owner from *Little Shop of Horrors* [1959]) gives a delightfully off-kilter performance as the "tetched" gravedigger fond of ghoulish ditties. Allison Hayes' scheming Livia is as convincingly evil as she is beautiful, and both Pamela Duncan and Val Dufour (as the confused heroine and fascinated psychiatrist) bring some much-needed sincerity to their roles of identity loser and identity facilitator. But toneless Richard Garland makes the most wooden hero since Pinocchio, and Richard Devon turns his Satan into a cartoon caricature of community-theater proportions.

While not exactly an overlooked classic, its offbeat approach and uniqueness make *The Undead* deserving of better than its current status as "The Unloved." —BMS

Uninvited, The (1944) [**possession; hypnotism**] (Paramount). *D:* Lewis Allen. *S:* Frank Partos and Dodie Smith, From the Novel *The Uninvited* (a.k.a. *Uneasy Freehold*) by Dorothy Macardle. *Cast:* Ray Milland (Rick Fitzgerald); Ruth Hussey (Pamela Fitzgerald); Gail Russell (Stella Maris); Donald Crisp (Colonel Beech); Alan Napier (Dr. Scott); Cornelia Otis Skinner (Miss Holloway).

The Uninvited is a favorite of mine. Not only is it one of the most well-conceived and executed of "ghost" movies, it is (along with some of the Val Lewton films), one of the very few horror pictures of the 1930s and 1940s that is actually scary. Siblings Pamela and Rick Fitzgerald buy a charming old house perched on a cliff overlooking the ocean. There they meet a beautiful but disturbed young girl named Stella, who was born in the house and now appears to be the victim of a resident supernatural oppressor.

A likable cast, sure-handed direction, effective score, and spot-on set design all contribute to the film's success—but nothing more so than the straight-forward manner with which the script approaches the subject matter. Are both Stella and the house truly haunted? Oh, hell yes! No discomfort with the material on the part of the studio or creators in this instance, *The Uninvited* is unabashedly in-your-face with its depictions of supernatural events and their causes.

Like *The Ghost and Mrs. Muir* (1947) and *Wuthering Heights* (1939), both from roughly the same era, there's a wistful, melancholy romanticism at work in *The Uninvited*. And part of that romanticism lies in the mystery surrounding Stella. On more than one occasion—and always while under the control of a supernatural entity—she nearly falls to her death from the cliffs. She is helpless to combat the ghost's pervasive influence—until she receives assistance from yet another supernatural entity. There's more than a hint of the Gothic to this whole aspect of the plot—right down to the de rigueur mysterious foreigner, albeit one who reaches for Stella from beyond the grave.

Stella's ordeal results not only in a loss of identity but the revelation and subsequent gain of another. For the idea of identity—who is who—lies at the center of *The Uninvited*. Stella has spent her life thinking she is the daughter of the saintly Mary

Dr. Scott (Ralph Napier), Roderick (Ray Milland) and Pamela (Ruth Hussey) Fitzgerald try to help Stella Meredith (Gail Russell) in *The Uninvited*.

Meredith, and the truth is slowly and cleverly revealed that Mary was neither saintly nor motherly (nor her mother!). And it is only through Stella's shedding of her false identity, and its accompanying set of self-limiting labels and beliefs, that she is able to survive and live her life to its fullest. The unhealthy Miss Holloway—who runs a sanitarium devoted to preserving the lie that was Mary Meredith—acts as the human agency to prevent Stella from discovering her true identity and those of the ghosts who haunt Windward House, and she finally succumbs to the madness that such a lie entails. Rick, who awakens to his identity as Stella's lover and protector, finds the courage to confront the malignant ghost and dissipate its evil energy, exposing the hollowness of its identity, thus destroying it once and for all.—*RJT*

Unsane. See *Tenebrae* (1982).

Vampire, The (1957) **[metamorphosis]** (United Artists). *D*: Paul Landres. *S*: Pat Fielder. *Cast*: John Beal (Dr. Paul Beecher); Coleen Gray (Carol Butler); Kenneth Tobey (Sheriff Buck Donnelly); Dabbs Greer (Dr. Will Beaumont).

Paul Landres' *The Vampire* attained the pinnacle of the 1950s subgenre that dealt with modern science discovering the means for man to regress to his primitive origins. [*Cf. Monster on the Campus* (1958 [*q.v.*]) and *Altered States* (1980 [*q.v.*]).] Made by the same team that created *Return of Dracula* one year later, *The Vampire* shines most brightly because of the nuanced performance therein by veteran actor John Beal, who did not project the image of the typical 1950s leading man. (Hunky supporting performer

Kenneth Tobey, as Sheriff Buck Donnelly, assumes leading-man responsibility here.) Beal plays small-town family physician Dr. Paul Beecher, pushing 50, who is widowed and raising a prepubescent daughter on his own. Beecher is always warm and personable, the type of old-fashioned medico who knows everyone in the town by their first name and who is more a friend than merely a coolly detached doctor. Beecher makes a house call on dying scientist Dr. Campbell at the man's creepy suburban home/scientific lab. (Besides housing typical lab animals, Campbell's lab contains vampire bats, instrumental in his experiments.) With his last ounce of strength, Campbell says all his years of work have paid off, and before he dies, he hands Beecher a container of pills. Unfortunately, Beecher suffers from migraines; when he arrives home and asks his daughter to get him his headache pills from his jacket pocket, we know from the get-go what pills she will fetch. Almost immediately, Beecher is addicted to the pills and finds he must take them by 11 o'clock every night. He also learns that, every time, by morning, another victim is dead. Beal gives a multilayered performance as the vampire (for it indeed appears to be the actor himself and not a stuntman in the vampiric regression makeup, looking like Mr. Hyde with a bad hangover)—more pill-addicted dope fiend than undead bloodsucker.

The Vampire shines, not only because of John Beal's standout performance, but because of several visually exciting and dramatic sequences that showcase that performance. First of all, after undergoing the transformation, Beecher follows Carol, his lovely nurse, as she walks the suburban streets after dark. In a sequence similar to one in *House of Wax* (1953), the young lovely realizes she is being pursued by a dark-cloaked fiend and runs toward her home, fumbling with the keys before getting safely inside. One of the town's beloved old ladies, accompanied by her faithful dog, is next pursued, and in a shocking sequence, Beal lurches toward the woman, knocking her down as he goes for her throat. The slightly fog-shrouded late-evening photography, with just enough close-ups of Beal to chill the blood, makes this sequence a standout.

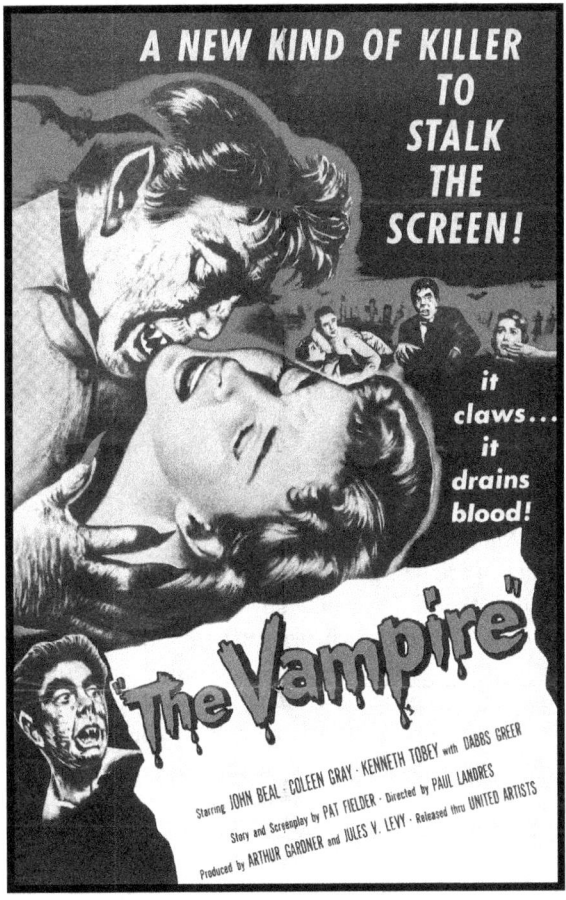

Later in the movie Beecher confesses his addiction to

Loss of Identity in the Horror Film

Campbell's pills to colleague and college buddy Dr. Beaumont, who vows to remain with Beecher until 11 o'clock at night, when his addiction reaches its highest urge level. Beal as Beecher is marvelous here, fidgeting with the desk drawer where Beaumont locked the pills away. Beecher grabs Beaumont's arms and pleads with his friend to allow him to have a few pills. Beaumont is folksy yet firm; Beecher is desperate and out of sorts. By 11:10, Beecher collapses at a desk and buries his face in his hands; Beaumont sees Beecher's hands and arms suddenly transform into something shrunken, hairy, and monstrous. With now-wide eyes, Beaumont backs off as the newly regressed Beecher lurches up from the desk and moves aggressively toward his friend, whom he attacks and strangles in moody silhouette, Beaumont pleading for his life the entire time. What a marvelous, well-acted and -photographed sequence, demonstrating why *The Vampire* is one of the better B horror productions of its decade, besides being an outstanding loss-of-identity entry. And such a loss of identity! Beecher goes from beloved, respected small-town doctor and single parent to pill-addicted, surly, and tormented man, who falls asleep at night only to recall the horrible acts he committed as detached dreams half-remembered the next morning!

Perhaps the most poignant sequence of the movie occurs when papa Beecher confronts his terminally cute daughter and asks her if she would agree to live with her aunt in another city, because he is ill. We can see how conflicted the father is and how difficult it is for him to give away his own daughter. She at first will not accept any thought of such a separation, and both father and daughter collapse in each other's arms, sobbing uncontrollably. Low-budget 1950s B productions seldom rose to this degree of sincere emotion. *The Vampire*'s abundance of talent and dedication makes it essential viewing.—*GJS*

Vargtimmen. See **Hour of the Wolf** (1968).

Videodrome (1983) [altered reality; brainwashing; eradication of self; metamorphosis; mind control] Filmplan International (Universal). *D*: David Cronenberg. *S*: David Cronenberg. *Cast:* James Woods (Max Renn); Sonja Smits (Bianca O'Blivion); Deborah Harry (Nicki Brand); Peter Dorsey (Harlan); Les Carlson (Barry Convex).

"I'm Max Renn. I run Civic TV. I don't… I don't kill people."

"You're an assassin now—of Videodrome."

"I am the video word made flesh."

Max Renn is perfectly comfortable in his identity as the head of a cable television outlet specializing in "softcore sex and hardcore violence." But his exposure to "Videodrome" (a completely plotless "program" consisting entirely of displays of realistic torture) changes everything. Convinced that he's found the "next big thing" for his station, Max has actually been fed a video signal capable of creating a hallucination-generating tumor in his brain. And at a point where he's already unable to trust his eyes, his very identity is stripped away by competing forces equally willing to manipulate him.

While the moral/ethical debate concerning extreme cinema/television imagery and its possible effects may be at the heart of *Videodrome*'s story, the Max Renn character is the heart of the film itself and the sole point of identification for the viewer, who must undergo his metamorphosis with him. With Max's mind all but erased by the signal,

Max Renn (James Woods) finds himself being manipulated by outside forces in David Cronenberg's *Videodrome*.

those who would force their vision of moral purity on the world program him like a VCR (this process is depicted with grisly special effects highlighting living, breathing cassettes being forced into Max's body), while the opposition is every bit as ruthless when it comes to changing the program and teaching Max to use his tormentors' own weapons against them.

No matter who's at the controls, Max is exactly who and what they say he is—and the fact that the film never cuts away to the "real" world for a glimpse of Max as others see him helps make *Videodrome* one of the most original, disturbing, and disorienting entries in the loss-of-identity field. Max isn't himself anymore. And neither is the viewer.—*RJT*

Virus (***Zombie Creeping Flesh; Night of the Zombies***) (1980) [zombification] Italy: Beatrice Film/Films Dara (Motion Picture Marketing, Inc.). *D:* Bruno Mattei (as Vincent Dawn) and Claudio Fragasso (uncredited). *S:* José Maria Cunilles, Rossella Drudi, Claudio Fragasso, and Bruno Mattei (as Vincent Dawn). *Cast:* Margit Evelyn Newton (Lia Rousseau); Franco Garofalo (Zantoro); José Gras (Lt. Mike London); Josep Lluis Fonoll (Vincent).

The tasteless tag-line for this movie just about sums it up: "If we don't feed the Third World, they'll come and feed on us!" Bruno Mattei, under the guise of one of his many directorial aliases (probably to avoid any legal ramifications), directed this piece of trashy exploitation which unashamedly attempts to steal the identity of many of its

Virus features lots of mindless zombies, and not only those in the audience.

superior forerunners, including the score composed by Goblin for *Dawn of the Dead* (1978 [*q.v.*]) and the dialogue and themes from both that film and its predecessor, besides "borrowing" a wide selection of uncompromising footage from the film *La Vallee* (1972) to pad out its running time.

In this movie as in most zombie films, there is a dual loss of identity, centering around both the unfortunate individuals who become mindless flesh eaters and, as initially explored by Romero, the erosion of humanity and its values that help maintain our own identities within a society crumbling under the strain of a zombie plague. However, in contrast to Romero's picture of decaying Western culture, Mattei focuses upon the breakdown of an arguably more "primitive," developing civilization, and pays particular attention to tribal rituals which see the bodies of the dead lying in state whilst decomposing, obviously allowing the corpses ample opportunity to reawaken and attack without any risk of being inconveniently entombed or cremated. It's just a pity that such an interpretation gives Mattei a little too much credit; it's doubtful that he made this film for any other reason than to cash in on the then success of American and Italian zombie movies.

Additionally *Virus* features the exploits and subsequent breakdown in discipline of a crack commando unit led by the redoubtable Lt. Mike London, whose men repeatedly fail to understand that headshots are required to take down their would-be predators. Much of the film is trite, dull, and very formulaic, but the amusing presentation within this piece (watch out especially for the commando truly losing his identity as he performs an incredible dance routine in a tutu) makes it worth watching—coupled with some utterly sickening scenes that are not for the faint of heart.—*AJB*

Walking Dead, The (1936) [**scientific manipulation**] Warner Bros. *D:* Michael Curtiz. *S:* Robert Adams, Ewert Adamson, Lillie Hayward, and Peter Milne; Story by Ewert Adamson and Joseph Fields. *Cast:* Boris Karloff (John Ellman); Ricardo Cortez (Mr. Nolan); Edmund Gwenn (Dr. Evan Beaumont); Marguerite Churchill (Nancy); Warren Hull (Jimmy); Barton MacLane (Loder); Henry O'Neill (District Attorney Werner); Addison Richards (Prison Warden); Paul Harvey (Blackstone); Robert Strange (Merritt); Joe Sawyer ("Trigger" Smith).

In the Buddhist tradition, loss of identity is something to be desired and sought, rather than feared. When the essence of one's self dissipates into nothingness, the individual soul merges into oneness with the eternal and divine—achieving nirvana, a state of supreme liberation and bliss.

Director Michael Curtiz's *The Walking Dead*, the most overtly spiritual of all the classic chillers from horror's Golden Age, hinges on a variation of this idea.

Mild-mannered musician John Ellman is falsely convicted of murder and is sent to the electric chair for a crime he did not commit. Scientist Dr. Beaumont, testing a

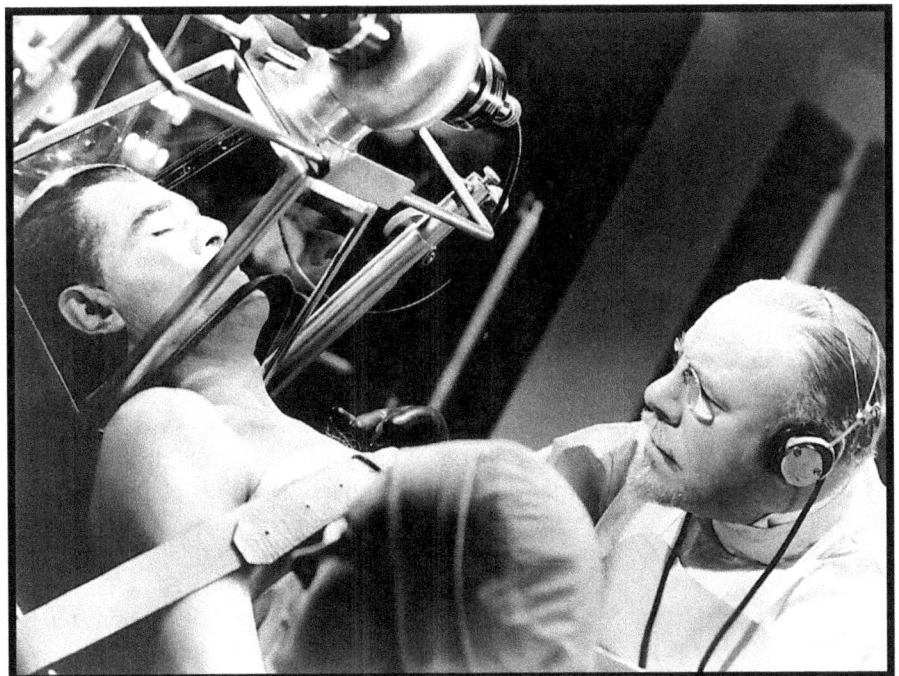

Dr. Beaumont (Edmund Gwenn) tries to bring convicted killer John Ellman (Boris Karloff) back to life in *The Walking Dead*.

radical new technique—which looks suspiciously similar to the "It's alive!" scene from *Frankenstein* (1931)—brings Ellman back from the dead. Or does he?

Ellman's body is revived, but only a thin ribbon of his personality remains because he briefly died and achieved union with the divine. The born-again Ellman proves something less than, or perhaps more than, fully human. He's a quiet, ghostly figure, an instrument of divine justice, which metes out punishment to the gang of racketeers behind his wrongful execution.

The only outward sign of Ellman's transformation is a new shock of gray hair. But Karloff's brilliant performance, which ranks among the very finest of his storied career, underscores the change in no uncertain terms. Early in the film, as the living Ellman, Karloff delivers intentionally broad and melodramatic line readings. After Ellman's revival, however, Karloff's delivery becomes hushed, reserved. He moves more slowly and carefully, in a way that at times recalls the eerie stillness of Karloff's Ardath Bey from *The Mummy* (1933 [*q.v.*]).

The revived Ellman also has access to information he never before possessed—presumably, as a result of his brief contact with the omniscient. The living Ellman knew nothing of the gangsters' plot against him. But the revived Ellman inexplicably knows the identities of those who framed him. In the film's most memorable scene, the scientist arranges a concert by Ellman—with all of the gangsters in attendance. Ellman plays robotically, without looking at the keys. Instead, he faces the crowd, selecting his enemies one by one and glaring at them in silent condemnation. His stare bores into his persecutors' very souls. (Photographer Hal Mohr nicely enhances Karloff's performance by illuminating his eyes with penlights.) The mobsters flee the auditorium.

Ellman tracks down and confronts his enemies. "You can't escape what you've done," Ellman warns the gunman who actually committed the murder. The terrified crook tumbles backward over a chair and accidentally shoots himself. Confronted by the cold stare of the all-knowing, all the criminals do themselves in, in one fashion or another: One flees into the path of an oncoming train; another has a heart attack and falls out a window. And so on. Through it all, Karloff maintains a baleful passivity.

Once justice has been served, Ellman returns to death—and unity with God. But not before cautioning the scientist against repeating his experiment: "Leave the dead to their maker," he says. "The Lord our God is a jealous God."

It's highly unlikely that Curtiz, Karloff, and company ever contemplated parallels with Buddhism. Nevertheless, *The Walking Dead* suggests that enlightenment lies in the dissolution of individual identity, through communion with the divine.—*MDC*

White Zombie (1932) [voodoo] Victor Halperin Productions (United Artists). *D:* Victor Halperin. *S:* Garnett Weston. *Cast:* Bela Lugosi (Murder Legendre); Madge Bellamy (Madeline); Robert Frazer (Charles Beaumont); Joseph Cawthorne (Dr. Bruner); John Harron (Neil Parker); Brandon Hurst (Silver); Clarence Muse (coach driver, uncredited).

The traditional zombie—not the cannibalistic monsters introduced by George A. Romero—the original concept of a human being reduced to a soulless automaton by means of voodoo, remains the movies' quintessential symbol of lost identity. And *White Zombie* remains the quintessential traditional zombie movie.

It's not just that *White Zombie* was the first zombie picture (even though it was), or that its eerie-looking, goggle-eyed undead defined the appearance of the movie zombie for a generation (even though they did). What makes *White Zombie* the text for its oeuvre is how powerfully it dramatizes the mute horror of zombie-ism.

To have Madge Bellamy (Madeline) for himself, Murder Legendre (Bela Lugosi) poisons Charles Beaumont (Robert Frazer) in *White Zombie*.

Beautiful, young Madeline comes to Haiti to join her fiancé Neil, but catches the eye of the couple's island host, the underhanded Beaumont. Beaumont tries to seduce Madeline but fails. In frustration, he turns to Murder Legendre, an evil sugar-cane magnate and voodoo practitioner. At Legendre's sugar mill, a legion of zombies silently goes about its chores, not even taking notice when one of the crew falls into a grinder!

Beaumont wants Legendre to kidnap Madeline and hold her captive for a month, in which time Beaumont intends to woo her away from her beloved. Legendre laughs off the idea. "Do you think she will forget her lover in a month? Not in a month, or even a year," Legendre says, smirking. "She is deep in love...but not with you."

"There must be a way!" Beaumont whines.

"There is...a way," Legendre intones menacingly. His scheme is to turn Madeline into the "white zombie" of the movie's title, using a voodoo doll and some mysterious zombie powder. Beaumont reluctantly agrees, and shortly afterward Madeline appears to drop suddenly, inexplicably dead. Later that night, Legendre and Beaumont remove her body from its crypt with the aid of Legendre's zombies. In short order Madeline is zombie-ized.

However, when Beaumont looks at the zombie-Madeline, as she stares speechlessly and mindlessly into space, he realizes that the woman he fell in love with is gone. Whatever his faults, Beaumont desired Madeline not only for her appearance but for her personality, her identity, which has been annihilated (or so it seems). He is mortified to see her reduced to an unthinking, unfeeling drone. Legendre, however, has no such scruples. He's interested in Madeline's body only.

Ultimately, Madeline is redeemed by her love for Neil, which enables her to overcome Legendre's spell. In the meantime, audiences may well ponder the film's bone-chilling and then-new-to-movies core concept. How agonizing would it be to see a loved one left alive (or sort-of alive), yet stripped of all the thoughts and emotions, all the facial expressions, tones of voice, laughter, sighs, and quirks—in sum, those things that make us love them? Or, how terrifying would it be to suffer that same fate ourself, to be stripped of everything that defines who we are? [It's a question that has real-life resonance in this day and age, when our bodies can be kept alive almost indefinitely on life-support systems, long after our brains are dead.]

It's an unnerving proposition—one that, if we think about, may prove scarier than a whole farmhouse full of intestine-munching, living-dead fiends.—*MDC*

Wolf (1994) [**metamorphosis**] (Columbia). *D*: Mike Nichols *S*: Jim Harrison and Wesley Strick. *Cast:* Jack Nicholson (Will Randall); Michelle Pfeiffer (Laura Alden); James Spader (Stewart Swinton); Kate Nelligan (Charlotte Randall); Richard Jenkins (Det. Bridger); Eileen Atkins (Mary); Christopher Plummer (Raymond Alden); Ron Rifkin (Doctor); David Hyde Pierce (Roy).

As with many good horror movies, *Wolf* is about the horror of loss of identity—*and* about the positive aspects of transformation and the discovery of one's true self. It is the story of the transformation—or, one might say, awakening—of Will Randall, a senior editor at a Manhattan publishing house, a man invariably courteous, decent, and urbane.

Will is driving his Volvo back to the city one full-moon night when he hits a wolf; as he tries to move it off the road, it bites him on the hand. This, it turns out, is just the beginning of a bad week; soon after, at a party thrown by his boss, he learns that he's

being removed from his job for being "a man of taste and individuality," qualities that are "something of a handicap" in business these days. To add insult to injury, he discovers that his replacement is his duplicitous former protégé, Stewart, who "pestered" the new boss until he got Will's job. Even this evidence of the backstabbing viciousness of business can't turn Will savage, though, and he refuses to shame or be rude to Stewart (a character whose loathsome, smarmy smoothness is played beautifully by James Spader). Will is so well-mannered, that even after a dizzy spell at the party, Laura, the boss's attractive black sheep of a daughter, who takes a liking to him almost in spite of herself, asks him incredulously, "What are you, the last civilized man?"

And he is—but, as he and we discover, that's not *all* that he is, especially as he develops more and more attributes of the wolf. Not all of these developments are bad: His senses are heightened, so that he can smell tequila on a coworker's breath, hear conversations across the building, and copyedit without his glasses. His new sense of smell precipitates his discovery of his wife's infidelity—with Stewart—and leads him, newly energized, to play into the cut-throat politics of publishing and win his job back/exact his revenge on Stewart—being bloodthirsty in the most civilized of ways. These changes also lead him to other encounters with Laura, a woman he takes a liking to.

But there are terrifying aspects of his transformation too, as his health and actions change: Animals are afraid of him, and horses will rear and plunge to escape him; he suffers occasional spells of short breathing, feverishness, and pain; and most terrifying, he goes on nocturnal rampages that we see but that he doesn't remember. He brings down a deer on Laura's father's estate; wanders Central Park, and savages a young mugger. Will has consulted, rather skeptically, with a professor and shaman who tells him that, yes, people can be transformed into animals, either through bites or simply "the passion of the wolf": For one who's bitten, a month after the bite, at full moon, the wolf "consumes him, eating all but his nature and his heart." Will remains doubtful until, in a horrifying moment, he innocently takes a handkerchief from his pocket and discovers two severed fingers wrapped in it. The suspense mounts as Will, Laura, and the audience begin to wonder whether Will's physical changes are also bringing about more substantial, and darker, psychological changes, making Will capable of brutally murdering his wife, who is found dead with her throat ripped out in Central Park.

In the end, however, we discover that the shaman was correct, and that Will's *nature* has not changed at all—he's no more evil as a wolf than he was as a man. In some ways, in fact, the film is the dream of every man having a mid-life crisis—the ability to bring out the wolf-ish qualities always present, but hidden, without giving up—unlike poor

Larry Talbot—one's "self." Still, few people would likely be willing to go through the chilling alterations Will is subjected to—and few would likely reveal themselves as being as inherently decent, well beneath the veneer of so-called civilization, as Will proves himself to be.—*OVA*

Wolf Man, The (1941) [**metamorphosis**] (Universal). *D:* George Waggner *S:* Curt Siodmak. *Cast:* Lon Chaney, Jr. (Larry Talbot); Claude Rains (Sir John Talbot); Ralph Bellamy (Paul Montford, chief constable); Patric Knowles (Frank Andrews); Warren William (Dr. Lloyd); Maria Ouspenskaya (Maleva); Bela Lugosi (Bela); Evelyn Ankers (Gwen); Fay Helm (Jenny).

Gypsy Maleva remains the heart and soul of Universal's classic *The Wolf Man*. Her profoundly sad face and even sadder voice convey the collateral damage of loss of identity—the sorrow and knowledge that Bela, her son, her flesh and blood, transforms into a werewolf, condemned by his blood curse to kill innocents whenever the autumn moon is bright. [In Universal lore, the Wolf Man was originally a *seasonal* beast—who developed into a monthly monster after the character caught on. By 1943's *Frankenstein Meets the Wolfman* (*q.v.*), it's a moon "*full* and bright" that effects his transformation.]

Larry Talbot returns home to Wales to be with his father, Sir John, after Larry's elder brother dies in an unexplained hunting accident. Taking some time off with Gwen Conliff, the girl he just met, and—to his chagrin—her friend and "chaperone" Jenny, Larry visits the nearby Gypsy camp. Werewolf Bela attacks Jenny; Larry tries to save her and, in the attempt, is bitten by the "wolf" he kills, thus inheriting the lupine curse.

Sir John (Claude Rains) morns his tragic son Larry (Lon Chaney, Jr.) in *The Wolf Man*.

Instead of resenting Larry for killing her son, Maleva—who understands the full import of the curse and sees Bela's death as a release, a ritual to be celebrated—transfers her fears and pain to her new "son," becoming a surrogate mother to Larry, and telling him about the curse and ways to protect himself.

Though very much aware of what physically happens to him when he transforms into a wolf, Larry is psychically powerless to fight the metamorphosis. He agonizes and grimaces with pain; however, he is doomed to slaughter—and to be tormented by the knowledge that he has killed and, sometimes, by the foreknowledge of whom he *will* kill, such as when he sees the sign of the pentagram in Gwen's palm. [Here, scripter Curt Siodmak seems to borrow a leaf from the earlier *Werewolf of London* (1935), wherein Dr. Yogami intones that "The werewolf instinctively seeks to kill the thing it loves best."]

So loss of identity becomes a pivotal theme in *The Wolf Man*, because Talbot fully understands what will happen to him at night—that his cultured and civilized person will become bestial and savage and give in to animal instincts beyond his control. His own body will betray him as he morphs from human to wolf in a matter of seconds. His own sense of self will be momentarily erased as he comes to realize that those he loves the most are in immediate danger.

The day after his wolf-self has murdered the cemetery caretaker, Larry—unable to cope with a mythology where evil becomes personified as a wolf, wishing his problem could be explained with "electric current, tubes, and wires"—seeks help from his father, who takes a decidedly psychological approach to lycanthropy, calling it a version of schizophrenia. Sir John discounts the idea of a man physically transforming into a wolf but states, "I believe most anything can occur to a man in his mind." Awful things occur in Larry's mind: Accompanying his father to church, Larry is convinced that everyone has turned around to stare at him, accusation in every eye—and he rushes out of the cathedral.

That very night Talbot, as werewolf, walks into an animal trap and writhes in pain until he loses consciousness. Maleva in her cart just happens to be passing by and comes to Talbot's rescue, bending over to stroke and comfort Talbot. "Find peace for a moment, my son," she states (soothing him more than his father ever does), and her magic transforms Talbot back into his human form. He runs off to avoid the dogs that are tracking him. Talbot goes to see Gwen to tell her he's decided to leave the village in order to protect her—and sees the dreaded pentagram in her palm. Talbot tells his father he is going insane, that he can no longer control himself. He demands that his father tie him to a chair, lock the windows, and bolt the door. Sir John believes his son's problems are all in his head but complies, and even acquiesces to taking Larry's silver-headed cane with him when his son (knowing full well that rope cannot bind him) begs him to.

So Talbot's internal struggle is between the powers of superstition and the powers of the diseased mind, and wherever Talbot attempts to seek help, he gets only skepticism. Only the lonely Gypsy woman understands the curse and what Larry must be undergoing, but her help is sporadic and limited. Thus, Talbot blacks out, awakening to find out another villager is dead or that he has been injured. He is not sure if he is losing his mind or if the curse of the pentagram is the cause of his problem. But in either case, Talbot suffers from loss of identity, a sense that he has become his own worst enemy and enemy to anyone who is close to him. Lon Chaney, Jr.'s acting is sometimes stiff, but his face and eyes register the horror of a man who is becoming a fiend he cannot understand. And in those tortured eyes and fearful face, audiences can truly understand the horror of loss of identity.—*GJS*

Yeux sans visage, Les. See ***Eyes Without a Face*** (1960).

Zombie (***Zombi 2; Zombie Flesheaters***) (1979) [**zombification**] Italy: Variety Film (The Jerry Gross Organization). *D:* Lucio Fulci. *S:* Elisa Briganti, Dardano Sacchetti (uncredited). *Cast:* Tisa Farrow (Anne Bowles); Ian McCulloch (Peter West); Richard Johnson (Dr. David Menard); Al Cliver (Brian Hull); Auretta Gay (Susan Barrett).

Originally penned by Lucio Fulci and Dardano Sacchetti before the Italian release of George A. Romero's *Dawn of the Dead* (1978 [*q.v.*]), *Zombie* came out in the aftermath of *Dawn...*'s success as an unofficial Italian sequel (hence its Italian title: *Zombi 2*) and went on to take over $30 million worldwide, which was surprising considering the extreme amounts of gore in this movie, with "barf bags" being thoughtfully placed in most cinemas for punters lacking intestinal fortitude. Interviews with Fulci and various members of the crew hint at their belief in the originality of their story; however, in the context of loss of identity, very little goes on here that doesn't occur in the Romero tetralogy.

The film does highlight a superb example of the zombie's complete lack of interest in anything but food, indicating the extreme loss of identity that the victims undergo in the transition from human to ghoul. Toward the end of the movie the creatures smash their way into a church hospital and, in their desire to satiate their hunger, stride heedlessly toward their intended victims through a hail of incoming fire and Molotov cocktails, paying little notice to the collapsing structure as it burns around them. It's a scene about the acute disparities between the undead—with their complete lack of self-preservation and their fearlessness and near indestructibility—and their living adversaries.

As the attack on the hospital continues, the human refugees fighting off the undead horde eventually break ranks, and once their unity of cause and purpose dissipates, they are divided and consumed. Peter, Anne, and Brian manage to escape the onslaught but, as they take off for the sanctuary of their boat, Brian's zombified lover, Susan, confronts him. This scene in particular provides another superb example of the contrast between the human, unable to relinquish his emotional urges, and the zombie, utterly bereft of former identity and simply looking for flesh to consume. Brian foolishly moves to hold Susan, and in response her reanimated corpse takes a large chunk out of his arm, thus condemning him to a zombified fate. He flees with the others but, as they sail in the hopes of finding salvation in the "land of the free," dies from the disease passed via his dead lover's saliva.

Zombie highlights the zombie's complete lack of interest in anything but food.

The final moments of the film see Peter and Anna recoiling in horror as they tune into a New York radio station, which frantically reports that zombies have taken over the city (during which the reporter forfeits his professionalism just before forfeiting his life). Then, from below deck, they hear the sound of Brian's cadaver, furiously attempting to escape the cabin's confines. Of course, the more astute viewers will wonder why the pair didn't simply dispose of Brian's corpse the moment he died, but they don't possess the same emotional pragmatism of, say, Ken Foree's Peter in *Dawn of the Dead*, who swiftly puts a bullet through buddy Roger's brain upon his reanimation. Their reluctance perhaps suggests here that Fulci's characters retain more of their humanity, although the ending proves that their noble action (or lack of it) won't assist them once those who have been killed get up and kill.

Zombie is a film that, despite not being particularly original in terms of content and storyline, features some incredibly gory moments and a bunch of disgustingly decayed and worm-ridden zombies. Thus the physical appearance and psychological impact of the flesh eaters is greatly enhanced, increasing their potential to make their victims forget themselves and fall to their knees in terror. Whereas in some other zombie movies the creatures often appear laughable, almost harmless and even pitiable, here they are simply abhorrent, evil creatures, with little resemblance to either humanity or anything else walking God's Earth—which is as it should be.—*AJB*

Zombie Aftermath (1982) [**zombification**] Nautilus Film Company (Goldscreen). *D:* Steve Barkett *S:* Steve Barkett. *Cast:* Steve Barkett (Lt. Newman); Sid Haig (Cutter).

Two astronauts crash land on their return from a dangerous space mission. They expect a hero's welcome, but their delusions of grandeur are rudely dispelled by the shocking realization that they have come back to a post-nuclear-war Earth. The dismayed and exhausted pilots must hastily swap their anticipated victory parade for a series of battles with a gang of raiders that has taken over the countryside. Steve Barkett's film presents the typical loss-of-identity characteristics associated with the end of the world: marauding barbarians who have risen from the gutter to prominence within a redefined society, unleashing their unfettered wrath upon shell-shocked refugees, who, in turn, are desperately trying to eke out a living on a barren landscape.

There are also a handful of zombies, mutated survivors of World War III, all of whom wander around the ruins, mindlessly scavenging for sustenance. Although Barkett's less-than-Dickensian storytelling style leaves a lot to be desired, we can surmise that everybody in this film, with perhaps the exception of the bad guys, suffers from a total loss of identity; the pilots struggle to accept that the President is not going to reward them with any medals for completing their hazardous space explorations, and the hapless survivors of the war have no identity except that of prey, for both the gang and the zombies. Not a great film by any stretch of the imagination, but if audiences ever wondered what a post-apocalyptic America would be like if it were taken over by a bloodthirsty, laser-wielding, joint-smoking Sid Haig, look no further.—*AJB*

Zombie Creeping Flesh. See ***Virus*** (1980).

Zombie Flesheaters. See ***Zombie*** (1979).

Zombies on Broadway (1945) [**voodoo; scientific manipulation**] (RKO). *D:* Gordon Douglas. *S:* Robert E. Kent and Lawrence Kimble; Story by Robert Faber and Charles Newman. *Cast:* Wally Brown (Jerry Miles); Alan Carney (Mike Streger); Bela Lugosi (Dr. Paul Renault); Anne Jeffreys (Jean LaDance); Sheldon Leonard (Ace Miller); Ian Wolfe (Prof. Hopkins); Darby Jones (Kolaga the Zombie); Sir Lancelot (Calypso Singer).

Inspired by the phenomenal success of Abbott and Costello at Universal, RKO formed its own comedy team by pairing funnymen Wally Brown and Alan Carney for a handful of films. But the team of "Brown and Carney" never caught on. For one thing, they lacked the years of practice that Bud and Lou had—together and separately—honing classic burlesque bits onstage and on the radio. They also lacked the timing and skills that Abbott and Costello naturally possessed. Though Brown and Carney physically resembled Bud and Lou, they were no competition for the superior comics. Still, their *Zombies on Broadway* remains a curiosity, not only as a rare chance to see Brown and Carney emulate Universal's comics, but also for the always welcome appearance of Bela Lugosi in one of his patented mad scientist roles.

Carney and Brown never imagined the zombie they would take back to the nightclub would be one of them in *Zombies on Broadway*.

In many ways, the film is a spoof of the Val Lewton–produced *I Walked with a Zombie* (1943 [*q.v.*]). It even features Sir Lancelot and Darby Jones virtually repeating their roles from that picture. Here, Brown and Carney play press agents Jerry Miles and Mike Streger. They're hired by ex-gangster Ace Miller to promote his new club, the Zombie Hut. Jerry and Mike have a brainstorm—they advertise that a *real* zombie will be present on opening night. The two have hired an actor, but when a local newsman finds out the zombie is fake, he threatens to expose Ace as a fraud. Naturally, Ace is upset by this, so he sends the two PR men to the Caribbean to bring back a bona fide example of the walking dead. After seeking advice from a loony museum curator, the two comics search out Dr. Renault for help. A beautiful cabaret singer supplies the love interest as the boys are menaced by Renault's zombie Kolaga. Using an experimental serum, the mad scientist plans to turn the boys into the undead, and he succeeds in zombifying Mike. (The effects of the serum include loss of free will as well as oversized eyeballs.) Escaping the island, Jerry plans to use Mike as the real zombie for Ace's club opening.

The zombies qualify this film for inclusion in this study of loss of identity. Under the control of Dr. Renault, the walking dead have no will of their own and are forced to carry out the mad doctor's orders. Just as in *I Walked with a Zombie*, Darby Jones, with his lanky frame and bulging eyeballs, makes a strikingly impressive emissary of the undead. But there is little background for the character. The audience has no idea how long he has been under Renault's control or what his true identity may have been in his pre-zombie days.

One would think in a comedy like this that there would be more jokes relating to zombies. But when Mike is transformed (and loses his identity), the situation is treated rather seriously. Though he is not above making Mike's transformation work to his advantage, Jerry shows real concern for his partner. Still, the audience keeps waiting for the picture to make light of what is happening.

But there exists a definite plan. Whether or not it was intentional, the film refrains from using the zombification for humorous purposes in order to hit the audience with a great fade-out gag. The serum (which Jerry has brought back to New York with him) wears off after a few hours and, just before his debut as the real zombie, Mike returns to his old self. Ace is incensed and is about to murder the agents when he is accidentally injected with the serum. To the delight of the gathered crowd—and especially the reporters—Ace himself becomes the promised zombie.

Not much is made of the loss-of-identity theme, though there are hints of menace surrounding Lugosi's Renault character, and the scenes where Kolaga rises from his crypt were shudder-inducing at the time. Still, RKO did not make many horror-comedies (though *You'll Find Out* [1940] is one of my all-time favorite films), and this is probably as close to a true spoof of the Lewton style as the movies ever came. Fans will want to check it out.

Brown and Carney appeared in another film with Lugosi, entitled *Genius at Work* (1946). This remake of *Super Sleuth* (1937) borders on horror territory and also features genre regular Lionel Atwill in one of his last screen appearances.—*JSM*

Zombi 2. See ***Zombie*** (1979).

Appendix I: LOI by Subject

Some titles show up more than once here because the films exhibit more than one type of LOI. Some of the categories are of necessity rather broad, but we balked at creating categories that were too discrete. (For one thing, it's sometimes hard to come up with these fine distinctions. For another, we wanted readers to see the similarities—and differences—within these categories.)

We debated long and hard over whether "eradication of self" should really be called "loss of individuality"—or if some "eradication of self" items weren't more properly "loss of individuality." For that matter, we wondered if "regimentation" wasn't more properly "loss of individuality." (Feel free to tell us if we've miscategorized any films—or left out some important categories.)

We tried to create categories that could comfortably house half a dozen pictures or more, but note that a few categories contain only one, two or three films ("body switching," "gender confusion," "impersonation," "soul transference," and "twins," for example). That's because we know there are other movies which *could* fit into those categories, but we couldn't fit them in—this time around, anyway. Case in point: Pictures like *Turnabout* (1940—also a gender-confusion film), *Vice Versa* (1948 and 1988), *Freaky Friday* (1977 and 2003), *Like Father, Like Son* (1987), and *18 Again!* (1988), to name a few, could swell our body-switching ranks. And certainly *All of Me* (1984—*also* gender confusion) would be a fine addition to the soul-transference films. Anyone just dying for a revised and expanded edition of *You're Next*?

alien possession
Alien³ (1992)
Alien Resurrection (1997)
Attack of the Crab Monsters (1958)
Brain Eaters, The (1958)
Brain from Planet Arous, The (1957)
Creeping Unknown, The (*Quatermass Xperiment, The*) (1955)
Creepshow (1982)
Enemy from Space (*Quatermass II*) (1957)
Five Million Years to Earth (*Quatermass and the Pit*) (1967)
Forbidden Planet (1956)
I Married a Monster from Outer Space (1958)
Invaders from Mars (1953)
Invaders from Mars (1986)
Invasion of the Body Snatchers (1956)
Invasion of the Body Snatchers (1978)
It Came from Outer Space (1953)
Thing, The (*John Carpenter's The Thing*) (1982)

altered reality
Carnival of Souls (1960)
Dark City (1998)
Door to Silence (1991)
Groundhog Day (1993)
Hour of the Wolf (*Vargtimmen*) (1968)
It's a Wonderful Life (1946)
Jacket, The (2005)
Jacob's Ladder (1990)
Machinist, The (2004)
Matrix, The (1999)
Matrix Reloaded, The (2003)
Matrix Revolutions, The (2003)
Performance (1970)
Planet of the Apes (1968)
Soul Survivors (2001)
They Live (1988)
Videodrome (1983)

amnesia
Angel Heart (1987)
Chump at Oxford, A (1940)
Clean Slate (1994)

Dead Again (1991)
Eternal Sunshine of the Spotless Mind (2004)
Fifth Element, The (1997)
Gorgon, The (1964)
Memento (2000)
Strange Possession of Mrs. Oliver, The (1977)

body switching
Black Friday (1940)
Mephisto Waltz, The (1971)

brain switching
Frankenstein Must Be Destroyed (1969)
Monster and the Girl, The (1941)
Revenge of Frankenstein, The (1958)

brainwashing
It's Alive! (1969)
Manchurian Candidate, The (1962)
Manchurian Candidate, The (2004)
Torture Ship (1939)
Videodrome (1983)

disfigurement/medical intervention
Eyes Without a Face (*The Horror Chamber of Dr. Faustus*; *Les Yeux sans visage*) (1960)
Face/Off (1997)
First Yank into Tokyo (1945)
Raven, The (1935)
Seconds (1966)
Tarantula (1955)

doppelganger
Day Mars Invaded Earth, The (1963)
I Married a Monster from Outer Space (1958)
Impostor (2002)
Invasion of the Body Snatchers (1956)
It Came from Outer Space (1953)
Student of Prague, The (1926)

dual personality
Bride of the Incredible Hulk, The (1978)
Dr. Jekyll and Mr. Hyde (1920)
Dr. Jekyll and Mr. Hyde (1931)
Dr. Jekyll and Mr. Hyde (1941)
Dr. Jekyll and Sister Hyde (1971)
Haunted Strangler, The (*Grip of the Strangler*) (1958)
Hulk (2003)
Incredible Hulk, The (1977)
Jekyll and Hyde... Together Again (1982)
Nutty Professor, The (1963)

eradication of self
Alien^3 (1992)
Altered States (1980)
Being John Malkovich (1999)
Devils, The (1971)
Eternal Sunshine of the Spotless Mind (2004)
Hour of the Wolf (*Vargtimmen*) (1968)
Invasion of the Body Snatchers (1956)
Invasion of the Body Snatchers (1978)
It's Alive! (1969)
It's a Wonderful Life (1946)
Minority Report (2002)
1984 (1984)
Oldboy (2004)
Omega Man, The (1971)
Planet of the Apes (1968)
Rollerball (1975)
Rosemary's Baby (1968)
Seconds (1966)
Son of Dracula (1943)
Star Wars (*Star Wars: Episode IV – A New Hope*) (1977)
Star Wars: Episode I – The Phantom Menace (1999)
Star Wars: Episode II – Attack of the Clones (2002)
Star Wars: Episode III – Revenge of the Sith (2005)
Star Wars: Episode V – The Empire Strikes Back (*Empire Strikes Back, The*) (1980)
Star Wars: Episode VI – Return of the Jedi (*Return of the Jedi*) (1983)
Videodrome (1983)

gender confusion
Goodbye, Charlie (1964)

hive mind
Attack of the Crab Monsters (1958)
Brain Eaters, The (1958)
Enemy from Space (*Quatermass II*) (1957)
Invaders from Mars (1953)
It Came from Outer Space (1953)
Thing, The (*John Carpenter's The Thing*) (1982)

hypnotism
Abbott and Costello Meet Frankenstein (1948)
Abbott and Costello Meet the Killer, Boris Karloff (1949)
Bride of the Incredible Hulk, The (1978)
Brides of Dracula (1960)
Cabinet of Dr. Caligari, The (*Das Kabinett des Dr. Caligari*) (1919)
Devil Commands, The (1941)
Devil Doll (1965)
Dracula (1931)
Fearless Vampire Killers, or Pardon Me, But Your Teeth Are in My Neck (1967)
Horror of Dracula (1958)
House of Dark Shadows (1970)
Hypnotic Eye, The (1960)
Man with Two Faces, The (1934)
She Creature, The (1956)
Son of Dracula (1943)
Svengali (1931)
Undead, The (1957)

impersonation
Black Room, The (1935)
Blade Runner (1982)

loss of affect
Carnival of Souls (1960)
Door to Silence (1991)
Jacket, The (2005)
Jacob's Ladder (1990)
Machinist, The (2004)
Soul Survivors (2001)

madness
Abbott and Costello Meet the Invisible Man (1952)
Dead of Night (1945)
Devil Commands, The (1941)
Dr. X (1932)
Gothika (2003)
Invisible Man, The (1933)
It's Alive! (1969)
Leopard Man, The (1943)
Mad Love (1935)
Peeping Tom (1960)
Pillow of Death (1945)
Pit and the Pendulum, The (1961)
Psycho (1960)
Raven, The (1935)
Rosemary's Baby (1968)
Secret Window (2004)
Tenebrae (*Unsane*) (1982)

metamorphosis
Abbott and Costello Meet Dr. Jekyll and Mr. Hyde (1953)
Abbott and Costello Meet Frankenstein (1948)
Alligator People, The (1959)
Altered States (1980)
Bride of the Gorilla (1951)
Bride of the Incredible Hulk, The (1978)
Brides of Dracula (1960)
Captive Wild Woman (1943)
Cat People (1942)
Cat People (1982)
Creeping Unknown, The (*Quatermass Xperiment, The*) (1955)
Creepshow (1982)
Cursed (2005)
Curse of the Werewolf, The (1960)
Dr. Jekyll and Mr. Hyde (1920)
Dr. Jekyll and Mr. Hyde (1931)
Dr. Jekyll and Mr. Hyde (1941)
Dr. Jekyll and Sister Hyde (1971)
Dr. X (1932)

First Man into Space (1959)
Frankenstein Meets the Wolf Man (1943)
Ginger Snaps (2000)
Ginger Snaps Back: The Beginning (2004)
Ginger Snaps: Unleashed (2004)
Gorgon, The (1964)
Horror of Dracula (1958)
Howling, The (1981)
Hulk (2003)
I Was a Teenage Werewolf (1957)
Incredible Hulk, The (1977)
Incredible Shrinking Man, The (1957)
Jekyll and Hyde...Together Again (1982)
Monster on the Campus (1958)
Nutty Professor, The (1963)
Performance (1970)
Pinocchio (1940)
Silver Bullet (1985)
Tarantula (1955)
Videodrome (1983)
Wolf (1994)
Wolf Man, The (1941)
Vampire, The (1957)

mind control

Buck Rogers (1939)
Ghidrah, the Three-Headed Monster (*San daikaijû: Chikyu saidai no kessen*) (1964)
Invaders from Mars (1953)
Invaders from Mars (1986)
Invisible Ghost, The (1941)
Manchurian Candidate, The (1962)
Manchurian Candidate, The (2004)
Mr. Vampire (*Geung si sin sang*)
Peeping Tom (1960)
Revenge of the Stepford Wives (1980)
Stepford Wives, The (1975) [*not!*]
Stepford Wives, The (2004)
Videodrome (1983)

possession

Being John Malkovich (1999)
Black Friday (1940)
Black Pit of Dr. M, The (*Misterios de ultratumba*) (1959)

Burnt Offerings (1976)
Dead of Night (1945)
Death at Love House (*Shrine of Lorna Love, The*) (1976)
Devils, The (1971)
Donovan's Brain (1953)
Exorcist, The (1973)
Gothika (2003)
Haunted Palace, The (1963)
Innocents, The (1961)
Killer Bees (1974)
Mephisto Waltz, The (1971)
Night of Dark Shadows (1971)
Nightmare Castle (*Amanti d'oltretomba, Gli*; *Faceless Monster, The*; *Night of the Doomed*) (1966)
Possession of Joel Delaney, The (1972)
So, You've Downloaded a Demon (2003)
Serpent and the Rainbow, The (1988)
Supernatural (1933)
Trilogy of Terror (1975)
Trilogy of Terror II (1996)

regimentation

Brazil (1985)
Devils, The (1971)
Handmaid's Tale, The (1990)
1984 (1984)

reincarnation

Chinese Ghost Story, A (*Sien nui yau wan*) (1987)
Dead Again (1991)
Goodbye, Charlie (1964)
Mummy, The (1932)
Night of Dark Shadows (1971)
She Creature, The (1956)
Undead, The (1957)

scientific manipulation

Alien Resurrection (1997)
Alligator People, The (1959)
Blade Runner (1982)
Captive Wild Woman (1943)
Clockwork Orange, A (1971)
I Was a Teenage Werewolf (1957)
Jacket, The (2005)

King of the Zombies (1941)
Mad Ghoul, The (1943)
Matrix, The (1999)
Matrix Reloaded, The (2003)
Matrix Revolutions, The (2003)
Minority Report (2002)
Revenge of the Zombies (1943)
Scanners (1980)
Torture Ship (1939)
Total Recall (1990)
Walking Dead, The (1936)
Zombies on Broadway (1945)

search for self

Matrix, The (1999)
Oldboy (2004)
Star Wars (Star Wars: Episode IV – A New Hope) (1977)
Star Wars: Episode I – The Phantom Menace (1999)
Star Wars: Episode II – Attack of the Clones (2002)
Star Wars: Episode III – Revenge of the Sith (2005)
Star Wars: Episode V – The Empire Strikes Back (Empire Strikes Back, The) (1980)
Star Wars: Episode VI – Return of the Jedi (Return of the Jedi) (1983)
Total Recall (1990)

soul transference

Black Pit of Dr. M, The (Misterios de ultratumba) (1959)
Devil Doll (1965)
New Mr. Vampire, The (Jiang shi fan sheng) (1987)

split personality

Dead of Night (1945)
Fight Club (1999)
High Tension (Haute tension) (2003)
Identity (2003)
Leopard Man, The (1943)
Machinist, The (2004)
Psycho (1960)
Secret Window (2004)

Trilogy of Terror (1975)

twins

Black Room, The (1935)

voodoo

Ghost Breakers, The (1940)
I Walked With a Zombie (1943)
King of the Zombies (1941)
Revenge of the Zombies (1943)
Scared Stiff (1953)
Serpent and the Rainbow, The (1988)
White Zombie (1932)
Zombies on Broadway (1945)

zombification

Beyond, The (E Tu Vivrai Nel Terrore—L'aldila) (1981)
Chinese Ghost Story, A (Sien nui yau wan) (1987)
Dawn of the Dead (1978)
Day of the Dead (1985)
Dead Next Door, The (1989)
Land of the Dead (2005)
Last Man on Earth, The (1964)
Man Made Monster (1940)
Mr. Vampire (Geung si sin sang)
New Mr. Vampire, The (Jiang shi fan sheng)
Nightmare City (Incubo sulla citta contaminate) (1983)
Night of the Comet (1984)
Night of the Living Dead (1968)
Omega Man, The (1971)
Return of the Living Dead (1985)
Return of the Living Dead 3 (1993)
Serpent and the Rainbow, The (1988)
Shaun of the Dead (2004)
28 Days Later (2002)
Virus (Zombie Creeping Flesh; Night of the Zombies) (1980)
Zombie (Zombi 2; Zombie Flesheaters) (1979)
Zombie Aftermath (1987)

Appendix II: LOI by Contributor

If readers have a favorite writer among the 17 who contributed to this book, or—if readers find themselves particularly enjoying the insights and style of one of these 17—here's a handy list of Who Wrote What, so one can read more entries by that person (or, conversely, if you hated him/her, so you can *skip* his/her work).

ABJ: Andrew (Barton) Jones
Land of the Dead (2005)
Omega Man, The (1971)
Performance (1970)
Possession of Joel Delaney, The (1972)
Psycho (1960)
Rollerball (1975)
Rosemary's Baby (1968)

AFA: Anthony (Frank) Ambrogio
Altered States (1980)
Buck Rogers (1939)
Chump at Oxford, A (1940)
Clean Slate (1994)
Cursed (2005)
Dead of Night (1945)
Devils, The (1971)
Dracula (1931)
Exorcist, The (1973)
Face/Off (1997)
Fearless Vampire Killers, or Pardon Me, But Your Teeth Are in My Neck, The (1967)
Forbidden Planet (1956)
Ginger Snaps (2000)
Ginger Snaps Back: The Beginning (2004)
Ginger Snaps: Unleashed (2004)
High Tension (Haute tension) (2003)
Howling, The (1981)
Impostor (2002)
Invsible Man, The (1933)
It's a Wonderful Life (1946)
Man with Two Faces, The (1934)
Minority Report (2002)
Pinocchio (1940)
Son of Dracula (1943)
Stepford Wives, The (1975)
Includes:
Revenge of the Stepford Wives (1980)
Stepford Wives, The (2004)
Total Recall (1990)

AJB: A(lex) J. Ballard
Beyond, The (E Tu Vivrai Nel Terrore— L'aldila) (1981)
Blade Runner (1982)
Brazil (1985)
Dawn of the Dead (1978)
Dead Next Door, The (1989)
Invaders from Mars (1986)
Matrix, The (1999)
Matrix Reloaded, The (2003)
Matrix Revolutions, The (2003)
Nightmare City (Incubo sulla citta contaminate) (1983)
Night of the Comet (1984)
Night of the Living Dead (1968)
1984 (1984)
Oldboy (2004)
Return of the Living Dead (1985)
Return of the Living Dead 3 (1993)
Virus (Zombie Creeping Flesh; Night of the Zombies) (1980)
Zombie (Zombi 2; Zombie Flesheaters) (1979)
Zombie Aftermath (1987)

AJL: Arthur (Joseph) Lundquist
Alien³ (1992)
Creeping Unknown, The (Quatermass Xperiment, The) (1955)
First Yank into Tokyo (1945)

Goodbye, Charlie (1964)
Hypnotic Eye, The (1960)
Invisible Ghost, The (1941)
It's Alive! (1969)
Killer Bees (1974)
Planet of the Apes (1968)
Seconds (1966)

BMS: Bryan (McCluer) Senn
Angel Heart (1987)
Brain Eaters, The (1958)
Bride of the Gorilla (1951)
Captive Wild Woman (1943)
Day Mars Invaded Earth, The (1963)
Devil Doll (1965)
First Man into Space (1959)
I Married a Monster from Outer Space (1958)
Last Man on Earth, The (1964)
Nightmare Castle (*Amanti d'oltretomba, Gli*; *Faceless Monster, The*; *Night of the Doomed*) (1966)
Serpent and the Rainbow, The (1988)
Silver Bullet (1985)
They Live (1988)
Torture Ship (1939)
Undead, The (1957)

CCS: Cindy Collins Smith
Chinese Ghost Story, A (*Sien nui yau wan*) (1987)
Clockwork Orange, A (1971)
Ghidrah, the Three-Headed Monster (*San daikaijû: Chikyu saidai no kessen*) (1964)
Groundhog Day (1993)
Identity (2003)
Memento (2000)
Mr. Vampire (*Geung si sin sang*)
New Mr. Vampire, The (*Jiang shi fan sheng*) (1987)
Star Wars: Episode VI – Return of the Jedi (*Return of the Jedi*) (1983)
    Includes:
    Star Wars (*Star Wars: Episode IV – A New Hope*) (1977)

Star Wars: Episode I – The Phantom Menace (1999)
Star Wars: Episode II – Attack of the Clones (2002)
Star Wars: Episode III – Revenge of the Sith (2005)
Star Wars: Episode V – The Empire Strikes Back (*Empire Strikes Back, The*) (1980)

GJS: Gary J(oseph) Svehla
Alligator People, The (1959)
Black Pit of Dr. M, The (*Misterios de ultratumba*) (1959)
Brain from Planet Arous, The (1957)
Brides of Dracula (1960)
Cat People (1942)
Day of the Dead (1985)
Devil Commands, The (1941)
Dr. X (1932)
Enemy from Space (*Quatermass II*) (1957)
Eyes Without a Face (*The Horror Chamber of Dr. Faustus*; *Les Yeux sans visage*) (1960)
Invaders from Mars (1953)
It Came from Outer Space (1953)
I Was a Teenage Werewolf (1957)
Leopard Man, The (1943)
Monster on the Campus (1958)
Mummy, The (1932)
She Creature, The (1956)
Tarantula (1955)
Thing, The (*John Carpenter's The Thing*) (1982)
Wolf Man, The (1941)
Vampire, The (1957)

JDT: Jeffrey (Dillard) Thompson
Burnt Offerings (1976)
Death at Love House (*Shrine of Lorna Love, The*) (1976)
House of Dark Shadows (1970)
Night of Dark Shadows (1971)
Strange Possession of Mrs. Oliver, The (1977)

Trilogy of Terror (1975)
Trilogy of Terror II (1996)

JML: Jonathan Malcolm Lampley
Fight Club (1999)
Frankenstein Must Be Destroyed (1969)
Haunted Palace, The (1963)
Manchurian Candidate, The (1962)
Manchurian Candidate, The (2004)

JSM: Jeffrey (Scott) Miller
Abbott and Costello Meet Dr. Jekyll and Mr. Hyde (1953)
Abbott and Costello Meet Frankenstein (1948)
Abbott and Costello Meet the Invisible Man (1952)
Abbott and Costello Meet the Killer, Boris Karloff (1949)
Bride of the Incredible Hulk, The (1978)
Frankenstein Meets the Wolf Man (1943)
Ghost Breakers, The (1940)
Hulk (2003)
Incredible Hulk, The (1977)
Jekyll and Hyde...Together Again (1982)
King of the Zombies (1941)
Monster and the Girl, The (1941)
Nutty Professor, The (1963)
Revenge of the Zombies (1943)
Scared Stiff (1953)
Shaun of the Dead (2004)
Zombies on Broadway (1945)

LJ-C: Laurel Jenkins-Crowe
Being John Malkovich (1999)
Eternal Sunshine of the Spotless Mind (2004)

MDC: Mark Daniel (aka "Danger") Clark
Attack of the Crab Monsters (1958)
Dr. Jekyll and Sister Hyde (1971)
Hour of the Wolf (*Vargtimmen*) (1968)
Incredible Shrinking Man, The (1957)
Mad Ghoul, The (1943)
Man Made Monster (1940)

Svengali (1931)
Walking Dead, The (1936)
White Zombie (1932)

OVA: Olivia V(lasopolos) Ambrogio
Alien Resurrection (1997)
Dead Again (1991)
Handmaid's Tale, The (1990)
28 Days Later (2002)
Wolf (1994)

RJT: Robert (John) Tinnell
Creepshow (1982)
Horror of Dracula (1958)
Innocents, The (1961)
Scanners (1980)
So, You've Downloaded a Demon (2003)
Tenebrae (*Unsane*) (1982)
Uninvited, The (1944)
Videodrome (1983)

SAS: Susan (Aurelia) Svehla
Fifth Element, The (1997)

SGT: Steven (Gary) Thornton
Black Friday (1940)
Black Room, The (1935)
Cabinet of Dr. Caligari, The (*Das Kabinett des Dr. Caligari*) (1919)
Cat People (1982)
Curse of the Werewolf, The (1960)
Dark City (1998)
Donovan's Brain (1953)
Dr. Jekyll and Mr. Hyde (1920)
Dr. Jekyll and Mr. Hyde (1931)
Dr. Jekyll and Mr. Hyde (1941)
Five Million Years to Earth (*Quatermass and the Pit*) (1967)
Gorgon, The (1964)
Haunted Strangler, The (*Grip of the Strangler*) (1958)
Invasion of the Body Snatchers (1956)
Invasion of the Body Snatchers (1978)
I Walked With a Zombie (1943)
Mad Love (1935)
Mephisto Waltz, The (1971)

Peeping Tom (1960)
Pit and the Pendulum, The (1961)
Raven, The (1935)
Revenge of Frankenstein, The (1958)
Student of Prague, The (*Der Student von Prag*) (1926)
Supernatural (1933)

SMD: Shane M. Dallmann
Carnival of Souls (1960)
Door to Silence (1991)
Gothika (2003)
Jacket, The (2005)
Jacob's Ladder (1990)
Machinist, The (2004)
Pillow of Death (1945)
Secret Window (2004)
Soul Survivors (2001)

If you enjoyed this book,
check out our other
film-related titles at
www.midmar.com
or call or write for a free catalog.
Midnight Marquee Press, Inc.
9721 Britinay Lane
Baltimore, MD 21234
410-665-1198
(8 a.m. until 6 p.m. EST)
or MMarquee@aol.com

www.ingramcontent.com/pod-product-compliance
Lightning Source LLC
Chambersburg PA
CBHW071219080526
44587CB00013BA/1432